Splintered Sisterhood

Splintered Sisterhood

Gender and Class in the Campaign against Woman Suffrage

SUSAN E. MARSHALL

The University of Wisconsin Press

The University of Wisconsin Press
114 North Murray Street
Madison, Wisconsin 53715

3 Henrietta Street
London WC2E 8LU, England

5 4 3 2 1

Printed in the United States

Library of Congress Cataloging-in-Publication Data
Marshall, Susan E., 1950–
Splintered sisterhood: gender and class in the campaign against woman suffrage / Susan E. Marshall.
360 pp. cm.
Includes bibliographical references and index.
ISBN 0-299-15460-2 (cloth: alk. paper).
ISBN 0-299-15464-5 (pbk.: alk. paper).
1. Women—Suffrage—United States—History. 2. Women political activists—United States—History. 3. Upper class—United States—Political activity. 4. Social conflict—United States—History.
I. Title.
JK1896.M38 1997
324.6′23′0973—dc20 96-43666

For My Parents

Contents

Illustrations

Tables

Preface

The investigation that culminated in this book began serendipitously when I came across a notice for the *History of Women* microfilm collection and became intrigued by the title of an antisuffrage journal. As a student of social movements with an interest in women's studies, I had read numerous histories of woman suffrage, but never realized that the suffrage opposition was sufficiently large or organized to produce its own journal. I soon discovered that women opponents were a dominant part of organized protest against the vote. Since I came of age during the 1960s, I regard feminism as the only logical choice for my gender, a clear expression of rational self-interest. Women's opposition to equal rights is more perplexing and thus of greater intellectual interest to me. The answers suggested in the rather cursory treatments of antisuffragism published at the time left me unsatisfied, certain that large pieces of the puzzle were still missing.

This book is an attempt to fill in some of those missing pieces about the mobilization of women against their own enfranchisement. It proposes an answer grounded in the politics of gender and class. My primary thesis is that a conservative urban elite regarded the extension of suffrage as antithetical to its interests. Already under siege by new wealth, immigration, and labor unrest, this group feared that progressive reforms such as woman suffrage would further diminish its power and endanger particularly women's status as political appointees, society volunteers, and custodians of propriety. I have hypothesized incentives for antisuffrage activism grounded in perceived self-interest rather than in cultural traditionalism, but acknowledge that attributing motives to social movement participants is highly speculative, especially for subjects no longer available for personal interviews. In recognition of this, my study places as much emphasis on the "how" of antisuffrage activism as on the "why." Like many of my colleagues working on social movements, I am interested in how organizations and networks shape individual discontent into coordinated protest action.

Aided by the surviving records of prominent antisuffrage organizations, I have documented at least some elements of that process, from emergence to eventual dissolution.

In the course of researching this book, I have gained a greater appreciation of the struggle and ultimate triumph represented by passage of the Nineteenth Amendment. I have also discovered an exciting body of literature in women's politics and history, pried into upper-class lifestyles of the Gilded Age, and chuckled (as one can only do from the safety of distance) at the specious rationales offered for denying equality to women and other minorities. I hope that readers will see in this historical example some disquieting parallels to our own era as well as a useful starting point for more critical scrutiny of antifeminism today.

This study would not be possible without the historical documents housed in various archives throughout the United States. I thank collectively those librarians whose kindness and expertise allowed me to gather much of my data by mail as well as those who assisted me in person. I am especially grateful to the Massachusetts Historical Society for preparing a microfilmed copy of the extensive records of the Massachusetts Association Opposed to the Further Extension of Suffrage to Women. The Maine Historical Society and the Alabama Department of Archives and History also provided invaluable historical documents. A National Endowment for the Humanities Summer Stipend gave this study its start, and the University of Texas Research Institute kept it going with three grants over a four-year period. I also thank the College of Liberal Arts at the University of Texas at Austin for providing summer support and research assistants. Two talented students, Snahel Patel and Kyong Murchison, cheerfully and accurately helped me with the tedious data collection. I acknowledge with gratitude the support of family, friends, and colleagues who have encouraged this work since its inception and the gracious forbearance of those associates held captive with me to this irony of women's history.

Splintered Sisterhood

1

Introduction: The Paradox of Antifeminism

> I cannot believe that the members of the Tennessee legislature, whom we counted upon, have allowed themselves to be swayed by petty politics and failed us.
>
> —Alice Hill Chittenden, President,
> New York State Association Opposed to Woman Suffrage

These somber words acknowledged the imminent enfranchisement of American women as Tennessee became the thirty-sixth and final state needed to ratify the Nineteenth Amendment to the U.S. Constitution in August 1920.[1] While euphoric representatives of the National American Woman Suffrage Association and the National Woman's Party celebrated their victory, a different group of activists headquartered at Nashville's Hermitage Hotel expressed bitter disappointment and vowed to fight on through the courts to stem "this feminist disease."[2]

The opponents of the amendment were not the constituency usually identified as the "invisible enemy" by the suffrage camp—they were neither brewery owners, saloon keepers, nor immigrant "wets," as male antitemperance voters were called. The national antiratification campaign was directed largely by women's organizations such as the National Association Opposed to Woman Suffrage and the Southern Woman's League for the Rejection of the Susan B. Anthony Amendment. Men's groups sporadically joined the protest, such as the American Constitutional League; led by wealthy New Yorker Everett P. Wheeler, this organization lobbied the Tennessee legislature under the banner of states' rights with the support of local university professors, attorneys, and politicians.[3]

Antisuffrage mobilization for the final vote in Tennessee was not an isolated event. Since the 1870s, opposition groups led by socially prominent eastern women had protested against woman suffrage in every form, from limited enfranchisement for female taxpayers or electors of local school boards to state constitutional amendments granting universal suffrage. Their efforts help explain why 480 legislative campaigns in the first forty years of suffrage agitation yielded only four full suffrage victories, all in the sparsely populated western states, instigating a refocused drive for a federal Constitutional amendment.[4]

Antisuffragists countered demands for women's enfranchisement by contending that political participation would coarsen the gentle female character and endanger the family, the bulwark of society. They repeatedly disclaimed any interest in politics and often delegated to men the front-stage management of referenda campaigns while continuing their work behind the scenes. They differentiated themselves from suffragists through an exaggerated discourse of femininity, defending their "birthright of beauty, of serenity, of faith" and entreating male voters for protection from "the life of manifold activities our modern sister would have us assume." They repeatedly affirmed their contentment with the status quo. We are women without grievance, declared National Association president Mrs. Arthur Dodge before the organization's annual convention in 1916, who "stand for the preservation of the home . . . and the conservation of the best of American womanhood." Scholars widely accepted their pledge to defend women's traditional place in the domestic sphere as the basis for female opposition to equal rights, and treatments of antisuffragism routinely dismissed the movement as static and culturally backward.[5]

This book presents an alternative interpretation of women's organized opposition to their own enfranchisement. It reconceptualizes women antisuffrage activists as political actors rather than retiring housewives, granting them their rightful historical place as counterparts to suffragists. It focuses on antisuffrage organizations to reveal movement strategies and activists' behaviors—what they did, both in public and behind the scenes—as well as the production of propaganda for mass consumption. Tracing the evolution of the movement over time, this study revises the static image of antisuffragism derived from its rhetoric proclaiming outright opposition to social change. I propose that antisuffragists' rhetorical arguments against the vote partly reflected their beliefs, but were also devised to obfuscate the true extent of their political activism, a contradiction that potentially undermined their entire argument against the vote. The exaggerated rhetoric of feminine domesticity functioned to shield activists from criticism while they petitioned legislators and voters for political demonstrations of masculine chivalry.

Wrapping themselves in the cloak of traditionalism, antisuffrage women entered the male world of politics, beginning with self-described "quiet work" and ultimately adopting tactics not unlike those of the suffragists whose behavior they scorned. They authored pamphlets, published journals, raised money to sustain as many as twenty-eight state associations, and toured the campaign states unchaperoned. They established the National Association Opposed to Woman Suffrage in 1911, which claimed a total membership of 700,000 women by the end of the decade.[6] Nor did the contest end with ratification of the Nineteenth Amendment. A diminished, more radical group of antisuffragists fought the federal amendment through the courts, blocked legislation proposed by new women's political organizations, and helped usher in the doldrums of the postsuffrage era.[7]

This study challenges the common answer to the puzzling question of female divisiveness over women's rights. Traditional views about women's roles may help distinguish antisuffragists from their prosuffrage counterparts, but this picture is incomplete and ignores the extent of traditionalism residing within the suffrage movement. I propose instead that antisuffrage women engaged in the protection of gendered class interests—that is, they were not merely conduits for the concerns of wealthy men, but fought suffrage as a threat to their own positions of privilege. The women who led the antisuffrage campaign were not a group of secluded homemakers, but a privileged urban elite of extraordinary wealth, social position, and political power. Contradicting their own rhetoric of domesticity, these were active women who maintained exclusive social networks that protected class hegemony and exercised political influence through informal channels derived from their proximity by kinship and marriage to powerful men officeholders at all levels of government. Appointed through these networks to serve on the boards of public agencies that regulated the poor, the sick, and the imprisoned, many among the antisuffrage leadership enjoyed public prestige as amateur experts in various fields. They were engaged simultaneously in the "hidden work of constructing class," a description by sociologist Arlene Kaplan Daniels of the significance of women's volunteerism in maintaining elite dominance.[8] Close to the centers of power, they perceived no need of the ballot for themselves, and, like many men of their class, regarded a mass electorate as a threat to their way of life. They revealed their class interests in statements decrying the expansion of the "ignorant vote" and declaring that only "women whose training and experience fit them for the task" should be active in public life.[9] Suffrage was a proposed progressive reform measure that jeopardized the female antisuffrage leadership particularly. A suffrage victory would legitimate women's employment and further the expansion of the social welfare state, supplanting the authority of the society volunteer with a cadre of female professionals bearing college credentials, relevant work experience, and liberal political agendas. In short, rather than contrasting enlightened suffragists and their misguided opponents, I contend that women activists on both sides of the suffrage issue pursued political self-interest.

This examination of a relatively neglected group of women activists contributes to ongoing historical revisions of the Progressive Era, which is now viewed as a more ideologically diverse period than was previously thought. It is, above all, a study of women in politics. Numerous anthologies of the era verify an impressive range of activities among women of different ethnicities and social classes on behalf of progressive reforms, but missing therein are the stories of women's groups that fought reform.[10] The unbalanced scrutiny of female political behavior has fostered a tendency to regard all women's politics as implicitly liberal and feminist. As a case study of a women's reactionary movement, this book underscores the diversity of female political ideology and also provides a new perspective from which to view the suffrage movement, which has undergone a recent round of critical reassessment. It contributes to a small but expanding body of work on the political activism of right-wing women that challenges stereotypes of female passivity and marginality, from Kathleen Blee's study of U.S. Klanswomen to research by both Koonz and Rupp on women's political roles in the German Nazi Party and Rebecca Klatch's contemporary analysis of New Right activism.[11]

Excluded from the formal political process, women's actions, whether for or against social change, have been privatized and domesticated. In shifting the locus of conflict over woman suffrage from cultural traditionalism to politics, this study also follows recent trends in feminist scholarship addressing women in public life and expanding the concept of politics beyond partisan and electoral participation.[12] This book examines not only the motives behind antisuffrage mobilization but also the political strategies that nearly succeeded in derailing woman suffrage. A basic premise of this research is that women activists on both sides negotiated within the restrictive cultural dictates of the ideology of separate spheres. This case study of a conservative women's movement predating enfranchisement demonstrates the creativity, complexity, and contradictions of female political behavior embedded in the social context of gender inequality.

Women's antifeminism is a paradox awaiting explanation. While there are other historical examples of reticent constituencies who feared retaliation after protest movement failure or of a relatively privileged few who sided with the majority out of personal self-interest, formal mobilization against proposed civil rights measures by beneficiaries is relatively rare. Yet antifeminist mobilization by women has happened twice in this century, testimony to the discomforting fact of an inchoate group consciousness that scholars have begun to address.[13] The reemergence of female antifeminist mobilization in the 1970s, which this time was able to quash the proposed Equal Rights Amendment and continues to threaten gains made by women's rights groups in employment and reproductive rights, augments the timeliness of this study. In a historical parallel to the suffrage era, the political acumen of the contemporary female backlash is often overlooked in favor of the traditional homemaker image promulgated by antifeminist organizations.[14] Unintentionally facilitating this benign interpretation is feminist scholarship, which has been reticent to direct its critical eye toward the female opposition.

The Feminist Dilemma

Female opponents have been relegated to a marginal role in most histories of the woman suffrage movement, exemplified by the assertion in a popular women's studies textbook that organized antifeminism is unique to the contemporary era.[15] This dearth of knowledge is especially curious given the explosion of feminist scholarship over the past three decades. Feminist analytical frameworks, grounded in the legitimation of women's experience and the social fact of gender inequality, are challenged by the existence of female antifeminists.[16] Faced with the choice of explaining women's opposition to enfranchisement as either a troubling manifestation of female political disunity or a legitimate grievance against a deeply flawed suffrage movement, it is not surprising that feminist scholars have tended to sidestep the question of women opponents. Critical reexaminations have focused on elitism within the suffrage movement and its impact on working-class and ethnic women, understandably more sympathetic research subjects compared with the relatively privileged leaders of the antisuffrage movement.[17] These revisions are long overdue, but so is the perspective on the women's movement afforded by comparisons with the reactionary forces against suffrage.

Treatments of antisuffragists have relied heavily on the opinions of suffrage activists, which partly explains the relegation of antisuffragism to the periphery. Suffragists' mention of their female rivals was sporadic and dismissive in tone, but careful reading also reveals changes in attitudes over time. This is evident in their multivolume work *The History of Woman Suffrage,* which remains the most comprehensive history of the U.S. suffrage movement.[18] First notice therein of the "remonstrants," the term favored through the 1890s, described them as "infinitesimal" in number and claimed that opponents actually benefited the cause of women's rights by bringing the suffrage issue to public attention, thereby mobilizing new legions of prosuffrage women to political activism. Suffragists asserted repeatedly that it was indifferent women, not remonstrants, who jeopardized the movement's goals. As the state-by-state amendment strategy stalled in the first decade of this century, however, suffragists' descriptions of their female adversaries became noticeably less benign. While continuing to downplay the role of women opponents in defeating state referenda, proponents began to characterize antisuffragists as misguided fronts for nefarious male corporate interests. Suffrage leaders Carrie Chapman Catt and Nettie Rogers Shuler concluded that the worst damage done by women "antis," as they were now called, was "to confuse public thinking by standing conspicuously in the limelight while the potent enemy worked in darkness."[19] They also dismissed women opponents as throwbacks to another century, clinging futilely to antiquated gender norms. This traditional label has profoundly influenced society's views of antifeminism to the present day, tilting analyses away from politics and locating the conflict in the realm of female culture, where it is reduced to a simple lifestyle struggle between homemakers and careerists, or, in the language of the suffrage era, between "true women" and "new women."[20] Suffragists were apparently unconcerned that, by applying patronizing gender stereotypes to discredit the female opposition, they might undermine their own claims of equality.

Despite their disavowals, suffragists campaigned with one eye on their female adversaries. Suffrage journals regularly reported on anti activities, if only to reassure their readers that such tactics were totally ineffective; suffrage leaders sent letters of correction to antisuffrage periodicals, revealing a higher level of scrutiny than was generally acknowledged. Women opponents were ridiculed, sometimes in theatrical skits, at annual suffrage conventions; as antis began to appear publicly at legislative hearings to protest proposed woman suffrage bills, suffragists carefully recorded their arguments and offered point-by-point rebuttals. More commonly, the antisuffrage position was articulated, albeit without attribution, and refuted in almost every suffrage speech. Late in the campaign, anti attacks on the patriotism of suffrage leaders during World War I were deemed sufficiently vitriolic to require direct public rebuttals that made headlines in urban newspapers.[21] These examples suggest that suffragists' indifference toward their female adversaries was more strategic than genuine.

The presence of organized female opposition to the woman's rights movement must surely have been awkward for suffragists. Confronted by the political embarrassment of women protesters and the practical reality that their fate rested in the hands of men, suffragists tended to focus more attention on the other gender. They analyzed many referenda defeats as votes against temperance, and often charged liquor interests with organizing an alliance of tobacco, railroad, manufacturing, cattle, and meat-packing interests whose main objective was trade protection. At the opposite end of the social scale, suffragists castigated working-class men for their prejudice against women, their intemperate drinking habits, or the corrupt practice of selling their votes to the shady alliance of corporate interests and political machines. Immigrant voters were identified as the deadliest foes of woman suffrage. Suffragists fumed at the decisive role played by "ignorant Americans and foreigners," particularly the German-American Alliance, which, they repeatedly claimed, was a front for the liquor and brewery trades. In the final decade of the campaign, entire political parties became the focus of suffrage protest action by its radical flank, the Congressional Union.[22]

Well-intentioned scholars have sometimes taken these suffrage accounts at face value to reconstruct the opposition movement, without giving due consideration to the political motives behind such allegations. They have often portrayed opponents as exclusively male, when they were mentioned at all. Eleanor Flexner's valuable history of woman suffrage, *Century of Struggle,* was one of the few to devote a full chapter to the female opposition, but it relied heavily on suffragists' reports, uncritically accepting the assertion that women antisuffragists were merely fronts for the economic interests of their wealthy husbands.[23] Unmentioned and apparently unnoticed was the suffragists' paradoxical denial of agency to women opponents.

The marginalization of women remonstrants is also a consequence of the image purposely created and maintained by antisuffragists themselves. Antisuffrage rhetoric proclaimed that the purity of true womanhood was at risk, and female remonstrants beseeched male voters to protect them from the degradation of politics and the misguided militance of a minority of their own sex. Those scholars who studied the antisuffrage movement firsthand rather than through the prism of suffragist interpretations tended to rely on such public rhetoric to explain women's protest mobilization. They identified the movement's primary motives as the maintenance of separate spheres, defense of the family from the divisive effects of female independence, and belief in inherent and immutable differences between the sexes.[24] These categories of public propaganda were rarely differentiated by gender or time period, and eventually took on the rigid characteristics of a stereotype, with the two groups of suffrage contestants dichotomized across a great divide into "new women" modernists and "true women" traditionalists. The antisuffrage movement, and antifeminism more generally, became frozen in time; cast as intransigent and retrograde, it attracted little scholarly interest.

If this were the final word on women's antifeminism, it is doubtful whether the study presented here would have been conceived. But feminist scholarship has been under way for three decades, and its maturation has recently produced a more complex picture of gender politics, raising questions that inform this investigation of the antisuffrage movement. Feminist revisions of women's history suggest that a simple dichotomy between the suffragist "new woman" and the antisuffragist "true woman" is simplistic and misleading. For one thing, histories of both sides reveal shared ideological roots. Numerous scholars have established the origins of American feminism in the traditional woman's sphere, which created a distinctly female culture, provided organizational experience in moral reform societies, and generated status discontent as women reformers increasingly chafed under restrictive seclusion norms. As historian Nancy Cott admits candidly, "What precipitated some women and not others to cross the boundaries from 'woman's sphere' to 'woman's rights' is not certain."[25]

Furthermore, suffrage ideology underwent a conservative shift by the turn of the century. Proponents downplayed the universalistic argument of natural rights in favor of the traditional belief in inherent gender differences; suffrage was now justified in terms of women's unique ability to solve the moral dilemmas of an increasingly complex society through municipal housekeeping. Resurrecting female virtue as the primary basis for citizenship, suffragists placed the canons of motherhood at the core of women's political personality. These apparent similarities between suffrage and antisuffrage rhetoric should not be overstated, since each side used these so-called essential feminine characteristics to pursue different political goals. Nonetheless, several observers claim that an essentialist suffrage ideology ultimately restricted women's political influence and also shaped national social welfare policies, based upon notions of female dependency, that persist to the present day.[26]

Finally, the suffrage movement, which harshly criticized opponents' elitism, was similarly flawed. Suffrage leaders not only railed against "the slum vote" that defeated woman suffrage referenda, but also stood in silent protest at naturalization ceremonies and considered supporting voting restrictions for black and foreign-born Americans for reasons of political expediency.[27] It is now generally acknowledged that, despite union endorsements and some recruitment success among the working classes, active suffragists were overwhelmingly native-born, middle-class women whose program benefited predominantly their own social stratum.[28]

In sum, feminist scholars have identified both differences and perplexing similarities between the two groups of political rivals. This research may not yet adequately explain women's mobilization against the vote, but it does cast further doubt on conventional explanations grounded in traditional woman's culture. Recent developments in research on stratification and women's politics suggest an alternative framework that guides the present study.

Gender, Class, and Social Movement Participation

Growing acknowledgment of the diversity of women's social location in the stratification hierarchy has opened the question of antifeminism to alternative interpretations. Early feminist revisions of mainstream theories of inequality, consciously making a case for the study of women as a "minority group" to a skeptical academic audience, contended that women constituted a separate class, or even a caste, that cuts across all socioeconomic strata.[29] In retrospect, such arguments overemphasized female homogeneity but at least questioned the dominant view that women's class interests derived from their male attachments. By the 1980s, however, mounting empirical evidence forced recognition of variations in social location among women and their consequences for gender solidarity.[30]

The next step was to identify the bases of differences among women. It was generally conceded that new ways of conceptualizing women's class position were needed, but there was less agreement about how to do this for women outside of the paid labor force.[31] A revised view of women as autonomous social actors implicitly challenges the notion that female political beliefs are identical to those of their male attachments. But proposed models to integrate gender, class, and ethnic dimensions of social inequality have tended to maintain each as a separate system, an approach that has been criticized for casting class and ethnicity as gender-neutral categories, for ignoring the gendered bases of men's behavior, and for locating women's subordination outside of the class structure.[32]

An alternative conceptualization posits that gender is embedded in the very process of class stratification. Following historian Joan Scott's contention that gender does not refer just to biological and cultural differences but is a primary way of signifying relationships of power, sociologist Joan Acker argues that gender is a "constitutive element" of organizations and social relations that affects the situations of men as well as women. The notion of gendered class positions "directs the analysis to gender as an integral part of all social existence in contrast to formulations of gender as analytically outside of other systems and impinging on those systems only at certain points."[33] This view of gendered stratification processes is compatible with earlier interactive models of ethnicity and class developed by Milton Gordon and H. Edward Ransford. It also broadens the notion of class beyond the conventional definition of market position, which is especially useful for the study of elite women.[34]

The concept of gendered class interests enhances the study of antisuffragism in several ways. First, it undermines the assumption that women antisuffragists were passively following the dictates of their husbands' economic interests. It suggests motives grounded in women's unique social location: protection of their own positions of privilege as elite volunteers, political appointees, and custodians of propriety. Class also shaped the development of a female countermovement that was distinct from men's protest activism in both form and content. The notion of gendered class position highlights the interaction between these two social locations, and recent scholarship has identified the contradictory effects of class—both opportunities and constraints—on the behaviors of wealthy women.[35] This study explores how antisuffragists' access to money, leisure, and extensive social networks facilitated the growth of the countermovement to suffrage; at the same time, the confines of class mandated a circumspect public image and an exaggerated rhetoric of true womanhood that undermined its political legitimacy and influence.

This research also benefits from increased scholarly focus on women as political actors, a development that supports a conceptual shift of the locus of conflict over suffrage from culture to politics. As Sara Evans recently observed, feminist historical analysis has made significant contributions to the study of women's activities in the private sphere of the family, sexuality, domestic labor, and sociability. Having documented the strength and vitality of a unique female culture and demonstrated how women's networks derived from traditional domesticity facilitated the development of political mobilization for women's rights, she suggests that it may be time to shift focus and elaborate similarly on women in public life. Historical accounts by Paula Baker, Nancy Hewitt, Mary Ryan, and Anne Firor Scott have broadened the scope of political studies beyond partisan and electoral participation to examine women's organizations, use of public space, and political activism in the period predating enfranchisement.[36] Collectively, these works have reconceptualized women as political actors and detailed the process by which gender is embedded in public rituals and political institutions. They have also contributed a more critical examination of the ways in which women's political activities have been obscured, legitimated, and contained through the ideology of separate spheres. My study applies these insights to identify female antisuffragists' subtle and strategic protests despite their avowed rejection of politics.

While feminist scholarship suggests new ways to think about women's political behavior, social movements research provides a conceptual framework for analyzing the politics of antisuffragism. Resource mobilization theory, in particular, underscores the social networks and organizational ties that facilitate social movement recruitment among women denied access to the formal political process.[37] Leadership, internal organization, financial support, recruitment strategies, maintenance of members' participation and commitment, goal transformation, and both competition and cooperation with other social movement organizations are some of the elements highlighted by this perspective. Instead of viewing rhetoric as simply an expression of members' ideology, resource mobilization theory redefines rhetoric to emphasize its strategic components, proposing that propaganda serves many social movement functions, including recruitment, self-affirmation, group solidarity, and separation from adversaries. Perhaps because of their typically conservative ideologies, countermovements have been a neglected topic of study, viewed as traditionalist, reactive, and static. The resource mobilization perspective advocates a dynamic approach that considers the trajectory of movement careers as well as interactions with the opposing side, manifested in competition for new recruits, public opinion, and state support. It has prompted reconsideration of the static concept of countermovements and renewed interest in the complexity of conservative political mobilization.[38]

The ideas of resource mobilization theory guide this investigation. Although several descriptive histories of the U.S. antisuffrage movement exist,[39] this study examines the subject from the perspective of the social sciences, using systematic techniques of data collection to address unresolved questions about the mobilization of women against equal rights. My primary focus is on antisuffrage organizations, which have received far less attention than public rhetoric, despite their central role in the campaign against the vote. This research systematically examines organizational documents to get a backstage view of antisuffrage political strategy. It breaks down the antisuffrage movement into its component parts, considering in turn its leadership, recruitment strategies, voting constituency, rhetoric, and campaign tactics. Investigation of changes through time demonstrates the complex interaction between the suffrage and antisuffrage movements and the extent to which antisuffrage women went beyond gender-appropriate "hidden work" to engage in political protest. The analysis thus builds on recent revisions of countermovement stereotypes and contributes to the ongoing elaboration of countermovements as proactive political phenomena.

Outline of the Study

At the heart of this study are a number of questions concerning the antisuffrage movement specifically and antifeminist mobilization more generally. What explains women's political protest against women's rights? What was the relationship of antisuffragism to the dominant impulse for reform during the Progressive Era? How did gender and class interests shape suffrage opposition? Who were the organizers and members of antisuffrage organizations, and what were their recruitment strategies? What were the relative contributions of men and women remonstrants, and did they present identical arguments against the vote? Who voted against suffrage, and why? How did the antisuffrage movement evolve from quiet work and parlor meetings to parades and national conventions? How did the movement react in the face of growing awareness of the inevitability of the Nineteenth Amendment's passage? And finally, what impact did interaction between the suffrage and antisuffrage movements have on their respective careers?

To address these questions, I utilize a diversity of methodologies and data sources. The primary data base is the organizational records of the Massachusetts Association Opposed to the Further Extension of Suffrage to Women, which was one of the oldest and most influential organizations fighting the eastward drift of female enfranchisement. The Massachusetts Association was instrumental in founding other state associations and directing referenda campaigns across the nation; as in similar organizations in other states, its membership and leadership were overwhelmingly female. Because of its primary significance for the development of the U.S. antisuffrage movement, the records of the Massachusetts Association yield information well beyond the state's borders that documents the national campaign against votes for women. For this study, these records, which include minutes of committee meetings, correspondence, and financial statements spanning over thirty years, have been coded, content-analyzed for more systematic study, and supplemented by various archival materials, including the records of other state associations and personal papers of antisuffrage leaders.[40] The backstage view provided by these documents is necessary for a critical examination of prevalent stereotypes about the antisuffrage movement.

This study systematically investigates the public face of the movement using a content analysis of over two hundred antisuffrage writings coded by author's sex and publication date.[41] Its leadership is identified through biographical encyclopedias, local genealogies, club records, newspapers, and population schedules of the U.S. Census.[42] In perhaps the first investigation of the antisuffrage membership, association records are matched with census data to identify the backgrounds of individual recruits and the community characteristics associated with the organization of local chapters. A sample of election outcomes for state woman suffrage referenda yields insights into the broader antisuffrage constituency. Along with secondary materials to place events in historical context, these diverse methods aim to present a comprehensive analysis of the U.S. antisuffrage movement, from the first published remonstrances after the Civil War to its end in the red-baiting decade of the 1920s.

As both a social history and a sociological study, this book is organized loosely in chronological order around the basic components of social movements to reassess old assumptions about antisuffrage mobilization. Chapter 2 examines the origins of antisuffrage mobilization and the social backgrounds of its female leadership, including family histories, marital patterns, and social and philanthropic activities that linked them in shared networks of interpersonal interaction and common interest. It addresses the questions of who orchestrated antisuffrage mobilization and how it was accomplished, given the gendered class constraints imposed by the ideology of separate spheres. Chapter 3 considers the role of men in the antisuffrage movement by identifying the social, political, and business interests of the male leadership and the relationship between men's and women's antisuffrage organizations. It reappraises the suffrage claim that men were the real power behind the opposition movement. Chapter 4 investigates the rhetoric of antisuffragism, using a sample of writings to identify differences in style and content by gender as well as changes through time as the movement matured. This analysis suggests revisions to conventional stereotypes about antifeminist ideology and women's gender consciousness. Chapter 5 examines the characteristics associated with the antisuffrage vote in states representing a diversity of regions, underscoring the influence of local political dynamics on the development of antisuffrage constituencies. It also explores the growth of the countermovement through individual recruitment and the organization of local chapters. Chapter 6 reviews the tactics adopted by the antisuffrage movement to win the battle of public opinion, with particular emphasis on the evolution of political strategies from dignified parlor meetings to full-scale political confrontation during the final antiratification drive against the Susan B. Anthony amendment, which activated southern opponents. It documents the phases of the movement from growth to decline, as internal conflict and defection of its leaders to partisan politics weakened its ranks and left a smaller, more radical cadre to make the last stand against suffrage and its reform political agenda. In conclusion, Chapter 7 summarizes the implications of these research results for the study of feminism, antifeminism, and countermovements more generally, and draws parallels between the antisuffrage movement and its modern successors.

2

"Women of High Social Standing"

> The anti-suffragist is the isolated woman, she is the belated product of the eighteenth century. She is not intentionally, viciously selfish, she has merely not developed into twentieth century fellowship.
>
> —Harriot Stanton Blatch

This description of the opposition by a prominent suffragist has endured largely intact since the battle over enfranchisement was joined in the nineteenth century.[1] The charge of "selfishness" is ironic, since this was the very term used to discredit suffragists and other women who deviated from traditional gender roles. Blatch's statement encapsulates other ideas that have shaped the direction of scholarship on women's politics. The stereotype of antisuffragists as a group of sheltered women bound to antiquated gender norms has deflected attention away from women's activism in favor of the male opposition, paradoxically denying agency to female remonstrants.[2] Antisuffrage associations are generally ignored in historical accounts of U.S. women's organizations, perhaps because they constitute an exception to the conventional view that such female cultures are latently feminist.[3] Even research focused on antisuffragism has shown a marked preference for rhetorical rather than organizational analysis, contributing to the impression of women's individualized and scattershot opposition to the vote.

The few studies of antisuffrage organizations that exist consistently identify its leadership as women of privilege. The most systematic analysis, by Louise Stevenson, examined the husbands of more than four hundred members of the standing and executive committees of the Massachusetts Association; she estimates that approximately forty percent of that organization's leadership belonged to the upper class.[4] Class-based ideologies upholding conservative views about gender, politics, and social change may help explain the contents of antisuffrage rhetoric advocating the continuation of separate spheres. But the elite composition of antisuffrage organizations poses further questions about political mobilization. If these women were as isolated as Blatch claimed, how were they able to coalesce against suffrage? And if they regarded women's public participation as antithetical to their own values, why would they want to engage in political protest?

Social movements research cannot easily resolve these apparent contradictions behind antisuffrage mobilization. It is commonly observed that countermovements organize in response to the success of the initial movement, but it is a giant step from sentiments of dissatisfaction to active protest, particularly among women who were constrained both legally and culturally from political participation. The documented importance of networks for social movement recruitment raises questions about the likelihood that isolated individuals would coalesce to found social movement organizations, and women were generally denied access to extant economic and political groups that served as key recruitment networks for men.[5]

This chapter addresses the origins of women's organized opposition to female voting rights. Like the suffrage movement, women's early mobilization against enfranchisement was episodic, and several distinct generations of antisuffrage activism can be identified. The analysis examines the first organized protests in the 1870s, the establishment of a few formal antisuffrage organizations in the 1890s, and the strategies pursued by these early associations, particularly in New York and Massachusetts, to establish antisuffrage organizations in other states by the turn of the century. We focus first on the female leadership of the antisuffrage movement, identifying their family backgrounds, civic and social activities, and class affiliations. This chapter addresses not only the question of who organized the antisuffrage movement but how they pursued initial mobilization efforts. It also considers the broader historical context of women's activism and assesses the accuracy of the stereotypes of women antisuffragists as isolated, retrograde, and marginal to the movement against enfranchisement.

The First Protests

Organized opposition to woman suffrage did not immediately follow the 1848 Seneca Falls convention inaugurating what was then called the "woman rights" movement. In the 1850s, political resistance consisted largely of adverse reports on the "suffrage question" filed by legislative committees in various states.[6] But it was condemnation by religious authorities that influenced more profoundly Americans' negative outlook on suffrage. Beginning with censure of women's abolitionist activities, ministers throughout the nineteenth century published addresses denouncing equal rights for women in the name of Scripture. This first phase of antisuffrage arguments tended to adopt punitive religious symbols, acknowledging legal inequality but stating that woman's subordination was decreed by God, as found in the Book of Genesis and the admonitions of Saint Paul. This "natural subordination of women" was an early reply to suffragist natural rights arguments, adding to antifeminist rhetoric a powerful moral claim. Prominent ministers and theologians of the day chastised suffragists for selfishly challenging the Divine Plan and warned society that women's inherent weakness, manifested in Eve's original transgression, would reemerge in corrupt and unstable female voters.[7]

Sacred ideology was also used in a positive way to prescribe women's seclusion from public life. The cult of true womanhood, which arose during the Jacksonian era, sought to upgrade women's domestic function and enhance the status of the newly leisured women of the ascendant middle class.[8] Turning submission into a noble virtue and self-sacrifice into a patriotic duty, the canon of domesticity defined a sphere where woman would demonstrate her moral superiority and power over men. Piety was the cornerstone of the cult of true womanhood; dispensing love and comfort from the quiet of the domestic sphere, women would bring "men back to God" and "raise up a whole generation of Christian statesmen."[9] Development of woman's religious and domestic virtues, especially for daughters of the new middle class, was the rationale for the establishment of female educational institutions, significantly called seminaries.[10] By mid-century this glorified domesticity had become a cultural ideal, generating a large market for magazines and manuals that taught women proper feminine conduct. Books like Lydia Maria Child's *The American Frugal Housewife* (1832), Catharine Beecher's *A Treatise on Domestic Economy* (1843), Sarah Josepha Hale's *Keeping House and House Keeping* (1845), and Rev. Horace Bushnell's *Christian Nurture* (1876) instructed woman in the art of her supposedly "natural" domestic functions and carved out a unique sphere of female influence by emphasizing gender differences.[11] Not surprisingly, the ideology of true womanhood was the basis for the first remonstrance against woman suffrage.

Women's antisuffrage mobilization officially began in 1871, when nineteen women published a petition to the U.S. Congress remonstrating against votes for women in the editorial pages of the popular *Godey's Lady's Book and Magazine.*[12] This monthly publication was a dominant proponent of the cult of true womanhood; Sarah Josepha Hale, its editor for forty years, frequently expostulated against the dangers of female voting.[13] The petitioners' brief "appeal" protested gently that they "shrink from the notoriety of the public eye," and act now only because of "grave perils" that threaten "women's higher sphere apart from public life." Expressing a mixture of self-sacrifice and self-interest, they justified their position on the basis of Holy Scripture, female physical frailty, children's welfare, marital stability, and social order. The editors of *Godey's* entreated the female readership to copy the petition and procure signatures from their own neighborhoods, a strategy that reportedly yielded almost five thousand names when presented to the U.S. Congress later that year.[14]

The signers of the first petition were not isolated women. To the contrary, they were at the center of American political and cultural influence, which explains their access to *Godey's* to publicize their cause. Their husbands included four Republican senators, Civil War general William Tecumsah Sherman, a former Ohio governor and cabinet member in the Grant administration, and the chaplain of the U.S. House of Representatives.[15] Although socially prominent and married to politically powerful men, few of the women were known for their own professional accomplishments. Only one signer was listed under her own name, and this because she was unmarried; she was Catharine Beecher, daughter of renowned evangelical minister Lyman Beecher, sister of suffragists Henry Ward Beecher and Harriet Beecher Stowe and great-aunt of noted feminist Charlotte Perkins Gilman. By this time an elderly woman, Catharine Beecher was a prolific author and educator, whose life mission had been the establishment of female seminaries to train teachers for the task of taming the West through moral education. Adopting political metaphors, Beecher's final works called upon women to eschew suffrage for the more powerful role of "chief minister" of the "family state."[16]

In addition to Catharine Beecher, several other leaders of the petition drive were women of accomplishment. They included the petition's reputed author, Madeleine Vinton Dahlgren, widow of a Civil War admiral, who was also a translator, novelist, and later etiquette book author, literary society founder, and president of the Ladies' Catholic Missionary Society in the nation's capital. Another signatory was Almira Lincoln Phelps, an educator and author, the second woman elected to the American Association for the Advancement of Science, and the sister of Emma Willard, founder of Troy Female Seminary, who was also an antisuffragist.[17] Mrs. Phelps was not an original signer of the petition, but as corresponding secretary of the Women's Anti-Suffrage Association for Washington City, the first known organization of its kind, she was probably responsible for its placement in *Godey's.* A few months after the petition appeared, *Godey's* published Phelps's strong antisuffrage message under the guise of a paean to a new edition of Sarah Josepha Hale's *Woman's Record,* which she lauded as "an antidote to the pernicious doctrines of woman suffragists."[18] Such sophisticated strategies to influence public opinion belied their own claims that women had no aptitude for politics.

Social movement success typically spurs the formation of countermovements, and the *Godey's* petitioners refer to "some danger that this question may be forced on Congress." As of 1871, however, there were few suffrage successes to report. Kansas had entered the union in 1861 with school suffrage for women in its state constitution, and the territorial legislatures of Wyoming and Utah granted women the vote in 1869 and 1870, although Utah's law was later revoked by Congress in the Edmunds-Tucker Act (1887) as part of an anti-Mormon strategy.[19] Significantly, Senator Edmunds was the husband of an original signer of the 1871 antisuffrage petition. It is unlikely, however, that these events alone were sufficient to incite antisuffragists to action. For one thing, the politics of remote western territories had little political relevance at this time, and the national suffrage leadership did not even campaign there, lending support to the view that the political issues underlying the suffrage question went beyond women's rights.[20] For another, these two victories were counterbalanced by stunning postwar suffrage defeats. In 1867, a highly publicized New York State constitutional convention and a state referendum in Kansas defeated woman suffrage.[21] The following year, the Fourteenth Amendment was ratified, for the first time defining U.S. citizenship as male; this was followed by the Fifteenth Amendment, which guaranteed voting rights to black men. These Constitutional additions helped split the suffrage ranks, incited by Elizabeth Cady Stanton and Susan B. Anthony's campaign against the Fifteenth Amendment and the subsequent departure of male abolitionist allies among the Republican party leadership. By 1870 the more conservative Boston-based American Woman Suffrage Association began the *Woman's Journal,* while the National Woman Suffrage Association ceased publication of the *Revolution* after becoming embroiled in scandal stemming from its association with the notorious speculator George Francis Train.[22]

With the suffrage movement in such disarray and its bases of support eroded, what were the "grave perils" to which the 1871 antisuffrage petition referred? The editorial introduction printed in *Godey's* expressed concern about the possibility of a federal amendment, and there was some slight progress in that direction. In 1868, the first measure for a woman suffrage amendment was introduced to the U.S. Congress. In January 1870, Stanton testified before a congressional committee considering a bill to extend the vote to women in the District of Columbia, claiming that women's citizenship rights were guaranteed in the U.S. Constitution. Neither of these measures was voted out of committee, but the federal strategy had been initiated, and it was not until 1874 in *Minor v. Happersett* that the U.S. Supreme Court ruled unanimously that suffrage was not identical with citizenship, necessitating what would become nearly a half-century fight for a federal woman suffrage amendment. A final precipitating event may have been Mrs. Victoria Woodhull's suffrage speech before a congressional committee in January 1871.[23] Woodhull, a champion of free love, was the antithesis of the true woman. Her unconventional lifestyle combined with a brief affiliation with the National Woman Suffrage Association would be cited repeatedly to tar the suffrage movement as radical and its followers as immoral and antifamily, in "rebellion against the laws, human and Divine." The dignified language of the 1871 petition stands in marked contrast to the scathing description of suffragists in Phelps's follow-up article in *Godey's*, which, in a veiled reference to Woodhull, condemned women who followed those "with whose names we would not soil this page."[24]

The moral indignation of the first remonstrants contained both strategic and ideological elements. Placed in historical context, the behavior of woman suffragists of the period, traveling independently, speaking in public, and challenging men on their own turf, was not just unconventional; to many it was also immoral. Scores of the most influential men of the day—ministers, politicians, educators, physicians, and authors—were either opposed or silent on the suffrage question, as were the major women's magazines and some of the most celebrated women of the period. Given this audacious configuration of antisuffrage sentiment, the woman's rights advocates were swimming against a powerful tide, underscoring the courageousness of their crusade. Both groups of contestants used moral suasion as a strategy, but only antisuffragists had religious orthodoxy on their side. Moreover, when the first women remonstrants claimed that woman's role as wife and mother was the source of her power, they had correctly assessed their own situation. Their status as wives of influential men gave them access to power enjoyed by few women of their time. While it is likely that many more women were offended or frightened by the agitation of suffragists, only elites had the resources to mount a challenge in relative anonymity through women's magazines, thus preserving their ladylike image.

This initial attempt at organized opposition failed to blossom into a full-fledged movement against woman suffrage. Between 1871 and 1873, the Washington City group published the first American antisuffrage periodical, the *True Woman*. This short-lived journal was based in Baltimore and edited by Charlotte E. McKay, a former Union nurse who aided Virginia freedmen after the Civil War.[25] It mixed political messages with the literary works of contributors like Madeleine Dahlgren, Almira Lincoln Phelps, and, surprisingly, Harriet Beecher Stowe. Interestingly, subsequent generations of antis seemed totally unaware of this first mobilization effort, while suffrage histories duly recorded the 1871 protest petition and acknowledged also the "solitary little monthly," noting smugly that it died from "inherent weakness of constitution."[26]

Building Institutions

By the mid-1870s, suffragists had made greater progress at the local than at the federal level, although a version of the woman suffrage amendment that would finally pass Congress forty years later was first introduced and adversely reported in the U.S. Senate in 1878. A diverse group of states passed laws permitting women to vote in school elections, including Minnesota and Michigan (1875), Colorado (1876), New Hampshire and Oregon (1878), Massachusetts (1879), and Mississippi, New York, and Vermont (1880). Women's participation in children's education was less controversial because it could be viewed as compatible with the duties of the true woman rather than as political activity, although some opponents warned that it was just the entering wedge in the campaign for universal suffrage. They were proved correct. After school suffrage, prosuffrage politicians introduced bills for municipal suffrage that incited opponents to organize.[27]

In 1882, a group of women met in a Boston parlor to defeat municipal suffrage, reportedly in response to prompting by state senator George G. Crocker. According to retrospective accounts, Senator Crocker warned the female assemblage that municipal suffrage was inevitable unless petitions were prepared; the women followed his suggestion and the pending measure was defeated. They subsequently appointed a thirteen-woman Committee of Remonstrants to monitor the Massachusetts legislature and remobilize whenever suffrage threatened; this was not difficult, since Mrs. Crocker was a founding committee member. There was no statewide organization in these early years, and activism typically consisted of yearly remonstrances (petitions of protest) submitted to the legislature to counteract suffrage petitions; these were plentiful in Boston, the headquarters of the American Woman Suffrage Association. Petitions were soon supplemented by formal addresses delivered to legislative committees by male representatives.[28] Slowly women began to write their own papers, although men still read them to the legislature. The Boston committee printed these addresses into pamphlets, recruited articles from prominent antisuffragists, and circulated them to legislators and newspapers.[29] They followed suffrage progress in other states and sent literature to fledgling activists, newspapers, and legislators where suffrage measures were pending. For such a small group, their efforts were surprisingly thorough and sometimes very demanding; in one year, they reported three separate mailings of antisuffrage literature to each of almost four thousand newspapers in Kansas.[30]

The Boston committee's efforts were rewarded by state legislative inaction. In 1887, a Rhode Island full suffrage referendum failed by more than a three-to-one margin, and municipal suffrage was defeated in the legislatures of Vermont and Massachusetts.[31] That same year, though, faraway Kansas became the first state to enact municipal suffrage. Antisuffrage activity escalated dramatically in 1889, as nineteen states considered various forms of suffrage legislation—school, municipal, tax-paying, and license suffrage, which was part of temperance reform. The measures were defeated by legislative vote in seventeen of the nineteen states and submitted to a popular referendum only in Washington State, where it was defeated decisively. The sole suffrage victory occurred in the new state of Montana, where the legislature passed suffrage for tax-paying women.

Woman suffrage proponents saw in these events a discouraging pattern of defeats, impelling them to reunite their two factions into the National American Woman Suffrage Association (NAWSA) early in 1890. But the Boston committee perceived the same phenomena as evidence of growing suffrage agitation, and, disturbed by events in South Dakota, where a referendum was scheduled that fall to strike the word "male" from the state constitution, they began publication of the *Remonstrance*. The new journal was "addressed to the Legislatures of the several states" by unnamed "Remonstrants in Massachusetts, Maine, Illinois, and other states," and included a special South Dakota issue for the November referendum. Out-of-state contributions to the *Remonstrance* consisted largely of a few newspaper clippings and an occasional article, but anonymity facilitated the impression of a larger group. The committee cleverly framed its purpose in traditional terms of public education rather than political propaganda, asking only for "a thoughtful consideration of their views in the interest of fair discussion," despite the fact that it aggressively distributed the journal in suffrage campaign states.[32] The *Remonstrance* was published annually until it became a quarterly in 1907; early issues were only four pages long. Until its final issue in October 1920, the journal catalogued suffrage defeats, presented evidence of the "failed experiment" from suffrage states, reprinted the antisuffrage views of prominent men, and scrutinized the suffrage movement for signs of weakness.[33]

In May 1895 the Boston Committee of Remonstrants formally organized as the Massachusetts Association Opposed to the Further Extension of Suffrage to Women (MAOFESW), forsaking anonymity and female modesty to print the names of the executive committee members in the next issue of the *Remonstrance,* although it would be two more years before they would elect a president of the organization. The precipitating event for the formation of the Massachusetts Association was the Wellman bill, finally passed by the state legislature earlier that month after years of suffrage petitions. The Wellman bill provided for a nonbinding referendum on women's municipal suffrage the following November, at which all those qualified to vote for school suffrage could register their opinion, and further mandated a separate ballot count by gender. This was a rare opportunity for women to vote on their own enfranchisement, and both sides wasted no time organizing a campaign strategy. A group of prominent male antisuffragists formed Massachusetts Man Suffrage and cooperated with the women's antisuffrage organization on an oppositional campaign strategy that asked women to stay home and boycott the election while "arousing men to vote against the proposal." The results of the first Massachusetts suffrage referendum were mixed: men voted two to one against the bill while over 96 percent of the women voters favored municipal suffrage. The Massachusetts Association pronounced its boycott a success and for the next two decades emphasized women's lower voter turnout as proof of its argument that the majority was uninterested in the vote.[34]

The founders of the Massachusetts Association explicitly credited their exemplars in New York, who had united scattered local activists into a state association just months before. Committees in Albany and Brooklyn had formed in 1894 after learning that suffragists were preparing petitions to introduce a woman suffrage amendment at a planned state constitutional convention. According to one opponent's recollection, a "handful of women" met and began a counterpetition drive, collecting eighteen thousand signatures in six weeks. The suffrage amendment was defeated, and the petition organizers decided to put an association in "good working order" to meet future emergencies necessitated by the persistent threat of suffrage agitation.[35] Maintaining the image of true womanhood, the New York Association claimed that its purpose was "to increase general interest . . . and to educate and stimulate public opinion to an opposition based upon intelligent conversation."[36] The New York and Massachusetts organizations were by far the two most influential U.S. antisuffrage associations; they communicated regularly and shared information, speakers, and campaign literature.

The proximate cause for the organization of New York and Massachusetts antisuffragists was the threat of woman suffrage in their respective states. Looming above the local emergency, however, was the progress of woman suffrage in the West. Wyoming had entered the union in 1890 with woman suffrage in its new constitution, although it was contested. Whereas in the 1880s universal suffrage went before the voters in only three states, in the decade of the 1890s ten state legislatures submitted suffrage bills to popular referenda, and suffragists recorded their first successes when the voters of Colorado, Utah, and Idaho approved women's enfranchisement. Despite public disclaimers that the western states were totally irrelevant to the situation in the more civilized east, in 1898 the Massachusetts and New York associations collaborated to send organizers west to defeat woman suffrage referenda for a second time in Washington and South Dakota. A "Western Report" prepared by MAOFESW that summer cautioned privately that it was the remonstrants' "first duty" to "prevent other states" from following the examples of the four suffrage states, those ever-present reminders of the dangers of complacency.[37]

To build a western antisuffrage movement, the eastern associations typically worked through prominent local women, who hosted parlor meetings. This strategy enabled them to reach a conservative female constituency and also promoted the appearance of grassroots opposition. On the latter point, their success is questionable. For example, when the Oregon legislature agreed to submit a referendum on full suffrage to voters in June 1900, a local suffrage leader reported that "the 'antis' of the East . . . sent a bright little schemer to Oregon in October, 1899, on an intended-to-be sub rosa mission, to organize an 'Association Opposed to the Enfranchisement of Women,' her salary and expenses being paid, as she alleged, by a society of wealthy women in New York and Massachusetts." MAOFESW records confirm this allegation, although they viewed their role less as meddling than as helping to defend the women of Oregon.[38] Their mission succeeded; the 1900 Oregon referendum was defeated narrowly by male voters.

No such impending referendum explains the formation of the Illinois Association Opposed to the Extension of Suffrage to Women in 1897. Illinois remonstrants had been loosely organized since 1886 by Caroline Corbin, who was an early contributor to the *Remonstrance*.[39] Illinois passed school suffrage for women in 1891, but contested interpretation of its wording went repeatedly before the Illinois Supreme Court and ultimately limited its scope. Township suffrage bills were presented to the state legislature between 1893 and 1897, but were thrice defeated. With the legislature ostensibly secure, other events may explain the mobilization of Illinois antisuffragists. One is increased attention by suffrage leaders. In 1897 a series of meetings was held throughout the state by the National American Woman Suffrage Association, culminating in a November conference in Chicago attended by luminaries Susan B. Anthony, Carrie Chapman Catt, and Anna Howard Shaw.[40] Antisuffragists may have perceived these meetings as preparation for an Illinois suffrage campaign and organized preemptively.

Chicago was also the site of numerous civil disturbances during this period, including the Haymarket riots in 1886, the Pullman strike in 1894, and the campaigns of the Woman's Christian Temperance Union, whose leader, Frances Willard, first declared herself a suffragist and later a socialist.[41] Illinois antisuffrage rhetoric, most of it authored by Corbin, was notable for its early vitriolic accusations linking woman suffrage and socialism.[42] Governor Altgeld was never popular with native-born elites, but their opposition increased when he pardoned some of the accused Haymarket rioters and refused to break the Pullman strike. The restoration of order was symbolized locally by Governor Altgeld's defeat in 1897 and nationally by the previous year's presidential elections in which Republican William McKinley triumphed over the populist challenger William Jennings Bryan.[43] These events were a setback for women's suffrage, prohibition, and other reform movements and perhaps a political opportunity for antisuffrage mobilization in Illinois.

By the turn of the century, women had organized antisuffrage committees in California, Iowa, South Dakota, and Washington State. They established formal associations in four states—Oregon, Illinois, New York, and Massachusetts—but only the latter claimed to be organizing beyond the major cities.[44] The repertoire of precipitating events behind antisuffrage mobilization seems more complex than is typically expected for countermovements; it included reactions to suffrage successes, but also more proactive strategies based on assessments of political climates favorable for a decisive stand against enfranchisement. In addition to these larger political grievances and opportunities, other lifestyle circumstances prompted individual leaders to channel antisuffrage sentiments into organized action.

Social Background of the Antisuffrage Leadership

Social movement activism generally requires resources such as time and money. This is especially true of women's activism, and it is not surprising that most of the founders of the first antisuffrage organizations were women of privilege. Few other women of the period had the requisite skills and networks to articulate publicly their political views. The female antisuffragists who built the first organizations constituted a particularly homogeneous group of elite women; they were members of an upper class that enjoyed unprecedented power in nineteenth-century society.

In Massachusetts, the antisuffrage leadership was drawn predominantly from the social stratum known commonly as Boston Brahmins, typically descendants of the first Puritan settlers who enjoyed political, economic, and cultural hegemony for over two centuries. Brahmin families ruled Boston society in the domains of law, medicine, politics, education, religion, and the arts. They founded universities, hospitals, museums, libraries, and numerous voluntary associations that preserved their power through informal networks. Harvard University, in particular, was a Brahmin stronghold; its sons were students, faculty, overseers, and even presidents. The group dominated city politics through the Civil War and served class interests by containing urban disorder through the construction of parks, jails, schools, and other public works and by improving the business district and adjacent exclusive neighborhoods. Residential propinquity, as Baltzell notes, limits social interaction and thus creates and preserves class cohesiveness. Boston Brahmins developed Beacon Hill and later Back Bay and Brookline as elite enclaves, in the process building fortunes in real estate, and used their power to locate the Massachusetts State House on Beacon Hill.[45]

Intergenerational dominance and a strong sense of clan consciousness were maintained through endogamous marriage patterns. By the 1820s, a Brahmin enclave of about forty families—the so-called Boston Associates—was firmly established. Some families made their fortunes early in the East India trade, real estate, and banking, and frequently compounded their wealth in textile manufacturing, shipping, mining, and finance capitalism. These interrelated Lowells, Jacksons, Lawrences, Appletons, Amorys, Dwights, Lymans, and Coolidges dominated the first American industry of cotton production, built railroads to transport their products, and established banking houses to fund new projects. Nearly every distinguished family furnished shareholders, officers, and trustees to manage vast family fortunes. The Boston Brahmins were more successful than the ruling elites of other regions in making the transition from mercantilism to industrialism, and their dominance lasted well into the Gilded Age.[46]

The social backgrounds of the organizers of the Massachusetts antisuffrage association identify them as members of the Brahmin clan. Table 2.1 summarizes the personal characteristics of the thirteen founding members of the 1882 Boston Committee of Remonstrants. First, they tended to reside in three exclusive Brahmin strongholds, stately Beacon Hill, nearby Back Bay, and the newly formed suburb of Brookline; residential addresses indicate that they were frequently neighbors. Two exceptions were Nancy Houghton and Mary Fisk, who lived across the river in Cambridge on either side of that Brahmin bastion, Harvard University. Despite their distance from Beacon Hill, their lifestyles were hardly bohemian; Mrs. Fisk, for example, wife of a wealthy cotton merchant, was ensconced on prestigious Quincy Street surrounded by illustrious neighbors, such as the families of author Henry James, Harvard president Charles W. Elliot, and geology professor Alexander Agassiz, creator of the famed Calumet and Hecla copper mines with the brother of G. Howland Shaw, whose wife was also a founding member of the Boston committee.[47]

Second, the women were born to the Brahmin aristocracy.[48] Their fathers were ministers, physicians, lawyers, politicians, gentleman scholars, and community leaders, whose activities were supported frequently by family fortunes. For example, Julia Coolidge's father was John Lowell Gardner, son of Samuel Pickering Gardner, one of the last great East India merchants. Miss Parkman was descended on her distaff side from the Rev. John Cotton and was also an heir to the mercantile fortune of her paternal grandfather, Samuel Parkman. Rev. Samuel K. Lothrop, father of the Homans-Peabody sisters, was a Unitarian

Table 2.1. Boston Committee of Remonstrants, c. 1882

Name	Lineage	Husband's lineage	Husband's status	Residence
Mrs. George G. Crocker (Annie Bliss, b. 1843)	Dr. Nathan Cooley Keep (Bliss)[a]	Uriel Crocker, publisher (Kidder) FF[b] 1843–1913[c]	Harvard, Harvard Law[d] politics, law[e]	Back Bay
Miss Sarah H. Crocker (1840–1917)	Uriel Crocker, publisher (Kidder) FF	n/a	n/a	Back Bay
Miss C. S. Parkman	Rev. Francis Parkman (Hall) FF	n/a	n/a	Beacon Hill
Mrs. J. Randolph Coolidge (Julia)	John Lowell Gardner (Peabody) FF	desc. Thos. Jefferson FF 1828–1925	Harvard, Harvard Law law	Back Bay
Mrs. Charles D. Homans (Eliza, 1832–1914)	Rev. S. K. Lothrop (Lyman) FF	prominent medical family 1826–86	Harvard, Harvard Medical medicine	Back Bay
Mrs. Oliver W. Peabody	Rev. S. K. Lothrop (Lyman) FF	Rev. W. B. Peabody, Springfield, Mass., FF	no college finance	Milton
Mrs. G. Howland Shaw (Cora)	Theodore Lyman (Russell) FF	Robert Gould Shaw, exporter (Parkman) FF 1819–67	Harvard banking	Back Bay
Mrs. Robert C. Winthrop (Adele Thayer, d. 1892)	Granger; husband John Eliot Thayer, financier	Lt.-Gov. T. L. Winthrop (Temple) FF 1809–94	Harvard, Harvard Law politics, philanthropy	Beacon Hill, Brookline
Mrs. William B. Swett (Susan, b. 1840)	Grenville T. Winthrop (Heard) FF	Newburyport, Mass. FF b. 1832	education unknown independently wealthy	Beacon Hill
Mrs. James C. Hooker (Elizabeth, b. 1833)	Grenville T. Winthrop (Heard) FF	FF b. 1824	education unknown banking	Beacon Hill
Miss Elizabeth Putnam Sohier (b. 1843)	William Davies Sohier, lawyer (Lowell) FF	n/a	n/a	Beacon Hill
Mrs. Henry O. Houghton (Nancy)	Weir (Manning)	Vermont tanner	no college publishing	Cambridge
Mrs. James C. Fisk (Mary, d. 1903)			education unknown cotton merchant	Cambridge

[a]Mother's lineage in parentheses.
[b]FF indicates founding family, arrival in colonies prior to 1650.
[c]Husband's birth and death dates.
[d]Husband's education.
[e]Husband's occupation.

minister and for forty years pastor of Boston's historic Brattle Square Church, and their mother was born a Lyman. Cora Lyman Shaw, who served as Massachusetts Association president between 1905 and 1910, was the granddaughter of Boston mayor Theodore Lyman and the daughter of a U.S. congressman and Harvard overseer who helped elect his cousin Charles W. Elliot to the Harvard presidency. The Sohiers were relative newcomers to Boston, having emigrated from the Isle of Jersey in the eighteenth century, but they produced generations of lawyers who intermarried with founding families; Elizabeth Sohier's mother, Susan Cabot Lowell, was descended from a long line of distinguished lawyers and jurists.[49] The committee list reveals a complex web of kinship ties uniting the group, including sisters, cousins, and in-laws.[50]

The pattern of upper-class endogamy was repeated in their own marriages.[51] Ten of the original thirteen committee members were married; the relatively high proportion of older, unmarried women within the upper class is consistent with the pattern Walter Firey identified for Boston many decades later, which he attributes to norms that forbid women from marrying outside their class.[52] Indeed, the husbands of committee members tended to be descended from the same local founding families of Winthrop, Parkman, and Peabody. The third and fourth columns of table 2.1 indicate husbands' parentage as well as their educational and career attainments. Spouses were generally educated at Harvard University, often followed by Harvard Law School and careers in banking and corporate law, frequently managing family fortunes.[53] Dr. Charles Homans was preceded by several generations of Boston physicians, while Robert Winthrop, descendant of the first governor of the Massachusetts Bay Colony and heir to a mercantile fortune, had an early political career followed by local leadership in philanthropic and civic affairs. True to their sober Puritan heritage, even the men who inherited family fortunes established ostensible careers, with the possible exception of William B. Swett, whom the 1880 census-taker listed as "living on his money" at the age of forty-eight.[54]

Only two husbands of the founding committee members appeared to deviate from the pattern of Boston Brahmin endogamy. These were Oliver W. Peabody, the son of a distinguished country cleric and author, who founded the investment firm of Kidder, Peabody, and publisher Henry O. Houghton, offspring of a Vermont tanner, who began working at age thirteen. Lacking college educations, both men could be described as "back-country Puritans," but the tight-knit economic hegemony of the Boston Brahmins nonetheless linked them to other committee members. Mr. Houghton began his publishing business by purchasing the firm of Crocker and Brewster, owned by Sarah and George Crocker's father Uriel, and Mr. Peabody's firm of Kidder, Peabody developed from an earlier company owned by Mrs. Winthrop's first husband, John Eliot Thayer.[55]

The spouses of the antisuffrage movement's founders were frequently outstanding social and civic leaders as well. Crocker and Winthrop served in the Massachusetts legislature, where they were useful to the antisuffrage cause. Most participated extensively in historical and genealogical societies, whose primary purpose was to document and celebrate the achievements of the founding families. These husbands were life members and frequently trustees of the Boston Athenaeum, the Bostonian Society, and the Massachusetts Historical Society; Robert Winthrop served as the latter's president for thirty years.[56] Private philanthropy was also an important Brahmin function; Mr. Winthrop headed the powerful Boston Provident Association and the Peabody Education Fund, while Dr. Homans was president of the Boston Humane Society. As urban development proceeded and public services expanded, they often became leaders in civic affairs. Winthrop headed the city's Board of Overseers of the Poor and the Board of Commissioners responsible for building the Boston Public Library, Homans was president of the Massachusetts Medical Society, and Crocker chaired the Boston Transit Committee and the Joint Board on Metropolitan Improvements.[57] Most of the husbands were Republicans, which after the Civil War became the party of tariff protection and fiscal stability that favored their economic interests.[58]

In contrast to the homogamy found among the Massachusetts antisuffrage leadership, the leaders of the suffrage movement had more varied backgrounds. Prominent members of the Boston-based American Woman Suffrage Association included fewer founding family names, and many of them, such as Lucy Stone and Elizabeth Palmer Peabody, tended to be from the hinterland rather than part of the tight-knit Boston ruling clan. Elizabeth Oakes Smith, for example, was a descendant of Puritan settlers of Maine, and Lucretia Mott's forebears were the oldest settlers of Nantucket.[59] Their spouses were also from more diverse family backgrounds compared with the husbands of antisuffragists; they tended to be more recent arrivals in the United States, from rural backgrounds, and less educated. Blueblood suffragist Julia Ward Howe, a close friend of antisuffragist Eliza Homans, illustrates the broader background of suffragists. She was a descendant of Rhode

Island's founder, Roger Williams, but was born and raised in New York as the daughter of a wealthy banker. Julia Ward married Samuel G. Howe, member of a well-known Boston family, who studied at Rhode Island's Brown University.[60] Other suffragists from prominent families often traded social position for social service; one such example was Josephine Shaw Lowell, Boston Brahmin turned New York suffragist, who was active in relief efforts during the Civil War and later organized the first Consumers' League.[61]

These examples illustrate significant differences between the two groups of leaders and support the contentions of suffragists that women opponents were members of the entrenched elite. Prominent suffragists may have been relatively privileged women compared with the general population, but they were trumped by the antisuffrage leadership, which was distinguished by homogeneity of class and kinship. Even Boston suffrage leaders with old Puritan family ties were more mobile, married men from less prestigious backgrounds, and seemed less interested in maintaining the exclusivity of their social circle. This distinction between the two groups of activists was reiterated elsewhere, with the opposition's founders drawn from the "old money" aristocracy, while wealthy women were relative latecomers to the suffrage movement and tended to represent the new wealth of the postwar Gilded Age. In New York, for example, DuBois finds that "society suffragettes" were not recruited until well into the first decade of the new century, helping to make suffrage "fashionable," a term scorned by the old guard prevalent among the antisuffrage leadership.[62] Examples of nouveaux riches socialite suffrage activists included Mrs. O. H. P. Belmont of New York and Newport, who had divorced a Vanderbilt, and Mrs. Leland Stanford of California, wife of the railroad baron. The early remonstrants, by contrast, were banners of old money and conservative propriety who expressed class allegiance without apology, confident of a respectful hearing from political institutions replete with friends and relatives. Describing their first legislative victory over suffrage in the 1880s, one woman opponent noted that "the rustle of Beacon Street silks at the doors of legislation drowned the appeals" of woman suffragists. Two decades later, New York City antisuffragists proclaimed confidently, "Newport is with us, body and soul."[63]

These social differences between suffrage contestants are significant, for affluent women from Brahmin families were more likely to uphold the status quo of class and gender relations. Rigid convention still governed social intercourse among the old elite of nineteenth-century

America; duty was more important than individual happiness, and divorce stigmatized the entire family.[64] Elaborate rules of etiquette dominated all aspects of social life and confined the activities of upper-class women to their own social circle, as portrayed in the novels of Henry James and Edith Wharton.[65] Broadly defined modesty norms proscribed "unseemly" or "conspicuous" behavior and restricted women's use of public space, particularly in cities where the masses teemed. Rules of chaperonage protected the reputations of young girls, and although private carriages permitted some unescorted urban mobility, women's social lives during the period were confined largely to parlor visits in each other's homes.[66] The daily consequences of these norms are illustrated by the recently published diary of a Brahmin social matron, the sister-in-law of a Massachusetts Association founder, who ruminated on the lack of etiquette observed at a local bathing beach, where women entered open carriages without collars, manifesting "a degree of negligence that was not becoming." True to the tenets of true womanhood, the diarist rejects equal rights for her sex, determining that women excel in the passive qualities and "deserve the greatest admiration" because it is "more difficult to obey than to disobey."[67]

Upper-class women of the day were partly compensated for these restrictions by their responsibility for status maintenance. As outlined by Max Weber, status, class, and political power are the three basic elements of social stratification.[68] Status honor is reflected through a distinct style of life that defines those within the social circle. Weber proposed that restrictions on social interaction through endogamous marriage patterns and control over the norms of social convention help maintain the group's privileged status. More recently, Pierre Bourdieu and his followers have developed the concept of cultural capital from Weber's insights about the importance of status groups and applied this perspective to study the power of Boston Brahmin elite men.[69] Missing from both Weber's discussion and many subsequent elaborations of cultural capital, however, is the recognition that group dominance is maintained through a gendered division of labor. While men have primary responsibility for the maintenance of economic or class hegemony, socially prominent women, by their restricted interaction with outsiders and by supervision of the rituals of social intercourse, help define and protect status boundaries from incursions from below.

Some contemporary scholars of stratification, most notably Domhoff, have recognized the functional roles played by upper-class women in the service of class hegemony.[70] He observed that women are the gatekeepers of upper-class social institutions; they also set cultural standards for the rest of the population and perform voluntary acts of charity that signify beneficence and forestall lower-class revolt. Domhoff's assertions have been confirmed and revised by recent studies of wealthy women's philanthropic activities, which adopt a more dialectical approach to the study of elite women that considers relations of gender subordination within class dominance.[71] The idea that upper-class women contribute to the maintenance of group hegemony helps explain antisuffrage mobilization in the late nineteenth century.

The Myth of the Isolated Antisuffragist

Although suffragists dismissed the remonstrants as isolated women, we have already seen that the first organizers of antisuffrage protest shared extensive kinship networks that facilitated their mobilization. Furthermore, they enjoyed proximity to power derived from their social class position. Upper-class norms may have moderated opposition rhetoric and confined their early activities to parlor meetings, but with the help of male relations who presented their petitions before legislative hearings, they were effective in keeping woman suffrage at bay.

But changes in the late nineteenth century would affect the lives of upper-class women. Class relations hardened in the 1880s as urban problems escalated, due partly to mounting labor disputes; by one estimate there were 37,000 labor strikes between 1881 and 1905.[72] The upper strata, fearing imminent class warfare, funded the construction of urban armories, and even Harvard University began drilling student riflemen to defend the propertied classes against rioting workers. In northern cities especially, the myth of community foundered in the face of increasing heterogeneity caused by an influx of industrial workers who were largely foreign-born. Attempts to restore the familiar social order took diverse forms in the last decade of the nineteenth century from various segments of U.S. society—including populism, temperance, nativism, and the restoration of racial hegemony through Jim Crow laws in the southern states.[73]

The population of Boston doubled between 1860 and 1880 as much from the annexation of surrounding communities as from the influx of new immigrants, and by 1884 the era of exclusive Yankee political control ended forever when the city elected its first Irish mayor. In the economic sphere, the New England textile industry was in decline, corporate mergers were replacing the family firm, and ambitious venture capitalists from outside the Brahmin circle competed successfully against the conservative investment strategies of old family trusts. Post–Civil War economic expansion created new wealth, and by 1892 only about one-third of Boston millionaires had kinship ties to previous generations of wealthy Brahmins.[74] Although they still held considerable power, the economic and political dominance of the ruling clans was receding. Brahmin Henry Adams noted the change, and the anxiety of the upper classes found its voice in the protagonist of Edith Wharton's novel *The Age of Innocence*, who fulminated that "the country was in possession of the bosses and the emigrant, and decent people had to fall back on sport and culture."[75]

As urban space became more densely and diversely populated, the upper classes did appear to retreat from urban life. Perhaps striving to preserve a sense of community, they separated themselves self-consciously from the masses by constructing suburban residential enclaves, exclusive rural New England boarding schools, and gentlemen's social clubs. Club membership was especially important as a "badge of social rank," an oasis of homogeneity amid the urban melting pot. As the new rich made claims to social honor, old elites in numerous cities closed ranks by making lists of members who were "in society" and by publishing social registers that formally delineated the boundaries of the status group.[76] Male cultural entrepreneurs established urban art museums, symphonies, and opera houses that increasingly segregated public entertainment by social class. This institutional dominion was accompanied by cultural authority, whereby elites, consistent with Weber's argument, first defined new symbols of social prestige and then preserved their value by restricting entrée to other members of their status group.[77]

Denied access to formal economic and political power, even wealthy women did not generally participate in the formation of institutions of high culture, but they helped maintain these institutions, along with group cohesion, through fund-raising entertainments. An increasingly ritualized social life drew affluent women out of domestic seclusion, and "society queens" received new public legitimation in local newspapers. Women organized most elite social events according to "seasons," with crowded calendars of parties, luncheons, tea dances, balls, and dinners before symphony and opera concerts. Women presided at these public affirmations of social honor and were themselves under scrutiny. The presentation of female debutantes to "Society" was formalized during this period to ensure elite marital homogamy. By the age of eighteen, young women became central players in class maintenance, exhibited before eligible men in the hopes of making a "brilliant" marriage to someone of impeccable social credentials, and throughout life maintained group solidarity through a host of social rituals.[78]

Elaborate rules of etiquette that increased the role of upper-class women in status maintenance were another elite response to the "excess of democracy." If the new rich could now purchase mass-produced goods that emulated the lifestyles of the ruling class and new urban residents could mingle freely with the gentry in bustling city streets, etiquette promised to "keep every cog and wheel in place." Etiquette facilitated social control by promising upward mobility in exchange for social conformity while simultaneously raising the stakes for elite membership from material achievement to personal governance and more subtle signs of "breeding." Parallel with elites' separation of popular and high culture, higher standards of etiquette distinguished the rustic and vulgar from the refined and genteel, and promised to unmask social counterfeits attempting entry to the higher circles. For example, a proliferation of new serving pieces reiterated the specialized industrial division of labor, and eating with one's knife, which was acceptable a century earlier, became taboo; the ritual of the dinner party, presided over by women, functioned as a test of pedigree.[79]

While men dominated institutions of high culture, women shaped the tastes of the masses. Women were both the primary authors and consumers of the many etiquette books published beginning with the Jacksonian period; these popular volumes as well as periodicals such as *Godey's* facilitated the cultural diffusion of the doctrine of separate spheres. Etiquette circumscribed the activities of "proper" women to shield them from the public gaze; sexual metaphors symbolized the problem of urban disorder, and modesty norms with moral overtones restricted women's use of urban space. Many studies of separate spheres have analyzed the home as a refuge from the impersonal marketplace, but it was also a place to rehearse public performance by practicing table manners and proper emotional display.[80] This new domestic function paradoxically increased the social value of female skills while restricting mobility, and also operated as a mechanism of social control against the lower classes.

Motherhood, in particular, was laden with new societal duties. Popular theories of child development held that children retraced the steps of human evolution from savagery to civilization and advised mothers to teach offspring the importance of self-discipline over self-gratification, the control of base appetites by the higher faculties. The expanded motherhood role affected all groups of women. Wealthy mothers were responsible for preparing children to take their places at the top of the social order, although nannies and governesses performed much of the daily labor; meanwhile, lower-class conformity to the behavioral standards of the ruling elite promised upward mobility. In the new gendered division of labor, elite men served class interests as institution-building entrepreneurs while women helped maintain group solidarity as cultural arbiters. These new female responsibilities required formal training, and private finishing schools, focused heavily on the social graces, taught young ladies the duties of their station.[81]

For adult women, the drive for self-improvement spawned the club movement. Much has been written about how ladies' clubs redefined the true woman beyond the domestic circle and laid the ideological and logistical groundwork for the development of woman suffrage as a mass movement. Less recognized is their function for organized antisuffragism. From the earliest women's benevolent societies through moral reform and municipal housekeeping, the doctrine of separate spheres expanded progressively to justify increased female community participation.[82] The earliest influential women's clubs were founded in 1868 in New York and Boston. Sorosis, founded by New York journalist Jane Cunningham Croly, broke gender conventions by meeting in public restaurants instead of private homes, paving the way for women's integration into urban life. Although its leadership and many of its members were suffragists, Sorosis eschewed controversial political topics; nonetheless, its appropriation of the word "club," heretofore associated only with male fellowship, was suspect, as was the organization of women without an ostensible philanthropic purpose. Local newspapers castigated the new organization for conspicuousness, selfishness, and household neglect.[83]

That same year, the New England Woman's Club (NEWC) formed to "organize the social force of the women of New England" and create a center "of comfort and convenience." To this end, they secured rooms in Boston, where, according to historian Anne Firor Scott, "women of the leading families, who were gradually moving to the suburbs, could restore the sense of community of an earlier day when they had been able to walk to each others' houses."[84] The membership composition of these two organizations differed slightly. The New York Sorosis served the professional interests of careerwomen, while the NEWC, led for almost thirty years by suffragist Julia Ward Howe, pursued social reform. Nonetheless, both organizations shared a vision of woman's virtue derived from her role as keeper of the hearth that would mediate the damaging effects of the competitive male sphere and thus improve society and the lives of women. Croly went on to help found the Association for the Advancement of Women (AAW), an alternative to suffrage agitation that lasted for twenty-five years, until it was eclipsed by the General Federation of Women's Clubs, which she was also instrumental in organizing.[85]

The General Federation of Women's Clubs knitted together local self-improvement societies and expanded the scope of traditional women's concerns and activities. It grew rapidly, from 160,000 members in 1898 to 500,000 women in 1905, and surpassed 1,000,000 by 1910.[86] The club movement did not so much abandon the ideology of separate spheres as extend it into public life by invoking themes of moral superiority and maternal devotion. Although it had somewhat of an elitist reputation, the federation made the transition from cultural self-improvement to municipal housekeeping by claiming that woman's traditional domestic skills were vital to the solution of new urban problems. In the process, it also gave women valuable experience in self-government; national and state federations routinely formed committees to study topics of special concern to women—education, child and maternal health, and consumer issues—that also had implications for public policy.[87]

The club movement was a common ground for women on both sides of the suffrage issue, at least in the early phases of the campaign. Several prominent Boston antisuffragists were active in the New England Woman's Club, and as early as 1896 MAOFESW leaders had earmarked women's clubs "as perhaps the most promising field for antisuffrage work at present."[88] Organizations representing both sides of the issue competed for the federation's support, and for three years the Massachusetts Association attempted unsuccessfully to affiliate. The General Federation's decision to endorse woman suffrage in 1914 embittered antisuffragists within its ranks; one Massachusetts officer even proposed that local clubs work to break up the federation entirely in retribution.[89]

By the turn of the century, the role of the affluent woman had expanded to include "her inherited obligations, her share of the working of the great civic machine, and all hung together in the solidarity of these traditional functions."[90] While some young socialites joined the settlement movement, by and large the charitable activities of society matrons had been redefined from Lady Bountiful into a managerial role—serving on the boards of various public commissions and private philanthropies and organizing fund-raising events.[91] One Brahmin antisuffragist wrote a journal article showing how the new clubwoman remained consistent with the true womanhood tradition, in part through her amateur status:

> The Boston clubwoman was never the aggressive, meddlesome, angular female of comic pictures . . . She is simple not complex, alert but patient, self-conscious and deprecatory; very moral and persistent . . . As a rule she is pre-eminently a religious woman, and, although gifted with facility in verse and prose, she is seldom a novelist or historian, but is always a good housekeeper.[92]

A women's club played a significant role in the formal organization of Massachusetts antisuffragists. It was the Mayflower Club, founded in 1893 by antisuffrage committee members Mrs. Charles Homans and her sister, Mrs. Oliver Peabody. Like its predecessor the New England Woman's Club, this self-defined "ladies' club" established rooms to accommodate the needs of suburban women restricted by social convention from using public restaurant and hotel accommodations. Unlike the NEWC, however, the Mayflower Club intentionally had "no literary, scientific, or even social reason for being," but "proposed to fashion itself after the manner of clubs heretofore enjoyed by men." In pursuit of these modest goals, it offered its members rooms and luncheon fare at the former Beacon Hill residence of John Amory Lowell, grandfather of antisuffrage leaders Elizabeth Sohier and Elizabeth Lowell Putnam, conveniently situated next door to an exclusive men's club. While women's clubs without a utilitarian function already existed in New York and Philadelphia, the idea was new to Puritan New England, and the *Boston Transcript* editorialized about the "experiment," pondering whether women could acquire through practice what men do by instinct—to "take pleasure in one another's society."[93] These musings about woman's selfish nature typified public responses to the club movement, and may indicate the stirrings of anxiety that increased female participation in urban life would exacerbate the processes of female independence, domestic abandonment, and societal disorder.[94]

Most striking is the deviation from the ideal of the self-sacrificing true woman proclaimed by the club's founders. "Without any pretense of service," the Mayflower Club operated according to the rule that "each member shall be in a manner independent, not expected to entertain any other, free to read, to be silent, to be alone."[95] As an expression of its intention to ensure female independence of thought and deed, the founding regulations of the club prohibited men and children. Social clubs apparently served gender-specific functions for affluent members; as exclusive men's clubs banned the discussion of business to preserve a protected sphere of fellowship untainted by the marketplace, those for women created a place of refuge from domestic responsibilities and an opportunity to practice the skills of self-government.[96]

The Mayflower Club predated the founding of MAOFESW by two years, but the organizations share a common history. Of the six women who hosted the organizational meeting for the new club, three were antisuffrage leaders and another was married to a prominent organizer of male antisuffragists.[97] In addition to presiding over the first meeting of the Mayflower Club, Eliza Homans was remembered as the "de facto leader" of the Boston Committee of Remonstrants and probably would have been named president when it reorganized into a state association had she not embarked on a world tour early in 1895.[98] Mrs. Homans "enlisted" Elizabeth Cabot to serve as the Mayflower Club's first president, the same office she would hold in the Massachusetts Association. In addition to Homans and Peabody, who also served as vice-presidents of the Mayflower Club, five other women from the early Boston committee were club members.[99] Mayflower membership was not restricted to antisuffrage women, but it attracted conservative women, facilitated their interaction, and prepared them for leadership roles; as antisuffragist Kate Gannett Wells observed a decade earlier, the fact "that clubs have taught women to work with one another alone justifies their existence."[100]

The second generation of antisuffragists who engineered the evolution from informal committee work to a state antisuffrage organization reflected these changes in women's roles. At the founding of the Boston Committee of Remonstrants in 1882, the organizers were in their forties and fifties, and by the mid-1890s the survivors were approaching old age. Although some of them, most notably Eliza Homans, Cora Shaw, and Elizabeth Sohier, remained active in the new state association, for the most part a new group of middle-aged women replaced them. Table 2.2 describes the leadership of the Massachusetts Association circa 1900. The social backgrounds of the women and their husbands manifest the continuity of Brahmin influence and clan homogamy, as illustrated by the repetition of founding family names among women as well as between spouses. The fathers of Elizabeth Dwight Cabot and Elizabeth Lowell Putnam had made fortunes in the textile industry, for example. Both Mrs. Putnam and her husband were Lowells, while Mary Lyman Guild and her husband Charles were Eliots on their distaff sides. Judge Francis Cabot

Table 2.2. Massachusetts Antisuffrage Association leadership, c. 1900

Name	Club activities	Family background	Husband	Residence
Mrs. J. Elliot Cabot (d. 1901)	pres., 1897–1901 chair, educ. comm., 1896–97 chair, Volunteer Aid Society Brookline School Comm. pres., Mayflower Club	Elizabeth Dwight FF[a] Husband: Perkins FF	Harvard, Harvard Law[b] architect, author[c] (1821–1903)[d]	Brookline
Mrs. Charles E. Guild	pres., 1902–5 v.p., 1897–1902, 1910–17	Mary Lyman (Eliot)[e] FF Husband: Eliot FF	Harvard	Brookline
Mrs. Henry M. Whitney	v.p., 1897–1917 Brookline Education Society Mayflower Club	Margaret F. Green Husband: New Hampshire	shipping, mining (1839–1923)	Brookline
Mrs. Robert W. Lord (d. 1904)	secretary, 1897–1904	Ella Green	lawyer	Boston
Mrs. James M. Codman (1838–1923)	pres., 1913–15 treas., 1901–19 exec. comm., 1895–1919 State Board of Lunacy & Charity Mayflower Club	Henrietta Gray Sargent	Harvard, Harvard Law lawyer (1831–1917)	Brookline
Mrs. Francis C. Lowell	v.p., 1912–17 exec. comm., 1895–1917	Cornelia Baylies, New York Husband: Cabot, Gardner FF	Harvard, Harvard Law jurist (1855–1911)	Boston
Mrs. William Lowell Putnam (1862–1935)	chair, E & O comm., 1910–1917 v.p., Household Nursing Assoc. pres., Am. Assoc. for Study and Prevention of Infant Mortality Mayflower Club	Elizabeth Lowell (Lawrence) FF Husband: Lowell FF	Harvard, Harvard Law lawyer	Boston
Miss Elizabeth H. Houghton (1858–1915)	exec. comm., 1895–1915 exec. comm., Consumers' League exec. comm., Cambridge Conference of Associated Charities Mayflower Club	Nancy and H. O. Houghton	n/a	Cambridge

[a]Founding family (see table 2.1).
[b]Husband's education.
[c]Husband's occupation.
[d]Husband's birth and death dates.
[e]Mother's family background in parenthesis.

Lowell, husband of Cornelia Baylies Lowell, was related to the Cabot and Gardner families. Still mostly Harvard-educated, many of the husbands were lawyers by training as well as community leaders. For instance, J. Elliot Cabot, a descendant of the Perkins mercantile fortune, studied law at Harvard and philosophy in Germany, was a well-known architect, explored Lake Superior with Agassiz, authored a memoir of his friend Ralph Waldo Emerson, and helped found the Boston Museum of Fine Arts and the Athenaeum Library.[101] As was true for the 1882 committee membership, the circle was not completely closed to outsiders, particularly if they were as successful as Henry M. Whitney, one of the first major international venture capitalists and a principal developer of suburban Brookline, whose wife was the sister of another association officer with more distinguished marital credentials.[102]

The greatest apparent change in the new generation of women leaders was their level of community participation. Two decades after the founding of the first antisuffrage committee, public anonymity was no longer the norm for upper-class women. The sphere of appropriate female influence had expanded even for elite women; whereas early antisuffrage leaders might be celebrated for their "character" and "piety," by the turn of the century the women at the forefront of the opposition were lauded for the "important positions" they filled in the community.[103]

This change is illustrated in the second column of table 2.2, which lists the positions held by each woman in the Massachusetts Association, followed by selected charitable and club activities. It indicates that some of these women officers were as involved in civic affairs as were the husbands of antisuffrage leaders a generation earlier. Elizabeth Cabot was not only president of two organizations, but also an overseer of the poor, chair of the Volunteer Aid Society, and, somewhat ironically, an elected member of the Brookline School Committee. Margaret Whitney, MAOFESW vice-president for twenty years, was also involved in community educational improvements, while Henrietta Codman, who served as both president and longtime treasurer of the association, was a member of the State Board of Lunacy and Charity; both Codman and Cabot were elected Brookline overseers of the poor in the 1880s. Some of the earlier Boston committee members who remained active in the Massachusetts Association throughout their lives also had appointments to state boards, although they were less active in community affairs than the succeeding generation of leaders. For example, Eliza Homans, a MAOFESW vice-president until her death in

1914, was a member of the state's Board of Prisons, and Elizabeth Sohier was one of the first appointees to its Library Commission.[104]

Despite their levels of civic participation, antisuffrage leaders were much less likely than suffragists to be college-educated and to pursue careers. None of the women founders of the Boston committee or the Massachusetts Association was a college graduate or engaged in paid employment, in marked contrast to Boston suffrage leaders like Alice Stone Blackwell, who graduated Phi Beta Kappa from Boston University in the 1880s.[105] In 1907 MAOFESW named as vice-presidents two prominent professional women with ties to elite women's colleges, neither of whom participated actively in the organization: Agnes Irwin, the first dean of Radcliffe College, and Anna L. Dawes, newspaper correspondent and Smith College trustee, both of whom were approaching retirement.[106] Moreover, only two other officers (and none of its fourteen presidents) were sufficiently prominent in civic affairs to be listed in the 1914 publication of the *Woman's Who's Who of America*. One was Elizabeth Lowell Putnam, sister of poet Amy Lowell and Harvard President A. Lawrence Lowell and first cousin of remonstrant committee member Elizabeth Sohier. Elizabeth Putnam was a national leader in child and maternal welfare, particularly the pure milk campaign, and president of the American Association for the Study and Prevention of Infant Mortality. She would later become active in the preparedness movement, appointed by the governor to supervise the compilation of male enlistees during World War I, head the Relief Department's Information Bureau for the troops, and represent her state on the Red Cross Casualty Bureau.[107] The second woman of national note was Elizabeth Houghton, daughter of the publisher, a second-generation antisuffragist, and head of the local Consumers' League, where her special interest was tenement housing. Houghton was also active in the Cambridge Conference of Associated Charities, the Cambridge Hospital League, and the Women's Auxiliary to the Episcopal Board of Missions; she participated in working girls' associations and founded a local boys' club.[108] These women were clearly exceptions, however; of the 102 MAOFESW branch committee chairs in 1915, only one was listed in *Woman's Who's Who*.[109]

The evolving female norm from seclusion to public participation percolated upward to the elite stratum and provided opportunities for antisuffrage mobilization. But important distinctions remained in the kinds of activities favored by the opposition leadership, reflecting the political orientations of their social class. The antisuffrage leadership did not participate in the Women's Trade Union League (WTUL), an early example of cross-class alliances among women that had early and active chapters in Boston, New York, and Chicago. This was partly due to the WTUL's association with the labor movement, about which antis expressed ambivalence and periodic hostility. Their own philanthropic choices demonstrated a clear preference for helping the poor in ways that upheld the status quo and sought to preserve private control over social welfare, as opposed to state action. Working girls' clubs were an expression of their gendered class interests. These associations were the province of wealthy women benefactors who saw themselves as the bearers of culture to the lower classes; according to Nancy Dye, their principal function was to imbue young working women with "good work habits and genteel notions of femininity," not to improve their economic position through collective action. Elizabeth Putnam's work for maternal and child health also favored a top-down approach, rejecting client education in favor of expanded medical services that were targeted, for a fee, at the more affluent middle class.[110] For the most part, though, the antisuffrage leadership pursued social club activities, building interpersonal networks that would prove beneficial for the long-distance recruitment of like-minded women.

Recruitment Networks of Class and Kin

While the officers of the Massachusetts Association were a particularly tight-knit group, the social backgrounds of antisuffrage leaders throughout the United States generally replicated these characteristics. This was no coincidence, because the Massachusetts and New York associations collaborated through their interstate committees to recruit "women of high social standing" for the purposes of founding antisuffrage organizations in other states. Club networks proved invaluable for this task; the national president of the General Federation of Women's Clubs, who also served on the executive committee of the New York Association, visited women's clubs in eleven states in 1903 and concluded that two-thirds of the federation's members were antisuffrage sympathizers. Both associations worked persistently to mobilize women across the United States, filing reports that "something needs to be done about Baltimore," that "interest seemed dead" in South Dakota and Washington State, and expressing relief when Maine asked for speakers "at last."[111] The many unsolicited requests for organizing assistance from residents of faraway states confirm their joint stewardship of the national antisuffrage movement.

One of the simplest recruitment strategies was to utilize kinship ties. The founder of the first Rhode Island antisuffrage committee in 1903, for example, was Mrs. William Ely, daughter of Massachusetts Association officer Henrietta Codman.[112] The chair of the Albany branch of the New York State organization, Mrs. John V. L. Pruyn, recruited her daughter for executive committee service, and Agnes Irwin's sister Sophy was a vice-president of the Pennsylvania Association, which organized formally around the time that Agnes relocated there in 1909. Some officers were daughters of famous male antisuffragists, such as Bishop William Croswell Doane of Albany, who preached against female public participation as early as the 1860s. Marital ties among the women officers were also common. A director of the New York Association and the president of the Rhode Island Association were both married to Hazard relations, and several Hoppin and Gammell women were officers of the latter group.[113] Among the leaders of the Pennsylvania Association were a number of Philadelphia founding family intermarriages among Biddles, Drexels, and Penroses.[114] The executive officers of the New York Association included sisters-in-law Jeannette L. Gilder and Mrs. Richard Watson Gilder, Mrs. Arthur M. Dodge and her daughter-in-law Priscilla Barnes Dodge, and numerous old Knickerbocker families, including Pruyns, Wheelers, and Van Rensselaers. Mrs. James Roosevelt, mother of future president Franklin Delano Roosevelt, served briefly as vice-president, but its officers also included the wives of wealthy industrialists, such as first-generation American Mrs. Fritz Achelis (the former Bertha Koenig), who frequently hosted annual meetings in her luxurious uptown mansion. The New York organization made full use of its cosmopolitan leadership by naming as its international secretary Mrs. Otto (Lilian Bayard Taylor) Kiliani, daughter of the well-known author; Lilian Kiliani's extensive experience living abroad served the cause by consolidating networks between U.S. and English antisuffragists.[115]

The influence of Yankee New England for antisuffrage mobilization reached well beyond these examples of parents, siblings, and spouses. The New York Association, in particular, was led by a number of women with extended kinship ties to Puritan Boston, such as its first state president, Mrs. Francis M. Scott (the former Lucy Parkman Higgins), Mrs. Lyman (Abby Hamlin) Abbott, state president from 1903 until her death in 1907, and Mrs. William A. (Carolyn Haines) Putnam, longtime chair of the Brooklyn auxiliary. The presidents of both the Illinois and Oregon associations were born in New England of Yankee ancestry.[116] Eastern ties facilitated long-distance mobilization in a period when much of the work was done through the slow method of correspondence; organizational records document the extent to which antis went about establishing new state associations by contacting women acquaintances.

It was not just the coincidence of heredity but the social significance attached to it that linked antisuffrage mobilization to the club movement of the 1890s. New patriotic-hereditary societies, organized typically in eastern cities like New York and Washington, were another response to the upheavals of the period. The defining characteristic of these organizations was renewed attention to the country's republican and revolutionary heritage, fused paradoxically with exclusive membership requirements based upon pedigree, a practice that in the previous century was attacked as antidemocratic and as imitating European aristocracy. The popular spread of Darwin's theories of evolution coincident with new waves of immigration from southern and eastern Europe reawakened interest in demonstrating genealogical superiority; some viewed it as the responsibility of the "best people" to "protect the purity" of American institutions. As with other urban social clubs described earlier, exclusiveness was a primary appeal; in addition to distinguished ancestry, for many societies "high social standing" was a prerequisite for membership.[117] Indeed, each subsequent organization seemed to compete with its predecessor by further restricting membership requirements; the Sons of the American Revolution (SAR), founded in 1889, was soon followed by the Society of Colonial Wars, which was open only to the descendants of soldiers and public officials who served before the Revolution.

Women's hereditary organizations enjoyed even greater popularity. The Daughters of the American Revolution (DAR), established in 1890, claimed over thirty thousand members by the turn of the century, the largest of any patriotic-hereditary society. In an obvious parallel to their male counterparts in the Society of Colonial Wars, the same year a group of New York "Knickerbocker aristocracy" led by a Van Rensselaer and a Gardiner organized the even more exclusive Society of Colonial Dames. Although such associations were more common in the urban northeast, the trend extended to the southern United States, where the United Daughters of the Confederacy was founded in 1894.

Not all were single-sex associations, however; the Society of Mayflower Descendants accepted both men and women who could meet the restrictive membership requirements.[118]

Regardless of gender, hereditary societies organized to commemorate their ancestors' contributions, much like the historical societies that predated them. But the newer associations had more ambitious social goals, convinced that patriotism could unite the heterogeneous masses and that early American roots uniquely qualified them to teach the duties of citizenship to the foreign born. Belief in the stabilizing influence of patriotism led these organizations to sponsor campaigns for public veneration of the flag, preservation of historic landmarks and monuments, and patriotic instruction through lectures and essay contests. They generally favored immigration restriction—as one DAR leader advised, "let the statue of Liberty put out her light"—but distanced themselves from nativist mass movements. Reflecting its conservative constituency, the DAR expressed suspicions about socialism and labor activism, but preferred a traditional nonpartisan role that extended to woman suffrage. Addressing a membership that included suffrage leaders Susan B. Anthony and Julia Ward Howe, one DAR leader advised her peers "to keep our Sisterhood of Daughters free from entangling alliances with bands of women aiming at any of the fads of the day."[119]

Another important function of the hereditary societies was the opportunity to socialize and celebrate superior breeding with others of similar background. This was especially true of the women's organizations, which developed concurrently with the women's club movement. The most exclusive women's hereditary societies such as the Colonial Dames sponsored elaborate teas where old letters were read and family heirlooms exhibited. Despite their nostalgic focus as "self-appointed guardians of the American past," these hereditary societies nonetheless constituted another institutional force propelling conservative, affluent women out of their homes into increasing involvement in social issues. Small numbers and regional concentration in the northeastern United States may have limited their influence, but DAR and SAR members frequently also "formed the socially ambitious local gentry in many a small American town."[120]

Numerous prominent antisuffragists participated in hereditary societies, especially in the hinterland. The Albany branch of the New York Association, which included among its officers the names of Gardiner, Sage, and Van Rensselaer, had proportionately more Colonial Dames members than the New York City branch, while the Boston Brahmin leadership rarely joined these societies, perhaps because in that locale it was not a particularly exclusive mark of social distinction.[121] Colonial Dames members were found among the officers of the Minneapolis, Maryland, Virginia, and Georgia antisuffrage associations.[122] Perhaps most striking is the finding that DAR members headed antisuffrage drives in at least fourteen states and the District of Columbia, and one president of the New York Association was a member of the Society of Mayflower Descendants.[123] Numerous husbands were also active in hereditary societies, heading Sons of the American Revolution and Society of Colonial Wars associations in New Jersey, Pennsylvania, and Minnesota. A particularly impressive antisuffrage couple were the McCamants of Portland, Oregon, one of whom served as SAR state president while the other was DAR state regent.[124]

Hereditary societies were not the only club activities to engage the interests of antisuffragists. Of the almost three dozen antisuffrage officers from around the country included in *Woman's Who's Who of America,* the majority were clubwomen rather than careerwomen. Of those with listed occupations, two were practicing attorneys, but most of the women were writers—poets, journalists, authors of children's books and songs—only a minority of whom supported themselves from their craft. These included Jeannette L. Gilder, founder of the *Critic,* and Mrs. Schuyler (Mariana Griswold) Van Rensselaer, dubbed "Newport's historian," who wrote on travel and art for *Century* magazine, which was published by Gilder's brother. Education was another calling that attracted women to antisuffragism as far back as Catharine Beecher and Emma Willard; in addition to Radcliffe dean Agnes Irwin, the presidents of the Southern California and Tennessee associations were educators, and a Georgia vice-president directed the Lucy Cobb Institute.[125] But fewer than half of the antisuffrage leaders listed in *Woman's Who's Who* were college-educated, whereas Kraditor's survey of suffrage leaders found the majority had college educations and a number of nationally prominent suffragists held advanced degrees.[126] Antisuffragists also manifested regional variations that paralleled changes in women's opportunities during the century. College attendance was rare among Boston women leaders, more common in New York and rural New England (where it was usually restricted to private single-sex institutions), while many educated women in the western frontier states were graduates of large public universities.

The typical antisuffrage leader was active in her community through membership in numerous local organizations, from study clubs to art guilds, religious and philanthropic activities, and civic affairs. A few were nationally prominent, and some evidenced a prior dedication to women's interests. The founder of the Illinois Association, for example, also helped establish the Association for the Advancement of Women in the 1870s, while the first two presidents of the National Association Opposed to Woman Suffrage (NAOWS) were leaders in the movements to establish day nurseries and community playgrounds.[127] The networks provided by the General Federation of Women's Clubs were an especially useful recruitment tool, drawing officers from distant states into the forefront of the antisuffrage movement.[128] As with their Massachusetts predecessors, devotion to good works did not distinguish antisuffrage leaders from their opponents, although the former tended to favor organizations that more assiduously observed the boundary between traditional philanthropy and social activism.

The participation of Boston antisuffrage leaders in the most exclusive social circles was reiterated elsewhere. Three-quarters of the officers of the New York Association were listed in the 1910 edition of the *Social Register.* The president of the Ohio Association was an active clubwoman "prominent in social life," and her Maryland counterpart was described as one of "the leaders of society in Baltimore, Newport, and Bar Harbor."[129] In the larger cities, exclusive social clubs similar to Boston's Mayflower Club served as sources of elite recruitment. Many of the New York antisuffrage leaders were members of the posh Colony Club, which in 1907 built a million-dollar clubhouse on Madison Avenue designed by McKim, Mead, and White to provide women with all the comforts of leisure—gymnasium, squash courts, running track, swimming pool, baths, tearoom, restaurant—so they would not have to mingle with "all classes of undesirable persons." While not all Colony Club members were antisuffragists, opposition leaders used the facilities to organize discussions on the suffrage question, garnering free publicity for the movement with a celebrated roster of participants; famed muckraker and antisuffragist Ida Tarbell presided at one hearing with Britain's duchess of Marlborough in attendance.[130]

The class position of antisuffrage leaders nationally is also explicated by examination of their parentage. They were most commonly the daughters of lawyers, bankers, and financiers, and to a lesser extent ministers, educators, and military officers.[131] Fathers included the first president of Johns Hopkins University, inventor and philanthropist Peter Cooper, and social reformer Jacob Riis.[132] Another well-represented occupation was politics; antisuffrage leaders included the daughters of Connecticut and Washington governors, several U.S. congressmen and senators, and presidential cabinet members. Perhaps not coincidentally, political offspring rose to the highest levels of antisuffrage leadership, including the first two presidents of the National Association Opposed to Woman Suffrage: Josephine Jewell Dodge, who accompanied her father during his term as U.S. minister to Russia, and Alice Hay Wadsworth, whose famous father, John Hay, served four presidents and was ambassador to the Court of St. James.[133] These findings suggest that some of the most prominent antisuffrage leaders, far from being isolated, were in fact steeped in politics from an early age. The movement also derived clear benefits from current paternal office holding; an Alabama officer was the daughter of U.S. Senator John H. Bankhead, and a National Association board member was the offspring of Senator Henry Cabot Lodge, both of whom were strong congressional foes of woman suffrage.[134]

As in Massachusetts, the husbands of the antisuffrage leadership elsewhere tended to be well-educated men from distinguished families; even those in the frontier states were often descended from old colonial stock. They were employed typically as bankers, lawyers, and industrialists, but they were also community leaders, active in politics, civic affairs, philanthropy, and patriotic-hereditary societies. The New York Association, in particular, was dominated by the wives of nationally prominent men, including politicians Elihu Root and Everett Wheeler, jurist Francis Markoe Scott, and magazine editors Richard Watson Gilder, Lyman Abbott, and Rossiter Johnson. Abram S. Hewitt, whose wife and daughter were officers in the New York organization, was a pioneer iron manufacturer, philanthropist, and former New York City mayor. This pattern was repeated in other states. For example, the antisuffrage movement in Rhode Island and Delaware was headed by the wives of prominent textile manufacturers, and the husband of the Pennsylvania Association president was a founder of Bethlehem Steel. The spouses of the Maine and Nebraska presidents were wealthy grain merchants, and the latter was also director of the U.S. Chamber of Commerce. A Minnesota officer was married to a founder of the Pillsbury flour mill conglomerate, and the husband of her Oregon counterpart owned one of the largest lumber mills in the Northwest. The Michigan Association was headed by the wife of a prominent surgeon, while the Connecticut leadership had strong marital ties to the Yale faculty.[135] Presidents of the Maine, Tennessee, and Oregon associations were the wives of well-known attorneys, and the leader of Wisconsin antisuffragists was the socialite wife of the state's attorney general; the husband of the founder of the Texas Association was a wealthy rancher, developer, and political boss of the Rio Grande Valley. Officers in at least eight state associations were married to railroad executives, and financiers were well-represented among the top leadership ranks.[136] These corporate connections may partly explain the suffragist claim that corporate interests were behind the antisuffrage movement. Governors' wives were also active in the antisuffrage movement, heading the Nevada Association and serving as state officers elsewhere. The New Jersey Association's roster of officers contained two high-status political widows, including the former wife of President Grover Cleveland. In addition, a NAOWS president was married to U.S. Senator James Wadsworth (New York), and one board member was the spouse of U.S. Congressman Augustus Peabody Gardner (Massachusetts), both of whom openly opposed suffrage.[137]

Elite networks for the most part facilitated the recruitment efforts of the antisuffrage leadership, but these class advantages also operated as constraints, a paradox observed in recent research on contemporary wealthy women.[138] At the turn of the century, upper-class norms still upheld traditional conventions of true womanhood, visible in the organizational practice of addressing antisuffrage leaders by their full married title rather than by Christian names. "Publicity is dreadful to a woman of refinement," proclaimed antisuffrage sympathizer Mrs. J. P. Morgan, wife of the celebrated Yankee financier, expressing succinctly the strategic dilemma confronting an antisuffrage leadership hoping to recruit among its own ranks. Their delicate task was to overcome female resistance to "conspicuous" behavior while simultaneously upholding traditional gender norms, a challenge exacerbated by the fact that some of them privately expressed ambivalence about the appropriateness of women's political mobilization.[139]

Their methods of resolving this dilemma were frequently quite ingenious. The New York organization held antisuffrage meetings at the exclusive Colony Club, claiming that this secluded site upheld proscriptions against female political activity. The Massachusetts Association monitored potential recruits discreetly and coaxed them slowly into political activism. In one case, they devised a "graduated plan" under which a woman who was a "strong antisuffragist, but not yet ready to undertake active work," could join the executive committee for a six-month trial period. The strategy for organizing neighboring Vermont was likewise planned carefully in stages: first, a lecture by a MAOFESW representative on "the responsibilities of the educated woman," which "almost invariably led to a direct antisuffrage talk later."[140]

Despite these clever strategies and the obvious benefits of access to elite resources, the constraints of social class contained the movement's development, especially in its early stages. For one thing, social obligations frequently superseded antisuffrage commitments. Some of the leaders went abroad for extended periods and were frequently absent during the summer as they retired to their country homes, upcoming referenda campaigns notwithstanding. For another, not all women were willing to risk the impropriety of public exposure, and hence the potential benefits of recruiting well-known women were not always realized. The recruitment speech of the Massachusetts Association, for instance, routinely promised potential members that they would "incur no publicity" because members' identities would remain confidential. It was often difficult to find women who were willing to speak at legislative hearings; one antisuffragist declined a request with the explanation that "her friends thought she cheapened herself" by speaking before a male audience.[141] For a long time, antisuffragists criticized the parades and mass meetings staged by suffragists as "spectacular and unwomanly," favoring instead private parlor meetings that yielded fewer opportunities for publicizing the movement and broadening its bases of support. As they would later realize, a self-proclaimed "silent majority" was of little use if it remained silent. And while the inclination to stay within their relatively homogeneous circle made some inroads among students at elite women's colleges, it also cost them missed opportunities among working women.[142]

Antisuffrage leaders periodically discussed the need to attract a "different class" of women to the group, but ambivalence about expanding their circle ultimately hindered the goal of diversification. One stark example of this occurred when the Massachusetts Association considered an offer from a "prominent stenographer in Baltimore" to found an antisuffrage organization there. They judged the woman "clever and able," but probably not the "best person" for the job, and the executive committee deferred the matter to a New York socialite, who "knows many people in Baltimore." An employee of the National Association complained privately that the New York leadership treated laboring women in the organization as servants, and wondered what difference it made, if people are willing to work against suffrage, "whether they came over in the Mayflower or not?"[143]

The privileged backgrounds of antisuffrage leaders also made them vulnerable to the suffragist charge that they were mere "butterflies of fashion . . . indifferent to the needs of society." Antis considered this description insulting, and rebuttals typically consisted of countercharges decrying suffragists' "bad manners" and "want of taste," although periodically they were compelled to publicize the work of antisuffrage leaders for "good causes."[144] Some attempted to surmount the constraints of class by devising means to obfuscate their political work under the guise of "public education," a more acceptable and traditional role for women of their social position. Although using the educational mantle for political activity was not unique to antisuffragists, they took this strategy a step further by establishing separate clubs for this purpose, such as the League for the Civic Education of Women, founded in 1908 by a trio of New York socialites. As one of them explained to readers of the *North American Review,* "Its purpose is to give women of the country the best possible means of obtaining information bearing on their rights, responsibilities, and economic position in the community," although she admitted privately to the Massachusetts Association that the work of the league was only "theoretically educational."[145] The same year, the Guidon Study Club, described as "an anti-suffrage, educational study club, for progressive, patriotic, and studious women" was also founded in New York City by author Mrs. Rossiter (Helen Kendrick) Johnson. Melding traditional femininity with conservative politics, they explained that the guidon "does not flaunt itself," but "is never absent from the fore-front of a marching column," pointing out the straight line, just as their group was against "the destructive spirit of state socialism."[146]

Antisuffragists also established ostensibly philanthropic societies to cloak their political work in a more socially acceptable form and defend themselves from suffragist charges of frivolousness and selfishness. The Great War provided a special opportunity for demonstrations of feminine self-sacrifice. In 1914, the Massachusetts Association constituted a companion organization called the Public Interests League for humanitarian service, especially war-related assistance to the Red Cross. While the Public Interests League raised money and rolled bandages for the war effort, behind the scenes the state antisuffrage leadership reported enthusiastically that it also brought them into contact with a new pool of potential recruits, and they were not averse to sending antisuffrage literature to western campaign states under the aegis of this supposedly charitable association.[147]

Despite these tactics to camouflage their political activities, there is no doubt that antisuffragists were adopting new roles and extending the boundaries of woman's domestic sphere. They were participating in what Paula Baker calls women's "political domesticity."[148] The paradox, of course, is that antisuffragists decried similar actions when perpetrated by suffragists and for the most part succeeded in obfuscating their own violations of traditional gender norms, a testimony to their considerable political acumen.

Conclusion

These findings suggest that the organization of antisuffragists to a great extent exemplified the patterns predicted by social movement theory. Mobilization against suffrage was precipitated by the perceived threat of the suffrage movement, but rather than suffrage successes, it was suffrage persistence that aroused antisuffrage organization. Quite simply, despite decades of defeat, suffragists would not go away. But victories in distant western states were less significant for the timing of antisuffrage organization than were local suffrage issues, such as state constitutional conventions, legislative bills, and popular referenda. On the positive side, enhanced political opportunities also spurred antisuffrage mobilization; a favorable political climate sometimes propelled antis to action in the hopes of winning a decisive victory and ending suffrage agitation once and for all.

The first organizers against woman suffrage did not conform exactly to the image conferred by suffragists that opened this chapter. Although upholding conventions about participation in public life for women of their social class, they were far from isolated. They resided in urban centers, enjoyed proximity to political and economic power by blood and marriage, and wielded considerable status and influence in their own right. They were early political appointees and benefactors of new charitable organizations, albeit always careful to present a benign amateur image. The female founders of antisuffrage organizations shared many leadership attributes with their suffragist sisters, with whom they competed for the support of clubwomen. The finding that women's clubs, heretofore regarded as latently feminist, constituted the basis of both suffrage and antisuffrage mobilization identifies a common history that defies facile explanations for why some women fought for the vote while others fought against it.

The women who founded antisuffrage associations were not drawn from identical social strata as the founders of suffrage, and suffragist characterization of antis as "butterflies of fashion" underscores significant differences between leadership cadres. Suffrage leaders were also overwhelmingly native-born women of Anglo-Saxon heritage, but they tended to come from the rural hinterland; while the national antisuffrage movement was dominated by New York elites throughout its existence, the leadership of the suffrage movement was far more diverse geographically and in social background. Even those with colonial lineage were from less illustrious and less prosperous branches of Yankee family trees. Significantly, they were more likely to have college educations and careers; in short, they embodied the independent "new woman" poised to replace the society volunteer in expanding social service occupations. Progressive reforms provided employment opportunities for educated suffragists, and the pursuit of social change was thus very much tied to their own self-interest.[149] Antis, on the other hand, actively maintained the relatively closed social networks of wealth and privilege that constituted the source of their power. Their support for the status quo likewise derived from gendered class interests.

Antisuffrage leaders used their privileged class positions to great advantage. As members of the American aristocracy, they played an important role in social status maintenance that became a valuable resource for antisuffrage mobilization. Kinship ties were also exploited to monitor suffrage activities, recruit additional officers, and establish organizations in other states. Ancestral associations drew like-minded women into political activism under the legitimating mantle of tradition, imparting useful leadership experience, chipping away at restrictive cultural norms, and defining a set of grievances and solutions that proved compatible with antisuffrage protest.

Class position operated as a constraint on political activity at the same time that it made available resources to circumvent these limitations. The contradictory effect of class membership on women's antisuffrage mobilization necessitated both discretion and innovation. Early antisuffrage organization efforts relied on interpersonal networks that obscured the extent of antisuffrage political activity. Women antisuffragists promoted an impression of more widespread, spontaneous female opposition than their numbers probably warranted and perpetuated a traditional, ladylike image belied by their own behind-the-scenes activities. In fact, the greatest success of women antisuffragists may have been their ability to pursue all the political activities documented in their own organizational records while at the same time convincing the American public and their suffrage adversaries that they were a group of isolated, inconsequential women who were merely fronts for the real enemy—men. In the next chapter, we reassess the accuracy of this impression by examining men's role in the antisuffrage movement.

3

Gentleman Suffrage

> The United States should guard against emotional suffrage. What we need is to put more logic and less feeling into public affairs. The country has already extended suffrage beyond reasonable bounds.
>
> —Nebraska Men's Association Opposed to Woman Suffrage

Men were widely regarded as the real power behind the antisuffrage movement.[1] In the view of many suffragists and contemporary scholars, men had both economic resources and motives—liquor profits, cheap industrial labor, lucrative municipal contracts—to fight votes for women. The memoirs of prominent suffragists unequivocally asserted that corporate interests, brewers, saloon keepers, and gamblers were the primary financial sponsors of antisuffragism, lobbying state legislatures and buying elections. The multivolume *History of Woman Suffrage*, still the most detailed state-by-state account of the suffrage campaign, documents the behind-the-scenes activities of liquor interests fearful of the enactment of prohibition by female voters, claims that were corroborated in part by a wartime report of the U.S. Senate Judiciary Committee and by the open opposition of liquor dealers' associations and the German-American Alliance. But proof that female opponents were merely fronts for "wets" is less conclusive, based on incidents such as the physical proximity of the two groups of legislative hearings.[2]

Allegations of a surreptitious conspiracy of corruption diminished the importance of men's antisuffrage organizations. Although a few studies have examined the votes of the male electorate on woman suffrage referenda, analyses of men's organized opposition to votes for women have been less systematic and limited for the most part to specific actions of prominent male antisuffragists and isolated key events in the campaign.[3] The history of male participation in the antisuffrage movement requires amplification, if only to clarify the relationship between women's and men's antisuffrage activism. Were women merely fronts for men, as suffragists claimed? How did men come to mobilize against woman suffrage and what interests united them? What contributions did men make to the opposition movement?

This chapter examines the men who mobilized against woman suffrage—their family histories, educational backgrounds, occupational pursuits, political activities, and organizational memberships. It explains male coalescence against woman suffrage as a consequence of shared social networks and political orientations that amalgamated class, ethnic, and gender interests. It also reviews the life cycle of men's organized antisuffrage activities, yielding a picture of behind-the-scenes gender conflict at odds with claims of female docility and male stewardship advanced by both sides during the suffrage campaign. Finally, it assesses the contributions of men affiliates of antisuffrage organizations as well as of prominent sympathizers whose critical essays in popular magazines influenced public opinion on the suffrage question.

A Cohesive Male Leadership

Men played key instigative and supportive roles in women's early mobilization against suffrage. In Massachusetts, State Senator George G. Crocker, whose wife and sister were founding members of the Boston Committee of Remonstrants, incited female organization by warning of the "considerable headway" made by suffragists in the legislature, where school suffrage had passed in 1879. Senator Crocker reportedly advised the women assembled in a Beacon Hill parlor in the winter of 1882 that "petitions in remonstrance were absolutely necessary, or they would wake up one fine morning and discover that the legislature had granted municipal suffrage to women."[4] Although hastily prepared petitions of remonstrance blocked a suffrage bill that year, suffragists' persistence kept the issue before the Massachusetts legislature. Male friends and relatives represented the antisuffrage cause at hearings on municipal suffrage. In addition to George Crocker, whose longtime service earned him accolades as "guide, philosopher, and friend," others who spoke against suffrage before the state legislature in the 1880s included Judge John Lowell, uncle of antisuffrage leaders Elizabeth Sohier and Elizabeth Lowell Putnam; lawyer Thornton K. Lothrop, brother of remonstrance committee members Homans and Peabody; lawyer and historian John Codman Ropes; civic leader Richard H. Dana; Rev. Brooke Herford; and Henry Harrison Sprague, president of the Massachusetts Senate.[5] As suffrage pressure escalated, the Boston remonstrants employed counsel "to conduct hearings before the legislative committee; to instruct the members who are ignorant of the bearings of the question; and to organize the debate." Among the men serving as antisuffrage counsel in the early years were state legislator Arthur Lord and lawyer Thomas Russell (both relatives of remonstrance committee members), and future Supreme Court Justice Louis Brandeis, who later reversed his position on suffrage.[6] Their political influence helped forestall the suffrage threat in a city that was a stronghold of the movement nationwide.

In the view of one Boston antisuffrage leader, the men worked "from conviction combined with chivalry" as "the protectors and defenders of the women entrusted to their political care." Monitoring the progress of woman suffrage legislation from within, lobbying among their peers, and skillfully wielding "the weapon of ridicule" against proponents at committee hearings, these men enabled the women remonstrants to maintain a discreet distance from the political fray.[7] In a period when public speaking was considered a breach of female etiquette, the men addressed legislative hearings on behalf of women remonstrants, and so preserved the genteel image of true womanhood. But the suffrage movement was persistent in Boston, and by 1895 the state legislature passed the Wellman bill submitting woman municipal suffrage to a popular referendum the following November by those qualified to vote on school committees, including women. The Wellman bill forced women antisuffragists into public acknowledgment as a formal organization, but they were still reluctant to campaign actively against the amendment. Their solution was ingenious. The newly formed Massachusetts Association Opposed to the Further Extension of Suffrage to Women (MAOFESW) called for a female boycott as a demonstration of protest and delegated to men the public campaign against the referendum.

The antisuffrage baton passed to the men, who responded by establishing the Massachusetts Man Suffrage Association for the duration of the 1895 campaign. Its executive committee consisted of State Senator Crocker; William D. Sohier, lawyer, former state legislator, and brother of remonstrant Elizabeth Sohier; manufacturers John T. Burnett and Eben S. Draper, a future Massachusetts governor; and lawyers John T. Wheelright and Charles Warren.[8] Chairman of the short-lived association was Francis Cabot Lowell, cousin of longtime antisuffragist Judge John Lowell, newly elected state legislator, and soon to be U.S. district court judge, whose wife Cornelia was a founding member of MAOFESW. The group's daily operations were ostensibly managed by the association's secretary, Charles R. Saunders, who would soon serve in the state legislature, where, one antisuffragist recalled, he used his influence as chairman of the Election Laws Committee to help the cause by firing "keen searching questions" at suffrage petitioners.[9]

As members of Boston's elite, early antisuffrage organizers were united by more than kinship. They enjoyed high social prestige derived partly from the achievements of their ancestors; Judge John Lowell, for example, sat on the same court as his great-grandfather, an appointee of President George Washington. Almost all attended Harvard College and Harvard Law, some later serving as Harvard Corporation fellows, overseers, and benefactors. Even exceptions to this educational pattern had ties to Harvard, such as British minister Rev. Brooke Herford, who preached there during his ten-year Boston stay, and Louis D. Brandeis, an outsider by virtue of his southern background and Jewish faith, who earned a Harvard law degree and subsequently practiced in Boston in partnership with a classmate from the prestigious Warren family.[10] Harvard credentials and family contacts helped establish lucrative careers, typically in legal practice with relatives or friends, later as corporate counsels, bank directors, and trustees of Brahmin family fortunes.

Beyond educational and economic advantages, Harvard conferred considerable social prestige on its graduates. Ronald Story documents the growing exclusivity of Harvard College during the nineteenth century, as students, faculty, and donors were increasingly drawn from the narrow tier of Boston Brahmin aristocracy. Recruitment patterns favored boys from expensive private preparatory schools, vocational goals shifted from ministry to business, and new campus construction turned inward, sequestering students from the larger community. Harvard's cultural identity was further enhanced by reorganizing college governance to favor alumni and reduce outsider influence.[11] Harvard's faculty secured its cultural leadership throughout New England as authors and editors of prestigious magazines such as *North American Review* and the more literary *Atlantic Monthly*.[12] In its evolution to a self-conscious elite institution, Harvard became a repository of upper-class cultural values, upholding refinement, character, and cultivation as attributes distinguishing the gentleman from the masses and the civilized from the rustic, described by one prep school headmaster as the "sheer restfulness of good breeding" that consolidated group solidarity. Heightened emphasis on transgenerational college traditions combined with explicit Anglophilism was a reaction to profound cultural changes of the period, functioning as an institutional "counterweight to social flux and intergenerational mobility" for the "domineering yet anxious elite."[13]

The male antisuffrage leadership represented well the Harvard ideal of the gentleman scholar. Many were authors by avocation, typically writing on historical or legal subjects, although one also published children's books.[14] Some were exceptionally prolific and talented, such as Man Suffrage leader Charles Warren, whose two-volume history of the U.S. Supreme Court would receive the 1923 Pulitzer Prize. Several were frequent contributors of political essays to popular Boston magazines, and one briefly headed a local newspaper.[15] They constituted what Paul DiMaggio calls "cultural entrepreneurs," dominating a network of status-defining private institutions that maintained the preeminence of the old elite.[16] They served as trustees of the Boston Athenaeum and the Museum of Fine Arts, raised funds to build a new concert hall for the Boston Symphony Orchestra, and headed the New England Conservatory of Music. They underscored distinguished ancestries through local voluntary associations, including the Massachusetts Historical Society, the Bostonian Society, and the New England Historical-Genealogical Society, and by founding the Military Historical Society of Massachusetts, the first of its kind in the United States. Community dominance was also enhanced through trusteeship of private charitable institutions that ultimately influenced national public policies toward the poor. Richard H. Dana, for example, organized and chaired Associated Charities of Boston, and others managed various local hospitals and relief associations.[17] Besides scholarly and philanthropic organizations, antisuffrage men were members of Boston's most elite social clubs, such as Somerset, St. Botolph, and the Union Club. In fact, the stationery of Man Suffrage Association listed the same Beacon Hill address as did the Union Club, which was located next door to the women's Mayflower Club that spawned MAOFESW.

Although a large network of exclusive institutions served largely to insulate Brahmins from social contact with the urban masses, the men who opposed woman suffrage were active in public life. Besides serving in the state legislature, they were often appointed to serve on commissions to oversee the expansion of government services and maintain order in the face of urban growth, positions of influence that favored their economic interests. For example, Man Suffrage leader John Wheelright chaired the state's utility commission, and Edward Sohier headed its highway commission. Their community activism also included pursuit of more partisan goals; they typically advocated civil service reform as a protest against Irish political ascendancy in the commonwealth, whose power was based largely on the patronage system. This late nineteenth-century movement sought to divorce government from politics and sometimes explicitly espoused the natural superiority of its social class, entreating "men of education and social position" into public service to replace "wretched, wire-pulling demagogues" with "wise, considerate, and temperate statesmanship." Several members of the Man Suffrage Association's executive committee were members of the Civil Service Reform Association and the National Municipal League. Richard H. Dana, an early antisuffrage representative in the state legislature, drafted the Massachusetts Civil Service Act of 1884 and edited the *Civil Service Record;* Sohier and Crocker each served as president of the state Republican Club during the 1890s, where they led the Yankee fight against the Irish Democratic political machine. Judge Francis C. Lowell gained notoriety for setting a punitively high bail following the arrest of the notorious Joseph M. Curley on corruption charges, while Charles Saunders, an ardent prohibitionist, fought ward bosses as a member of Boston's Board of Election Commissioners. Charles Warren chaired the Massachusetts State Civil Service Commission until repeated clashes with skilled Irish pol Boston Mayor John ("Honey Fitz") Fitzgerald over the fitness of his agency appointments generated so much controversy that the governor allowed Warren's term to lapse.[18]

Demands for political reform to improve the quality of local government and check the corrupt power of ward bosses and urban political machines were compatible with the platform of the progressive movement. But the Massachusetts male antisuffrage leaders represented the most conservative wing of the early impulse toward reform, and their goal was to reduce rather than increase popular control of government. They were generally opposed to progressive reforms such as the referendum and initiative, direct election of U.S. senators, and the federal income tax. Their hostility to popular democracy reflected both class interest and ethnic prejudice. The gubernatorial tenure of Man Suffrage officer Eben S. Draper, for example, was marked by repeated conflicts with organized labor, which protested the policy of his family's manufacturing business to hire only nonunion workers, and Governor Draper twice vetoed bills mandating tougher enforcement of an eight-hour law for public employees. Their self-described conservative views were expressed by Brahmin historian Francis Parkman, whose influential 1878 article in the *North American Review* criticized universal suffrage for producing bad voters, decried the "slow but ominous transfer of power from superior to inferior types of men," and located human failing in moral character rather than in inadequate education. Parkman rejected the goal of cultural assimilation for American immigrants in favor of the elite view that character is the product of generations of careful breeding.[19]

These sentiments later found political expression in the formation of the Immigration Restriction League, founded in 1894 by three recent Harvard graduates, one of whom organized the Massachusetts Man Suffrage Association. This was Charles Warren, whose 1889 Harvard commencement speech, entitled "The Failure of the Democratic Idea in City Government," denounced the political power of immigrants who voted for taxes that others had to pay. The Immigration Restriction League, which recruited its officers from the Brahmin elite, viewed itself as a patriotic organization whose goal was to save the nation from foreign infiltration. The league expanded nationally, with some branches started by Harvard alumni. It favored an immigration policy barring those without skills, which it commonly equated with the upper-class shibboleth of genetically based "character," and, according to Barbara Miller Solomon, pursued the "ingeniously snobbish" strategy of a coalition between urban elites and skilled laborers. The league favored a literacy test as the basis for the exclusion of foreigners, and its greatest congressional advocates were Senator Henry Cabot Lodge and Representative Augustus P. Gardner, two antisuffrage men linked by both ideology and kinship. Although Charles Warren was defeated in his earlier struggle with Boston's Mayor Fitzgerald, his antiforeign sentiments were later placed in national service when, as assistant attorney general under President Woodrow Wilson, he drafted wartime measures against enemy aliens, most notably the Espionage and Trading with Enemy Acts of 1917. Another officer of the Immigration Restriction League was Harvard president A. Lawrence Lowell, cousin and former law partner of Man Suffrage president Francis C. Lowell and brother of MAOFESW leader Elizabeth Lowell Putnam. In the 1920s, President Lowell investigated the "race distribution" within Harvard College and recommended a restrictive quota for Jewish students.[20]

The Man Suffrage Association's 1895 campaign against the Wellman bill, like the Immigration Restriction League's crusade for immigration restriction, relied heavily upon social rank to sway public opinion. The organization distributed a poster listing "over one hundred of the most prominent men of the State" who opposed the Wellman bill. Should the recipient fail to note the high caliber of this nonpartisan appeal, an accompanying letter pointed out the names of college presidents, former governors, and "many others whose names are household words to you."[21] Man Suffrage also used its considerable legal expertise to publish a pamphlet listing women's privileges in both state and federal statutes, and the stated objections to woman suffrage reflected their supreme position in the economic hierarchy:

> Our city and town governments are great public business corporations. So long as the relative inexperience of women in business affairs continues, it is not to be expected that the combined vote of men and women will give as good results as the vote of men alone . . .[22]

The Man Suffrage 1895 campaign was apparently carried out with the quiet dignity befitting their high social status and accompanying disdain for the hurly-burly of mass politics; their tactics rarely extended beyond posters and mailings, which were reprinted at no cost by local newspapers interested in the views of such prominent citizens. The men resisted public antisuffrage activism and seemed as concerned as the women with a prospective loss of prestige, although they were not similarly constrained by gender seclusion norms. Their concerns were justified, for newspapers as far away as Chicago editorialized about the Boston group's published antisuffrage "manifesto," with the more liberal publications charging them with hypocrisy and alleging a historical connection to the proslavery sentiments of their famous ancestors.[23] The Man Suffrage Association disbanded after defeating the Wellman bill with a majority of a hundred thousand male votes, and it took fifteen years to assemble a new men's list and almost twenty years to remobilize Man Suffrage in Massachusetts.

Owing to its national prominence in the antisuffrage movement, the Massachusetts men's organization influenced the mobilization of opponents in other states. Preexisting networks favored an elite leadership cadre, and membership lists of local Harvard clubs were used to recruit men and their wives in the nation's hinterland.[24] As in Massachusetts, men elsewhere typically did not organize until an emergency threatened, such as state legislative passage of a woman suffrage bill subject to voter approval. The strategic mobilization of well-known, powerful men underscored their utility for the antisuffrage campaign by dint of experience and name recognition; the practice also allowed women's organizations, at least in the early phase, to remain true to their professed goal of remaining politically aloof and thus pure.

While Massachusetts represented the most extreme case of a cohesive homogeneous elite and, perhaps not coincidentally, the maintenance of female seclusion norms that increased antis' dependence on men, the circumstances behind the founding of male antisuffrage associations were similar in other states. New York's first state suffrage referendum was not held until 1915, but in 1894 mounting pressure to include woman suffrage in the state constitution precipitated antisuffrage mobilization. Some women remonstrants addressed the state's constitutional convention, but public endorsement by male delegates who could sway votes was vital for success. One convention delegate who gave an address opposing woman suffrage was Francis Markoe Scott, future state supreme court justice, whose wife, the former Lucy Parkman Higgins, chaired the fledgling New York Association.[25] Another antisuffrage speaker was Elihu Root, chairman of the convention's judiciary committee and future secretary of war (1899–1904), secretary of state (1905–9), U.S. senator (1909–15), and recipient of the Nobel Peace Prize. Like his Massachusetts counterparts, Root was descended from early colonists and began his career as a corporate lawyer, representing the Havemeyer sugar refining conglomerate in its attempt to circumvent the Sherman Anti-Trust Act. A self-described conservative Republican, Root defined U.S. colonial policy in Cuba, Puerto Rico, and the Philippines and helped negotiate the so-called "gentleman's agreement" with Japan restricting the flow of immigration to the United States. As an early member of the anti-Tammany Union League, Root denounced political corruption, labor movement agitation, and the political apathy of the "better classes."[26] He was also a cultural entrepreneur, helping to establish New York's Metropolitan Museum of Art and later serving as president of the prestigious all-male Century Association, described by Root as a sanctuary for "the unruffled harmony of modest friendship" and an antidote to the "rude alarums and excursions of the turbulent world." The house rules of the Century Association exemplified the ideal of the gentleman's club as urban refuge, restricting access of female visitors and requesting that members refrain from publicizing the association to shield it from possible controversy.[27]

The primary organizer of the national men's antisuffrage movement was New York corporate lawyer Everett P. Wheeler. Wheeler inherited a distinguished family lineage; he was the grandson of a diplomat who served under Presidents Jefferson and Madison, son of a corporate attorney, and educated at Harvard Law School. Wheeler was among the initiators of the civil service reform movement, and chaired both the state's Civil Service Reform Association and New York City's Civil Service Commission. He was active in the formation of the Citizen's Union that supported reform candidate Seth Low for mayor in the election of 1897, serving on its executive committee with a number of prominent antisuffragists, including Elihu Root. In 1913, Wheeler organized and chaired a state men's antisuffrage association, which he shortly renamed the Man-Suffrage Association Opposed to Political Suffrage for Women.[28] The similarity to the earlier Boston-based men's group was no coincidence, for Wheeler regularly corresponded and shared literature with the Massachusetts antisuffragists. The New Yorkers copied many of the tactics of their Massachusetts predecessors, advertising the "prominent men and women" opposed to woman suffrage, publishing pamphlets, and even sponsoring a survey of college professors to demonstrate the extent of experts' opposition to the vote.[29]

As in New England, the task of assembling prominent opposition to woman suffrage was relatively easy for New York's Man-Suffrage Association, because its executive committee was replete with important men from old Knickerbocker families. These were neither self-made men nor the expanding class of newly rich industrialists; most had attended New England prep schools and Ivy League colleges such as Amherst, Princeton, Columbia, or Harvard, followed by law school at Harvard or Columbia. Corporate law was the dominant profession identified on the executive committee, which included Robert K. Prentice, an insurance company director; Francis Lynde Stetson, general counsel of U.S. Steel; and Herbert L. Satterlee, counsel to railroad and banking interests and son-in-law of financier J. P. Morgan. Charles S. Fairchild, who headed the reorganization of Man-Suffrage into the American Constitutional League after New York's 1917 state referendum, was a corporate lawyer, railroad and bank president, and former secretary of the treasury under President Cleveland. Another executive committee member, George W. Wickersham, served as U.S. attorney general under President Taft and was a well-known transportation industry lawyer. Merchant and corporate trustee Cleveland H. Dodge, manufacturers Fritz Achelis and Frank L. Babbott, and Columbia University professors Munroe Smith and Talcott Williams, dean of the Pulitzer School of Journalism, represented other interests on the committee.[30] A number of their wives were leaders in the women's state antisuffrage association, and Dodge's Aunt Josephine presided over the National Association Opposed to Woman Suffrage.

As further testimony to its impressive pedigree, the New York Man-Suffrage leadership was socially prominent as well as professionally successful. Two-thirds of its founding committee members were listed in the New York *Social Register.* They were active clubmen, including among their memberships the exclusive Century, Union, and University clubs in addition to patriotic-hereditary societies, literary and artistic organizations, and yachting and country clubs. Their wives were likewise generally from distinguished American families and members of organizations such as the Colonial Dames. As in Massachusetts, these were not elites in total retreat; they were active in political and civic affairs, joining partisan political organizations like the Republican Union League and Democratic Manhattan Club, serving on the city's Board of Education, leading civic reform associations, and even directing a fund-raising drive to refurbish Grant's tomb. Many were active in professional organizations, especially state and local bar associations. Almost all were well-known philanthropists, college trustees, officers of relief societies, hospitals, and libraries, and founders of settlement houses and museums. They were art collectors and institutional benefactors, and their generous donations sometimes attracted publicity, such as Frank Babbott's posthumous bequest of over three million dollars to numerous museums and schools, including all-female Vassar College.[31]

Less is known about the organization of men in other states, but their social backgrounds, economic status, and political affiliations appear similar to those of the northeastern leadership. For the 1913 Michigan referendum on full suffrage, a men's association organized at Detroit's University Club with local attorneys as leaders. The Nebraska Men's Association Opposed to Woman Suffrage, which appealed publicly to voters shortly before the 1914 suffrage referendum, was led by bank president and former U.S. senator Joseph H. Millard and other well-known lawyers, bankers, and businessmen.[32] The New Jersey Men's Anti-Suffrage League, established in 1915 to defeat the state referendum, was headed by distinguished men of colonial ancestry and drew heavily from Princeton University faculty and administrators, although corporate law was represented by men like Edward Q. Keasbey, who was also an author and philanthropist. The Iowa Association of Men Opposed to Woman Suffrage, formed to defeat the 1916 state suffrage referendum, was headed by New York born Frank D. Jackson, a former Republican governor of Iowa and head of a large insurance company. Other "prominent men of the state" listed as leaders of the Iowa organization included a real estate tycoon, a banker and railroad president, and a Harvard-educated oil company lawyer, as well as Ford Automobile Company executive and future Iowa governor and U.S. senator Clyde L. Herring.[33] Although brewery, labor, and immigrant organizations such as the German-American Alliance also mounted active campaigns against both suffrage and prohibition, especially in the midwestern states, suffragist charges of a direct tie to antisuffrage organizations remain speculative, and their divergent class interests and political ideologies argue against the likelihood that these elite men served as fronts for working-class interests.[34]

Men's mobilization against suffrage, like that of their female counterparts, illustrates the importance of preexisting networks for social movement organization. These men shared professional and business interests, social club memberships, and colonial family histories; they were sometimes also linked to the antisuffrage cause by kinship or marriage to women antisuffrage activists. Another common characteristic was a political ideology that frequently involved them in civic reform organizations. Besides woman suffrage, these men also opposed corrupt urban political machines and mass politics driven by the interests of labor. They lamented the passing of Yankee stewardship, attempted to reverse the expansion of immigrant influence, and exhorted others of their class to assert civic responsibility while they sought partial refuge from urban strife through membership in exclusive organizations. Their high social positions and professional credentials rendered them valuable to the antisuffrage cause, but also hesitant about creating permanent formal protest organizations that might draw controversy.

The Reluctant Organization of Men

Most men's antisuffrage organizations had brief life spans, typically limited to the duration of state referenda campaigns and lasting a year at most. There were basically two reasons for men's formal involvement in the antisuffrage movement: political expertise and financial support. We have already seen that men's achievements as legislators, educators, and businessmen made them valued antisuffrage activists, particularly useful for lobbying against prosuffrage petitions in legislatures and, when that failed, campaigning publicly against forthcoming suffrage referenda. Even after Massachusetts Man Suffrage had disbanded, its secretary, Charles Saunders, served as paid counsel for the women's antisuffrage association until his death, monitoring the progress of suffrage legislation, addressing hearings on the question, and writing pamphlets that were distributed nationally.[35] Women antisuffragists regularly sought men's advice on how to present their case most effectively to the state legislature and keep suffrage bills off the ballot. By the turn of the century, they were already conferring with Senator Henry Cabot Lodge to develop opposition strategies against a federal amendment. Lodge and his colleagues, including U.S. Senator James Wadsworth of New York, husband of the National Association president, aided the cause in later years by speaking against a federal woman suffrage plank at national Republican Party conventions.[36]

Women's antisuffrage organizations also relied on men for financial support. One favorite suffragist tactic for neutralizing the female opposition was to claim that they were merely the fronts for a well-financed campaign of male liquor interests and other capitalists. These data lend little support to that claim.[37] Not only did inadequate financial resources plague the Massachusetts women from their earliest organization as a local committee, but their meeting discussions reveal considerable resentment of the yoke of financial dependence on men. While campaigning under the banner of traditional womanhood, the female leadership struggled privately to remain autonomous from male control. An early address reveals the careful strategies behind their fund-raising efforts. Written for presentation before a men's group, the prepared text reveals numerous deletions of direct requests for money. In its final form, it first flatters profusely the men "who have stood by us so steadfastly and borne with us so patiently," then explains that, as public leaders, men would be most adversely affected by the "hideous complications" of woman suffrage, and finally indirectly asks for male help by stating plaintively, "There is one thing—which certainly should not be expected any longer of us women—and that is to raise the funds necessary to carry on the work."[38]

Persistent financial crises and the impropriety of public fund-raising were probably major factors behind the women's decision to designate a male treasurer when they organized the Massachusetts Association in 1895. He was Brahmin Laurence Minot, Harvard-educated lawyer, estate trustee, and future head of the Good Government Association, a largely Republican civic reform society.[39] Even with Minot's guidance, the balance in the MAOFESW treasury remained modest, hovering around $100 at the turn of the century, with women's recorded contributions totaling about seventy-five percent of men's. By spring 1901, facing a budget deficit and having discussed and abandoned several fund-raising strategies, the executive committee acted. In May, they gently "relieved" Mr. Minot of the job as treasurer, replacing him with Henrietta Codman, but asked Minot to retain the official title of auditor as a sign of organizational stability. After receiving several large donations from leaders of both sexes, the Massachusetts Association embarked on a subscription campaign and swelled its treasury to over $1,000 by September. This respite proved short-lived, however, and the executive committee was soon struggling to find a more lasting solution to its financial dilemma. They proposed a permanent fund of $25,000 to be raised by "the gentlemen"; this group of supporters, led by State Senator Crocker and Judge Lowell, met periodically to replenish the empty treasury, but the endowment goal was quietly dropped.[40]

By early 1906, the MAOFESW executive committee decided upon an organizational solution. They would form a men's advisory committee under the leadership of George Crocker, with names recruited from the 1895 Man Suffrage list of one hundred prominent Massachusetts antisuffrage men, because their "habit of calling upon a few men each year to make up the sum necessary was too haphazard to be depended upon any longer."[41] At a special meeting called in Judge Lowell's parlor, Mrs. Guild appealed to male protective impulses by invoking the traditional stereotype of female incompetence, acknowledging that running the treasury down to empty was "improper and unbusinesslike" and projecting an image of female helplessness. "But our hands are full," pleaded Mrs. Guild, "the work is not easy, and we ask that we be relieved of at least part of the burden." Despite the tone of supplication, the women were unwilling to extend full organizational membership to men, proposing instead the formation of two men's committees, one "to confer with us occasionally" and the other "to help us raise money systematically." This was done, but in exchange the men attempted to impose businesslike discipline by requesting a written statement of the organization's needs, including a proposed annual budget.[42]

The relationship between the men's and women's antisuffrage organizations was marked by periodic tension. The women members of the Massachusetts Association's executive committee proposed additional members and pressed the men to expand in order to increase their effectiveness, expressed dissatisfaction with the progress of male fundraising efforts, and discussed "unsatisfactory" correspondence from the "gentlemen's finance committee." For their part, the men were often frustrated with the difficulty of recruiting more volunteers, and they once canceled a planned conference because the women's failure to develop "definite propositions" for men's antisuffrage work "would mean an unsatisfactory expenditure of time for all concerned."[43] The men's committee periodically sent out circulars to prominent acquaintances and raised some money, but never succeeded in establishing a permanent financial base for MAOFESW. By 1909, the women's organization concluded that the level of male financial and political support was insufficient and that "the men should come out actively for antisuffrage." That fall, they met with members of the men's committee and repeated their need for "financial assistance" and "moral backing," offering this time the concession of a men's auxiliary. The men rejected the implicit subordination of this arrangement, canceled a planned organizing meeting, and prepared instead a new publicity list of prominent male remonstrants that they declared "adequate for present needs."[44]

The conflict surrounding men's unwillingness to organize formally against woman suffrage reveals the prerogatives and constraints of their class position. For men of their background and social status, the notion of a subsidiary relationship to anyone, especially women, was unfamiliar and unacceptable. They were also unwilling to suffer the indignities of public political activism, but preferred to assist behind the scenes through donations and the distribution of circulars to other men of their social circle. Judge Lowell reportedly told Mrs. Guild "that his zeal for the cause had carried him as far as his position would allow him to go," and he decided against attending the men's organizing meeting. These concerns were not unfounded, given the mixed public reception to their 1895 "manifesto" and the changed political climate in Boston, where the Irish political machine of Mayor John Fitzgerald was already engaged in battle with Brahmin antisuffragists like Judge Lowell and Charles Warren. Nor was the problem limited to Massachusetts; the 1915 annual report of the Maine Association summarized acidly the dearth of male interest: "Indeed, we find them, as a rule, very willing, both personally, and politically, to leave the subject alone."[45]

The reluctance of men to advocate publicly against woman suffrage seems especially surprising when contrasted with the willingness of their female peers. Elite women were actually more willing than men to form antisuffrage organizations, perhaps aided by gender norms that legitimated opposition under the traditional mantles of education and the preservation of female seclusion. Women's reticence about public antisuffrage activism, often interpreted as signifying conformity to gender constraints, is shown, when men are examined, to reflect in good measure the influence of social class. Men of high social position also sought to stay above the "clamor of the streets," where lower visibility rendered their actions less controversial and enabled them to save face in the event of failure. Studies of more recent history have documented the proclivity of male elites to adopt covert methods of wielding power.[46] The finding that privileged male antisuffrage sympathizers considered the impact of open activism on their public positions supports the concept of a gendered class structure.[47] The behaviors of both men and women antisuffragists reflected somewhat different concerns, each traced to the gender-specific demands of class location. Whereas women worried about losing the social prestige derived from norms prescribing female modesty and decorum removed from public participation, antisuffrage men were concerned with protecting their public image as civic-minded nonpartisans. The effects of social position on both sexes were thus dialectical, facilitating as well as constraining antisuffrage mobilization.

The suffragist tendency to dismiss women as passive fronts for men is belied by MAOFESW organizational records documenting the extent to which they functioned autonomously. Although they used male associates as point men in the state legislature or during referenda campaigns, they did not, like dutiful wives, follow blindly the directives of men. If anything, they engaged in a quiet but resolute struggle to maintain control of the antisuffrage movement. The breakdown of efforts during 1909–10 to form a men's auxiliary was partly the consequence of women's competition with men for scarce revenue; according to a frustrated Mrs. Guild, the MAOFESW leaders "threw cold water on the whole scheme, and were afraid they would lose financial support if another committee were in the field." The continuing pressure of suffrage petitions to the Massachusetts State House finally convinced the executive committee of the need for a men's league, but it took considerable diplomatic effort and the initiative of someone unconstrained by public office to bring the gentlemen to the same conclusion.[48]

The Massachusetts Men's Association against the Extension of Woman Suffrage was finally formed in the spring of 1912, due largely to the efforts of William T. Sedgwick, MIT biology professor, curator of the prestigious Lowell Institute, and past president of the Boston Civil Service Reform Association.[49] By the time of the organization's founding, the older generation of antisuffrage leaders was passing away. Judge Francis C. Lowell and Charles Saunders had died, followed the next year by George Crocker. New committee members included corporate lawyer Richard M. Saltonstall, wealthy manufacturer A. H. Parker, and banker Henry Parkman, who was treasurer of the Provident Institution for Savings, a major source of Brahmin financial power whose State Street headquarters also housed the Massachusetts Historical Society. A frequent adviser on financial and staff issues was James M. Prendergast, a wealthy Boston stockbroker active in city government.[50]

While still working closely with the Massachusetts Association through a joint committee structure for financing and planning referenda campaigns and through shared paid counsel that represented both organizations at legislative hearings, the men's association occupied separate offices and collected money independently, regularly contributing shares of their proceeds to the women's organization. The men's association discussed a statewide recruitment campaign, including a plan to invite "representative men from the principal cities and towns" to a luncheon meeting. The proposed event was not mentioned again, and the fact that they continued to call themselves a committee suggests that subscription efforts did not move far beyond members of their elite circle.[51]

The women leaders of MAOFESW welcomed the new organization with an announcement in the *Remonstrance* that omitted any references to names and addresses, thus precluding either recruitment or financial donations, and subsequent journal issues ignored the men entirely, perhaps owing to competition for scarce resources. The female leadership generally confined its private discussions of the men's committee to its utility as a source of desperately needed funds, particularly since the formation of the National Association Opposed to Woman Suffrage (NAOWS) constituted an additional drain on its treasury. The women's meetings verify constant crises over budget deficits, and the men's committee frequently bailed them out by paying staff salaries.[52] In exchange for this support, the men attempted to exercise veto power over the women's decisions; they refused the pay the rent on association headquarters because they thought the price too expensive and disputed a large bill from legislative counsel. These actions threw the women into a panic, but they usually stood firmly behind their decisions, and the men's committee often acceded, although not without protracted negotiations. The men's committee also tried to exercise financial leverage by requesting that the women prepare budget statements for projected expenses and by labeling contributions as loans rather than donations. Partly as a defensive measure, MAOFESW developed alternative sources of funding by tithing its branch associations.[53]

The timing of the formation of the men's committee coincided with an impending state suffrage referendum. By early 1913 the Massachusetts legislature was shifting in favor of suffrage, necessitating regular strategy sessions between the two groups. During the summer of 1914, the *Remonstrance* prepared its readers for legislative action on a woman suffrage constitutional amendment, which passed early in 1915 and went before the male voters the following November. The two associations joined forces to defeat the referendum, but in truth the major share of campaign work was completed by jointly paid staff, including press agents, professional speakers, and a male lawyer hired as a state organizer who shifted the organization's resources to voting men and announced his intention to secure "the cooperation of important men in every town." To this end, he directed the production and distribution of new campaign literature—with titles such as *Votes for Men, Men's Manual to Voters,* and *Why a Man Should Oppose Woman Suffrage*—targeted explicitly at those who would decide the question. As election day approached, he sent cadres of male canvassers to get out the opposition vote. High expenditures on salaries and publicity explain the persistence of budget crises despite escalating revenues, and the joint committee frequently discussed fund-raising appeals aimed at well-heeled men of the state, including bankers, businessmen, and "influential manufacturers."[54]

Taking charge of the 1915 political campaign, the men's association supervised the state organizer and removed many of the campaign decisions, especially those directed at men, from MAOFESW knowledge and control. One of these concerned fund-raising, and the unsettled women warned that the association "could not receive help from any doubtful sources." This is the only suggestion in MAOFESW records of possible financial impropriety and provides no clear support for suffrage charges of liquor interest involvement in the female antisuffrage movement; if they funded the Massachusetts organization, it was through donations to the men's committee and was likely unknown to the women. Male control for the duration of the referendum campaign extended beyond money, moreover. The state organizer requested reports on the women's committee activities and instructed the leadership to undertake no policy without consulting him, increasing the tension between the two groups.[55]

After the defeat of woman suffrage in the November referendum by a margin of almost two to one, the primary contact between the men's and women's associations was through the paid organizer, whose major activity now shifted to development of a national men's organization. During the 1915 referenda campaign in the four populous eastern states of New York, Massachusetts, New Jersey, and Pennsylvania, NAOWS president Josephine Dodge had begun requesting lists of "prominent men" from the state associations, intending to constitute a men's advisory council as a means of encouraging other men to "come out" against suffrage during that crucial election season and to raise funds for future campaigns. The Massachusetts staff collaborated with the New York Association to develop a national men's committee, chaired by former U.S. Treasury secretary Charles S. Fairchild, "to relieve the women of the political work." Its secretary was Professor

M. W. Jacobus, dean of the Hartford Theological Seminary and New Testament scholar, and serving as treasurer was his former Princeton classmate, manufacturer Henry B. Thompson, whose wife, Mary Wilson Thompson, headed the Delaware women's antisuffrage association and was NAOWS finance chair. In a clever display of image manipulation, Mrs. Dodge announced the committee's formation at the national convention, expressing gratitude to the men for "this spontaneous offer of co-operation."[56]

The ambitious plan for building the men's committee was to recruit two representatives from each of eighteen states; at most, seven states participated, although they collected an illustrious roster of "supporters" that included former governors, judges, industrialists, and railroad presidents. The organization soon reformed as the Men's National Anti-Suffrage Association, and its work consisted almost exclusively of sending paid political organizers to take charge of opposition campaigns in various states voting on suffrage.[57] The new association was heavily supported by MAOFESW; its executive secretary was the male organizer who directed the 1915 state referendum campaign, and its business was managed from Boston. By 1917, the tables had turned. Women no longer could look to men for financial assistance in their antisuffrage crusade; instead, the state organizer requested that MAOFESW tithe its local branches to support the men's work nationwide. Furthermore, local men no longer served as advisers, and when it came time to fight the federal amendment in 1919, the remaining women in the Massachusetts Association constituted a new men's committee to assist them.[58]

Men's antisuffrage mobilization in New York experienced a parallel faltering pattern of development. In 1909 and again in 1911, the Massachusetts Association received information that the New York men were organizing, but it was not until May 1913 that Everett P. Wheeler established the New York State Association Opposed to Political Suffrage for Women at the request of NAOWS president Josephine Dodge. Like his Massachusetts peers, Wheeler determined to be prepared for a referenda fight he regarded as imminent; his organization officially began the campaign with a Brooklyn antisuffrage meeting in September, where Wheeler described the organization's purpose as charitable, "to prevent the burden of political activity on mothers of the state," and euphemistically dubbed his group the "Society for the Prevention of Cruelty to Women."[59] A few months later, however, when addressing the U.S. House Committee on Rules, Wheeler's rhetoric became noticeably less chivalrous as he warned the suffragists:

The manhood of this nation has been trained to respect and revere womanhood. And I claim that for American manhood today. But if we are challenged to fight this movement there will be blows to give as well as blows to take.[60]

Displays of masculine power became more explicit in 1914, when Wheeler changed the name of the organization to Man-Suffrage Association Opposed to Political Suffrage for Women in time for referenda opposition in the four eastern states. Wheeler prepared a campaign manual that included a checklist for effective debating, statistics demonstrating the deleterious effects of suffrage in the western states, a summary of state laws favorable to women, lists of prominent men and women opponents, an antisuffrage bibliography, and New York census data underscoring the high percentage of foreign-born residents. The manual was sold to other organizations, as were reprints of Wheeler's numerous antisuffrage addresses, Professor Sedgwick's letter to the *New York Times* stating that woman suffrage will set human evolution back "a thousand years," and selected newspaper editorials denouncing votes for women.[61] One anonymous essay, entitled *Woman Suffrage: Some Underlying Principles and Comments,* linked woman suffrage to immorality through innuendoes against its female leadership, a breach of male etiquette that garnered notoriety for Man-Suffrage when NAWSA president Carrie Chapman Catt demanded and received a public apology from the association, which even the antisuffragist *New York Times* denounced as "half-hearted."[62]

To defeat the 1915 referenda, men's antisuffrage associations in Massachusetts, New York, and New Jersey formed campaign committees that supplied speakers, literature, and publicity. The Men's Anti-Suffrage League of New Jersey lobbied heavily among labor unions, and its efforts were rewarded when the New Jersey State Federation of Labor rescinded its support for woman suffrage. Political affiliations sometimes facilitated alignments with influential organizations; while Boston's Good Government Association endorsed woman suffrage, New York's anti-Tammany Union League, after "spirited discussion," went on record opposed. The men's tactics were often inventive as well as economical; Wheeler's regular letters to local newspaper editors, for example, garnered free publicity for the cause, and an interstate exchange of antisuffrage speakers pooled resources.[63] They raised money in sizable amounts from wealthy members, although Man-Suffrage reported total campaign expenditures of less than one-quarter of the amount spent by the women's state association.[64] For the moment, at least, the feared eastern migration of woman suffrage was checked as voters rejected all four referenda.

Another common trait between New York and Massachusetts antisuffrage organizations was periodic conflict with their female counterparts, but in New York it was the women who seemed to have the upper hand. During the 1915 referendum campaign, the New York Association leadership ignored attempts by Man-Suffrage to coordinate activities. In 1916, Everett Wheeler was temporarily replaced as head of Man-Suffrage by the younger Ezra P. Prentice, chairman of the State Republican Committee. A male worker for NAOWS blamed the women antis, who had " 'knocked' him so much with some of the men that they will not help him out, as they should." Wheeler regained the headship of the organization, but by the next year its treasury was down to "a few dollars in the bank," its chief staff assistant had resigned, and the office lease was about to expire. As the 1917 New York referendum approached, Wheeler wrote the president of the New York Association, detailing the crises afflicting Man-Suffrage and asking the women to decide the future of the men's organization. The state association responded by sharing its campaign headquarters and giving Man-Suffrage a major role in preparing antisuffrage propaganda; Wheeler later claimed that his group produced a hundred thousand pieces of literature for the 1917 election.[65]

The New York suffrage victory that November proved to be a turning point that incited a last-ditch coalition among men antisuffragists. Within weeks of the election, the Man-Suffrage Association and the Men's National Anti-Suffrage Association were reconstituted as the American Constitutional League under Fairchild's leadership. Its field secretary, J. S. Eichelberger, was also in charge of publicity for the women's National Association Opposed to Woman Suffrage, reiterating the pattern of interlocking staff.[66] Its object was the defeat of a federal suffrage amendment under the banner of states' rights, which Everett Wheeler attached to patriotic sentiments during wartime:

> Compelling another State to adopt your own ideals is the essence of the German Kultur which is bringing woe to the world. It would be particularly unjust to impose it upon the Southern States involving, as it would, the votes of the negro women.[67]

The rhetoric became increasingly strident as antisuffragists' desperation grew. Early in 1918, the women's New York Association and the American Constitutional League jointly announced a two-pronged campaign to stop ratification of federal suffrage and rescind the recently passed state amendment. Speaking at a rally at the posh Biltmore Hotel, league president Charles Fairchild, whose wife would shortly assume the leadership of the reorganized New York women's antisuffrage association, warned of the dangers of immigrant women voters, and Henry A. WiseWood declared that "American Bolsheviki are running away with the country." With the socialist connection to newer eastern European immigrants and the labor movement, antisuffragists explicitly transformed exacerbation of ethnic and class conflict into acts of patriotism.[68]

Such inflammatory wartime rhetoric derived in part from antisuffragist participation in the preparedness movement. An important organizational tie to the suffrage opposition was the National Security League (NSL), founded in 1914; several members of New York's Man-Suffrage Association were NSL officers, including George Wickersham, Herbert Satterlee, and Talcott Williams. Antisuffrage leader Elihu Root succeeded his mentor Joseph Hodges Choate as honorary league president in 1917; as chairman of the Carnegie Corporation, Root helped sustain the NSL with foundation grants, while Man-Suffrage member Cleveland Dodge was also a major donor. By 1916 the NSL claimed to have fifty thousand members in forty-two states, and its Iowa state chairman served concurrently as an officer in the men's antisuffrage association. Women antisuffragists were also connected to the league, such as Mrs. A. J. George, longtime paid public speaker for the Massachusetts Association, who, as the league's "authority on patriotic education," designed a program for military preparedness in the public schools. The organization's two greatest congressional supporters were Representative A. Peabody Gardner and Senator Henry Cabot Lodge, also strident foes of woman suffrage and immigration. Henry A. WiseWood, who coordinated the activities of all patriotic societies for the Conference Committee of National Preparedness, spoke out frequently against woman suffrage as propacifist and a danger to national security.[69]

The NSL's patriotism campaign relied heavily upon antiforeign, antisocialist, and antisuffrage rhetoric along with a muscle-flexing masculinity. For example, the league called for an Americanization program in all public schools that included a ban on German language instruction. Root criticized President Wilson's neutrality policy for damaging America's prestige among all "virile" peoples of the world and glorified the war as a moral battle for the survival of superior Anglo-American civilization. According to these wealthy eastern men, the battle for the future of America was also being waged inside the United States, which was threatened by the growing political power of "pacifists, slackers, and hyphenates." Masculinity themes predominated in the discourse used to decry the wartime threat to the United States: prosperity had rendered America "soft," foreign immigrants were indolent, and woman suffrage risked the nation's decline before a "wave of effeminacy." Their proposed solutions included a resounding military defeat abroad, an ethnically homogenized America "swept clean of foreign tongues," and a male electorate remasculinized by victories abroad and at home.[70] The declining years of the men's campaign against woman suffrage were characterized by a relationship to reactionary patriotic organizations that exploited wartime anxieties and cast further doubt on suffragist charges that they were front organizations for the ethnic interests of the brewery trade.

After converging on Nashville in an unsuccessful effort to block ratification of the federal woman suffrage amendment, the final tactic of the American Constitutional League employed its leaders' occupational expertise—the law. As Tennessee was about to become the final state to ratify the Susan B. Anthony Amendment, Charles Fairchild filed suit for an injunction preventing U.S. Secretary of State Bainbridge Colby from officially proclaiming the amendment ratified because some states had not held popular referenda on the question. Everett Wheeler helped prepare a supporting brief and wrote to the *New York Times* praising the suit's defense of home rule.[71] Fairchild lost, but appealed the case with the financial support of the women's antisuffrage associations, and it took a few years for *Fairchild v. Colby* and a related suit brought by a group of Maryland men cooperating with the league to proceed to the Supreme Court. In 1922, the Court ruled unanimously against both plaintiffs and upheld the constitutionality of the Nineteenth Amendment. In an ironic end to the antisuffrage campaign, both unfavorable decisions were written by Justice Brandeis, former antisuffrage lobbyist.[72]

Opinions of Eminent Persons

Not all men aided the antisuffrage cause by joining organizations. Others wrote essays about the dangers of woman suffrage, many of which were distributed by antisuffrage associations. Although both sexes wrote articles for the cause, men tended to be more widely known and possessed the professional credentials that added weight to their arguments, particularly among the male electorate who by and large decided the question. Women's organizations actively recruited famous men to produce antisuffrage literature and sometimes packaged it in volumes with names such as *Opinions of Eminent Persons against Woman Suffrage* that were distributed throughout the country.[73]

Elite networks again proved useful in recruiting authors to prepare antisuffrage tracts. In Tennessee, for example, the husband of the state antisuffrage association president and a prominent Nashville lawyer authored a 1916 pamphlet addressed "to the men of Tennessee" that was used in the last-ditch fight against the federal amendment.[74] For decades the most popular publication of the Massachusetts Association was Francis Parkman's *Some of the Reasons against Woman Suffrage*, a condensed version of a longer article published in an 1879 issue of *North American Review*.[75] Parkman, related to a founding member of the Boston Committee of Remonstrants, was the archetype of the Brahmin gentleman scholar: a graduate of Harvard, where his father endowed a divinity chair, a leading historian of the American frontier, and an expert horticulturist who briefly held a professorship at his alma mater. Parkman's position on "the woman question" sounded themes similar to those of his argument against universal suffrage published the previous year, warning that "the coarse and contentious among women would be drawn to politics" and that "rash legislation," "one of the chief dangers of popular government," would be a heightened risk "if the most impulsive and excitable half of humanity had an equal voice in the making of laws."[76] Parkman died before the 1895 referendum on the Wellman bill, but MAOFESW used his essay and his prestigious name throughout its long existence.

Women antisuffragists preferred to give the impression that antisuffrage endorsements were offered spontaneously, but their organizational records document extensive behind-the-scenes efforts to recruit men's literary assistance. One female leader boasted many years later that "inducing" Parkman to write the *North American Review* article was the remonstrants' "first achievement." The Massachusetts Association's executive committee sometimes suggested topics, identified suitable authors, and edited drafts of essays before approving them for printing.[77] With the help of personal networks and a professional clipping service, they identified well-known sympathizers and sent notes of appreciation that frequently included invitations to write testimonials for the cause or speak at antisuffrage functions. Some of the men accepted, while others demurred, citing pressing work commitments or, in the case of Senator Lodge, the constraints of public office.[78] Antis donated propaganda to public libraries, mailed them to state legislators and residents of campaign states, and sold them to other antisuffrage organizations, with the revenues constituting a much-needed source of income.[79]

The men who contributed antisuffrage essays were drawn generally from three occupational groups: religion, journalism, and education. The clergy had been the most outspoken group against suffrage in its earliest phase, and its statements possessed the additional pressure of moral suasion. By the end of the century, however, attitudes were changing among the religious leadership. The Methodist ministry reportedly went on record for suffrage for the 1895 Massachusetts referendum, the American Unitarian Association endorsed suffrage in 1912, and a council of reform rabbis did the same in 1917 "by a substantial majority." Pockets of antisuffrage sentiment remained, however, particularly among elite social networks. Rev. O. B. Frothingham, Harvard-educated Unitarian clergyman of radical views, had written antisuffrage articles for a quarter of a century, and although he also died before the 1895 Massachusetts referendum, his *Arena* essay praising the remonstrants was cited for years afterward.[80] Another longtime advocate of separate spheres for women was Episcopal bishop William Croswell Doane of Albany, New York, whose daughter was a leading antisuffragist. His article "Why Women Do Not Want the Ballot" appeared in the influential *North American Review* shortly before the 1895 Massachusetts referendum. James M. Buckley was one Methodist clergyman who opposed woman suffrage; his writings on the issue in the prestigious *Century* magazine were expanded subsequently into a popular book.[81] Congregationalist pastor Henry A. Stimson of the prestigious Manhattan Church contributed a previously published essay to the New York Association, of which his wife Alice Bartlett Stimson was an officer; the liberal-sounding title inquired whether woman suffrage was an "enlightened" policy, but its conclusion evoked the biblical image of Eve by stating that suffrage would bring women "new temptations" and "unanticipated evil."[82]

Roman Catholic prelates generally opposed woman suffrage, and although they had fewer ties to the remonstrant leadership, they constituted an important bridge to immigrant populations. The most valued antisuffragist among the Catholic clergy was James Cardinal Gibbons, archbishop of Baltimore, whose political views were otherwise at variance with those of native-born elites. The son of Irish immigrants, Cardinal Gibbons was on record as opposed to immigration restriction and prohibition and in sympathy with the labor movement. He had authored a number of articles criticizing the "restlessness" of suffragists, and was invited to attend a 1913 antisuffrage meeting by Baltimore socialite leader Mrs. Robert Garrett; Gibbons declined, but explained in written detail the reasons for his opposition to votes for women.[83] His subsequent open letter to a New Jersey Democratic leader before that state's 1915 referendum was reproduced, translated into Italian, and distributed widely in other campaign states, where it incited some priests to denounce suffrage from the Sunday pulpit.[84] As the ranking prelate of the Roman Catholic Church in the United States and a friend of presidents, Cardinal Gibbons exercised considerable influence, which the antisuffrage associations used to their advantage. They read a message from him at their 1916 national conventional and published at least two anthologies of antisuffrage statements by well-known religious leaders, one of which focused on Roman Catholics.[85] Antis must surely have become anxious when it was widely reported in 1917 that Cardinal Gibbons was visited by a group of prosuffrage Roman Catholic women and declared himself "impressed" by their arguments.[86]

Two other religious figures were especially important antisuffrage allies owing to their influence on public opinion through the mass media. The first was Rev. Lyman Abbott, protégé of Henry Ward Beecher and his successor as pastor of Brooklyn's Plymouth Congregational Church and as editor-in-chief of the weekly *Christian Union.* Abbott changed the journal's focus from religion to public affairs and literary criticism, renamed it the *Outlook* in 1893, and presided as editor until his death in 1922. He was tied to the Boston elite through ancestry and marriage as well as professionally, having presented a celebrated lecture series at the Lowell Institute and served on the Harvard College board of preachers. A follower of the "new theology" pioneered by antisuffragist minister Horace Bushnell that placed more responsibility for individual salvation and social progress on humankind, Abbott was an early advocate of civil service reform and economic justice for workers. But by the 1890s he also supported immigration restriction, promulgated the manifest destiny of American imperialism derived from the superiority of its Anglo-Saxon heritage, and endorsed early U.S. military action in Cuba and then against Germany as a necessary defense of civilization against "barbarism" and "lawlessness." Abbott was also a strong advocate of the National Security League co-founded by his son Lawrence, calling it "the greatest peace society in America."[87]

According to his biographer, Lyman Abbott was an early sympathizer with equal rights for women until converted by his wife, who later became president of the New York Association. His father, Jacob, had established girls' schools in Boston and New York, and Abbott showed an early interest in higher education for women that the antisuffrage movement utilized by sending him to lecture at female colleges.[88] During his tenure as *Outlook*'s editor-in-chief, Lyman Abbott authored more than two dozen antisuffrage editorials and articles, published timely exhortations for rejection of state referenda, and put the magazine on record as "opposed to woman suffrage primarily because it is an advocate of woman's rights"; he also contributed a scholarly rebuttal to suffragist arguments in a special 1910 supplement of the *Annals of the American Academy of Political Science.*[89] Correspondence with the Massachusetts Association resulted in publication of "Why Women Do Not Wish the Suffrage" in the Houghton-owned *Atlantic Monthly* magazine (subsequently reprinted by MAOFESW), and a paean to traditional womanhood entitled *The Home Builder,* published by Houghton Mifflin. Abbott was also one of the first magazine editors to cover women's antisuffrage organization as a news story, furnishing free publicity for the fledgling movement.[90]

Another religious personage whose antisuffrage position was widely accessible to American women was moral crusader Rev. Charles H. Parkhurst, pastor of New York City's Madison Square Presbyterian Church, who rose to prominence in the 1890s when he assumed the presidency of the reformist Society for the Prevention of Crime. Parkhurst demonstrated the complicity of New York's police in the vice industry and led a victorious campaign against Tammany in 1894, which was extensively covered in the *Outlook.* Fresh from his highly publicized victory against urban corruption, Rev. Parkhurst authored a monthly column in the *Ladies' Home Journal* that during 1895 regularly lambasted suffragists and endorsed the opposition.[91]

The *Ladies' Home Journal* represents the second category of influential antisuffrage sympathizers, that of journalists. This magazine succeeded *Godey's Ladies' Book* as the preeminent women's magazine in the United States and was a leading publication in the transition to mass-market publishing. Started in 1883, fifteen years later it had attained monthly circulation of almost a million readers, thanks largely to the genius of Edward Bok, originator of the "woman's page" in newspaper publishing, who became its editor in 1889.[92] Bok added many features new to women's magazines, including a pseudonymous romantic advice column, true-life stories about and by daughters of famous men, and experts' writings on health, beauty, and household management. He would sometimes diverge from convention and embroil the magazine in controversy; for example, at the urging of his friend Lyman Abbott, Bok took up the fight against venereal disease as an issue of women's and children's health, despite considerable loss of advertising revenue. Bok more typically aimed to educate American women on how to dress, raise their children, feed their families, and decorate their homes; like other cultural entrepreneurs, this Dutch immigrant aimed to shape the tastes of the emergent middle classes. The magazine offered inexpensive architectural plans and extensive photos of home interiors with captions instructing readers in the differences between "ugly" and "beautiful" furnishings. Bok also sought female involvement in municipal housekeeping, at least in its aesthetic dimension, by printing pictures of unsightly billboards in a "Beautiful America" section.[93]

The *Ladies' Home Journal* was equally opinionated on the subject of women's rights. Bok personally authored over twenty articles on the topic during the suffrage campaign. He opposed not only woman suffrage, but any activities that diverted women's attention away from domestic duties, including employment, clubs, and education.[94] He complained that female housekeeping skills had deteriorated in the modern era and blamed a host of social problems on household neglect—saloons, he wrote, are prevalent because women are incompetent cooks—and cautioned women to resist the temptations of feminism or risk divorce, ill health, and perhaps death.[95] Bok also helped focus public attention on antisuffragism by recruiting opinion pieces from influential Americans, including former presidents Grover Cleveland and Theodore Roosevelt, who later reversed himself and supported suffrage.[96] The *Journal*'s popularity among middle-class American women, coupled with its intimate editorial style and use of modern imagery, made it a valuable ally of the antisuffrage movement.

Another influential journalist and antisuffrage sympathizer was Richard Watson Gilder, editor of *Century* magazine (formerly *Scribner's Monthly*) from 1870 until his death in 1909. Like Lyman Abbott, Gilder was the son of a minister who had established all-female schools and related to prominent antisuffragists: his wife, socialite Helena de Kay Gilder, and his sister, journalist Jeannette Gilder, were both active in the New York Association. Gilder was also involved in civic affairs as an anti-Tammany Republican; he was an early advocate of tenement reform, a topic *Century* addressed with reports by his friend Jacob Riis. Although he kept the magazine nonpartisan, Gilder was active in the reformist Citizen's Union along with Everett P. Wheeler and Elihu Root; his son Rodman, also affiliated with *Century,* was executive secretary of the National Security League. *Century* equivocated on U.S. imperialism and immigration policy and preferred to take positions on less controversial issues like conservation and currency reform, although after the Haymarket riots Gilder blamed labor violence on subversive foreigners and sounded much like Francis Parkman when he editorialized that what the United States needed was citizens of "character, ability, and training."[97]

As one of many popular magazines to originate in the postwar decade, *Scribner's*, which was renamed *Century* after the prestigious New York men's club, tried to edge out the competition by building a niche among middle-class subscribers. Gilder's editorial strategy was to position the magazine as an arbiter of culture. *Century* was renowned for spending large sums on elaborate artwork and stories by famous authors. Gilder had the credentials to become a crusader for good taste: his wife, Helena, had studied painting in Europe and was one of the founders of New York's Art Students League; both the Society of American Artists and Authors Club of New York were established at the Gilders' residential salon. Consistent with his religious background and interest in the "new theology" movement, Gilder viewed *Century*'s artistic contents as a vehicle of moral uplift and public education, "not as indulgence, but to improve American society." Its aesthetic orientation was antimodern and reverential toward European culture; not surprisingly, the magazine lauded the romanticized White City of the 1893 Chicago Columbian Exposition as the "apogee of Hellenism in modern America."[98]

Women were central to Gilder's marketing strategy. *Century* magazine published women's poetry, employed female writers such as art critic and antisuffragist Mariana Griswold Van Rensselaer, and instituted a "Home and Society" feature addressing domestic concerns that was unique for its time. He regarded women as guardians of the nation's morality and intentionally excluded from the magazine material that might "offend" mothers or "corrupt their daughters." The magazine expressed ambivalence toward female role expansion; its editor approved of women's increased educational opportunities and participation in community affairs, yet other articles attacked divorce and fulminated over the low marriage rates of college-educated women.[99] While *Century* presented both sides of the suffrage question during the 1894 New York constitutional convention, Gilder editorialized against woman suffrage as a threat to the "home woman," idealizing the female function as a necessary anchor of stability in a changing world.[100]

Antisuffrage advocacy by journals and newspapers facilitated greatly the movement's stated goal of public education. Besides editorial endorsements and antisuffrage testimonials by prominent men, some of which were reprinted and distributed by women's antisuffrage organizations, these magazines also published articles by female antisuffrage sympathizers and activists.[101] Even anti leaders with few journalistic credentials placed articles in periodicals friendly to the cause; for example, New York antisuffrage leaders Mrs. Gilbert E. Jones and Mrs. William Forse Scott wrote articles for *North American Review,* and Mrs. Lyman Abbott's views were featured in "Just among Ourselves" in the pages of the *Ladies' Home Journal.*[102] Family ties were also called into service. Longtime chair of the Massachusetts Association's printing committee, Elizabeth Houghton used Houghton Publishing (later Houghton-Mifflin), operated by her father and brother, for printing association documents, and the Massachusetts executive committee discussed placing antisuffrage articles in the Houghton-owned *Atlantic Monthly.* The aforementioned Mrs. Jones was married to a son of the founder of the *New York Times,* an important antisuffrage ally. Male talents were also exploited behind the scenes in the preparation of antisuffrage journals. For years, the *Remonstrance* was edited anonymously by journalist Frank Foxcroft, who was assistant editor to William Sohier at the Boston *Journal* and author of several antisuffrage essays under his own name.[103] The fact that the Massachusetts Association cultivated the pretense that women produced their house organ underscores their political aptitude in presenting an image of female self-sacrifice and commitment to the cause.

The third group of men who authored articles expressing antisuffrage views were academicians from distinguished institutions of higher learning. In addition to Man-Suffrage organization members Professors Munroe Smith, Talcott Williams, and William T. Sedgwick, other antisuffrage sympathizers contributing articles and speeches included Harvard professors William Watson Goodwin, Barrett Wendell, and Ernest Bernbaum, who edited a MAOFESW volume of antisuffrage views.[104] Although these classical and literary scholars lent considerable prestige to the antisuffrage movement, the most effective arguments were probably contributed by scientists. Scientific opinions on the suffrage question reflected the nation's transition to an industrialized, secular society. As the U.S. population became more diverse in religious affiliation, arguments based ostensibly on reason and science supplemented traditional pulpit rhetoric exhorting obedience to God's law. While numerous journals in the latter half of the nineteenth century continued to promulgate Christian viewpoints, a spurt of national scientific interest is evidenced by the addition of science departments in mainstream periodicals such as *Atlantic Monthly, Scribner's,* and

Harper's and the appearance of specialized magazines like *Popular Science Monthly.*[105]

The influence of Darwin's evolutionary theory was reflected in the antisuffrage writings of scientists, such as University of Pennsylvania paleontologist Edward Drinker Cope. Cope was a leader of the American school of neo-Lamarckians, advancing the argument that acquired characteristics were transmissible and concluding that women's "degenerative" practice of adopting so-called male characteristics of political participation would be inherited by their daughters.[106] More commonly, Social Darwinism melded the interests of ethnicity, class, and gender. Two favorite British experts among antisuffragists were social philosopher Herbert Spencer and historian Goldwin Smith, both of whom championed the superiority of the Anglo-Saxon race while paradoxically expressing concerns about its numerical and physical weakness. Harvard English professor and antisuffragist Barrett Wendell illustrates this contradiction, praising the literary genius of Anglo-Saxon ancestral culture yet voicing anxiety about "being strangled by invading aliens" and observing ruefully in 1893 that "we Yankees are as much things of the past as any race can be."[107]

Herbert Spencer, who reportedly coined the term "survival of the fittest" commonly attributed to Charles Darwin, visited the United States in the 1880s and expressed concerns about the deterioration of Anglo-Saxon stock. His ideas led some Americans to question the value of assimilating immigrant populations and influenced the Brahmin founders of the Immigration Restriction League.[108] According to Allan Chase, there were good reasons why Spencer was "the favored philosopher of the affluent":

> He not only proclaimed the moral rights of the Deserving Rich to heaven; Spencer also denounced the immorality and impracticality of health, education, safety, and welfare programs that would have materially increased their taxes here on earth.[109]

Goldwin Smith addressed the failure of universal suffrage in the *Atlantic Monthly* shortly after Francis Parkman's 1878 *North American Review* article on the same theme. Both Spencer and Smith had earlier discussed the issue of woman suffrage in *Popular Science Monthly,* declaring her unfit for political participation on the basis of evolutionary specialization: arrested mental development imposed by nature to preserve her energy for reproduction.[110]

Spencer and Smith were cited frequently in antisuffrage literature, and local scholars with compatible views produced essays purporting to demonstrate the scientific basis of separate spheres. Distinguished Harvard psychologist Hugo Münsterberg, who also gave public speeches for the Massachusetts Association, wrote that the women's movement would cause race suicide by undermining the attractiveness of marriage, feminizing higher culture, and, by making women "pathologically tense," would render them unfit mothers.[111] Münsterberg's writings underscore two additional elements of the scientific rationale against woman suffrage. One is the interest in eugenics derived from Galton's research asserting the genetic basis of hereditary achievement patterns among Britain's upper classes, documenting declining birthrates among urban affluent families, and proposing a strategy of racial improvement based on higher fertility among the wellborn. Galton's ideas reflected class anxieties about the social changes of industrialization in a tripartite argument that linked class with a narrowly defined racial superiority and asserted the primacy of women's reproductive role at a time when elite women were challenging traditional norms of genteel confinement. The three interlocking ideas of race, class, and gender superiority found expression in antisuffragism. Brahmin leaders of the Immigration Restriction League increasingly used eugenics arguments, and New York Man-Suffrage office Frank Babbott was president of the Eugenics Research Association.[112]

Münsterberg's discussion of feminization and nervous disorders also alluded to neurasthenia, a disease named by George Beard in 1869 that constituted a common diagnosis for turn-of-the-century physicians serving the leisure classes. The symptomology of neurasthenia reflected ambivalence about the quickening pace of industrial society in general, but its discourse was further bounded by class and gender. For upper-class women, the disorder was believed to be brought on by too much worldly activity—in their terms, by masculinization—and the prescribed treatment was rest and quiet, a return to traditional female seclusion. For men, the diagnosed cause was just the opposite—excessive exposure to mental labor and feminized, refined culture—and the cure was exercise and rugged travel westward to remasculinize the self. Antisuffragists Elihu Root, Francis Parkman, and Thomas Russell were known sufferers from the disorder, as were Theodore Roosevelt, Henry James, and Edith Wharton. Neurasthenia was simultaneously a critique of the hectic pace of modern life, a paradoxical claim to racial superiority, and a mechanism of adjustment to social change circumscribed by class and gender. Since sexual differentiation was regarded as a key component of evolutionary law derived from specialization of function, the health risks of elite women's higher education, employment, and political participation ostensibly endangered both genders and the future well-being of the Anglo-Saxon race. S. Weir Mitchell, the Philadelphia physician who invented the rest cure for women neurasthenics made famous in Charlotte Perkins Gilman's "The Yellow Wallpaper," warned *Ladies' Home Journal* readers of the perils of competing with men and claimed to have observed the ruined health of many "ambitious" women.[113]

Scientific themes of male superiority were reiterated by biologist and antisuffragist William T. Sedgwick, whose *New York Times* essay, reprinted by New York's Man-Suffrage Association, asserted that sex differences affect "every organ, every tissue, and every cell of the entire body" and judged women's competition with men "regrettable from a physiological and medical point of view." According to a Massachusetts Association officer, Professor Sedgwick's "scientific and biological knowledge of women's lives and duties brought in a new element," and MAOFESW made full use of his talents. His wife, Mary K. Sedgwick, published an article in *Gunton's,* "Some Scientific Aspects of the Woman Suffrage Question," that was probably ghostwritten by her husband; Mary Sedgwick was also named chair of the Massachusetts Association's education subcommittee, whose primary functions were publicity and the production of antisuffrage propaganda.[114] More generally, the New York and Massachusetts associations published anthologies of the statements, letters, and articles of prominent men, sometimes repackaged as local products for distribution in western campaign states.[115]

Perhaps more than the content of these literary contributions, the mere fact of an antisuffrage endorsement from a "man of importance" was newsworthy and could potentially influence public opinion. To get such testimonials, women antisuffragists were not above pursuing the wives of influential men. They made one woman an officer of the Massachusetts Association in 1902 because of the "great influence" of her husband, a future governor, and identified other possible female recruits whose husbands "would do much for us." Even deceased men could be useful; the 1915 campaign issue of the *Remonstrance* advertised widows among the "wives of leading statesmen" who were active opponents of woman suffrage. One Massachusetts Association officer admitted that the habit of constituting lists of prominent men opposed to woman suffrage was "not for the legislature alone, but for use at all our meetings, and to influence women as well as men."[116] This explains the penchant of both men's and women's associations for publishing anthologies of antisuffrage opinions by eminent persons.

Conclusion

Male antisuffrage leaders were not unlike their female peers in social class background; they were largely native-born, wealthy, socially prominent, and accomplished in their professions. These similarities are not accidental, as the antisuffrage leadership included numerous married couples and other relatives. Homogeneity of social background was also a consequence of the importance of social networks for recruitment. Female antisuffrage organizations utilized local university clubs to start new state associations and courted prominent clergy in the hopes of receiving endorsements in Sunday sermons. Male antisuffragists shared a large network of social clubs, cultural and philanthropic activities, hereditary societies, and civic and professional organizations. These activities brought together men with similar worldviews and a proclivity toward political activism, a combination that proved favorable for antisuffrage mobilization.

The male leaders of the antisuffrage movement were defenders of class and ethnic privilege to a great extent inherited from their ancestors. These were typically not self-made men, but graduates of private preparatory schools, Ivy League colleges and law schools, and members of exclusive social clubs and hereditary societies. Although frequently employed as counsel for new industrial giants and railroad monopolies, their lives reflected ambivalence about changes in U.S. society. They were a distinctly urban elite that was unsettled by the disorder wrought by industrialization and urbanization. At the top of the economic and social hierarchy, they nonetheless expressed anxiety about the future and looked backward for comfort and guidance.[117] This antimodern impulse found expression elsewhere in American culture, and drew some to the antisuffrage movement.[118]

The men involved in antisuffragism responded in particular ways to the perceived disorder of class mobility and ethnic diversity. Physically, they walled themselves away from the masses, women, and the marketplace in exclusive all-male clubs where rules prohibited luncheon shoptalk in order to preserve the "unruffled harmony of modest friendship."[119] Socially, they established and supported charitable institutions that defined poverty as an individual problem of character and discouraged structural solutions. Politically, their fight against the corruption of urban machines reflected a basic distrust of "ignorant" voters, and they favored immigration restriction as the long-term solution to the perceived alien threat. Their response to labor unrest was more likely to dismiss strikers as un-American than to call for government regulation of business practices. Antiforeign, antidemocratic, and antipopulist themes peppered their writings, and their opposition to woman suffrage constituted part of a larger reaction against universal suffrage. As Barrett Wendell stated, they were "the last of the tories."[120]

The genteel dominion enjoyed by previous generations of American elites was indeed ending, but the genteel response was multifaceted.[121] Some became progressives, confident in their ability to educate the masses for greater participation and seeking the order imposed by bureaucratic control. Others participated in reactionary organizations, ruminating wistfully on past glories. Examining the male participants in antisuffrage mobilization leads to the conclusion that it is very unlikely that they were mere fronts for liquor interests. Neither did they control female antisuffragists; if anything, men were used as covers for women's political activity. Female antisuffrage associations operated autonomously and struggled to stay that way while selectively soliciting male assistance. Surviving records suggest that women frequently tried to instigate men's mobilization, but they also feared competition over resources and resisted male attempts at fiscal control.

Men were major contributors to the antisuffrage movement. They lent their names, expertise, and money, essential resources given cultural constraints on women's public participation. But class position also constrained male behavior; professional propriety and public stature made some male public figures chary of formally affiliating with antisuffrage organizations. Social position also shaped the campaign strategies of male activists, who typically eschewed the unseemly rabble of mass politics. The advantages of class permitted the antisuffrage leadership to wage rigorous campaigns while upholding the dictates of convention by hiring staff to conduct the less elevated aspects of campaign work. Instead of rallies and speaking tours, male antisuffrage leaders often preferred to wage dignified campaigns of mailed circulars, letters to the editor, and scholarly articles in popular magazines, maintaining distance from the source of their disquietude. For antisuffragists to succeed, however, they needed to extend their message beyond the inner circle and engage the interest and sympathy of the broader public. The next chapter examines the rhetoric of antisuffrage as both ideology and strategy.

4

A Menace to Civilization

> We antisuffragists stand for the conservation of the best of American womanhood . . . We do believe that woman has more power in uplifting civilization through the home than man has through the vote.
>
> —Mrs. Arthur M. Dodge, NAOWS annual convention

The most scrutinized aspect of the antisuffrage movement is its rhetoric.[1] Repeated public pronouncements that enfranchisement threatened to erode gender differences and female virtues derived from domestic seclusion are the basis for widespread consensus that antisuffragists were traditionalists engaged in the defense of separate spheres.[2] Jensen summarized the philosophical basis of antisuffragism as "conservative and reactive . . . aimed at maintaining the nineteenth-century ideal of the woman in the home and the man in the world," and Howard concluded that opposition arguments remained "largely the same from Catharine Beecher's remarks in 1870 to the last issue of the *Remonstrance* in 1920." Some have offered psychological analyses, characterizing women's protest against the vote as "almost entirely irrational," reflecting antisuffragist fears, fantasies, personality disorders, self-worth issues, or status conflicts.[3] Reductionist treatments of antisuffrage rhetoric perpetuate movement stereotypes as static, particularistic, and single-issue.

While it is clear that antisuffrage rhetoric included a defense of separate spheres, numerous questions remained unanswered. For example, what were the relative frequencies of the various arguments against the vote? Few studies of antisuffrage writings attempt to prioritize rhetorical themes, and fewer yet utilize systematic data collection techniques to support their conclusions.[4] Did antisuffrage arguments change over time? Perhaps one of the most significant insights about suffrage rhetoric is Kraditor's discovery of its evolution from natural rights to expediency claims. But despite the fact that the opposition developed in reaction to suffrage successes and necessarily fashioned a rhetoric of rebuttal, scholars have yet to conduct dynamic analyses charting the rhetorical career of the antisuffrage movement. Moreover, gender differences in antisuffrage propaganda have not been examined thoroughly. Some of the earliest and most influential treatments of antisuffrage rhetoric either confined their focus to one gender or failed to distinguish between men's and women's arguments.[5] Identifying such differences in antisuffrage propaganda may uncover complexities in the opposition campaign on a par with those revealed in histories of the woman rights movement.

A more general issue concerns the significance of social movement propaganda. Most previous studies have used antisuffrage rhetoric to assess individual motivations for joining the cause, and there is some basis for this conclusion in rhetorical and social movements scholarship. Rhetoric does function as an expression of ideology; it crystallizes discontent, defines the problem as well as the solution, promotes individual identification with the group, and impels protest action through shared meanings.[6] Because its purpose is to articulate personal grievances and link the individual to larger social issues, rhetoric has been used frequently to draw inferences about individual motivations for joining social movements. Some have cautioned against a simple reflectionism between literature and values, however, and have underscored the disparity between the views of the leaders who manage movement propaganda and their target audience.[7] Recent developments in social movements scholarship reject the view of public propaganda as simple ideological expression. Rhetoric serves multiple strategic functions, not only attracting potential recruits, sympathizers, and organizational allies, but also competing with adversaries to influence public discourse and state policy.[8] These revisions suggest a wider conceptual framework for rhetorical analysis of the antisuffrage movement.

This broader perspective informs the following analysis of antisuffrage rhetoric. We consider both ideological and tactical meanings of the propaganda campaign against women's enfranchisement. The strategic challenges confronting the female-dominated antisuffrage movement were formidable. As the presumed beneficiaries of the woman rights campaign, women antisuffragists had to justify their opposition and simultaneously mobilize others of their sex for a political battle whose ostensible goal was to keep women out of politics. Male propagandists, meanwhile, had to convince others of the probity of their case for denying political rights to a category of citizens. Finally, women's exclusion from politics required rhetoric that reached a larger audience of male voters and politicians.

The data for this analysis are a sample of 214 antisuffrage writings spanning the woman suffrage debate from 1867 until the immediate aftermath of the passage of the federal amendment. This was a purposive rather than a random sample, with particular efforts made to include the most popular materials and to represent a diversity of media sources, time periods, and geographical regions.[9] The sample includes speeches from legislative hearings on the suffrage question, pamphlets published by numerous antisuffrage organizations, contemporary popular magazine articles, and books written by famous antisuffragists. Content analysis yielded a total of 242 theme categories and 2,054 theme units, which have been condensed for greater reliability and ease of presentation.

To examine gender differences in antisuffrage rhetoric, each selection was coded by author's sex. The sample represents almost equal numbers of women and men; women authored 114 books, articles, and speeches, while men contributed 100 entries. Authors among both sexes included a mix of organizational leaders and distinguished sympathizers such as muckraker journalist Ida Tarbell.[10] To compare rhetorical arguments over time, the entries were divided into three time periods that coincide with significant phases in the development of the antisuffrage movement: the nineteenth century, 1900–1912, and 1913–1921.[11] During most of the nineteenth century antisuffragists were sporadically organized, while the 1900–1912 phase marked the rise of numerous state antisuffrage associations and the heyday of the campaign to oppose woman suffrage at the state level, and the final period saw the battle transformed into a larger contest for a federal amendment. Men's writings were evenly divided among the three periods, while the middle period was the modal category for entries authored by women.[12]

Countermovement Competition

As table 4.1 indicates, the total number of theme units was fairly evenly split between male and female authors, and the overall distribution of major themes demonstrated striking gender similarity. For both sexes, about one-third of theme units involved explicit comparisons to the suffrage movement: rebutting suffrage arguments, attacking suffrage proponents, and articulating a unique counteridentity. The remaining

Table 4.1. Major themes in antisuffrage rhetoric, by gender

Themes	Female authors	Male authors
Comparisons to woman suffrage	37%	34%
Rebut suffrage arguments		
Justice	10	11
Expediency	6	6
Attack suffragists		
Politics	9	7
Personality	5	8
Antisuffrage counteridentity	7	2
Gender issues	33%	38%
Separate spheres	4	8
Family welfare	5	7
Male-female relations	5	7
Female character	4	6
Domestic roles	8	5
Female employment	7	5
Political issues	30%	28%
Female political influence	10	8
Unqualified female electorate	8	7
Not a social panacea	6	5
Nation's strength	4	5
Elite dominance	2	3
Total	100%	100%
N	1074	980

themes elaborated on the antisuffrage rationale against the vote. Another third of theme units focused specifically on gender issues, such as family preservation and the gender division of labor. The final third addressed political issues, which were ostensibly the heart of the suffrage question.

A substantial portion of antisuffrage rhetoric made invidious comparisons to the suffrage campaign, rebutting proponents' arguments for the vote, criticizing suffragists as a group, and differentiating antisuffragists from their competitors. Like all countermovements, antisuffragists organized explicitly for the purposes of protesting an existing movement, typically one agitating for social change. These conditions foster a tendency for countermovements to be ideologically reactionary and strategically reactive.[13] The antisuffrage movement was no exception; to the contrary, the delicate paradox of their political position made antisuffragists dependent on public confrontations with the suffrage movement. If their defense of normative restrictions against women's political participation were taken too literally, antisuffragists would undermine their own recruitment goals. On the other hand, if they appeared to brush aside these restrictions too readily, they would erode the ideological roots of their opposition to women's enfranchisement.[14] These exigencies increased pressures on the antisuffrage movement to elaborate upon the suffrage threat. Depicting suffrage as a pending national crisis helped overcome both ideological and strategic dilemmas.

The most common counterassault was repudiation of suffragists' rhetorical claims. According to Kraditor's groundbreaking analysis of suffrage rhetoric, there were two major types of suffrage arguments: justice and expediency. The suffrage movement's earliest justification for women's enfranchisement was based on the Enlightenment philosophy of natural rights that had been used a century earlier in the U.S. Declaration of Independence, the very document paraphrased in the Declaration of Sentiments produced at the first Women's Rights Convention in Seneca Falls, New York, in 1848.[15] Evoking republican principles of equal citizenship rights, individual liberty, and the consent of the governed, suffragists contended that women were entitled to political equality with men by virtue of their shared humanity. No further basis for their claim was deemed necessary; moreover, denying the ballot to female taxpayers replicated Britain's violation of democratic principles that provoked the American Revolution. According to the justice rationale, any state true to its republican ideals must extend the franchise to women.

The expediency rationale began to dominate suffrage rhetoric around the turn of the century, coinciding with the passing of the torch to a new generation of suffrage leaders, although the rhetorical transition was gradual and the justice argument never disappeared. The distinction between the two arguments may be summarized as a dichotomy between intrinsic and instrumental rationales; demanding the vote as an issue of abstract justice emphasized the democratic principle of "consent of the governed," whereas the expediency argument legitimated women's enfranchisement in terms of what the vote would do for women and for society. Expedient suffrage rhetoric typically claimed that women needed the ballot to fulfill individual duties of citizenship and represent their collective interests, while later arguments expanded on the idea of municipal housekeeping, alleging that female moral superiority and maternal skills would upgrade society.

As table 4.1 indicates, antisuffrage rhetoric produced by both sexes refuted the justice argument more frequently than the expediency argument. Women's most popular counterargument to justice applied the "majority rules" standard, claiming that suffrage was desired by a small minority and therefore constituted an undemocratic demand forced upon their sex. The typical supporting evidence was a lengthy catalogue of legislative and electoral woman suffrage defeats, most of which, of course, represented the views of the male electorate. Doubtless aware of this logical weakness, many antisuffragists cited the 1895 Massachusetts referendum in which very few eligible women voted (although those who did favored suffrage by a wide margin) to demonstrate the "profound indifference" and "apathy" of women to the ballot, a self-serving strategy that was incidentally used to explain the small numbers of organized female opponents. Molly Seawell, for example, claimed that antisuffragists are "in an enormous majority . . . This is why you don't see much attempt by them to acquaint the public with the anti-suffrage side."[16] Antisuffrage writings challenged suffragists' claims that women were victims of injustice by portraying suffrage proponents as aggressors and democratic society as their prey; for instance, a NAOWS pamphlet dismissed an important suffrage victory by declaring, "Woman suffrage was imposed upon the state of California by a minority of the voters." Beyond assertions that most women were "perfectly satisfied and content with their present circumstances" and thus felt "no sense of injustice" with the current political system, another common tactic was to declare that enfranchisement would bring about the oppression of nonsuffragists.[17] One popular antisuffrage pamphlet asked, "Why Should Suffrage Be Imposed on Women?" and another demanded more plaintively, "Must All Women Bear the Burden of the Ballot to Give Some Women Political Prominence?"[18]

The obligation of the ballot was another common antisuffrage rebuttal to the argument that suffrage was a natural right. In listing "ten good reasons" for opposing woman suffrage, Grace Duffield Goodwin declared, "The ballot is not a right denied; it is a burden removed." More often, however, antisuffrage rhetoric disputed the natural rights argument by asserting that voting was a privilege rather than a right, sometimes citing support for its position in U.S. Supreme Court decisions reaffirming the constitutionality of women's exclusion from voting. They frequently pointed out that suffrage is "a granted right, not a natural one," and "is conferred by general consent."[19] The view of suffrage as an inalienable right is "anti-republican," another popular antisuffrage tract stated, "for the very essence of republicanism is that power is a trust to be exercised by the common weal. Suffrage does not exist for the benefit of the individual, but of the state."[20]

In rebutting the natural rights argument, antis pressed for an expediency justification for female enfranchisement, demanding that suffragists demonstrate the benefit to the state, either that it is "necessary to the cause of good government" or "that it will promote the welfare of society." Dismissing the natural rights argument as "vague" "metaphysics," some men adopted a practical approach to politics based on traditional male expertise, invoking "good government" themes of order and efficiency to argue that "the ballot is simply a method of conducting public business."[21] While a few male opponents avowed a willingness to change their opinion upon presentation of evidence by suffragists that voting would "be for the real benefit of their sex," women antisuffragists tended to eschew explicit self-interest in favor of societal well-being, asserting allegiance to the ideal of female self-sacrifice by claiming the central question was not women's interests, but "the greatest good to the greatest number."[22]

The expediency response shows up in antisuffragists' rhetoric as early as the 1860s, and by the 1890s they were using the term explicitly as a prerequisite for female enfranchisement in direct rebuttal of the suffragists' natural rights argument.[23] This suggests an explanation for the suffrage movement's shift from natural rights to expediency rationales additional to those proposed by Kraditor. She explains the change as a way of exploiting the reactionary shift among middle-class, native-born men prompted by foreign immigration and worker unrest and perhaps also as an indication that women's equality was no longer contested, given female progress in education and the professions during the century.[24] These results suggest that the antisuffrage rebuttal against natural rights may have also influenced the transition to expediency rationales. Antisuffragists explicitly used the term expediency in two highly publicized and successful campaigns against women's enfranchisement: Elihu Root used the term in a speech at New York State's constitutional convention in 1894, which was reprinted and widely distributed by the New York State Association Opposed to Woman Suffrage; and it was used again during the victorious 1895 Massachusetts campaign against a municipal suffrage referendum, which occasioned a published collection of essays entitled *Woman Suffrage, Unnatural and Inexpedient*.[25] Despite proponents' alleged dismissals of antisuffragists, their own literature reveals the extent to which they monitored the opposition, and it is likely that suffragists shifted toward expediency arguments partly as a response to the perceived success of the antisuffrage rebuttal strategy.[26]

Antisuffragists contested other elements of the justice argument, particularly after the turn of the century, when attention turned away from the natural rights issue. Addressing the suffrage demand for equal rights, female antisuffragists tended to acknowledge past inequities but asserted that these had been rectified, and that women, "the already overburdened mothers of the race," now enjoy "the right to be exempt" from the obligations of citizenship imposed upon men, such as military service. Male authors tended to emphasize the many privileges enjoyed by women, with some arguing that demands for both rights and privileges constitute "more than they are entitled to." Suffrage thus represented simultaneous threats to both masculine equity and feminine privilege.[27] Women's inherent equality was a delicate issue, and these findings confirm Kraditor's observation that the basest assertions of female inferiority were limited to the mid-nineteenth century. Most authors sidestepped the issue of gender equality and emphasized equality of function, wherein each gender excels in its own sphere: "Should a woman, gifted with a wonderful soprano voice, waste her life trying to sing bass!" mused one male opponent. Others conceded that women were not the physical equals of men and thus needed continued protection by the stronger sex, "instead of being thrown into hopeless political competition with men!"[28] Antis also derided the suffrage rallying cry of "No Taxation without Representation," another piece of rhetoric borrowed from the American Revolution, as "un-American" and "elitist," because only under the old aristocratic system was taxation tied to voting rights. Some male authors took particular pains to state that political representation is a group rather than an individual issue and self-servingly praised men for representing women's interests so well.[29]

Although antisuffragists used expediency to rebut the justice rationale for extending votes to women, they were no more receptive to the more practical expediency claims of their rivals.[30] Rebuttals of the justice argument continued to be popular, while expediency rebuttals increased along with suffragists' adoption of that argument. This is shown in table 4.2, which examines the distribution of antisuffrage arguments by author's gender and time period. Contesting the claim that suffrage would help women, anti rhetoric denied that women needed the ballot for self-protection. Men expressed particular indignation at the suggestion of lapsed chivalry and warned suffragists that a shift from a "natural" to a legal basis of ordering gender relations would result in a "chilling of sympathy rather than any increased protection."

Table 4.2. Antisuffrage arguments, by time period

	Females			Males			Total		
Themes	1[a]	2[b]	3[c]	1	2	3	1	2	3
Suffrage comparisons	29	41	38	24	41	37	27	41	37
Rebut justice	8	10	11	10	13	9	9	11	10
Rebut expediency	5	6	6	4	8	7	5	7	7
Attack politics	9	8	10	4	9	9	7	8	9
Attack personality	4	7	5	3	9	11	3	8	8
Counteridentity	3	10	6	3	2	1	3	7	3
Gender issues	40	32	26	39	39	38	40	35	33
Separate spheres	6	5	3	7	9	8	7	6	6
Family welfare	6	5	7	7	5	9	7	5	8
Male-female relations	7	4	4	10	6	6	8	5	5
Female character	6	2	2	8	5	6	7	4	4
Domestic roles	9	6	6	4	4	7	6	5	7
Female employment	6	10	4	3	10	2	5	10	3
Political issues	29	26	36	36	20	25	32	23	30
Female influence	10	9	9	10	7	6	10	8	7
Unqualified voters	7	7	10	10	5	5	8	6	7
No social panacea	5	5	10	8	3	5	6	4	7
National strength	4	3	3	5	3	5	5	3	5
Elite power	3	2	4	3	2	4	3	2	4
Total	98%	99%	100%	99%	100%	100%	99%	99%	100%
N	353	463	258	309	314	357	662	777	615

[a]1867–1899
[b]1900–1912
[c]1913–1921

Women antis, meanwhile, attempted to mollify men by declaring their contentment with the status quo and holding their own sex responsible for any male injuries against them, since "women's task" is "to form and train, inspire and reward the executive sex."[31]

Opponents of both sexes rejected the argument that enfranchisement was necessary for women to achieve equal opportunities in employment and education. They generally affirmed the fairness of the labor market and rejected suffrage claims that the ballot was a self-improvement measure for women, countering with scientific experts from women's colleges that women must be educated differently from men for the "all-important" "work of the wife and mother," "to train the coming generation in mind and morals and social philosophy."[32] Women's rebuttals of the self-protection claim diminished over time, however, while male authors made increasing use of this tactic as the campaign proceeded. Female antisuffragists were more likely than males to credit the women's rights movement with helping women progress and, in their view, attain equality. Their acknowledgment of the contributions of what had now evolved into the suffrage movement constrained women opponents from contesting that part of the expediency argument.

Women remonstrants focused over time on the second dimension of their rivals' expediency arguments: societal benefits. They repeatedly cited evidence from the "experiment stations" of the western suffrage states to conclude that women were "indifferent voters" and that the cleansing of social evils—intemperance, prostitution, juvenile crime, child labor, inadequate public health—was making more headway in the eastern nonsuffrage states. Both male and female authors turned increasing attention to refuting suffrage claims of societal benefits as these became more prominent in suffrage literature, illustrating the "tango" of the movement-countermovement dynamic.[33] The primary counterargument by female antisuffragists was that women's traditional charitable and civic activities effect more social reforms than does the ballot. Male writers protested defensively that their gender was also interested in social welfare, at the same time declaring that the most important function of government was maintaining "law and order," an allusion to men's military service. Women opponents, meanwhile, blamed persistent social problems on female domestic neglect, proclaiming that "women can serve the country better through the home than through the ballot-box."[34] Finally, while acknowledging that the suffrage movement had captured the "tactical advantage" by its monopoly of the "progressive" label, antis cautioned against becoming "hypnotized" by "rash ventures" that ultimately signify "moral retrogression" and deviation from the "natural laws" of evolution.[35] This rhetorical device clearly reversed the meaning of progressivism and invoked the legitimating power of modern science.

Antisuffrage rhetoric also attacked suffragists as a group in an attempt to discredit their rhetoric. Moving the debate from issues to individuals took one of two general forms: personal or political. Attacks on suffragists' political ideologies typically tarred them as radicals, a common strategy against movements for social change. More personal denunciations of suffragists' character were surprisingly common and tended to utilize traditional gender stereotypes, condemning suffragists for both conforming to and deviating from prevailing images of femininity.

Accusations of political radicalism encapsulated a broad spectrum of issues, most of which impugned the patriotism of suffrage activists. Antisuffrage writings portrayed suffragists as aligned with "uncertain and dangerous elements in our political life," including socialists, anarchists, communists, atheists, populists, "radical labor movements," and all kinds of "contagious unrest" that threaten republican government. Others derided Mormons, early suffrage advocates in some western states, as radicals for their alleged opposition to the Constitutional separation of church and state, while southern writings quoted northern suffrage leaders' intention to enfranchise "2,000,000 negro women."[36] Antis were enamored of certain controversial quotations from suffrage leaders and repeatedly described the violence of militant British "suffragettes" to warn of extreme tactics to come. The New York Association produced a pamphlet for the 1915 referenda campaigns that identified a number of alleged socialists among the woman suffrage leadership, asserting, "We are indeed threatened by a red peril in a yellow cloak," the latter being an allusion to the official suffrage color.[37]

Antis foresaw social revolution also in the shocking spectacle of new suffrage tactics that deviated from the norms of feminine propriety. As one woman antisuffragist opined, "The bare-footed hike, the street procession, the soap-box oratory, the suffrage 'melting pot,' prove only the extreme methods to which agitators are forced in their efforts to recruit."[38] They deemed suffragists' unladylike demands as portents of economic, political, and social upheaval. "Its advocacy of equal industrial rights" and female "economic independence," which would "depose man as the head of the home" and replace the "sacred marriage tie" by a "mere partnership contract," reflected an ideology "borrowed directly from socialism" and godless "materialism." The "feminism" label was not always equivalent to suffragism, but emerged in the new century as a derogatory shibboleth meaning radical and dangerous; the title of one antisuffrage volume published during the critical campaign year of 1915 aligned the "terrible triplets" of socialism, feminism, and suffragism.[39]

Antis used other rhetorical strategies to assail suffragists' politics. They invoked proponents' critiques of the institution of marriage and women's economic dependency to denounce proponents as either antifemale or antimale; although these might seem at first glance to be contradictory arguments, they were in fact complementary and about equally likely to appear in antisuffrage literature. Antifemale charges often highlighted quotations from famous suffragists to demonstrate their "sex disloyalty" and "disrespect," leading publisher Edward Bok to affirm, "There is no greater enemy of woman than woman herself."[40] They were particularly incensed by Charlotte Perkins Gilman's writings describing married women as "slaves" and "parasites" and repeated indignantly her assertion that "even a kitten could be a mother." Many of these suffragist comments were allusions to women's social inequality, but opponents interpreted references to gender subordination as "belittling" statements that did "incalculable harm" by minimizing the "dignity and value" of woman's traditional work.[41] Likewise, when suffragists complained of male social superiority, antis chastised them for envying the other sex, rejecting their feminine natures, and using suffrage to betray women in the service of an "imitation-of-man" movement.[42]

The antimale epithets, ironically, derived from some of the same suffrage quotations: if woman is a slave, then man is an "oppressor" and "tyrant." Such accusations, claimed antisuffragists, destroyed harmony and spawned a "sex battle." Male authors were especially colorful in describing the alleged man hatred of suffragists, some asserting proponents' desire to "take him and kill him" and charging that their ultimate plan was "to wipe men from the face of the earth." By this rhetorical reversal, men were converted into the true victims and women into oppressors; observed one male antisuffragist, "All this modern talk of sex antagonism comes not from men but from women."[43]

The third political criticism of suffragists undermined antis' own charges of political radicalism. Opponents condemned "rich" suffragists for using working-class women to serve their own selfish ends and for considering class-based qualifications on enfranchisement, such as taxpayer suffrage. They also claimed that by advocating economic independence for all women, suffragists compete with female wage earners and also "crowd out some responsible father or husband on whom a family is ever dependent."[44] These charges of elitism meshed poorly with other accusations that suffragists were allies of radical groups, and by the last phase of the suffrage campaign the former argument diminished sharply in frequency, partly because of increased cross-class alliances among suffragists and also because the conservative wartime climate and political reactions to the Bolshevik revolution made allegations of radicalism more advantageous.

Male and female antisuffragists pursued slightly different strategies in denouncing proponents. Women showed a strong preference for criticizing suffragists' politics, and men slightly favored personal over political accusations; men in particular showed a sharp increase in attacks on suffragists over time. Denunciations of suffragists' character and personality fell into two broad categories, based on either their perceived conformity to or deviance from prevailing gender stereotypes. Women antisuffragists tended to dismiss proponents in the trivializing language of feminine incompetence: suffragists were either childishly naive and ignorant of the full consequences of political equality or victims of their emotions and thus not in full control of their logical faculties. Because of woman's impulsiveness, explained one anti, "the ballot in her hands is a dangerous thing." A few women characterized proponents as the "dupes of men," ironically the same term used by suffrage leaders to describe them. Others, often men, built on traditional beliefs about female physical frailty to diagnose woman suffrage as an illness akin to neurasthenia, a "fever" caused by the "excessive development of the emotional in her nervous system."[45] In all of those characterizations, women suffragists were portrayed as wrongheaded but as not fully responsible for their mistakes.

Antisuffrage rhetoric also derogated suffragists for failing to conform to gender stereotypes, especially when written by men. They labeled female proponents as unfeminine, mostly for their aggressive tactics, although some men paradoxically attacked male supporters of women's rights as "feminine men and mollycoddles," a "deplorable spectacle of human weakness." While women's rhetoric chided female suffragists for their "would-be imitation of men," men's language was considerably more strident and escalated over the length of the contest, labeling proponents as "freaks," "hybrids," "Amazons," and a "third sex."[46] Another common mode of character denunciation was to tar suffrage activists as self-absorbed, a clear deviation from the feminine norm of self-sacrifice. Suffragists were found guilty of pursuing political self-interest instead of modest retirement and service to others. Refuting the expediency claim, antisuffragists charged that proponents were "not seriously interested in political reform," but were drawn to politics by "selfish ambition, political intrigue, and noisy notoriety," or, in the words of one male opponent, by "monomania."[47] As table 4.2 illustrates, male attacks on suffragists' personality escalated over time.

Countermovements also respond to the initial movement by defining themselves in contrast to it. Opposition rhetoric included lists of significant events in its history, identification of well-known remonstrants, and analyses of antisuffrage tactics and membership. Women antis were far more likely than men to participate in such public self-scrutiny; the few men's comments tended to focus on lists of famous male sympathizers or on critiques of the movement, usually for being too quiet.[48] What really differentiated male and female authors were affirmations of a unique identity in contrast to suffragists. Women took great pains to define female remonstrants in conformity to the traditional feminine image of true womanhood—nurturing, domestic, philanthropic, quiet, pious, and unselfish. As Mrs. Lyman Abbott noted, "The position of defence is never easy, and our duty requires patience that is not experience, it calls for readiness which is not aggressive, and vigorous expression of our views which must never be acrimonious." The New York Association reprinted an account of antisuffrage leader Mrs. W. Winslow Crannell's 1905 speech to the state legislature that described her, in explicit contrast to the "new woman," as "a gentle woman . . . who spoke . . . evenly, with the calm wisdom of fireside women to grown sons." Public speeches underscored the point that antisuffragists are women who "do not crave publicity or notoriety" and seek only to serve society and the home by doing "the neglected work . . . not for their own sakes or their own glory, but for the common good," justifying their foray into politics as a "painful sacrifice" and "a sacred duty" for "the welfare of the state and race."[49] These self-descriptions served multiple purposes; they helped explain the countermovement's lower visibility relative to the alleged publicity-seeking suffragists and hoped to mobilize reluctant women to political activism by justifying deviations from the norm as ideologically consistent with the mission of true womanhood.

Despite a strategy that portrayed opposition to the vote as the consummation of female self-sacrifice, mobilizing their quiet supporters was apparently not a simple task, as antisuffrage writings repeatedly acknowledged the reluctance of "home-loving" women to engage in political protest. Some attempted to motivate sympathizers with alarmist recitations of crises, ominously reminding women that "Silence will be counted as consent." Other leaders rejected the traditional feminine ideal of self-sacrifice, urging women to forget the well-being of others and focus on their own political interests. Recruitment appeals sometimes deviated from gender stereotypes by declaring, "Reason not sentimentality should be our motto" and announcing the intention to refrain from "hysterical quarreling with our opponents." They also attempted sporadically to coopt the contested term "progressive," proclaiming that societal progress depended upon conformity to gender segregation and specialization of function. Despite this rhetorical parrying, there is no indication in antisuffrage literature of an alliance with the progressive movement. To the contrary, antisuffragists identified as conservatives while updating the traditional image of womanhood to fit modern times; they were "for the retention of the best ideals of the preceding generations adapted to the advantages and opportunities given to them under modern conditions."[50]

These rhetorical tactics of comparison, contrast, and cooptation suggest the degree of competition experienced between the two groups of contestants. Antisuffrage rhetoric discussed and rebutted suffrage arguments, analyzed and criticized suffragists' personalities and character, and defined an identity for countermovement participants in explicit contrast to that of the "new woman" suffragist. Part of their focus outward can be explained by the need for countermovements to articulate the threat of the initial movement. Antisuffragists were especially challenged, confronted by the potent democratic rhetoric of equality coming out of the suffrage camp. This may explain why antisuffrage writers continued to prefer rebuttals of justice arguments, even after suffragists shifted to expediency rationales. Moreover, early antisuffrage demands for demonstrations of pragmatic benefits to women or society may have influenced the suffrage transition from justice to expediency, underscoring the relationship of mutual interaction between the initial movement and its opposition. The larger political opportunity structure also influenced the contents of antisuffrage rhetoric. In the reactionary political climate of World War I, antisuffragists increased attacks on suffragists' patriotism, a strategy enhanced by socialist endorsement of woman suffrage and the participation of prominent suffrage leaders in the peace movement.[51]

Another important function of movement rhetoric is to articulate grievances; such crystallizing of discontent helps attract new recruits and mobilize public support. Conventional wisdom states that countermovements invoke the potent "established myths of society" to oppose change.[52] In this instance, however, suffragists laid claim to the Enlightenment theme of equality, necessitating a more complex response by the opposition. They essentially rejected the suffragists' grievance by denying that women were suffering from inequality. In some cases, this rebuttal required antisuffragists to credit their opponents for recent gains made by women. But merely denying grievance was apparently judged insufficient for member recruitment, and antisuffrage rebuttals also began to articulate a set of grievances against the suffrage movement itself. These included allegations that enfranchisement would overburden women, embitter relations between the sexes, and jeopardize American democracy. In addition, antisuffrage rhetoric included a wide range of character denunciations against suffragists, from personality to politics.

One of the most unexpected findings is that men were slightly more likely to lodge personal allegations against suffragists, while women manifested a marked preference for political attacks. Moreover, men's attacks on suffragists' personality increased over time. Since politics was a male domain, men might be expected to manifest greater conformity to the rules of public debate; and given the prevalence of the fragile stereotype of womanhood, the relative dearth of male chivalry is surprising. Turner and Killian propose that countermovement rhetoric reflects perceptions of the initial movement's success or failure; when they assess the movement as weak, opponents are likely to adopt derogatory language, but when it is judged to be strong, opponents cannot risk direct confrontation and show more restraint and respect, labeling proponents as misguided rather than malevolent.[53] It may be that male antis perceived the suffrage movement as weaker, while women had more respect for suffragists as formidable political opponents.

It is also likely that male antisuffrage writers had greater difficulty accepting women as political actors. Perhaps they held more rigid views of electoral politics as a male domain than did their female colleagues in the antisuffrage movement. This conclusion is suggested by Paula Baker's study of rural New York State, which showed how the rise of party politics in the nineteenth century reinforced the doctrine of separate spheres by making partisan loyalty a male virtue and defining office holding as a just reward for good character and hard work. Baker finds that political rhetoric increasingly focused on the candidate's character, whose attributes—courage, loyalty, industry, independence—were associated with manhood, thus reinforcing the notion that politics was a man's business. Militaristic campaign terminology lauded successful candidates for waging "manly" battles and derided foes with feminine epithets. Those who deviated from the major parties (such as political independents) or from issues defined as the appropriate business of politics (such as social reformers) were called "Miss Nancies," "namby-pamby, goody-goody gentlemen," "political hermaphrodites," and "the third sex," the identical term used against suffragists. As war in Europe threatened, critics of the preparedness effort were discredited with sexual epithets, underscoring the extent to which electoral politics and military service were regarded as fundamental components of manhood.[54]

The historical context in which the suffrage question was embedded suggests an interpretation of men's preference for personal over political attacks as well as their greater use of sexually derogatory remarks compared with that of female remonstrants. The issue of character had by this time become part of formalized political rhetoric, somewhat paradoxically linking men's private and public lives at the same time that it supported a gendered separation of spheres. Male political culture promoted such personal attacks as a means of reinforcing male unity in the face of an expanded and increasingly diverse electorate. It necessarily barred women from exercising the franchise, because defining manhood by participation in electoral politics depended on female exclusion for its maintenance. The Illinois Association noted this fact in one of its publications, stating, "Most men regard the ballot as the badge of their manhood and prize it accordingly." Men probably attacked the character of female suffragists because such tactics had become an accepted part of political discourse and because voting was deemed logically incompatible with femininity. This may account for men's greater attention to suffragists' alleged deviance from gender stereotypes. These findings also support the argument of Ann Douglas that some men of the period reacted against women's growing influence on American culture, which ironically derived from the ideology of separate spheres.[55]

Domestic Relations and Women's Roles

The remaining arguments presented in antisuffrage writings elaborated more affirmatively on the remonstrants' alternative worldview. Roughly one-third of their rhetorical contents addressed gender issues; as table 4.1 illustrates, gender was a more common theme among men than women. Antisuffrage arguments rested upon the societal necessity of a gendered division of labor, otherwise known as the ideology of separate spheres, which female authors not only invoked less frequently than did males, but lost interest in over time.

The basic argument for a division of labor rested on inherent differences between males and females: men reason, women feel; men are practical, women are idealistic; "Man is the expression of divine truth; woman of divine love. Man is the active element, woman the passive." The Pennsylvania Association president asserted, "Both men and women have the same stake in the government—and that stake is the family and the home." Man protects the home on the battlefield and in politics, which is modified warfare, and woman preserves it "as a refuge of pleasure and peace." Female authors elevated woman as the "power behind the throne," because her dependence on man inspires

Count the Cost!

YOU CANNOT double the electorate without *increasing the cost of government.*

YOU CANNOT increase the cost of government without *increasing taxation.*

YOU CANNOT increase taxation without *raising the cost of living.*

Count the Cost

Work Against Woman Suffrage!

For information and literature apply to

PENNSYLVANIA ASSOCIATION OPPOSED TO WOMAN SUFFRAGE

1108 FINANCE BUILDING, PHILADELPHIA

Figure 1. Prepared for the Pennsylvania campaign of 1915, this antisuffrage broadside appeals to male voters' class interests. Woman's Suffrage and Women's Rights Collection. Courtesy of Special Collections, Vassar College Libraries.

THE PITY OF IT!

Figure 2. This popular broadside produced by the Massachusetts Association was distributed widely throughout the United States. An ostensibly sympathetic image of suffragists, the cartoon exploits female fears of abandonment as well as male voters' prejudices about female incompetence. Swann-Cavett Family Papers. Courtesy of Mitchell Memorial Library, Mississippi State University.

Figure 3. This *Remonstrance* cartoon from October 1912 presents the antisuffrage case as an issue of female self-interest by suggesting that suffrage increases women's labor. Sophia Smith Collection. Courtesy of Smith College.

Figure 4. By 1916, the antisuffrage image of the suffragist has shifted. This cartoon from the April *Woman's Protest* is a comment on the errant lifestyles of the "new woman." Library of Congress.

Figure 5. From an antisuffrage campaign handbook prepared by the Man-Suffrage Association, the male perspective predicts the loss of femininity for women voters. Everett P. Wheeler, *The Case against Woman Suffrage: A Manual for Speakers, Debaters, Writers, Lecturers, and Anyone Who Wants Facts and Figures* (New York: Man-Suffrage Association, 1915). Library of Congress.

To the Rescue

Figure 6. A prize-winning antisuffrage cartoon published in the sympathetic *New York Times* counters arguments that women voters will relieve "Uncle Sam" of his burdens by depicting suffragists as helpless infants. *New York Times,* 5 February 1911, sec. 5, p. 6.

THE "THREE IMMEDIATE WOMEN FRIENDS" OF THE ANTHONY FAMILY. SEE BIOGRAPHY OF SUSAN B. ANTHONY, PAGE 1435, BY MRS. IDA HUSTED HARPER.

CARRIE CHAPMAN CATT The Rev. ANNA HOWARD SHAW "Mrs. R. JEROME JEFFREY" (NEGRO)

From Left to Right: Carrie Chapman Catt: The Rev. Anna Howard Shaw; Mrs. R. Jerome Jeffery, Negro woman of Rochester, N. Y. Often "Guest in Anthony Home" with Mrs. Shaw and Mrs. Carrie Chapman Catt, President of National Woman Suffrage Association, to which all Southern Suffragettes belong.

"Suffrage Democracy Knows no Bias of Race, Color, Creed or Sex."—Carrie Chapman Catt.

"Look not to Greece or Rome for heroes, nor to Jerusalem or Mecca for saints, but for all the higher virtues of heroism, let us WORSHIP the black man at our feet."—*Susan B. Anthony's Official History of Suffrage.*

Figure 7. As the suffrage campaign moves to the southern United States, broadsides exploit racist sentiments and regional loyalties. Swann-Cavett Family Papers. Courtesy of Mitchell Memorial Library, Mississippi State University.

America When Femininized

The More a Politician Allows Himself to be Henpecked
The More Henpecking We Will Have in Politics.

A Vote for Federal Suffrage is a Vote for Organized Female Nagging Forever.

"American pep which was the result of a masculine dominated country will soon be a thing of the past. With the collapse of the male ascendancy in this country we can look forward to a nation of degeneration. The suppression of sex will ultimately have its harvest in decadence, a phenomenon already beginning. The effect of the social revolution on American character will be to make "sissies" of American men—a process already well under way."—Dr. William J. Hickson, Chicago University.

WOMAN SUFFRAGE denatures both men and women; it masculinizes women and femininizes men. The history of ancient civilization has proven that a weakening of the man power of nations has been but a pre-runner of decadence in civilization.

Will you stand for this? Prove that you will not by voting to **Reject** the Federal Woman Suffrage Amendment to the Constitution of the United States.

SOUTHERN WOMAN'S LEAGUE FOR REJECTION OF THE SUSAN B. ANTHONY AMENDMENT

WE SERVE THAT OUR STATES MAY LIVE, AND LIVING, PRESERVE THE UNION

Figure 8. The final stand against the federal amendment brings out the most extreme rhetoric. Antisuffragists reverse gender roles and men now require protection from "hen politics." Courtesy of Josephine Pearson Collection, Tennessee State Library and Archives.

THE SIFTER

All the Little Antis Fall Through

Figure 9. The National Association Opposed to Woman Suffrage published this cartoon shortly after the ratification of the federal amendment to honor the loyal senators who voted against suffrage and threaten the "little" turncoats with political defeat. The giant-sized suffragist (Elizabeth Cady Stanton) presents a potent but less attractive feminist image. *Woman Patriot,* 25 September 1920.

Figure 10. With the suffrage question decided, the remaining antis take revenge on male politicians. Here a congressional co-sponsor of both education and social welfare legislation is portrayed as a frazzled mother while progressive reformists are infantilized. *Woman Patriot*, 5 March 1921.

him to noble purposes, and some men agreed that "the world is governed by heart," asserting the centrality of the family institution. The question of equality was typically resolved with a declaration of separate but equal, based on each gender's "particular capacity for a particular kind of work"; "it cannot be said that the root is superior to the branch or the branch to the root."[56] Women's physical inferiority was one common exception to antisuffragists' avoidance of explicit statements of gender ranking, but it was an important one, because it justified men's political authority by virtue of military service.

The rationale for separate spheres rested on differential capacities between the sexes, typically explained as a product of the fundamental "laws of nature," not "man," although early writings commonly referred to "the great plan of God" sealed by "divine fiat," and religious justifications never completely disappeared. The main point was the immutability of gender differences; as Francis Parkman noted in the 1880s, "Neither Congress, nor the states, nor the united voice of the whole people could permanently change the essential relations of the sexes."[57] The suffrage experiment was therefore doomed to failure by the eternal truths revealed in Scripture and later, by science—in the twentieth century, even ministers were using science to justify assertions about gender differences.

The most common scientific argument, based on Herbert Spencer's adaptation of Darwin to human social organization, emphasized specialization of function as an indicator of societal progress and compared separate spheres to the efficiency of the modern industrial system. Applying evolutionary theory to the question of gender differences, antisuffragists concluded that the higher up the "social scale," the more separated are the sexes "in their quality, aptitude, and mission." Such statements carried double meanings; gender differentiation was an indicator of a society's level of civilization and also signified ethnic and class superiority. Antis declared that "the nobler and higher the type, the greater the difference in function."[58] Following this line of argument, "The vital fact in all organic life is not equality, but diversity," and suffrage demands for equality "would arrest all progress." In the final analysis, stated the president of NAOWS, woman suffrage "is a retrogressive movement toward conditions where the work of man and woman was the same because neither sex had evolved enough to see the wisdom of being a specialist in its own line."[59] Antisuffrage arguments thus blended traditional arguments with modern ones and drew analogies between the domestic and industrial divisions of labor.

Assertions of separate spheres as a natural and necessary part of civilization laid the basis for consideration of suffrage's impact on family welfare. In broadest terms, antisuffragists argued that women's enfranchisement imperiled the institution of the family, the "safeguard of the state."[60] Reasons given for the deleterious effects of female political participation on family life included marital discord, divorce, domestic neglect, and rampant individualism. Men's arguments tended to emphasize the increased domestic conflict caused by divergent political affiliations: disunity, rivalry, and strife were common descriptions of the prospective marital unhappiness wrought by suffrage. Men regarded the costs to husbands as especially dear, because male authority as well as the peace and harmony of his domestic refuge would be compromised; terms such as "the family state" and "individual man's own government" suggest support for domestic patriarchy, where men exercised "natural sovereignty" through affection and cooperation in contrast to force and competition that governed relations in the public sphere. As one Nebraska minister implored, "We want more love, not more politics, in the homes of this country."[61] Not only did men address the deleterious impact of suffrage on family life more often than women, but their attention to this topic increased over time.

Women authors also mentioned these domestic issues, but they were more likely to see the "decay of family life" as emanating from their gender's pursuit of the "false doctrines concerning the emancipation of women" and consequent neglect of home duties, especially the religious and moral education of children. While men saw the breakdown of the marital relationship as the outcome of "political disputes," increased "incompatibility," and "the unmanly surrender of leadership to the women," women tended to blame the "national leprosy" of divorce on "lax marriage and divorce laws" promulgated by suffragist reformers.[62] Some also charged that the loosening of the marriage bond espoused by radical feminists exposed women to the risk of "illicit relations" and "the free-love doctrine."[63]

The broader philosophical issue underpinning the antisuffrage defense of the family—its "keynote," stated one leader at a legislative hearing—was individualism. Antisuffragists linked women's political independence to economic independence and more generally to the pursuit of self-gratification over self-sacrifice. Emily Bissell's charge that woman's desire for the vote represented "an impatience of ties and responsibilities, a restlessness, a fever for 'living one's own life' " was repeated in other writings. Antisuffrage rhetoric warned that "the future of the race depends" on children's proper upbringing, and if women sacrifice the "sacred duties" of the home to the "more engrossing excitements of politics . . . we will have a grotesque, ill-formed nation" undermined by "race suicide and ruined offsprings." The deterioration of women's moral influence in the home affects all classes, they charged, not only harming children but also increasing husbands' vulnerability to drink and crime. Moreover, they blamed affluent women who sought the limelight for being poor domestic role models for the lower classes, where the lack of household training is responsible for "so much that is deplorable to-day in the lives of the very poor."[64] While denouncing the individualism of suffragists, opposition rhetoric continued to attribute social ills to individual flaws and failures.

Antisuffrage arguments addressing the effects of suffrage on gender relationships reiterated these themes of family and societal breakdown using a slightly different tack. They predicted that woman's increasing abandonment of the domestic sphere would diminish her civilizing influence. Men and women authors agreed that the destabilizing brutality of gender conflict was a certain outcome of women's entrance into the political arena, not only because of domestic neglect and spousal conflict, but also owing to suffragists' use of the expediency claim that women need the vote to protect their own interests. Alluding to contemporary concerns about labor unrest, Mariana Van Rensselaer predicted that the results of calling "women a separate 'class' will be sex antagonism," and the president of the Pennsylvania Association linked the suffrage battle to the European conflict by warning of a domestic "sex war" if the state referendum passed. Calling the potential crisis of gender conflict instigated by suffragism a "race danger, a national danger, a world-peril," Virginia Association leader Emily Bissell labeled suffrage a "return to barbarism, not an advance in civilization."[65]

Men's arguments reiterated these themes with ominous descriptions of the retrogression to barbarism. They warned that chivalry, which tamed the "wild beast" of man through woman's love, would be lost, because the sight of voting women would "excite the brutal in men," and "privilege, courtesy, chivalry, and respect" will be abolished. Chivalry, they explained, is an "elevated gratuity which is due, if due at all, from the strong to the weak" and comes from "women's dependence on man." By encouraging women to "enter the fierce battle of modern competition" in politics and in the labor market, suffrage fosters sex competition instead of cooperation, which "will usually result in her discomfiture and humiliation." The cautionary tale of the Amazons was a frequent reminder that entrance into the masculine domain would "unsex woman" and produce a "counterfeit man," "monstrosities of nature," "touched with blight and fallen out of luster," who would no longer compel male protection. An antisuffrage tract printed by a group of Nebraska ministers for the 1914 state referendum campaign was perhaps the most threatening rejoinder to the perceived imminent sex war, asking "Must men put on the iron glove?"[66] While women authors used flattery to appeal to male legislators and voters, asking for continued protection and courtesies at which "the American man . . . is ahead of any man in the world," men's rhetoric made it clear that chivalry was conditional: "We men have put women on a high pedestal . . . and she will have to be infinitely careful or she will knock herself off . . ."[67] Both sexes manifested decreasing interest in the question of male-female relationships as the century proceeded, perhaps an indication that the "new woman" was gaining widespread acceptance.

The nature of womanhood, the presumed basis for the separation of spheres, was another issue addressed in antisuffrage rhetoric. Men were more likely than women writers to analyze the female character, and women's attention to this question diminished markedly over time. The same three themes dominated the writings of both sexes, however: emotionality, intellectual underdevelopment, and physical weakness. The argument that women are more emotional than men, which "is a great source of strength in women's sphere," justified their exclusion from public power. Women authors more frequently than men used the language of victimization when discussing the implications of this alleged gender difference, arguing that her quicker "sympathies" would place the female voter "more at the mercy of the will of others." Her "impulsive" and "impressionable" nature makes "the ballot in her hands a dangerous thing," because women "can be deceived and misled by the baser sort." Several remonstrants made a biblical analogy to Eve's temptation and subsequent fall, predicting that the "gilded pill of suffrage" would turn out to be "as fatal a snare and delusion" as the serpent's beguiling message in the Garden of Eden.[68]

Men writers showed a continued preference for stronger language to describe the female temperament, describing "hot flashes, aberrations of mind and hallucinations" that may reach the level of permanent insanity and render women "as unfit for public life as children." Rather than depicting women as more vulnerable because of their sympathetic natures, men portrayed them as petty, jealous, and mean-spirited, lacking in "judicial fairness," and more likely to indulge their animosities in political decisions as compared with the "coolness of judgment" of *some* male voters. "Emotional suffrage," an allusion to the mass politics of the lower classes as well as women, was labeled the "greatest danger to democratic governments," and the addition of female voters augured a "greater danger of state insurrections and seditions." This gender difference, derived from nature's plan for separate spheres, rendered women more particularistic, whereas men have a greater ability "to plan for the good of the whole." While lauding woman for her "unselfish devotion to her children," male antisuffragists commonly claimed "abstract justice" as a male virtue.[69]

The correlate of women's heightened emotionality was a deficient rationality, and antisuffrage rhetoric also cited men's higher intellect as justification for a restricted franchise. Different mentalities, both sexes claimed, were a consequence of the evolution of separate spheres, and even female antisuffragists noted that the "average woman" lacks the "power of consecutive thought upon any intricate problem." A few male remonstrants were more definitive, stating bluntly that "woman is man's intellectual inferior." The feared results were the same: ignorant and incompetent feminine voters, adding to a preexisting problem that already endangered American democracy.[70] Her alleged physical weakness also limited woman's ability to participate in politics, taxing her more delicate system, especially a greater susceptibility to nervous disease and mental breakdown. This disability, linked to the female reproductive role, was touted paradoxically as an indicator of racial advancement, an allusion to class superiority. Both sexes agreed that suffrage would have "disastrous" effects on women's health and proclaimed their unselfish concern for the very survival of womanhood.[71]

Antisuffrage assessments of female character were based increasingly on contemporary scientific doctrines that prescribed a racial and gender hierarchy as a conservative reaction against the changes wrought by immigration, political democratization, industrialization, and agitation for women's rights. This scholarship adapted Darwin's evolutionary theory to construct a psychology of sex differences that legitimated the doctrine of separate spheres. Darwin's hypothesis that intelligence was passed exclusively from men to male offspring not only justified ideologies of gender superiority but also encouraged others to identify a host of "secondary sex characteristics" as inherited traits that constituted evidence of evolutionary advancement. The concept of recapitulation, which posited that every individual organism recreates the evolution of its race, was elaborated by the renowned scientist and antisuffragist Edward Drinker Cope; his book *The Origin of the Fittest* suggested that men passed through a "woman stage" of character when emotionality prevailed, while women's development was arrested at this lesser stage of evolution. Cynthia Eagle Russett documents the "remarkable unanimity" of this "sexual science" in the late nineteenth century, which derived its power from empirical evidence that was, in hindsight, quite suspect.[72]

One of the earliest forms of "scientific" investigation of female inferiority involved detailed comparisons of skull sizes and brain weights to demonstrate male intellectual superiority. A dominant view at least until the end of the century, the idea that bigger is better was reiterated by Harold Owen in a popular 1912 antisuffrage tract, *Woman Adrift*, which articulated the dangers of deviation from nature's evolutionary plan. Owen asserted women's lesser intelligence, "even if the standard be set by sheer pound and ounces of brain"; he also advanced the neo-Lamarckian view that, by duplicating man's experiences, woman would "educate herself out of all her secondary sex characteristics." As the new science of anthropology broadened the study of physiological determinism to encompass the entire human body, scholars linked many supposedly feminine traits to their skeletal and metabolic similarities to children, "savages," and apes. A surprising source of antisuffrage quotations on women's emotionality was controversial British sexologist Havelock Ellis, who emphasized the significance of the "sexual periodicity" of the human female for differentiating the personalities and behaviors of men and women.[73]

By far the most influential scientific figure on antisuffrage writings was Herbert Spencer, who popularized the notion that women's status indicated the level of societal evolution, and that sex specialization resulting in female seclusion connoted a more advanced civilization. Spencer departed from Darwin by emphasizing organic harmony and cooperation rather than competition, which better fit the romanticized image of separate spheres; he also used the laws of thermodynamics to draw an analogy between the human body and the machine that emphasized the importance of energy conservation. Spencer's ideas not only found their way into the new medical diagnosis of neurasthenia but also justified restrictions on female activity due to their alleged extra energy expenditure during menstruation. Antisuffrage articles warned of women's "regular periods marked by mental and nervous irritability," which, if the strain were not alleviated by domestic seclusion, could "explode in violent paroxisms," an implicit allusion to political instability. Although by the turn of the century experimental research and Mendelian genetics undermined the recapitulation theory that the female was an underdeveloped male as well as Spencer's fixed-energy conception of the body and Darwin's hypothesis of a sex-specific transmission of intelligence, the antisuffrage and eugenics movements continued to advance ideas of male biological superiority based on scant empirical evidence.[74] It should be noted, however, that women antisuffragists were less likely than men to discuss the female character, and their attention to the topic declined markedly during the latter years of the antisuffrage campaign.

By contrast, female remonstrants manifested a greater interest in women's domestic and work roles. Of utmost concern to women authors was that suffrage would impose more work on their gender, and they invoked the justice argument to defend women's interests. Lamenting the "exhaustion" that would surely occur from "the addition to our already sufficiently heavy burdens of the duties and cares of the state," women antisuffragists like Mary MacIntire protested that "office-holding is incompatible with woman's proper discharge of her duties as wife and mother." Since man "cannot by any possibility" relieve women of their reproductive duties, "he commits a palpable and a monstrous injustice" if he "demands that women participate in external duties." Later arguments linked women's roles to new standards of industrial organization; one woman cautioned that "if the highest efficiency in private life is to be striven toward, women must regard themselves as a sort of emergency corps, prepared to meet the unexpected," and this "private duty" superseded the public responsibilities of citizenship. Eschewing sentimentality, another argued that "the business of women must be to . . . standardize the family life with their new understanding of the importance of the product of every separate family to the state."[75]

Male antisuffragists concurred that women's domestic, social, and philanthropic duties were "essential to the well-being of the state," and that the feminine "inspiring and ennobling influence" also "keeps all the busy wheels of industry revolving" by serving as the "moral support, the spiritual mainstay of their men and of the race." They contended that the motherhood role benefits society by inculcating in future citizens the character traits—honor, uprightness, purity, truth—that produce "the public spirited, right minded man, whose vote registers the fact that the mother in that home has done her job faithfully and well." According to Elihu Root, "The highest exercise of power is that which forms the conscience, influences the will, and controls the impulses of men, and there to-day woman is supreme and woman rules the world." Lawyer John Dos Passos warned that any interference that "diminishes her influence as a mother is a direct blow at civilization. . . . After all, the veil of civilization which keeps men and women within decorous bounds is not very thick." Such statements expressed a tenuous assessment of societal well-being, based partly on the pessimistic view that civilized manhood was, according to Cynthia Russett, but a "thin veneer over the savage self." If the virtuous woman behind the male citizenry ensured the nation's stability and prosperity, her devotion to marriage and motherhood meant that "the destiny of the race is in her hands." This effort required a biological as well as a moral contribution, and women authors in particular reminded the reader of the necessity to reject the temptations of the "new woman," conserve her energy, and reproduce the race, perhaps even in service to class interests represented by the budding eugenics movement.[76]

Antisuffrage acknowledgment of the growing popularity of new womanhood revealed a less confident view of the female domestic role, typically involving the status loss of the homemaker. Growing ambivalence among women remonstrants to domestic occupations is suggested by reduced attention devoted to that theme over time, while men increased their coverage of female household responsibilities. Both sexes conceded that "the present disinclination for motherhood," "the dissipated thirst for public ovations," and the "unrestful desire for life outside the home" "have dulled the sober sense of national obligation" among women. They concurred that mother's work "everywhere needs strengthening," lest homes become "dreary" and woman sinks "into an ignominious grave," but only women antis elaborated a specific solution—scientific motherhood. Domestic science appeared as early as the writings of antisuffragist Catharine Beecher, although it was promulgated by suffragists as well. This was a way of elevating housework into a profession, engaging women's commitment to the domestic sphere, and including them in the improvements of modern technology. Science has much to teach, claimed Helen Kendrick Johnson, including "how to dress sensibly, cook wholesomely, make the home sanitary," and Ida Tarbell professed astonishment that "the varied, delicate and difficult problems which crowd the attention of the woman in her social laboratory should ever be considered unworthy of first-class brains and training." Antisuffragists emphasized the challenges of homemaking, asking, "what woman is equal to it all? What greater problem could a woman desire? All that a college girl can get in her four year's course is not sufficient for its demands in science and in art."[77] Despite their boosterism for female domesticity, however, antisuffragists could not ignore the expansion of women's roles in the public sphere.

Antisuffragists professed certainty that enfranchisement would be of no benefit to women workers. They generally justified employment inequality by contending that women are less skilled, less committed, and therefore less valuable workers or that women create their own problems by crowding into a limited number of occupations, whereupon the universal economic laws of supply and demand depress wages. Very few authors expressed support for the principle of equal pay for equal work, and all of these were women writing in the nineteenth century; one early antisuffragist even advocated paying women more because their weaker constitution required twice the exertion to produce the same output as a man. By the new century, however, the idea of pay equity was firmly associated with suffragists, and opponents' views had hardened. Another reason for the apparent change of attitude may have been the altered composition of the female labor force; sympathetic female discourse of the nineteenth century focused on women in the professions, especially teaching, whereas subsequent antisuffragist discussions of pay equity for the most part addressed the industrial labor force. Interestingly, nineteenth-century male writers, who also concentrated on professional women when discussing employment issues, expressed the most overt gender prejudice, conceding that females were qualified for lower-status jobs, but standing firm in the view that most women lacked the logical skills to be doctors, lawyers, and administrators—in other words, to compete with men of their class.[78]

Antisuffragists' rejection of the principle of employment equity was stated most succinctly by Molly Seawell, who declared that women's work is not as good as men's and that suffrage will not raise wages because it will not make women better workers. Women cannot compete with men because they are physically weaker and are "transient" and "uninterested" workers who fail to acquire skills before they leave jobs to marry; after marriage, they are less "serious" workers whose diversion of energy to the home constitutes an "insurmountable handicap" in the labor market. Women also "gravitate toward certain employment requiring no particular skill nor extended training," and the joint effects of "overcrowded trades and unskilled workers make low wages." Since pay is determined largely by the available supply of labor, "voting can no more influence supply and demand than it can change the phases of the moon."[79]

Having diagnosed the problem of women's lower wages as being due to either the "ruinous competition" of women themselves or the "universal equity" of the industrial labor market, antisuffragists had few remedies to offer. Those of a more liberal orientation suggested that women take a page from men's labor history and organize. A few noted that the ballot is a poor remedy for working women because most of them are ineligible to vote by either age or nativity; some went further and expressed classist views that enfranchised female labor "will not know enough to help intelligently." Countering the suffrage claim that the ballot would have ameliorated the working conditions that led to the Shirtwaist Strike of 1909–10 and the subsequent Triangle Fire that killed over one hundred women garment workers, one antisuffragist argued that women workers "need the protection of laws made by an electorate as free as possible from corrupt and ignorant voters."[80] Several others, mostly women, contended that improvements in the labor conditions of female wage earners could easily be accomplished by entering domestic service, where, they claimed, the dearth of native-born, "self-respecting American women" had driven up wages "year after year, without a struggle." Apparently oblivious to their own ethnic prejudices or the self-serving solution they offered to the "servant problem," antisuffragists lamented that "ignorant and uncleanly" foreign workers had driven "the native-American girl from her natural vocation of housekeeping," and made enlistment appeals for the "profession" of domestic service, "offering to women high wages, a comfortable room, good food, and a sheltered life." In a candid expression of class insularity, one female antisuffragist ruminated, "Until woman settles the servant question, how can she ask to run the government?"[81]

While only a minority of antisuffragists espoused radically conservative views such as opposition to the minimum wage or support for child labor, most who discussed women's employment at least implicitly blamed workers rather than employers for inequities in the labor market.[82] Some were quite blatant, alleging that the real issue is not the amount of the wage, but "how the money is spent," and offering to laboring women the observation that " 'the simple life' is the weapon needed to fight their battles and protect them from what seems injustice and discrimination." Another located the problem in poor female money management: "If an increase in wage simply means another feather in the hat . . . how has she been benefited?" A few others, predominantly men, denied that any problem existed and contended that women have already gained employment equality, citing protective and limited equal pay laws in some states.[83]

Most antisuffragists recommended that women retire permanently from the labor market to help raise the pay of male breadwinners and strengthen the family unit. Economic independence, in their view, discouraged young women from marrying and caused married women to neglect their family duties; both trends do "grave injury to the state" because they threaten to "dissolve the family." Antisuffragists defended a particular kind of family, characterized by hierarchical relations; they worried that, as a result of wives' employment, "the children are growing up unruly, ill-mannered, disrespectful," undermining husbands' "influence" and "authority in their families." Women's employment was judged an "unhealthy" and unnatural condition that contradicts evolutionary law and thus has a "deteriorating effect" upon the human species. Denouncing competition in relations between the sexes, they predicted a return to "old barbaric conditions" as wives pursue careers and husbands live off women's wages. This scenario, of course, presumed a fair labor market for women and an adequate living standard for the working class. Their negative view of the modern woman was summed up by one California antisuffragist, "The pendulum has swung too far. We have too much new era and too much new woman."[84]

Gender issues were a more common theme among male than female authors. Given prevalent notions of antifeminist women as self-interested defenders of the traditional domestic sphere, this is a surprising finding. Not only did women address the family, gender relations, separate spheres, and female character less frequently than did men, but women's attention to most of these topics diminished over the life of the antisuffrage movement. Perhaps women writers were less concerned about the impact of suffrage on gender relations because increased participation in mainstream women's organizations had broadened their own notions of domestic roles over time.[85]

Men's discussion of gender issues reflected overt self-interest; they expressed concerns about the impact of women's economic independence on patriarchy, the so-called "family state," which provided a refuge from the competitive relations that increasingly characterized economic and political life. Men and women differed in their treatment of gender issues; men used more threatening and misogynistic rhetoric, underscoring the extent to which cultural rituals such as chivalry are also social control mechanisms that reinforce status hierarchy.[86] Women's language was more deferential toward men, but also extolled the social contributions and power of the female domestic role. Women expressed at least an inchoate gender consciousness in reframing the ballot as an issue of labor equity and attempting to reverse the declining status of the homemaker with the aid of science. But class interests mediated their support for women industrial workers, manifested by defense of employer discrimination, naive recommendations that married women retire permanently from the paid labor force, or self-serving appeals for native-born women to pursue domestic service. The blinders of privilege often inhibited acknowledgment of the necessity for women's paid labor and the realities of employment injustice, and thus antisuffragists could offer little sympathy for and no realistic solutions to the problems of working-class mothers.

Despite their differences, male and female antisuffragists shared a larger vision of the impact of changes in gender relations on American society. The rhetoric of both sexes was a mixture of sentiments; men swung from chivalrous hyperbole over the sanctity of motherhood to ominous boasts of certain victory in the impending sex war, while women blended traditional self-sacrifice with self-interest, manifesting less than total conformity to the true womanhood ideal. Antisuffragists expressed considerable anxiety, forecasting society's transition from order to conflict, cooperation to competition, duty to restless individualism, and civilization to barbarism. They were apprehensive about the instability wrought by industrial expansion and political democratization, and their assessment of the tenuousness of civilization's progress, predicated upon assertions of group superiority and fears of race suicide, impelled a search for order through containment.

Antisuffragists acknowledged America's increasing diversity as a problem and tried to repress it by uplifting universal motherhood as a social solvent. Presenting idealized images of the traditional family and gender relations, they asserted the necessity of female domesticity to help "tame men for citizenship through family life" while paradoxically attributing to women the very characteristics of inferior citizenship—emotional instability, vulnerability to corruption, intellectual incompetence—leveled against the lower classes. As the mediating institution between the individual and society, the family and its female custodians were regarded as both the saviors and the scapegoats for social, political, and sometimes economic ills. Suffragists and antisuffragists may have held similar views of women's moral superiority, but they saw divergent political implications: proponents argued that women needed the vote "to control men's excesses . . . and infuse civic virtue into politics," while opponents contended that women could best achieve these goals through the roles of wife and mother.[87] For antisuffragists, concern about the future of the family and concern about the nation's political well-being were inseparable.

The Politics of Republican Motherhood

The disparate gender roles endorsed by antisuffrage writers did not absolutely deny women a political role, but limited severely their political opportunities. In *Woman and the Republic,* a major antisuffrage tract published in 1897, Helen Kendrick Johnson identified women's unique political contribution: "to train up statesmen who will be the first to do us honor. The American Republic depends finally for its existence and its greatness upon the virtue and ability of American womanhood." Linda Kerber has labeled such sentiments the ideology of republican motherhood, which emerged in the wake of American independence as a means of reconciling traditional restrictions on women's political participation with the egalitarian ideals of the new republic. Virtue is the basis of a republic, declared Benjamin Rush in 1778, and some political scientists have argued that the cultivation of female virtue in the privacy of the domestic sphere may have been one solution to the enduring tension between the philosophies of Lockean liberalism and republicanism upon which the United States was founded. According to this view, the home was not so much a retreat from corrupt commercialism and rampant individualism as a corrective for it, elevating motherhood into a "civic calling."[88]

Women's contributions as keepers of republican civic virtue legitimated expansions in educational, religious, and social participation, but suffrage threatened to destroy "domestic virtue and exacerbate the individualism, fragmentation, and conflict endemic in liberal America." One antisuffragist summarized fears that women's enfranchisement represented the triumph of individualism over republican virtue, characterizing it as part of the general trend of "contagious unrest" "for more liberty, more justice, more opportunity, more to eat, more money to spend, more fun, more leisure, more knowledge" by people who "don't know what is right or wrong in the world at present."[89] The moralistic tone of the suffrage debate thus reflected not only contention over gender roles but also deeper philosophical cleavages.

Women remonstrants addressed the political consequences of enfranchisement slightly more frequently than men, but the most common theme among both sexes was the preservation of woman's political influence, which, antis believed, rested upon her exclusion from partisan politics. Women authors, in particular, emphasized the great public contributions made by women in philanthropy, social reform, and the shaping of public opinion, all because women are nonpartisans. Some women referred to their political role as a "third estate" or even an "independent party," and established the source of their power in the fact that, standing outside of politics, "we have no favors to give and none to ask." Contrasting themselves with the "clumsy" and "indirect" male ballot, they asserted confidently the power of women's direct political influence; "we go straight to the governor, attorney general, or chairman of the committee," one wrote, seemingly unaware that few women enjoyed such privileges. They cited legal reforms granting married women property rights and guardianship of children as testimony to the effectiveness of women's direct appeals as well as the immediacy of men's responsiveness. In their view, women enjoyed a less contentious and more efficient version of democracy. Rather than eschewing power, the antisuffragist watchword was "power through independence."[90]

While women underscored the positive aspects of disfranchisement, men tended to stress the negative, elaborating on the prospective loss of female influence under suffrage. Male antis warned that a deterioration of women's moral power would result if she abandons her "high pedestal of alabaster" for the foul stream of the political pit; "platform virtue" was no substitute for the reverence derived from the purity and innocence of the domestic sphere. The voting woman, they charged, "abdicates her throne and throws down the scepter of her power," and men's retraction of chivalry will eradicate the legal privileges that protect her and discriminate in her favor. Women shared these concerns about a loss of female influence with enfranchisement, although they often foresaw this outcome as a consequence of reduced time for the noble work of public service and of partisanship's destruction of feminine unity forged through social and philanthropic associations.[91] For both sexes, though, these negative predictions diminished over time.

A second popular argument against the vote questioned the citizenship qualifications of the prospective female electorate. One concern was women's inexperience in public life, which somewhat contradicted the assertion that they were already effective political actors. Some writings alluded to the nation's political turmoil, warning that it would be a "folly" at "this time of great peril" to submit the government to "unskilled apprentices." A related concern was that female exemption from military service produced a more cavalier attitude about the consequences of their political decisions and a lower aptitude and inclination for the "conflict of wills which is the essence of politics." Female enfranchisement therefore jeopardized democracy, because adding to the electorate "a large body of stay-at-home voters would result in bad government." An increasingly popular tactic, especially among women remonstrants, was to muster statistical evidence of low female voter turnout from full- and partial-suffrage states and municipalities to demonstrate the "evil of an irresponsible or disinterested voting class"—"government by a minority."[92]

For the most part, though, antisuffragists worried less about woman's low voter turnout than the corruptibility of her ballot, reflecting a pessimistic view of contemporary American democracy. The "lack of decorum" of contemporary politics, the "canvassing, heckling, button-holing, street-speaking, megaphoning," the "mixing with all sorts of men . . . and playing such intrigues of candidacy," would contaminate female purity and "introduce an unspeakable element of public demoralization." They regarded mass political participation with distaste, if not disgust; during the pivotal 1915 campaigns, NAOWS president Mrs. Arthur Dodge cautioned, "It is easier to soil and spoil the woman's spotless cloak of reputation and character than it is to use it as a mop for the mud of politics." By the time that women have purified politics, asked another, "who shall purify the women?" Allegations of women's stuffing ballot boxes, selling votes to ward bosses and saloon keepers, and, as new officeholders, partaking in the corrupt spoils system illustrated how voting women "become potential reinforcements to the forces of vice."[93] In general, antisuffragists saw some categories of women as more corruptible than others, and fulminated that the reluctance of "good women" to "get out and mix with the men and vote" would enhance by default the political power of "ignorant and vulgar women," by which they meant the lower classes.[94] Writing for the Massachusetts Association, New York journalist Carl Schurz reasoned:

> If woman suffrage meant only the enfranchisement of the women of high character and good education, there would be little opposition among the men, provided such women actually desired the ballot. But the introduction of woman suffrage means also the enfranchisement of those classes of women who correspond in character and education to the plantation negro and the ignorant immigrant.[95]

Schurz's statement summarized the class, race, and ethnic prejudices behind antisuffrage rhetoric. Although alarms concerning "ignorant" female voters typically referred to the urban poor, antisuffrage associations also tailored their arguments to local concerns. In the northern states, for example, where there was already considerable anxiety about immigrant men who "know little and care less about the government of their adopted country" and are easily manipulated by scheming urban ward bosses, antisuffragists declared bluntly that foreign women are "much more backward." Appearing before the New York legislature in 1909, speakers from the state association warned that the immigrant woman "would show a criminal disregard for American institutions," and was, furthermore, "a fickle, impulsive creature, irresponsible, very superstitious . . . in many things much resembling a sheep." A NAOWS slogan for use in California, "Down with the Yellow Peril, Woman's Votes," invoked the double meaning of anti-Asian and antisuffrage sentiments. Southern writings emphasized the risks of extending the same civil rights "to the recently emancipated slaves, only a few generations removed from cannibalism, as to the highest type of the Caucasian race, with a thousand years of civilization behind it."[96]

A third argument offered was that female enfranchisement would not solve the problems of U.S. society. This rhetorical tactic became increasingly popular with women writers over time, in the face of increasing evidence from full suffrage states that social ills persisted unabated. Antisuffragists' beliefs that women could effect more social reforms without the ballot derived from the power of republican motherhood:

> Temperance? It would come to-morrow in our cities if every mother, every sister, every wife, believed deeply in it. Social purity? It would have to come, if all women resolved upon it. Wages? They would rise at once if women forswore bargains. Asylums, courts, jails, would no longer be needed if every home had a wise mother in it.[97]

Temperance was by far the social issue of greatest concern to antisuffragists, and there is no evidence that they supported "wets"; to the contrary, antis often blamed suffragists for exacerbating intemperance by courting the liquor vote and by encouraging women to abrogate their moral duty and abandon the home. "The truth is," submitted one male antisuffragist, "the prime cause of our troubles in government and society is not bad legislation, but bad morals," and "whenever the great women arise to make society in that high key," they can accomplish it "by simply making a right, clean atmosphere." In contrast, the ballot is a limited solution, because women voters "could not pass laws to abolish all forms of evil."[98]

The experiences of suffrage states constituted proof that "hen politicians" are neither better nor worse than men, at best duplicating the ballot with only one effect—the great additional expense when taxpayers' money could be better spent elsewhere. The doubled vote was both inefficient and profligate, the antithesis of good government. In a blunt appeal to class interests, one male antisuffragist calculated that the additional costs of enfranchising women in New York State would pay to endow "a college like Vassar every five years." The president of the Pennsylvania Association predicted that the expenses of hiring more public employees to meet women voters' demands for expanded social services would decrease the number of female appointments "to high public places."[99]

Antisuffragists also defended the supreme power of male citizens, mostly by reaffirming the classical republican belief that the obligations of citizenship include the physical defense of liberty.[100] "Force converts law into government," declared Molly Seawell, rephrasing Horace Greeley's colorful rejoinder to Susan B. Anthony that "Behind the ballot lies the bullet." Women's physical and temperamental inability to serve as soldiers and police was assumed, and so woman suffrage would be simply "the blank-cartridge ballet," asserted Rossiter Johnson in a popular essay distributed by the New York Association, counting "for nothing until each is backed by a pellet of lead and a pinch of powder ready to enforce its decree." The physical force argument fell into disfavor among women in the latter phases of the movement, while men consistently sounded the theme. Some contested the justice of granting women full citizenship if they "shirk the utmost that it involves," while others predicted the nation's slide into anarchy as men ignore "women's laws" with impunity. Alluding to the constant pressure of "turbulent elements" in society and the lessons of the Great War, antisuffrage writers in the later phase of the contest wondered how far from barbarism were even the most civilized nations and stressed the enduring need for force to maintain order.[101]

Men especially enlarged upon the theme of "emasculated government," worrying that suffrage would further the process of feminization begun by boys' subordination to women teachers, a dispiriting condition in education or politics. The results, they concurred, threatened the future of American democracy. Equating citizenship with manhood, one antisuffragist proclaimed, "Woman suffrage has made cowards and puppets of men. It has coarsened and cheapened women." More positively, both sexes attempted to demonstrate the "identity of interest" between men and women of the same social class and the fine political representation done by men, "whose zeal for the highest welfare of their mothers, sisters, wives, and daughters is surpassed by no other state in the civilized world." Because women are ultimately responsible for rearing the male citizenry, they claimed that "household suffrage" is more in keeping with democratic principles than is redundant "double suffrage."[102]

The final major political consequence of woman suffrage, according to the opposition, was to imperil group dominance. Challenges to the status quo would jeopardize democracy itself by enabling the less stable elements of society. The endangered group was not usually identified, but was alluded to vaguely as the "righteous and public-spirited" or "educated voters." The menace was variously depicted as "undesirable classes," "the indolent and the vicious," or simply "unintelligent voters," but it was clear that for the most part antisuffragists were referring to the "plug-ugly" foreign born, whose quality, they suggested, has been "steadily deteriorating" in the new century as immigration flows shifted away from northern and western Europe. One antisuffragist bluntly asked, "Where would New York and Chicago be with a doubled ignorant vote?" and others warned of the political menace to white supremacy in the southern states, where blacks outnumbered white citizens. It would be incorrect to infer that racist statements were limited to the southern states, however, although antisuffrage pamphlets produced by organizations such as the Southern Woman's League for the Rejection of the Susan B. Anthony Amendment contained some of the most strident rhetoric evoking the specter of sexual as well as political mixing.[103] Northern luminaries such as Elihu Root, Everett P. Wheeler, Mrs. Lyman Abbott, and Grace Duffield Goodwin also expressed concerns about the calamity of doubling the power of the "ignorant and helpless" Negro population, a political menace due allegedly to its vulnerability to exploitation and bribery. Northern antisuffragists likewise waved the banner of "states' rights" as the campaign switched from state suffrage to a federal amendment, invoking the federalist tradition of local self-government, a "Saxon principle."[104]

Most commonly, antis expressed fear of the tyranny of immigrant "alien races," which they saw as swamping superior Anglo-Saxons. They regarded the foreign-born as one alarming mass, voting "as a unit" and able to "swing issues of trade, war, and peace." Anti-Catholic rhetoric, often an expression of anti-immigrant sentiments, appeared only occasionally in antisuffrage literature, perhaps because eminent church leaders opposed suffrage. Anti-Mormon comments were surprisingly common; as a concentrated population distant from major suffrage battles, Mormons represented an easy target for anti-alien sentiments, and their religious doctrines permitting polygamy were interpreted as antifamily, communistic, and consistent with the "free-love" programs of radical feminists.[105] The immigrant population was feared for many reasons, not the least of which was its supposed importation of radical ideologies like socialism and anarchy. These themes were especially prevalent in the final years of the suffrage campaign, owing partly to increased xenophobia during the war years and a conservative shift toward law and order. Antisuffragists, longtime commentators on the "boiling mass of unrest and disquiet" captivating America, exploited popular fears by warning that the suffrage experiment represented "radical and violent changes" in the U.S. Constitution, expansion of "the revolutionary vote," and the nation's imminent decline from democracy to "mobocracy."[106]

Antisuffrage arguments underscored the political significance of the doctrine of separate spheres. By the turn of the century, even labor had entered the party system as an organized interest group, further revealing the diversity of national culture and the increasingly divisive and competitive relations that characterized the American workplace and polity. Threats from below had rendered the maintenance of order by physical force an increasingly salient issue. The virtuous republican mother was needed to tame male passions and supply an ideal of self-sacrifice and cooperation to help smooth tensions. Antisuffragists thus lauded female nonpartisanship as a counterbalance to political conflict and emphasized women's patriotic service as inculcators of the moral values and self-restraint believed necessary to maintain public order. The republican mother, notes Kerber, was a citizen but not a constituent.[107] Women remonstrants nonetheless used the discourse of partisan politics to define women's role in public life, even referring to the benefits of women's independence, a core component of citizenship; through time, moreover, their vision of the realm of republican motherhood broadened. Men, by contrast, emphasized the exclusively masculine nature of politics and its polluting effects on women, demonstrating less confidence in the permanence of female virtue. Men's protectiveness toward women was accompanied by a self-interested territorial defense, expressed by pejorative references to the feminization of American culture and pointing to the crudeness of the political domain with a certain measure of intimidating pride.[108]

An overarching political concern uniting men and women antisuffragists was the growing power of the "ignorant vote." Republican motherhood was widely perceived as a way to Americanize the immigrant, and antisuffragists blamed a deficient home life for the purported corrupt values and radical ideologies of the lower classes.[109] The flip side of republican motherhood made women the scapegoats for men's perceived misdeeds, as antisuffragists scolded upper-class women to provide more virtuous role models and asked laboring women to return to their homes and better train future citizens. While bourgeois and racist rhetoric was not exclusive to antisuffragists, they held somewhat darker opinions of the immutability of human character and, skeptical of assimilation efforts, viewed the continued disfranchisement of lower-class women as a necessary security measure.[110]

Conclusion

Analysis of this sample of antisuffrage rhetoric finds support for the general observation that opponents of women's enfranchisement upheld the doctrine of separate spheres. This conclusion should not be applied narrowly to depoliticize the interests of remonstrants as simply defenders of the traditional female lifestyle, however. Although antisuffrage rhetoric frequently reiterated conventional ideas about woman's virtue derived from domestic seclusion, their notions of appropriate female activities expanded during the long campaign to include the roles of scientific homemaker, producer of obedient workers, and even independent political actor. Antisuffragists used the ideology of separate spheres to justify increasing political influence for women of a certain class—those with "leisure, opportunity, and experience," stated NAOWS president Mrs. Arthur Dodge—while supporting the continued disfranchisement of poor women.[111]

Antisuffrage rhetoric selectively changed over time. While many arguments remained long-term staples of the antisuffrage arsenal, others shifted in frequency as a strategic reaction to altered political opportunities and the actions of proponents. For example, attacks on suffragists increased while religious legitimations diminished over the length of the suffrage campaign. Antisuffrage rhetoric, such as their early use of the expediency rationale as a rebuttal, also provoked responses from the suffrage movement; this suggests that the opposition was not solely a reactive movement, but could also impel suffrage innovation.[112]

Men and women authors shared many rhetorical themes but diverged in others. The general pattern of the opposition argument varied little by gender, although male writers showed a slightly greater proclivity to address gender issues and to attack opponents' personality. Men were more likely to focus on the preservation of separate spheres, traditional family organization, and questions of female character, all of which upheld domestic patriarchy. Women, meanwhile, ostensibly defending their gender from additional labor burdens, often expounded on the multiplicity of feminine roles—domestic, economic, and political. The political implications of enfranchisement were of escalating interest to women writers, while men increasingly aimed their vituperation at suffrage activists.

In matters of style, gender differences were more apparent. Male remonstrants used sharper rhetoric to condemn suffragists for violating gender stereotypes and to affirm female incompetence for the ballot. Men's discourse was also more threatening, reminding women of the dire consequences of leaving the pedestal and competing with men. Female antis, on the other hand, more positively depicted woman's traditional domestic power base, social contributions, and labor output, even presenting antisuffragism as an issue of gender equity by defending women's right not to be further burdened with men's work. But women also used more deferential and flattering language to make their claims, perhaps cognizant of the need to appeal to male voters and politicians who would ultimately decide the question.[113] These gender differences provide further evidence that women antisuffragists were not simply the puppets of men and also indicate that strategic concerns at least partly shaped the tone and contents of antisuffrage rhetoric.

Antisuffragists used the doctrine of separate spheres to emphasize the political dimensions of republican motherhood that supported their position. Revised and expanded to fit new circumstances, republican motherhood linked woman's patriotic service to the domestic sphere, provided a rationale for the mobilization of women antisuffragists, and asserted a level of political independence at odds with traditional gender norms. Its cultural appeal as a venerating symbol of women's contribution to social harmony was a comfort to segments of the population concerned about exacerbating societal conflict. At variance with their traditional stereotype, antisuffrage writers increasingly based gender differentiation on scientific theories of biological determinism that also affirmed racial, ethnic, and class superiority.

If antisuffragists were to have any chance of success in stopping the suffrage movement, they had to reach beyond elites to the mass electorate. Essays in prestigious journals like the *North American Review* might generate donations and attract influential sympathizers, but popular referenda ultimately decided the question. To assess the movement's success in building the constituency required for victory, we next examine election results and organizational recruitment strategies.

5

Mobilizing a Majority

Stand by the Women! Vote for Women's Rights!

The man who opposes women's so-called emancipation is the far-sighted lover of his country and his kind . . . Her right is the right to protection. The whole duty of man toward woman is to protect her, even against herself, if need be.

—Pennsylvania Association Opposed to Woman Suffrage

Most social movements confront the necessity of expanding beyond the cadre of true believers to convince a broader constituency of the imperative of their cause.[1] This was especially true of suffrage, where women activists were denied formal access to the political system they were trying to influence as well as party networks that facilitated recruitment efforts. Both sides worked to build strong women's organizations that could sway the opinions of male legislators and voters through self-described campaigns of public education. Given societal constraints on female comportment, persuading potential women recruits of the virtues of shifting from quiet sympathy to public activism was a difficult task for both groups.[2]

One way to distinguish constituencies on either side of the suffrage question is suggested by the finding that woman suffrage drew support from other reform movements. Scholars have traced the origins of suffrage agitation to female participation in nineteenth-century moral reform societies, abolitionism, and the temperance crusade. These experiences helped women build networks, develop the requisite political skills, and construct new ideologies that challenged the status quo.[3] The rise of progressivism at the turn of the century, which opened the political process to direct citizen action and extended the reach of government into the traditional female domains of education, health, and social welfare, suited changing rationales for women's enfranchisement and generated new consumer and working women's organizations that enabled suffrage recruitment.[4]

If the reform impulse explains the sources of suffrage support, who constituted the opposition constituency? Elite dominance of antisuffrage organizations and the class and ethnic prejudices expressed in movement rhetoric would seem to deter mass recruitment to the remonstrants' cause, especially after the turn of the century when arguments for a restricted electorate and political representation by proxy ran counter to the national trend, exemplified by adoption of the direct primary, the initiative and referendum, and the popular election of U.S. senators. It is curious that a movement with such a narrow base of support could succeed for so long at obstructing the goal of woman suffrage.

This chapter addresses the paradox by identifying the voting constituency opposed to women's enfranchisement. Both sides of necessity made direct appeals to the male electorate, ranging from obsequious entreaties for masculine protection to more reasoned disputations on voter self-interest.[5] But how did male voters respond to such rhetoric at the ballot boxes? To assess the demographic and political characteristics of the antisuffrage electorate, we begin with an examination of voting patterns in state suffrage referenda, including one election in which women participated.

In order to reach the voting masses, antisuffrage organizations also needed to expand their organizational base. Even in the early stages when remonstrants disclaimed any interest in political activism, women recruits could write letters to editors, canvass friends and family members, contact legislators, and contribute money to print large quantities of literature distributed throughout the country. We also consider the recruitment strategies of antisuffrage organizations and evaluate their success by reconstructing membership profiles from the records of two eastern state associations. This study provides a rare look beyond the leadership cadre of the antisuffrage movement to identify its wider network of female followers.

Women's Vote on the Suffrage Question

Neither suffrage successes nor failures were randomly distributed, and the pattern of early western breakthroughs for female enfranchisement, its slow movement eastward, and the collective intransigence of the southern states indicate that the campaign for women's rights may be better understood within a broader political context. The acceleration of suffrage successes coincident with the rise of the Progressive Party and successive congressional passage of prohibition and woman suffrage amendments within a short time span support the argument that partisan competition and the reformist political climate of the period influenced the strategic choices of both sides and, ultimately, the outcome of the long campaign for women's voting rights.

Richard Hofstadter's influential study *The Age of Reform* provides the basis for linking the constituencies of populism, progressivism, and suffragism in terms of the desire to restore America to an earlier, simpler time when certain groups dominated society. Alan Grimes extended the Hofstadter thesis to explain the early victories of woman suffrage in the western states as a consequence of the political actions of members of old-stock pioneer families threatened by the influx of disruptive transients to the frontier territories. Grimes proposed that Yankee settlers, motivated by status discontent, advocated a host of reforms to assert symbolically the superiority of their value system and to secure status group dominance. Temperance and suffrage were related value symbols of the Puritan ethic; sobriety symbolized civic virtue and public order, while woman suffrage hoped to attract scarce female settlers, increase the number of married householders, and enhance community stability beneficial to local business interests.[6] This model identifies the constituency for woman suffrage as native-born Anglo-Saxon Protestants, rural settlers, and residents of areas with a relative oversupply of men. Conversely, greater opposition to woman's enfranchisement would be expected among the foreign-born, Catholics, urban dwellers, and residents of communities where women were relatively plentiful.

The Hofstadter thesis gains some support from the fact that woman suffragists and other reformers often targeted immigrant voters as particular obstacles to reform. Suffrage leaders frequently claimed that naturalized male citizens came from cultures that were less democratic, more resistant to gender equality, and intemperate in their drinking habits, voting down suffrage because of prejudice against women and fears that enfranchised women would install dreaded prohibition. Owing to their urban concentration, immigrants were also seen as contributing to societal decay through their support of corrupt political machines, allegedly selling votes or following mindlessly the directives of local party bosses and liquor interests. Leaders of suffrage campaigns in the western states credited victories to the presence of "so few foreigners" and blamed referenda defeats in other locations on the "slum vote" and "the ignorant, the vicious, and the foreign born."[7]

What we have learned about the antisuffrage movement so far raises questions about the validity of these generalizations concerning the bases of suffrage support and opposition. If the Hofstadter thesis is correct, the social backgrounds of antisuffrage leaders and their rhetorical appeals to class and ethnic prejudice suggest that both sides drew from the same constituency. In arguing that reform movements of the period represented the preservation of the status quo, the Hofstadter thesis blurs the distinction between these two groups of adversaries and may understate the extent of controversy generated by suffragists demanding what many viewed as disruptive changes in women's status. Second, referenda results in numerous states undermine assertions of universal immigrant and urban opposition to women's enfranchisement.[8] The different demographic and political contexts of the sparsely populated western territories as compared with those in the more urban, industrialized eastern states, where suffrage referenda often did not reach the voters until decades later, render suspect sweeping assessments of male sentiments on the issue. Given the growing diversity of the U.S. population by the turn of the century, the suffrage opinions of the masses need more systematic examination.

Even less is known about women's views on the suffrage issue. First-person suffragist accounts and scholarly reconstructions generally confirm Hofstadter's thesis, identifying a fairly homogeneous group of middle-class women activists for the vote, although in its latter stages the movement formed temporary cross-class alliances. The characteristics of antisuffrage recruits, on the other hand, remain largely a mystery; the same can be said for female sympathizers on either side of the suffrage question, although it is generally assumed, perhaps incorrectly, that women shared the political opinions of their male counterparts who voted on suffrage referenda.[9] Before the development of sophisticated survey techniques, referenda results constituted the primary mechanism for assessing public opinion and took on significance far beyond state boundaries. Both sides used ballot results repeatedly in campaign propaganda and of necessity focused on men.

One of the few indicators of women's public opinion on the suffrage question is the 1895 Massachusetts referendum on the Wellman bill. After more than a decade of suffrage agitation in the Massachusetts legislature, a municipal suffrage bill passed the house in 1894 and came within seven votes of success in the Senate. An amended Wellman bill passed the following May. It called for a nonbinding referendum that November on the question "Is it expedient that municipal suffrage should be extended to women?" to be decided by all persons qualified to vote for school committees. This included women, although with restrictions that included a poll tax for nonpropertied women.[10] Suffrage proponents objected to the nonbinding referendum as an antisuffrage plot, calling it a "sham test vote" that required the effort of a "campaign for a popular majority which, if we get it, gives us nothing." After some debate, suffragists finally decided to organize a state committee to work for its passage.[11]

Opponents were privately no more pleased with the Wellman bill, which caught them unprepared for a statewide campaign. They hastily established MAOFESW but acknowledged in retrospect that "the suffragists were thoroughly organized and . . . it was impossible for us to arrive at a similar position in so short a time." They grumbled publicly in the *Remonstrance* that only taxpaying women were "entitled" to vote and castigated suffragists for including in their petition "the corrupt as well as the pure, the irresponsible as well as those who have something at stake in the welfare of the community." Perhaps fearful of the broader female electorate, antisuffragists' strategy "expressly discouraged" women from voting and focused efforts on "arousing the men of the state to vote against the proposal." A boycott by women antis obscured their own lack of organization while at the same time aimed to deter the political mobilization of the distrusted female masses. By ostensibly removing themselves from the political fray, remonstrants also maintained consistency with the true womanhood ideal while operating behind the scenes to assist the newly formed Massachusetts Man Suffrage Association in defeating the Wellman bill.[12]

From its headquarters in downtown Boston, the men's organization waged largely a propaganda campaign against the referendum. Refusing public debates, they mailed literature throughout the state, ranging from lists of prominent local male opponents to Mary A.J. MacIntire's popular tract *Of No Benefit to Women,* which warned of doubling the "ignorant vote," weakening the family, and jeopardizing the temperance cause. Suffragists nonetheless indicted the opposition as a front for liquor interests. Both major parties were divided on suffrage, and labor leaders were generally quiet on the question; only the Women's Garment Workers' Union of Boston publicly endorsed the bill. Influential newspapers like the *Boston Herald* editorialized against suffrage and urged women not to vote. The religious leadership was split, with prominent Unitarian, Universalist, and Methodist clergy supporting the Wellman bill while the Episcopalian and Roman Catholic hierarchies typically opposed it. According to James J. Kenneally, this unlikely coalition of antisuffragists, representing the disparate interests of Irish Catholic immigrants and Brahmin aristocracy, is explained by the involvement of nativist groups in the 1895 referendum campaign. The American Protective Association urged municipal suffrage to reduce Catholic influence on the local school boards, and reactionary women's organizations such as Loyal Women of America sponsored suffrage rallies for "patriotic women" and endorsed the Wellman bill as a way of saving the commonwealth from "Romanism."[13]

Antisuffragists won a decisive victory in the November 5 referendum. Among the nearly three hundred thousand who registered their views, over 63 percent statewide voted against the Wellman bill. Separate tabulation of men's and women's ballots found early evidence of a gender gap, with more than 68 percent of male voters but fewer than 4 percent of female voters rejecting municipal suffrage for women. Both sides tried to use the election results to best advantage. Suffragists emphasized the nearly unanimous affirmative vote among women and claimed that the primary opponent of women's rights was the urban "ignorant vote." Conversely, MAOFESW stressed the strong opposition among men and women's overwhelming lack of interest, manifested by low voter turnout, while the Man Suffrage Association issued a postelection statement suggesting hopefully that the question had been settled and "further agitation at present is uncalled for."[14]

We examine the 1895 vote on the Wellman bill through election returns of all Massachusetts cities and towns.[15] Men's vote against the referendum varied from 33 to 89 percent, and male turnout averaged 44 percent (see Appendix 1). Female preferences varied more widely, as might be expected from a turnout estimated at only 4 percent of those eligible; in forty-five towns, no women's votes were recorded at all.[16] Given the higher turnout of male voters, the referendum's outcome was largely determined by men's opinions on suffrage. The strongest predictor of the election result was men's voting behavior; higher male turnout was associated with a larger male negative vote and a higher total margin of referendum rejection.[17] Women's turnout was slightly lower in towns where the male vote was more antisuffrage; moreover, where fewer eligible women voted, the total margin against suffrage was greater. These results lend some support to MAOFESW claims that their boycott strategy aimed at women was effective.

Table 5.1 presents the results of regression analyses that simultaneously assess the influence of various town characteristics on the percentage of voters rejecting the Wellman bill. Male and female negative votes are examined separately;[18] of course, we have no way of identify-

Table 5.1. Predictors of women's and men's opposition vote by town, 1895 Massachusetts referendum

	Female "No" vote				Male "No" vote			
	(1)		(2)		(3)		(4)	
	b	Beta	b	Beta	b	Beta	b	Beta
Sex ratio, total	−.014	−.013	.021	.020	.074	.104	.102	.143*
Foreign-born	.104	.288**	.130	.362**	−.026	−.140*	−.018	−.096
Foreign-born voters	−.143	−.105	−.233	−.171*	.335	.339**	.251	.254**
Population, total	.004	.036	−.007	−.072	−.020	−.274**	−.023	−.315**
Farm	.022	.027	.174	.217*	−.183	−.324**	−.111	−.196*
Single adults	.359	.162*	.190	.086	−.049	−.032	−.094	−.061
Irish	.102	.129	.099	.125	.075	.133*	.077	.137*
British	.142	.127*	.118	.106	.028	.036	.008	.010
French Canadian	.074	.087	.034	.040	.039	.066	.003	.006
German	.089	.050	−.004	−.002	−.077	−.058	−.108	−.082
Male employment			−.678	−.245**			−.144	−.076
White-collar			.337	.187*			.071	.054
Female employment			.488	.245*			.306	.214*
White-collar			−.121	−.183			−.112	−.253**
Manufacturing			−.068	−.127			−.053	−.145
Intercept	−.241*		.241		.730**		.851**	
Adjusted R^2	.08		.16		.21		.25	
N	308				353			

*$p \leq .05$
**$p \leq .01$

ing individual voters, but this aggregate analysis does indicate patterns of suffrage support and opposition. Panels 1 and 3 consider the effects of the Grimes-Hofstadter factors on men's and women's negative votes: male numerical dominance, immigrant political power, population size, rural residence, and share of unmarried adults.[19] We hypothesize that suffrage rejection rates will be higher in towns with lower male-female sex ratios, more immigrant voters, larger populations, fewer farmers, and more single adults. To consider suffragist claims of opposition among some ethnic groups derived from cultural and religious prejudices, table 5.1 includes measures of ethnic origins for the foreign-born residents of each town.[20] To permit direct comparisons of the relative strengths of these community characteristics on voter behavior, both unstandardized (b) and standardized (Beta) coefficients are presented.

When we compare suffrage opposition by sex, the Hofstadter thesis is revealed as a relatively poor predictor of women's behavior. Female opposition to municipal suffrage was greater in towns with more single adults and more male-skewed immigrant populations, findings contradictory to expectations. Towns with British immigrants were also more opposed to suffrage, not generally a group targeted as opponents by suffragists. The model better fits men's voting preferences; as seen in the third panel of table 5.1, male voters in communities with more foreign-born voters, immigrant sex ratios favoring women, and fewer farmers were more opposed to suffrage, as were those with larger Irish immigrant populations. Male opposition was more pronounced in smaller towns than in larger cities, however, which is contrary to the Hofstadter thesis as well as to suffragist postreferendum recriminations.[21]

To examine an alternative thesis that referendum voting patterns reflected gendered class interests, the remaining panels of table 5.1 expand the model to include estimates of women's and men's labor force participation rates,[22] white-collar employment, and, for women, manufacturing activity.[23] Antisuffrage rhetoric invoking fears of gender strife and male abandonment suggests that communities with lower female employment rates and less skilled women workers would be more opposed to enfranchisement. Their warnings about the erosion of the male breadwinner role might also increase opposition in towns with lower men's employment rates. The predicted interaction between gender and class may produce divergent effects of white-collar employment, with larger community stocks of high-status men associated with suffrage opposition and those with more women in better jobs evincing higher suffrage support at the polls.

The gendered class interests model helps explain women's opposition in particular, as shown in the second panel of table 5.1. Occupational characteristics are useful predictors of female voting patterns; where men's labor force activity is lower and women's employment is higher, women voters rejected suffrage in greater numbers. These results suggest that the repeated warnings of antisuffragists that labor market competition with men would ultimately harm their own sex may have resonated with women workers, few of whom in 1895 brought home wages that rendered the suffrage ideal of economic independence a realistic goal.[24] But women also cast relatively more negative votes where employed men had better jobs, identifying another more privileged antisuffrage constituency among women. Further casting doubt on the applicability of the Hofstadter thesis to eastern women voters, fewer foreign-born voters and rural residence were also associated with greater female opposition.

The pattern of men's votes in the 1895 Massachusetts referendum is quite different. Among the labor force characteristics, only traits associated with women's employment were relevant to men's voting patterns: towns with higher female employment rates recorded higher male rejection rates, while those with greater proportions of employed women in white-collar occupations reported lower male opposition. This finding suggests that men in communities with more "new women" pursuing careers were more supportive of equal rights. Contrary to the Hofstadter thesis, though, communities with sex ratios favoring men also recorded higher male opposition.

A second way to describe the suffrage constituency, especially among women, is voter turnout. Since MAOFESW asked women to stay home, while suffrage proponents tried to draw women to the polls, low female turnout on the Wellman referendum may indicate suffrage opposition.[25] This interpretation is supported by our finding that female voter turnout rates were higher in towns that voted more favorably on the Wellman bill, while male turnout was positively related to antisuffrage voting. Table 5.2 examines selected community characteristics as explanations of variations in estimated men's and women's voter turnout in 1895, with some variables altered to measure more directly the impact of age and family structure on voting behavior.[26] To assess the effectiveness of divergent antisuffrage strategies for each sex, female boycott and male turnout rates are presented.

Table 5.2 reveals that our models are better predictors of referendum turnout than of voter preference for both sexes.[27] Women were less likely to vote on the Wellman bill in towns where the native-born population had relatively more women, consistent with the Hofstadter thesis, but also where the foreign-born population was more skewed in favor of men. Communities with older and more married populations also had lower female turnout rates; this indication that age and family status are associated with women's conservatism on gender issues was repeated more recently in public opinions on the proposed Equal Rights Amendment.[28] Ethnicity was irrelevant to women's voter turnout, and only men's employment characteristics were significant: communities with lower male economic participation and fewer professional men had higher female boycott rates, indicating that antisuffragists may have successfully aroused women's fears concerning loss of male support.

Men's voter turnout is associated with different community charac-

Table 5.2. Predictors of voter turnout, by gender, 1895 Massachusetts referendum

	Female boycott				Male turnout			
	(1)		(2)		(3)		(4)	
	b	Beta	b	Beta	b	Beta	b	Beta
Sex ratio								
Native-born	−.143	−.271**	−.157	−.296**	.039	.042	.084	.089
Foreign-born	.026	.211**	.032	.261**	−.021	−.096	−.013	−.061
Foreign-born voters	.042	.065	.030	.047	.527	.459**	.440	.383**
Population, total	−.001	−.028	−.000	−.003	−.009	−.107	−.017	−.207**
Farm	−.033	−.091	.001	.004	−.034	−.051	−.008	−.013
Youth	−.152	−.103	−.313	−.213**	−.208	−.079	−.046	−.017
Married adults	.296	.337**	.326	.372**	−.002	−.001	.097	.062
Irish	.025	.070	.020	.055	.149	.227**	.146	.222**
British	.016	.031	.007	.015	−.070	−.077	−.078	−.087
French Canadian	.031	.079	.005	.013	.064	.092	.049	.070
German	.060	.070	.051	.060	.196	.128**	.163	.107*
Male employment			−.279	−.226**			.046	.021
Professional			−.728	−.150*			1.942	.224**
Female employment			.022	.023			.572	.345**
White-collar			−.033	−.114			.057	.111
Manufacturing			.010	.042			−.018	−.041
Intercept	.940**		1.174**		.456**		.220	
Adjusted R^2	.17		.21		.30		.35	
N	353				353			

*$p \leq .05$
**$p \leq .01$

teristics, and again the models explain town variations in men's voting patterns better than they do women's. As shown in table 5.2, ethnicity was a significant predictor of male behavior: towns with higher percentages of naturalized voters and those with greater Irish and German concentrations among the foreign-born population had higher male turnout rates. Women's labor market activity continued to influence men's behavior, predicting higher likelihood of voting, although those from towns containing more higher-status men were also more likely to vote on municipal suffrage.

Election returns for an early suffrage referendum strongly challenge the assumption of uniformity in male and female antisuffrage constituencies. Even in the tradition-bound northeastern United

States, women's voting patterns did not duplicate those of their male counterparts. In fact, men and women shared only one community trait: female employment increased rejection rates of the Wellman bill for both sexes. Considering the contents of antisuffrage rhetoric, the motives behind this apparent consensus may have varied, with women voters responding to elevated anxieties about male abandonment and men voters reacting to threats of labor competition. Ethnicity was of very limited utility for explaining women's voting, but suffragist allegations of immigrant opposition fit better male voters of the commonwealth in 1895. These results point to an early manifestation of the recently identified gender gap and imply divergent interests between the sexes.[29]

The Hofstadter thesis performed poorly as a predictor of women's antisuffrage votes. Even for men, however, the results underscore the significance of local political context for shaping constituencies for and against suffrage. The Massachusetts municipal suffrage referendum became embroiled in an ethnic and class struggle for control of local school boards; these results corroborate Kenneally's claim that the prosuffrage mobilization of nativist groups impelled a cross-class coalition of elite Brahmin and Irish immigrant voters, at least among men.[30] While Brahmins provided leadership and organizational expertise to the antisuffrage campaign, men in foreign-born, Irish, and working-class communities both opposed the referendum and turned out in higher percentages to defeat it.

The findings for women point to a broader antisuffrage constituency of both privileged and working-class negative voters and referendum boycotters. In addition to the positive relationship between women's employment and antisuffrage voting for both sexes, lower men's labor force participation rates were consistently associated with suffrage opposition and referendum boycott among women. It appears that antisuffrage arguments warning of the deleterious effects on male breadwinners and family well-being resounded among some segments of the female populace. But women from more privileged towns—those with higher shares of male white-collar occupations—were also more likely to vote "no" on the Wellman bill. Conversely, men tended to support woman suffrage in towns with higher percentages of female professional employment. This disparity may identify dialectical effects of gendered class location on political opinion. It is also paradoxical that male labor force characteristics were more influential on women's referendum ballots, while the opposite was true for men, whose voting preference on woman suffrage was shaped more by the patterns of female economic participation in each town.

The 1895 Massachusetts referendum provided crucial ammunition for the antisuffrage cause nationwide. It was a rare test of public opinion on the question in the eastern states and the sole referendum where women voted. Antisuffrage activists cited these election results repeatedly in speeches and campaign literature to bolster their claim that the majority of American women did not want the vote, while some famous male sympathizers publicly credited the Massachusetts referendum as influential in forming their antisuffrage position.[31] As a mechanism for identifying the popular bases of antisuffragism, however, these findings are limited both temporally and geographically. The 1895 referendum on the Wellman bill predated extensive antisuffrage mobilization and the rise of other political movements that would become important to shaping opinions on suffrage in the new century. To examine these dynamics, we turn to a larger sample of states for a later time period and concentrate on male voters, who were necessarily the primary focus of suffrage contestants.

Antisuffrage Voters in the Progressive Era

The resounding defeat of the Wellman bill in Massachusetts had a chilling effect on legislative action in the eastern United States, despite the continued efforts of petitioning suffragists. Over the next twenty years, the only eastern state where a suffrage bill passed the legislature and progressed to the electorate was New Hampshire, where a referendum was defeated in March 1903 by a margin of almost two to one. Further west, suffragists found a more receptive political climate, and before the century was over four states—Colorado, Utah, Idaho, and Wyoming—had implemented universal suffrage.[32] During the same period suffrage was defeated in popular referenda in California (1896), Washington (1898), South Dakota (1898, 1910), and Oregon (four referenda between 1900 and 1910). These events are an important reminder that while suffrage was more successful in the western states, its progress was slow everywhere.

The logjam was finally broken in 1910, when the voters of Washington State enfranchised women on the third try, followed by California (1911); Arizona, Kansas, and Oregon (1912); and Nevada and Montana (1914). During this four-year period, thirteen other referenda went down in defeat, and 1915 proved to be an important year for the opposition campaign, when voters in the four populous eastern states of Massachusetts, New York, New Jersey, and Pennsylvania rejected woman suffrage.[33] Yet only two years later, the momentum would shift again as New York became the first eastern state to approve a suffrage referendum and help usher in a federal amendment.

The timing and geographic pattern of suffrage successes and defeats support the impression that public opinion reflected the cultural and demographic attributes of voting constituencies. Western and rural states were the first to adopt woman suffrage, while the southern and eastern states, with large nonwhite and foreign-born populations, voted down suffrage proposals in their respective legislatures and in the few referenda that were placed before the electorate. But systematic analyses of various state referenda results reveal less consistent conclusions about the characteristics of antisuffrage voters. The generalization that urban residents disapproved of woman suffrage while farmers favored it was not upheld in all states, nor did foreign-born voters universally oppose female enfranchisement.[34] Despite overt opposition to the 1915 New Jersey referendum by associations representing state liquor dealers, German Catholics, and organized labor, urban immigrant voters were not solidly antisuffrage, but generally replicated the voting patterns of the native-born urban electorate. In the defeated Iowa referendum of 1916, an urban-rural split on suffrage was not evident, and immigrant opposition was largely confined to Germans and Catholics. The results of the successful 1912 Arizona referendum indicate that foreign-born miners and native-born prohibitionists constituted two disparate sources of suffrage support.[35] In the most extensive study of voting patterns on woman suffrage to date, McDonagh and Price examined the election results of thirteen state referenda between 1910 and 1917. In general, they identified German Catholics and urban dwellers as the most consistent opponents of suffrage, while supporters included Scandinavian and English immigrants and residents of more affluent communities. They also found regional variations in the effects of numerous community characteristics on voter preference.[36]

The following analysis empirically reexamines the bases of suffrage support and opposition. Table 5.3 presents the results for nine woman suffrage referenda grouped into four geographic regions: the three western states (Washington, California, and Oregon) where suffrage victories beginning in 1910 reenergized activists on both sides; the four eastern states (Pennsylvania, Massachusetts, New York, New Jersey) where definitive referenda defeats made 1915 a banner year for antisuffragism; Kansas, the first midwestern state to pass suffrage in 1912 and where the question was first put before voters in 1867;[37] and finally, the rare southern state where a suffrage bill passed the legislature and was placed before the electorate, the failed Texas referendum of 1919.[38]

The sampled states have diverse political histories on the suffrage issue. Among the three western states studied, Washington voted suffrage in first and with the largest margin (64 percent), perhaps owing to a plethora of local interest group endorsements that included the state's Grange, Farmer's Union, and Federation of Labor. California passed woman suffrage in 1911 with a bare majority, while Oregon experienced the most consistent suffrage agitation, with five previous referenda. Antisuffrage organization in the western states was sporadic and typically limited to committees located in the major cities, heavily supervised by the Massachusetts and New York associations. A New York antisuffrage leader sent to help Oregon in the 1906 campaign complained that one Portland woman was working "almost single-handedly" to defeat suffrage. Another frustrated antisuffrage worker reported to the MAOFESW executive committee in the wake of the 1910 Washington election, "It was impossible to get the women to organize in opposition," and the next year wearily described the California campaign as "uphill work" because the people were "very difficult" to arouse.[39]

In the nation's heartland, Kansas voted for suffrage in 1912 with a small 52 percent majority; this marked the third suffrage referendum in that state, although the last attempt was almost twenty years earlier. The eastern antisuffrage establishment was not very involved in the Kansas campaign, perhaps because its attention was diverted by six other state referenda that year.[40] Antisuffrage organization was sporadic and relatively late in Texas, where no association formed until 1915; its president announced plans for extensive statewide organization, but these objectives were never realized. The Texas Association held no state conventions, apparently had no organized local chapters, and primarily functioned as a distributor of antisuffrage literature from its Fort Worth headquarters, some of which was tailored to local concerns about the preservation of racial dominance. Despite these limitations, suffrage was defeated in Texas by a 54 percent majority.[41]

The 1915 campaigns in the four eastern states took place on the home turf of the antisuffrage movement, with well-funded and well-organized state associations. Pennsylvania organized in 1909, and its association grew large enough to hold a statewide convention to inaugurate the campaign against the referendum; New Jersey's antisuffrage association, established in 1912, was a relative latecomer in the region but nonetheless claimed thirty-four branches by the October election.

These four state associations benefited from their close proximity to coordinate literature and speakers.[42] In addition, the National Association Opposed to Woman Suffrage, whose governing board was dominated by eastern women, took an active role behind the scenes to direct the four campaigns, and in its private communiqués to the state associations clearly viewed the 1915 elections as a do-or-die crossroads of the movement.[43] Only Massachusetts had held a previous referendum on the question, and the commonwealth's voters again rejected suffrage in 1915 by the widest margin of 65 percent, followed by New York and New Jersey at about 58 percent, and Pennsylvania with a 54 percent majority against suffrage.

We again examine the impact of community characteristics—this time at the county level—on state referenda outcomes, measured as the percentage of male voters rejecting suffrage in each county.[44] The two models tested are loosely based on the ideas that guided the Massachusetts analysis, although the choice of indicators is modified by the data collection procedures of the U.S. census. County demographic traits include sex ratios, urbanization level, population growth, ethnic and racial distribution, and school enrollment (as a proxy for social class).[45] Because concerns regarding the potential political power of nonwhite populations were especially relevant to electoral behavior in the western and southern states, relatively larger populations of nonwhites may have incited antisuffrage voting as a way to protect racial hegemony.[46] The second model includes more detailed indicators of cultural heritage in order to assess the impact of religious and ethnic traditions and the threat of prohibition on suffrage voting patterns.[47]

Voter opinions on suffrage referenda were not randomly distributed, and states that rejected suffrage showed wider intercounty variations than did those where it passed (see appendix 2). Moreover, opposition counties, regardless of the referendum's outcome at the state level, tended to be clustered geographically, forming contiguous pockets of dissent. In California, for example, the strong antisuffrage counties largely encircled the Bay Area of San Francisco; in New York, the most prosuffrage counties were located in western, rural portions of the state, while the upper Hudson Valley voted down the referendum by the widest margins. Demographic and ethnic characteristics also varied by state and region; for example, sex ratios were more unbalanced in the west, while the eastern states were the most urbanized, Texas counties had the largest proportion of nonwhites, and average school enrollment was highest in more homogeneous Kansas (appendix 2).

Table 5.3 finds that demographic characteristics, tested in the first

Table 5.3. Predictors of opposition vote on state suffrage referenda, by county, 1910–1919

	Suffrage passed							
	West				Kansas			
	(1)		(2)		(1)		(2)	
	b	Beta	b	Beta	b	Beta	b	Beta
Demographic variables								
Male/female ratio	.003	.008	.034	.103	−.118	−.140	−.132	−.156
Urban	.056	.184	.037	.121	−.034	−.099	−.024	−.071
Growth	−.019	−.370**	−.019	−.371**	−.030	−.168	−.005	−.026
Foreign-born	−.053	−.048	.064	.058	.811	.500**	.887	.547**
Nonwhite	−.641	−.311**	−.594	−.289**	.306	.111	−.128	−.047
School enrollment	−.581	−.318**	−.476	−.261*	−.165	−.089	−.000	−.000
Ethnicity								
German			.253	.169			.252	.301**
Irish			−.215	−.110			.393	.149
Scandinavian			−.154	−.189			.049	.068
Catholic			.301	.281**			.420	.248**
Intercept	.865**		.710**		.667**		.462**	
Adjusted R^2	.19		.30		.29		.45	
N	123				105			

	Suffrage failed							
	Texas				East			
	(1)		(2)		(1)		(2)	
	b	Beta	b	Beta	b	Beta	b	Beta
Demographic variables								
Male/female ratio	−.419	−.291**	−.313	−.218**	−.506	−.352**	−.541	−.376**
Urban	−.103	−.132*	−.101	−.129*	−.023	−.062	−.034	−.092
Growth	−.000	−.066	−.000	−.107	−.023	−.107	−.035	−.162
Foreign-born	−.316	−.183	−.242	−.140	.118	.104	.128	.113
Nonwhite	.132	.145*	.115	.127	.468	.103	.541	.118
School enrollment	−.461	−.299**	−.503	−.327**	−.144	−.055	.050	.019
Ethnicity								
German			.231	.217**			−.110	−.097
Irish			−.066	−.016			−.255	−.196*
Scandinavian			−.138	−.052			−.758	−.364**
Catholic			−.063	−.050			.211	.174
Intercept	1.257**		1.130**		1.174**		1.139**	
Adjusted R^2	.22		.26		.10		.23	
N	235				159			

*$p \leq .05$
**$p \leq .01$

panels, poorly explain the antisuffrage vote in the eastern states, better fit voting outcomes in Texas and the western sample, and perform the best in Kansas, where they explain 29 percent of county variation on the suffrage question. No variable had consistent effects across the four regions, although many operated in the expected direction. In the East and Texas, for example, counties with relatively more women were more likely to vote against suffrage, corroborating the Hofstedter thesis that women benefit from the situation of relative scarcity. Somewhat surprisingly, however, this pattern was not found in the western states, where the hypothesis originated and where county sex ratios showed more variation (see appendix 2). Perhaps this explanation for western suffrage success is more useful in cross-regional comparative studies that in intraregional comparisons such as these. As for class differences in suffrage constituencies, the results for school enrollment indicate that antisuffrage balloting was relatively higher in poorer counties, at least in Texas and the western states. And only in Kansas were counties with higher percentages of foreign-born residents more likely to vote against suffrage, further evidence that immigrant opposition to suffrage has been overstated. The effects of race varied by region; in Texas, larger nonwhite populations predicted antisuffrage voting, confirming the racial hegemony hypothesis. In the western states, however, where the nonwhite population was predominantly of Asian origin, larger stocks of nonwhites strongly increased county margins for suffrage, perhaps signifying the mobilization of disparate constituencies for reform in different political climates.

Urbanization was weakly related to voters' suffrage opinions; a significant relationship is found only in Texas, where the least urban counties tended to vote antisuffrage. Population growth was only negatively associated with referenda rejection and only in the western sample. These findings contradict arguments that antisuffrage voting constituted reactions by groups most disoriented by industrialization and urbanization. It seems that, at least by this later phase of the debate over enfranchisement, antisuffrage voters came from more traditional communities further removed from disruptive social change.

Ethnic heritage is more useful for explaining men's suffrage voting patterns than is foreign birth, as shown in the second panels of table 5.3. The addition of religion and national origin increases the explanatory power of the model, especially in the eastern states, while in Texas its effects are quite modest. These findings corroborate earlier research that areas with higher proportions of Germans and Catholics were more antisuffrage, but even this relationship is not universal across all regions. Voters of German background were a larger percentage of the foreign-born and foreign-parentage population in the two states (Kansas and Texas) where they constituted a relatively potent opposition force against suffrage. But the effects of ethnic heritage in the eastern United States were negative; counties with more Scandinavian and Irish residents recorded more prosuffrage votes, the latter at variance with the results of the 1895 Massachusetts referendum. Suffragist denunciations of immigrant voters are rendered more suspect by these results. More generally, ethnicity explains a larger percentage of opposition voting where suffrage referenda passed, which may indicate that some groups were easier to convert than others.

The results of table 5.3 fail to identify a universal set of demographic and cultural correlates of suffrage support and opposition and, in some regions, leave a large share of variation in voting behavior unexplained. This suggests that additional factors contributed to suffrage electoral outcomes. Voter turnout is one such element of political contests; regardless of public opinion on an issue, sympathies must be translated into behavior at the ballot box in order to influence state policy. In the Massachusetts referendum of 1895, we found that getting out the vote was an important element of campaign strategy among both groups of contestants, and ultimately worked to the benefit of antisuffragists. Not all electoral conditions are under activists' control, however; external events, such as presidential elections and the presence of multiple issues on the ballot, may heighten voter interest and increase turnout.

Table 5.4 adds voter turnout to the model and finds that the antisuffrage cause was often its beneficiary.[48] Voter turnout was strongly and positively associated with antisuffrage preference in three of the four regions. Except for Kansas, which had by far the highest voting rates of any region, counties with higher turnout tended to record more antisuffrage votes. And its impact is quite strong; the inclusion of voter turnout typically boosts by about a third the explanatory power of each model. This positive association between voting rates and antisuffrage preference may appear contradictory in the three western states where all suffrage referenda passed; it means that higher voter turnout produced lower suffrage support, not necessarily a majority against the referendum. Further, it is consistent with the fact that the states with the largest prosuffrage margins typically had the lowest voter turnout.[49] The conclusion that the suffrage movement in the West generally benefited from low voter turnout is supported by the memoirs of local suffragists who seemed cognizant of the need to keep

Table 5.4. Impact of voter turnout on antisuffrage vote, by county, 1910–1919

	Suffrage passed				Suffrage defeated			
	West		Kansas		Texas		East	
	b	Beta	b	Beta	b	Beta	b	Beta
Male/female ratio	.056	.168	−.102	−.120	−.294	−.205**	−.439	−.305**
Urban	.049	.161	−.014	−.040	−.069	−.089	−.000	−.002
Growth	−.013	−.259**	−.005	−.029	−.000	−.125*	−.037	−.174
Foreign-born	.321	.291**	.893	.551**	−.211	−.122	.025	.022
Nonwhite	−.521	−.253**	−.029	−.011	.130	.143*	.541	.118
School enrollment	−.428	−.235*	−.024	−.013	−.522	−.358**	−.208	−.080
German	.256	.171*	.233	.279**	.143	.134*	−.181	−.160*
Irish	−.138	−.071	.397	.150	−.033	−.008	−.496	−.381**
Scandinavian	−.215	−.264**	.046	.065	−.209	−.079	−.760	−.365**
Catholic	.177	.165*	.432	.255**	−.050	−.040	.224	.184
Voter turnout	.211	.413**	.078	.107	.286	.249**	.306	.408**
Intercept	.538**		.390*		1.058**		1.115**	
Adjusted R^2	.40		.45		.30		.34	
N	123		105		235		159	

*$p \leq .05$
**$p \leq .01$

from rousing the opposition. One leader's account of the successful Washington State effort credited its tactful campaign management and the fact that the ballot's wording did not mention women, while California suffragists planned an "inoffensive campaign" in 1911 that was ultimately victorious.[50]

Voter turnout also altered the impact of constituent characteristics on antisuffrage voting, depending upon election outcomes. For example, in the two locations that passed suffrage, the inclusion of voter turnout strengthened the relationship between the size of the foreign-born population and suffrage opposition. Conversely, the two areas that defeated suffrage seem to have little in common, except that higher voter turnout helped the opposition (especially in the eastern states) and greater male numerical dominance predicted suffrage support, as Hofstadter theorized. In Texas, counties that were poorer, more nonwhite, slower growing, and German recorded larger antisuffrage margins. In the eastern states, though, ethnicity continued to reduce suffrage opposition when voter turnout was controlled.[51]

The eastern antisuffrage establishment deserves some credit for getting out the opposition vote in 1915. Adopting a proactive approach, by 1913 the Massachusetts Association was already prepared to "bring out our vote" should a suffrage bill pass the legislature. It judged conditions as "entirely different from those of 1895"; for one thing, it had since built "an organization covering the state," so a "courageous stand" was possible without fear of humiliating defeat. In contrast to its shadowy participation in the first referendum, MAOFESW went after male voters with gusto, posting antisuffrage messages in ballparks and accosting "Mr. Voter" with signs on urban streetcars. New York antisuffragists canvassed election districts and mailed a weekly antisuffrage update to five hundred newspapers in the state, while New Jersey activists spoke at local political clubs and fraternal organizations. Pennsylvania antisuffragists made the circuit of Grange picnics and instituted a chain telephone strategy, whereby each man was responsible for producing five opposition votes and each woman pledged to get one antisuffrage voter to the polls.[52]

Voter turnout was only one political dynamic that influenced the outcomes of suffrage referenda. Another was the temperance issue, which evolved into prohibition during the Progressive Era. Although both temperance and prohibition emphasized the deleterious effects of excessive drinking on women and families, the latter movement sought to exercise the power of government for social reform by mandating abstinence instead of leaving the matter to individual self-control. The issue was a double-edged sword for suffragists. The Woman's Christian Temperance Union, the first mass movement of American women, gave suffrage an early endorsement in 1881, produced a number of prominent suffrage leaders, and was active in several state campaigns for the vote. But the union's support also provoked the active opposition of powerful business interests; by the 1890s some suffragists became wary and blamed association with the temperance cause for numerous referenda losses, while others denounced foreign-born "wets" and "the invisible enemy" of brewery and liquor interests lurking behind the antisuffrage movement.[53] There is evidence that both industries worked against female enfranchisement, especially in the midwestern states, from legislative lobbying to propaganda production and possibly the purchase of opposition votes. The prohibition issue alarmed groups involved with the brewery trade, producing the overt antipathy of the German-American Alliance as well as that of some labor unions that viewed suffrage as a threat to working-class interests. But suffragists' allegations of collusion with "liquor forces" also impelled defensive reactions among antisuffrage organizations, some of whom forbade their male workers from leaving materials with bartenders or saloon men.[54]

McDonagh and Price's study of several state suffrage referenda results found regional variations in the salience of the prohibition issue. Where prohibition appeared on the same ballot with woman suffrage, it strongly influenced voter turnout, with varying effects on suffrage referenda outcomes, depending upon the sizes of constituencies for and against temperance. In the successful 1912 Arizona woman suffrage referendum, for example, native-born prohibitionists constituted an important source of suffrage support, and settling the issue for prohibition in the midwestern states removed a potent source of opposition and paved the way for woman suffrage in the latter half of the decade.[55] The varying influence of the prohibition debate on suffrage balloting is illustrated in our sample. The 1896 California referendum was defeated in part because of its connection to temperance, but the prohibition issue was settled before the 1911 election when the state legislature voted in a local option law. German-language newspapers nonetheless denounced the California referendum as a threat to brewery jobs and a way of life that included visits to the neighborhood tavern, and our results confirm that western voters in more heavily German counties showed greater suffrage opposition (see table 5.4).[56] In Texas, on the other hand, statewide prohibition and woman suffrage shared the ballot in the 1919 election, over the protests of local suffrage leaders and despite the fact that the Eighteenth Amendment to the U.S. Constitution had already rendered superfluous a state vote on prohibition. The presence of prohibition on the ballot drew out prohibition opponents who managed to defeat woman suffrage while prohibition carried by a small majority.[57]

The impact of prohibition on the Texas suffrage vote is illustrated in table 5.5. These results suggest that the prohibition vote had a major direct influence on the suffrage election outcome.[58] Antiprohibition voting in 1919 had by far the strongest effect on Texans' antisuffrage balloting, and its inclusion more than doubles the explanatory power of the model. It seems that opposition to prohibition mobilized antisuffrage voters when both issues appeared on the same ballot and mitigated the impact of demographic and cultural background characteristics on woman suffrage opinion. Table 5.5 shows that the inclusion of antiprohibition balloting reduced the direct effect of German heritage on the suffrage referendum's outcome, because heavily German counties were also strongly antiprohibition. Likewise, the previous relationship between voter turnout and referenda opposition disappears, con-

Table 5.5 Impact of prohibition and partisanship on antisuffrage vote, Texas and New York, 1915–1919

	Texas		New York			
	1919		1915		1917	
	b	Beta	b	Beta	b	Beta
Male/female ratio	−.266	−.153**	−.206	−.230	−.156	−.156
Urban	−.130	−.177**	−.110	−.519*	−.066	−.283
Growth	.000	.047	−.006	−.066	.000	.008
Foreign-born	−.352	−.217**	−.013	−.019	−.022	−.029
Nonwhite	−.010	−.011	−1.177	−.185	−2.401	−.340**
School enrollment	−.217	−.147**	−.444	−.292*	−.522	−.310*
German	−.003	−.003				
Irish	−.081	−.020				
Scandinavian	−.041	−.016				
Catholic	−.149	−.128**				
Voter turnout	.058	.051	.087	.132	−.036	−.079
Antiprohibition	.805	.834**				
Democratic vote			.265	.348*	.101	.172
Third party vote			−.334	−.287*	−.507	−.401*
Intercept	.574**		1.110**		1.100**	
Adjusted R^2	.78		.33		.28	
N	215		61		61	

*$p \leq .05$
**$p \leq .01$

firming speculation that prohibition was responsible for increasing the turnout of opponents.[59] With the influence of prohibition balloting controlled, rural counties voted antisuffrage, while those with higher percentages of Catholic and foreign-born voters were more prosuffrage.

A third political dynamic that influenced voters' opinions on the suffrage issue was party politics. Despite claims of nonpartisanship, leaders from both sides spoke frequently at national conventions and competed for endorsements from the major parties; the controversial assault on the Democratic Party by the suffragist Congressional Union beginning in 1914 was a negative example of a long-standing political strategy. Political reform movements, because they challenged the status quo, frequently became suffrage allies. The early passage of woman suffrage in the western states can be credited partly to the regional strength of the Populist Party, which placed an equal suffrage plank in its 1893 national platform. The newly formed Socialist Party endorsed equal rights in 1901 and inserted a suffrage plank in 1908, followed by the Progressive Party in 1912.[60]

Swayed by the expediency claims of the suffragists that women possessed a higher morality, reform movements often endorsed suffrage as way to double their voting constituencies. Political exigencies help explain the success of woman suffrage in California, which followed on the heels of a clear victory for Republican Progressives and the Anti-Saloon League in the 1910 state legislative elections. Passage of state suffrage referenda in Kansas, Arizona, and Oregon in 1912 can be credited in part to the strong showing of the Progressive Party in that presidential election year, when Theodore Roosevelt tried to recapture the White House as a third-party candidate. In 1913, the Illinois legislature bypassed the referendum process to vote in presidential woman suffrage as a result of the rising political clout of the Progressives in state government. And in a one-party state like Texas, the election of a reform Democratic governor and legislature in 1918 was followed quickly by passage of a law granting women the right to vote in primary elections, which was tantamount to full enfranchisement; this surely palliated suffragists' disappointment over the referendum defeat the following year.[61] These events are not without irony, as reform-minded administrations sometimes circumvented the electoral process in the interest of political democratization. Nonetheless, presidential suffrage by legislative enactment, which escalated during the war years, instilled women with new political value and generated partisan competition for their support.[62]

Arguably the most significant outcome of political reform movements is the impact of third-party competition on the platforms of mainstream political parties. Suffragists could not control the emergence of this political situation, but some astute groups seized the opportunity for suffrage. Janet Boles found that state legislatures with higher levels of interparty competition were more likely to pass suffrage bills. For example, Populist Party support for suffrage during its heyday in the 1890s forced other contesting political parties jockeying for state control to endorse it as well, which depoliticized the issue and gained women the vote early in some western states. In order to have positive outcomes for suffragists, though, partisan rivalry had to be carefully brokered. The failed 1894 Kansas campaign demonstrated the negative results for suffragists of misplaying interparty competition. Taking Populist support for granted, suffragists first approached Republicans for an endorsement; after they were rejected, suffrage lost its political cachet and received only lukewarm Populist referendum support.[63]

To demonstrate the critical role of partisan politics, we consider the results of the 1915 and 1917 suffrage referenda in New York, a state that experienced a rapid turnaround on the issue. Historian Paula Baker attributes the change in voter sentiment to partisan politics. She observes that suffrage support in 1915 was most pronounced in the counties where third parties ran well, garnering as much as 36 percent of the vote. Seeing that suffrage siphoned voters to third-party candidates, both major parties endorsed the 1917 suffrage referendum. Not only did New York women win the vote, but the share of third-party votes declined in 1917 by more than half. Somewhat bucking the trend, the popularity of the Socialist Party choice for New York City mayor compelled the remaining three candidates to follow his lead and endorse the 1917 referendum, a tactic born of partisan competition that probably helped carry the city for suffrage.[64]

Table 5.5 tests Baker's thesis by including the percentage of Democratic and third-party votes received in the general elections nearest in time to each referendum.[65] These results confirm the importance of partisan politics for suffrage voting. In both New York elections, counties with larger percentages of third-party ballots realized larger margins for suffrage. Democratic Party voting was related to suffrage opposition in 1915, but two years later the opposition of Democratic voters was neutralized by the party's endorsement of woman suffrage. These data also confirm that in both New York referenda it was the less affluent counties that manifested higher voter opposition.[66] It appears that partisanship shaped public opinion on the suffrage question, but party dynamics were themselves responsive to changing exigencies: then as now, political survival required organizational flexibility in response to shifting issue relevance, constituency demands, and interparty competition.

The fluid dynamics of partisan politics are underscored by our earlier finding that immigrant voters in the eastern states were not more likely to reject suffrage referenda, challenging the reactionary stereotype of urban political machines. In Massachusetts, for example, historical accounts observe that foreign-born sentiments had shifted in favor of suffrage by 1915, possibly in response to more assiduous cross-class mobilization efforts by suffrage activists and revised positions by urban political machines. Both Republican and Democratic party organizations were neutral on the Massachusetts referendum in 1915, but the state AFL-CIO and Boston's flamboyant Mayor Curley endorsed it.[67]

Nationally, historians document an "abrupt and startling reversal" on the suffrage issue by political bosses at about this time and link it to various factors, but especially the recognition that Progressive reforms, by democratizing politics and expanding the electorate, potentially enhanced rather than jeopardized the power of urban machines.[68]

This investigation of eleven referenda in ten states finds few universals in the politics of woman suffrage. Constituencies for and against female enfranchisement varied across regions and, indeed, shifted through time within the same state. Neither urban residents nor rapidly changing populations were more likely to oppose suffrage. If anything, the reverse is true, suggesting that antisuffrage balloting reflected the fears of populations further removed from social change, who were perhaps trying to keep distant daunting disruptions to their way of life. Consistent with Hofstadter's proposition, male numerical dominance was associated with prosuffrage balloting, but only in the states where suffrage failed. Larger concentrations of foreign-stock residents constituted pockets of suffrage resistance where suffrage referenda passed. Counties with more people of German heritage manifested greater suffrage opposition in states west of the Mississippi, whereas the reverse was found in the eastern states. These regional variations in antisuffrage constituencies are testimony to the significance of local political exigencies.

Interrelated political dynamics such as voter turnout rates, prohibition issue relevance, and partisan competition condition the impact of community characteristics on suffrage referenda outcomes, challenging the notion of stable constituencies opposed to woman suffrage on cultural or ideological grounds. Progressive politics played a role in mobilizing both suffrage support and opposition; the emergence of third parties as well as reform elements within the two major parties promoted suffrage endorsements and neutralized partisan sources of opposition. On the other hand, demands for prohibition, where they occurred simultaneously with woman suffrage, tended to increase opposition turnout. The influence of partisan politics on the suffrage issue underscores the uphill task for women activists who sought to influence the political process as outsiders.

Building a Female Constituency

The results of the 1895 referendum on the Wellman bill convinced Massachusetts antisuffragists of the importance of building effective organizations. The state association's executive committee examined the election districts that voted for suffrage and concluded that "in almost every case there was little or no antisuffrage membership behind them or there had been very great efforts made by suffragists." As this statement indicates, antisuffrage expansion efforts were impelled in part by competition with proponents, who annually petitioned the state legislature until they finally gained passage of a woman suffrage bill in 1914. Realizing early that the opposition was undeterred by defeat, antisuffragists began a recruitment campaign in 1901 with a mailing to women statewide—clubwomen, those with influential spouses, or the few professional women, mostly in education—inviting them to join the MAOFESW standing committee. Husbands were from the beginning an important element of antisuffrage strategy, and all published organizational materials listed married women leaders by their husbands' full names. This practice not only reflected gender conventions but also served numerous strategic functions. It was a backhanded criticism of proponents' alleged rejection of traditional marriage, subtly signifying that antisuffrage women were proud to be married and bear their husbands' names. More pragmatically, in an era of considerable gender segregation, a roster of prominent men had more influence on the wider public, especially voters. Its official brochures, updated annually, individually listed by town the names of the standing committee, even when the numbers ran into the hundreds. Through careful selection and subsequent publication of the names of people of "weight and influence," the Massachusetts Association hoped to convert reluctant sympathizers to active work.[69]

Diversity was another goal behind the expansion of the MAOFESW standing committee. The Massachusetts leadership privately discussed the desirability of getting names from "new places" beyond Boston and augmenting Boston committee representation with "ladies belonging to a different class." In pursuit of geographic diversity, they repeatedly sought women from rural western Massachusetts and Cape Cod, tracking potential recruits through intricate networks of family and marriage. Broadening social class representation on the committee was more difficult, since kinship networks were of little use. They requested nominations by mail and asked public speakers employed by the organization to "make inquiries," but the Boston names on the standing committee continued to represent primarily elite Brahmin families. The task of expanding the leadership was arduous, as numerous women responded to invitations by reaffirming their support for the cause but lamenting that they were not yet ready to "come out."[70] Sometimes recruitment methods appeared overzealous and cast doubt on the accuracy of the printed list; one Brookline woman, who was apparently added to the standing committee without her knowledge or consent, protested to MAOFESW that she had "no interest in the subject whatsoever," unleashing further recruitment attempts. By early 1904, the Massachusetts Association proclaimed its leadership drive a success, with sixty new members on its two major committees.[71]

The top panel of table 5.6 evaluates the results of efforts to expand and diversify the MAOFESW standing committee. It counts the total number of committees and the number of towns represented for three time periods at five-year intervals.[72] It also describes the geographic distribution of the standing committee by separating Massachusetts into five major regions: the municipality of Boston, the greater Boston area, defined as a twenty-mile radius from the city center, and the central, western, and eastern sections of the state (excluding metropolitan Boston).[73] The results reveal fluctuations in the association's recruitment drive. In its first ten years (1895–1905), the size of the standing committee grew by 50 percent. From 1905 to 1910, committee membership increased by 11 percent, but in the next five-year period preceding the referenda campaign it increased by a third, to 457 women.[74] The number of towns represented on the standing committee actually decreased between 1905 and 1910, perhaps connoting resignations from reluctant committee members ensnared by the first overzealous recruitment drive. Between 1910 and 1915, there was a 50 percent increase in the number of towns on the committee, reflecting organizational preparation for another referendum battle.

Attempts at regional diversification were somewhat less successful. While the percentage of Boston members on the standing committee declined slightly, this loss was counterbalanced by additional women from towns closely surrounding Boston, a trend that paralleled the migration of elite families to the posh suburbs. Nearby Brookline and Cambridge continued to dominate the leadership cadre, peaking at 35 percent of greater Boston standing committee members in 1910. Throughout all periods examined, fully two-thirds of committee members resided in Boston and surrounding towns. While the eastern region increased its share of committee members over time, representation from the hinterland declined during the decade. Central Massachusetts, in particular, reduced its representation on the standing committee by about a third, while delegates from western Massachusetts remained a small minority. The western two-thirds of the state constituted at most 21 percent of standing committee members, and by 1915

Table 5.6. Geographic distribution of antisuffrage organization, Massachusetts, 1905–1915

	MAOFESW standing committee		
	1905	1910	1915
Boston city	27%	27%	21%
Greater Boston	38	42	45
Eastern region	14	15	17
Central region	13	10	9
Western region	8	6	8
	100%	100%	100%
Total members	309	343	457
Total towns	96	83	130

	MAOFESW branch committees	
	1906	1915
Boston city	10%	8%
Greater Boston	50	45
Eastern region	13	28
Central region	13	7
Western region	13	12
	99%	100%
Total committees	30	102
Total members	12,150	28,420

its share had declined to 17 percent. Although stocking the leadership ranks with women who lived in close proximity to MAOFESW headquarters no doubt enabled greater participation in the organization, it is directly at odds with the organization's self-declared goals of expanding into enemy territory; rural men, as we have seen, voted more prosuffrage in the 1895 referendum.

In practice, the members of the standing committee were generally not expected to participate in organizational decision making. Their primary functions were ostensibly to serve as role models for coaxing other women into activism and to assist in the formation of branch committees; this is probably why organization brochures always listed committee members by town. Placement on the standing committee was probably part of a graduated recruitment plan, for these women typically served as the contact person whenever the executive committee decided that a town needed to be organized into a branch committee. An early MAOFESW pamphlet in uncharacteristically candid fashion describes the process of starting a branch committee: first, invite a small number of women to a parlor meeting to hear an association speaker describe its aims and activities; the speaker shall then help the assembled group choose a branch committee composed of at least three women; finally, call a larger general meeting of women from the community, at which organizers collect signatures on membership cards.[75]

The assertiveness and confidence of the female antisuffrage leadership are evident in the organization of local chapters, which was predominantly directed from above and rarely developed from women's grassroots mobilization. Paid organizers embarked on state tours, and executive officers took personal responsibility for forming branches in particular towns, sometimes courting prominent women to host the all-important first parlor meeting in a new locale. During one progress report on branch committee organization, an officer opined that a new branch "could be formed in Quincy if Mrs. Brooke Adams, the most influential woman there, would open her house for a meeting. Miss Ames [MAOFESW president] will ask her."[76]

The bottom panel of table 5.6 assesses the progress of the Massachusetts Association in establishing new branch committees.[77] In the first ten years of mobilization, MAOFESW grew to thirty committees statewide; in the second ten years, the number of branch committees more than tripled. Their locations replicated the geographic distribution of the standing committee, testimony to the effectiveness of the association's graduated plan of community mobilization. Over half of all branch committees were established in close proximity to Boston, and regional expansion over time was concentrated in the growing metropolitan area of eastern Massachusetts. The central and western regions remained underrepresented, and the proportion of committees from the hinterland diminished through time. These data provide ample evidence that antisuffrage mobilization, partly by design and partly by necessity, was predominantly an urban phenomenon. But it was by no means an inner-city movement; in 1909, for example, the suburban Brookline chapter counted a thousand members, and the entire Boston chapter numbered only sixteen hundred.[78]

The first panel of table 5.7 further examines the characteristics of Massachusetts towns associated with the development of antisuffrage branch committees.[79] These results confirm that antisuffrage organization was largely an elite, urban phenomenon. Branch committees were more likely to be found in larger towns and those with higher percentages of male professionals but lower female employment rates. Towns with higher proportions of unmarried adults were also more likely to

Table 5.7 Correlations and consequences of antisuffrage organization, Massachusetts, 1915

	Branch committee organization		1915 negative vote	
	b	Beta	b	Beta
Male/female ratio	.014	.003	−.029	−.051
Single adults	1.887	.163**	−.003	−.002
Foreign-born voters	.280	.038	−.142	−.197*
Population, total	.291	.537**	−.009	−.171
Rural population	.527	.125	.089	.211*
Irish	−.034	−.008	.032	.075
French Canadian	−.295	−.066	.081	.173**
German	.032	.003	.174	.187**
Male employment	−.550	−.039	.081	.054
Professional	13.291	.238**	.516	.090
Female employment	−1.840	−.172*	.166	.155
Professional	.126	.038	−.079	−.241*
Manufacturing	−.176	−.064	−.088	−.320**
Negative vote, 1895	.750	.115*	.133	.201**
Male turnout, 1895	−.017	−.003		
Female turnout, 1895	−.071	−.006		
Organization			.007	.071
Intercept	−2.653**		.651**	
Adjusted R^2	.38		.17	
N	353		289	

$^*p \leq .05$
$^{**}p \leq .01$

be organized. Immigrants were largely irrelevant to the location of branch committees; neither the town's share of foreign-born voters nor the relative concentration of specific ethnic categories was related to branch organization. Although rural towns voted more favorably on the 1895 Wellman bill, the MAOFESW plan did not target farming communities or towns in need of conversion to the antisuffrage point of view. Instead, these results show that branch committees were more likely to be placed in sympathetic towns, that is, those with higher rates of opposition voting in 1895. These community traits explain over a third of the variation in branch committee organization statewide.

The impressive growth of branch committees belies the behind-the-scenes difficulties involved in keeping them operating. Almost from the inception of MAOFESW, its leaders privately expressed concerns about the inactivity of local chapters, commenting about their poor attendance at annual meetings and deliberating the adoption of new policies requiring branch committees to meet at least once yearly and to file reports of their activities.[80] As early as 1903 the executive committee attempted to assign membership quotas to branch committee chairs. A 1906 in-house report described numerous branches in gentle euphemisms as "resting" or "very sleepy" and expressed disappointment at the futility of efforts to rouse interest in several chapters. By 1913, a revamped state organization committee reported its intention to prepare and distribute a paper on the "duties of branches." At any given time, numerous chapters were privately declared inactive, although they were still listed in official propaganda. On the eve of the 1915 state referendum campaign, the chair of the county committee, which was constituted in 1913 as part of a plan to mobilize antisuffragists by senatorial district, reported that twenty-eight branches had already been reorganized and another thirty-nine were currently being "worked on"; this indicates disarray in more than half of extant branch committees.[81]

The instability of local chapters can be traced partly to the hazards of a top-down organizational style, which left branch committees vulnerable to the motivation and political skills of their handpicked chairs; progress reports often linked declines in committee activity to chairs' travel plans or physical ailments, and the state headquarters typically tried to rejuvenate sagging chapters by replacing chairs. The Massachusetts Association leadership remained perplexed about how to incorporate input from local committees, which, they acknowledged, often felt excluded and "of little importance" to the organization. To build commitment, they experimented with chairman's luncheon meetings and more frequent updates from association headquarters, but even these tactics were designed more to impart directives than to receive feedback from below. Despite the image of genteel femininity, the women who headed the antisuffrage movement did not shrink from exercising their authority and seemed to prefer hierarchical organizational structures, extending even to such details as requiring executive approval for all local fund-raising entertainments.[82] Whether it was shipping literature and workers to mobilize protest in the western states or directing the operation of local committees, the management style at the top of the organization more closely resembled elite confidence than feminine retirement.

The weaknesses of antisuffrage organizing strategies are illustrated in table 5.7, which assesses the impact of branch committee location on the 1915 Massachusetts suffrage referendum.[83] As the second panel demonstrates, the organization of branch committees had no effect on male voter preference, although towns rejecting the 1895 referendum were slightly more likely to do the same in 1915. Other findings suggest an altered antisuffrage constituency from that of the previous referendum, with increased opposition among men in farming communities. While towns with larger stocks of German and French Canadian immigrants showed more negative votes in the 1915 referendum, communities with more foreign-born residents were now more likely to favor enfranchisement. Women's employment in both professional and blue-collar occupations reduced men's opposition voting, while men's employment continued to have negligible effects on male opinions. Collectively, these town attributes are relatively poor predictors of referendum preference, explaining only seventeen percent of the variance in town outcomes.

These data confirm that the Massachusetts Association placed branch committees in communities friendly to their cause—towns that had voted against the 1895 suffrage referendum in higher percentages—ignoring its own advice to infiltrate prosuffrage territories. It also paid less attention to both immigrant and farm populations, two constituencies that continued to influence the outcome of state referenda. The fact that community organizing strategies by MAOFESW had no independent effect on their victory in the 1915 referendum underscores the extreme centralization of antisuffrage campaign efforts.

If the selection of standing committee members and the organization of branch committees manifested elitism, the third strategy of antisuffrage mobilization, the direct recruitment of individual members, was considerably more ecumenical. At its first annual report in 1896, statewide membership in MAOFESW was listed at 1, 560 women; six years later, the association had grown to about 9,000 members. By 1906, reported membership was over 12,000 and at the start of 1915 it had more than doubled, to more than 28,000 women (see table 5.6). Over the course of the referendum campaign MAOFESW claimed to have added another 8,000 members to its rolls. In truth, the membership requirements for the Massachusetts Association were not stringent. Official membership figures included all women over twenty-one years of age who signed cards; no annual dues were required, and it appears that, barring written notice of resignation, a woman's one-time registration rendered her a MAOFESW member in perpetuity. Official membership tallies were cumulative counts, and it is likely that their rosters contained the names of deceased women. Although its final recruitment campaign ended with the 1915 election, its last reported count, in the spring of 1917, was about 40,000 women.[84]

The plan to build the organization was hatched by the association's education committee, which in 1896 charted a comprehensive campaign to recruit from a broad spectrum of groups that included women's clubs, college students, and factory workers. Women's clubs were deemed the "most promising field," compatible with existing networks of the antisuffrage leadership; in addition, the suffrage issue could be introduced benignly as a topic for group study. The executive committee prepared a list of women's clubs and sent letters offering to send speakers, but responses were "generally unfavorable," as most clubs either failed to respond or rejected the topic outright as unsuitable. The association continued to send antisuffrage speakers and pamphlets when requested, but ultimately devised a more subtle recruitment strategy through the pursuit of individual conversion instead of official club endorsement. Even in the waning days of the suffrage fight, when Massachusetts organizers could find only one new recruit in a particularly partisan blue-collar town, she was described propitiously as "a prominent DAR and Federation woman."[85]

In targeting students at elite women's colleges, antisuffragists were grooming a younger version of the same affluent constituency. The antisuffrage leadership had strong links to female educational institutions, extending back to Emma Willard, and they remained strongly opposed to coeducation for women. In addition to MAOFESW officer Agnes Irwin, dean of Radcliffe College, the president of Wellesley College was the sister-in-law of the Rhode Island Association president, and prominent New York antisuffragist Annie Nathan Meyer was a founder of Hunter College.[86] They began by sending speakers and soon progressed to mailing packets of literature to entire classes of Radcliffe, Wellesley, and Smith colleges, among others. The education committee tailored the selection of materials to the presumed modern ideas of college students, explicitly avoiding those that placed "such emphasis on woman's physical disabilities that it would immediately prejudice active and ambitious young women against the antisuffrage cause."[87] MAOFESW subsequently formed a college committee, for which alumnae contacted faculty and administrators, who often seemed more sympathetic to the remonstrant point of view than did their students. For a brief period after the 1915 referendum they experimented with a College Anti-Suffrage League, but more successful in both New York and Boston were junior leagues that recruited young society women for antisuffrage work.[88]

Opposition leaders recognized early the necessity of wage-earning women for the group's success. Instead of being invited to join the executive committee, however, they were recruited primarily for the education committee, which directed the production and distribution of antisuffrage propaganda. The MAOFESW officers, out of their element, struggled to identify influential employed women. They prepared special pamphlets on wages and the ballot for distribution at working girls' associations and periodically opened shops in mill towns with large concentrations of laboring women. Through connections with business owners, they also sent paid speakers to employees' meetings at downtown department stores as well as factories throughout eastern Massachusetts.[89] They reportedly found "much interest" at these talks, but encountered persistent problems recruiting wage earners for committee work. After fifteen years with few results to show for its efforts, the leadership formed a special subcommittee to locate working women and voted to hold evening meetings to accommodate their schedules. This strategy lasted only until the antisuffrage victory in the 1915 referendum, however, after which interest in working-class women waned and morning meetings resumed.[90]

Outreach to minority women, including immigrants and women of color, was similarly motivated by expediency and concentrated in the months preceding the 1915 election, partly because of ignorance and a paucity of contacts among the lower classes. The difficulty of crossing the chasm of social class was illustrated by an incident in which one woman got "a good many" of her fellow African Americans to sign antisuffrage cards and subsequently requested payment to oversee the "state organization of colored women." Accustomed to the volunteerism of women of a certain class, the executive committee was appalled that the organizer "seemed to expect to make money out of it," and resolved to have "nothing more to do" with her. They tended to adopt indirect recruitment strategies to reach immigrants, placing antisuffrage advertisements in foreign-language newspapers and translating leaflets into French, Italian, and Yiddish. They periodically targeted professional women such as nurses and public school teachers, although from the standpoint of the elite MAOFESW leadership these occupations were undifferentiated from the masses of working women. It was not until the end of 1917 that they sponsored a businesswoman's supper against suffrage, which ran a deficit.[91]

Recruitment was a top priority for antisuffrage associations, despite their class and ethnic biases. While reserving the highest positions in the organizational hierarchy for their own clan, they nonetheless recognized the need to reach broader segments of women. The following comments by the chair of the education and organization committee at the 1913 annual meeting of the Massachusetts Association show that she clearly appreciated the potential power of female mobilization:

> Public opinion, not the ballot, is the great force in the world to-day, and public opinion requires organization to make it effective. We want to strengthen our organization this year until we cover every town of any importance in the state.[92]

Their meeting records demonstrate the seriousness with which they pursued organizational growth. Every month the Massachusetts Association tallied the number of new signatures collected and routinely visited towns with lagging membership. They also took their responsibility personally; on several occasions MAOFESW assigned quotas for sponsoring new members, and the Maine Association experimented with a penalty fee of ten cents for each number short of the assessed goal of fifty recruits per woman.[93]

Antisuffrage recruitment strategies were aggressive and diverse, but they were not unaffected by the social class background of those in charge. Organizational records demonstrate that leaders had more extensive personal contacts with other elites than with the masses, and those networks facilitated entrée into certain groups and caused persistent problems in reaching others. They were most comfortable with clubwomen and society matrons; even elite women's colleges—those "hot-beds of suffrage," complained one leader in 1916—presented challenges. Contacts with wage earners often required paid intermediaries, and reports that factory audiences were not as "unfeeling" and "unintelligent" as anticipated reveal insurmountable biases of class and ethnicity. Meanwhile, agricultural communities were "scattered" and difficult to reach, even with the cooperation of local Grange associations. Employed women often had no spare time to give to antisuffrage work, and organizers might visit a farming town to find that "everyone is canning and will not even attend a meeting before October." Recruitment among their own class was not without difficulties, either; the summer vacation season emptied affluent communities for months at a time, and substantial prejudice prevailed that, as one would-be organizer of an old-line Massachusetts community observed, "it was neither dignified nor 'Peabodyfied' to mix in politics."[94]

The social backgrounds of individual recruits are further delineated by examination of surviving membership lists of the Maine Association Opposed to Suffrage for Women (MAOSW). Maine had been an early locus of remonstrance activity, extending back to 1889 when groups of Portland and Bangor women petitioned the state legislature against a municipal suffrage bill. The formation of the Maine Association in late 1913 was instigated with MAOFESW assistance, and its organizational structure, with branch committees and antisuffrage junior leagues, replicated in miniature that of its progenitor.[95] Its leadership, stocked with names celebrated as much for their own accomplishments as for those of their Puritan forebears, included the wives of politicians, jurists, and corporate executives; the president of the Augusta branch, the widow of a former governor and financier, was reportedly the highest woman taxpayer in the state.[96] MAOSW was not a large organization, claiming slightly fewer than 2,000 members in 1914, but an aggressive recruitment campaign for the 1917 referendum on woman suffrage managed to increase it size to over 3,500 registrants. Antisuffragists and the presence of a prohibition amendment on the ballot helped defeat that bill, but the state legislature subsequently enacted presidential suffrage for women in 1919.[97]

The analysis is based on a sample of MAOSW members residing in Portland, which was the center of antisuffrage organization in the state; over half of the signatures collected were from that city.[98] Portland was Maine's largest city in 1910, although it was relatively small, numbering about 58,000 residents. It was a regional center for shipping, manufacturing, and commerce, and its residents were more likely to be native-born than was true for Boston at the time, although almost half were first- or second-generation Americans. Of the 21 percent of the city's foreign-born population, one-third had emigrated from Canada, another 25 percent came from Ireland, and 11 percent were of Russian origin. Thus, Portland was a small city, but relatively diverse demographically.[99]

The Portland sample represents a majority of state antisuffrage members and was collected in a two-stage process.[100] Because of the difficulties in matching addresses on membership cards to census data, it is of necessity a selective sample.[101] The results, shown in table 5.8, nonetheless provide more systematic information than has previously been collected about the social backgrounds of antisuffrage activists below the leadership tier. A comparison of these findings with a 1917 state organizer's report permits some assessment of sample quality. The Maine Association permitted male members, and, as the first panel indicates, about five percent of the Portland sample was male, compared with the

Table 5.8. Description of antisuffrage organization membership, Portland, Maine, 1910

Sample			Women: Married	Women: Single
Sex		Occupation		
Female	95%	None	91%	50%
Male	5%	Blue-collar	3%	16%
		Sales, clerical	5%	25%
Employed	32%	White-collar	1%	9%
		Head's occupation		
Marital status		None	8%	32%
Single	43%	Blue-collar	17%	33%
Married	45%	Sales, clerical	11%	10%
Widowed	12%	White-collar	65%	25%
Household position		Household position		
Head	14%	Head	—	7%
Wife	38%	Wife	89%	—
Child	32%	Child	7%	66%
Other kin	10%	Other kin	4%	16%
Nonrelative	7%	Nonrelative	—	11%
Nativity		Nativity		
Born U.S.	89%	Born U.S.	88%	93%
Head U.S.	82%	Head U.S.	89%	75%
Father U.S.	74%	Father U.S.	82%	65%
Household composition		Household composition		
Male head	79%	Male head	98%	71%
Servants	33%	Servants	46%	18%
Antisuffragists	27%	Antisuffragists	17%	38%
Size	4.7	Size	4.9	4.9
Number of kin	3.8	Number of kin	3.9	4.3
Age		Age		
Member	41.2	Member	44.7	33.5
Head	54.8	Head	52.0	57.0
N	252		105	103

statewide average of fourteen percent male members. The sample's percentage of employed members was identical to that reported for the overall Maine membership.[102]

Our demographic sketch of the Portland sample finds that its members were about evenly split between married and single individuals, revealing that antisuffrage organizations recruited more widely than their homemaker image predicts. This diversity is illustrated in the breakdown of members according to their position in the household. Wives represented the most frequent membership category, but almost a third were resident offspring of the household head; members also included household heads, other relatives, and a small share of unrelated boarders and servants. Members were disproportionately native-born, even when compared with the overall population of Portland, and the heads of their households were only slightly less likely to be born in the United States. About one-quarter of antisuffrage members were second-generation Americans, a figure that matches closely the statistics for Portland as a whole. Antisuffrage members were fairly affluent, judging by the fact that servants resided in one-third of their households. Antisuffrage mobilization was also partly a family affair, since over a quarter of the members coresided with another MAOSW member. Average household and family size was smaller than average for the period and reflects the older ages of the antisuffrage membership.

The second panel of table 5.8 examines in more detail the two core groups of organized antisuffragists: married and single women.[103] Married women members were overwhelmingly homemakers; 91 percent had no paid employment. Their husbands were most likely to be employed in professional or managerial occupations, grouped here under the white-collar category; two-thirds of their husbands were engaged in white-collar employment, constituting a far higher percentage than that of Portland's male labor force.[104] Based on their husband's jobs, we estimate that slightly more than one-quarter of the married women were working class or lower middle class. Their relative affluence is also indicated by the fact that almost half of them had servants. The average age of about forty-five years for married female antisuffragists in 1910 suggests that for the most part they had completed their childbearing. Women's political activism, then as now, required leisure time, and the married women members sampled here were endowed with this resource both by class position and by life cycle stage.

Single women antisuffrage members present a somewhat different demographic profile. They were more likely than married members to be employed, but not at levels indicating widespread self-support. Half of them engaged in no paid employment at the time of the 1910 census, and only a few of those with jobs were in prestigious white-collar occupations.[105] But neither were they likely to be mill girls; half of the employed women were in sales or clerical jobs, which carried more prestige than factory labor. Their social class backgrounds were more diverse and lower status compared with those of the married women members, judging by the occupations of the household head. The greater share of retired or nonemployed heads of households among the single female members is explained by their family position; two-thirds of them resided with at least one parent, often a widowed mother. Less than twenty percent of these women lived on their own, and the remainder shared the households of other relatives. The lower social class backgrounds of unmarried antisuffragists compared with those of members is also indicated by the smaller percentage residing in households with servants.

Unmarried MAOSW members were more likely to be native-born as compared with married members, but they were also more likely to be second-generation Americans; about one-third of their parents were born outside of the United States. The households of single antisuffragists were also more likely to contain other members of the Maine Association, implying that family ties constituted an important mechanism for recruiting younger women, even below the elite leadership tier. Although younger than their married peers, their marital and labor force statuses were probably not transitory conditions. The membership profile suggests that antisuffrage organizations found allies not only among urban matrons, but also among native-born women from blue-collar backgrounds whose experiences with limited upward mobility may have attracted them to a movement extolling the virtues of true womanhood and the superiority of Anglo-Saxon culture.

Conclusion

Social class exerted both opportunities and constraints as the privileged antisuffrage leadership sought to expand beyond its inner circle and build effective political organizations. At a time when social restrictions limited female political access and influence, the Massachusetts Association used existing networks of kinship and social class to construct an organizational hierarchy of considerable size. The resulting committee structure reflected these interpersonal contacts, overrepresenting more affluent communities and largely encircling Boston. While antisuffrage leaders viewed the appointment of socially prominent women to committee posts as an advantage in the contest for public opinion, they also recognized early the need to recruit from the working classes. Class prejudice, inadequate networks, and occasionally high-handed tactics made this task difficult, however, and their efforts were repeatedly confounded. The records of the Maine Association demonstrate that antisuffragists had greater success attracting older, native-born, economically advantaged women. Portland remonstrants were married homemakers with professional husbands, but also upwardly mobile single women for whom elitist messages may have conferred symbolic prestige.

A direct connection between female antisuffrage mobilization and state referenda results is difficult to establish. In the 1895 Massachusetts referendum, women antisuffrage sympathizers were rural and working-class, at variance with the pattern of organizational growth in the state. Nor did the location of MAOFESW branch committees have a significant effect on town voting patterns in the 1915 referendum. Elsewhere, regional analyses of eleven suffrage referenda found that smaller, slower-growing, and poorer counties rejected suffrage at higher rates, belying claims of urban and immigrant opposition. Counties with more foreign-born and Catholic voters constituted pockets of resistance only where suffrage referenda passed, although German ethnicity was most consistently associated with negative voting. The weak and varying effects of most social background community attributes cast doubt on fixed cultural explanations for suffrage opposition, whether it be the Hofstadter thesis concerning elites' status discontent or suffragists' assertions of immigrant prejudice against women.

The antisuffrage constituency can be better understood within a broader political context. An antisuffrage vote tended to be an antireform vote, whether from immigrants fearful that women voters represented incipient nativism or misguided attempts to alter the urban spoils system, antiprohibitionists who resented state interference in personal lifestyle choices, or rural residents who viewed suffrage as a symbol of creeping social instability. At a period when proposed reforms were sometimes motivated by class and ethnic prejudices, the association between the woman suffrage and progressive movements may have inclined some groups nearer the bottom of the social hierarchy against the female ballot. It appears that this elite-led antisuffrage movement paradoxically found considerable popular support among less affluent voters, although we found no direct evidence linking movement organization and opposition balloting among the working classes. The antisuffrage propaganda campaign, at least in Massachusetts, extended far beyond the placement of local chapters, with posters and billboards on mass transit and at popular recreational sites using simple appeals to get out the vote. The antisuffrage cause also benefited from the efforts of other groups that opposed suffrage, such as ethnic heritage societies and corporate organizations whose involvement in the antiprohibition campaign helped the antisuffrage message reach the masses. It is not inconceivable that disparate constituencies bore different grievances against suffrage, and that less advantaged and rural voters rejected suffrage referenda in order to contain the prerogatives of the urban ruling classes while those in charge of the antisuffrage movement sought to check the power of the restive masses.

If suffrage opposition is best explained in political terms, the churning environment of early-twentieth-century partisan politics also accounts for changes in public opinion. Shifting dynamics of controversy and resolution on such matters as prohibition, third-party challenges, and the stance of urban political machines mediated community demographic characteristics to shape suffrage opinions. While even suffrage leader Alice Paul conceded that there was no association between women antisuffragists and liquor interests, the presence of prohibition on the ballot increased opposition turnout and contributed to many suffrage defeats.[106] Where upstart political parties challenged the political status quo, the resulting competition often pressured the two major parties to conciliatory positions on the suffrage issue. Urban political machines also responded pragmatically to the success of the reform movement by reversing their opposition to female enfranchisement. As constituencies changed with altered political circumstances, so too did the tactics of antisuffrage organizations.

6

From Parlors to Parades

If we fail to vote, we are moral shirkers.

—Women Voters' Anti-Suffrage Party

Antisuffragists' rhetoric convinced many voters, suffragists, politicians, and pundits that they were traditional homebound women who eschewed politics.[1] Public statements and literature articulated for public consumption their tactics as well as beliefs. Antisuffragists effectively distinguished themselves from their female opponents, whose behavior they denounced as a violation of gender norms, by recasting their own political activities in traditional terms. Their retiring image, largely undisturbed to the present day, is testimony to their political skills. But it also suggests a limitation of studies of the antisuffrage movement, which too often represent only this public side.

Like all social movements, antisuffragism had a backstage, where leaders planned various responses to the suffrage threat and devised skillful rationales to legitimate and obfuscate deviations from traditional gender arrangements. Using the organizational records of several state associations, this chapter reconstructs behind-the-scenes deliberations that challenge the passive stereotype of antifeminist political behavior. It also shows that women's opposition campaign strategies were not simply a reaction to the suffrage movement. They constituted a more complex response that involved competition with suffragists, organizational exigencies such as membership retention and leadership composition, and emergent political demands. While the ideology of true womanhood continued to shape the tactics of the antisuffrage movement until the end, it was only one factor among many and its influence waned over time.

Despite its conservative ideology and self-presentation, the antisuffrage movement was far from static. As election returns documented, the Progressive movement was a great boost to the suffrage campaign, and women remonstrants could not remain in their parlors and hope to achieve their goal of arresting the momentum of political reform. This chapter traces the reluctant adoption of tactical innovations that reduced stylistic differences between the two sides, identifying four distinct stages of the antisuffrage movement's career. Shifting fortunes characterized the long campaign, taking its toll on the opposition and finally forcing them into more overt political confrontation; conversely, the effectiveness of antisuffrage tactics at blocking state referenda convinced suffragists to pursue a new winning strategy through a federal amendment. We examine the antisuffrage campaign through its decline and ultimate defeat and follow the small cadre of remaining Woman Patriots who fought the suffragists' reform agenda in the decade following passage of the Nineteenth Amendment.

The Early Phase of Quiet Protest

The ideology of separate spheres influenced not only the rhetoric of the antisuffrage movement, but its organizational development as well. The first local antisuffrage committees avoided public political activities, relying instead on personal interviews with legislators and the use of proxy speakers before legislative hearings.[2] Their wealth, high social status, and personal contacts with influential male politicians enabled antisuffrage leaders to conduct a quiet campaign through paid intermediaries and preemptive actions that defeated suffrage bills before they proceeded to public electoral contests. The small Boston committee that met sporadically during the 1880s to remonstrate against suffrage proposals at the neighboring State House disavowed any interest in permanent organization, manifesting early what would become a routine practice of differentiating its group through invidious comparisons with suffrage proponents:

> You may perhaps ask—but why not some anti-suffrage organization also? . . . We cannot originate one. It requires more time and exclusive interest than we can give. Anti-suffrage is one of the great interests and responsibilities of our lives, but not the only one. To the suffragist it is the supreme thought, and babies may go unwashed, and husbands' dinners uncooked, if the interests of suffrage requires [*sic*] their time.[3]

Less than a decade later antisuffragists did organize formally, often over their own public protestations. The founder and longtime leader of the Illinois Association, for example, presented herself as "not a believer in the organization of women," but they typically justified new levels of mobilization as a necessary defense against heightened suffragist activism. The New York Association explained its founding as a response to a perceived "emergency" engendered when suffragists raised a $60,000 war chest to honor Susan B. Anthony. This fund, recalled socialite antisuffrage leader Mrs. Barclay Hazard, "immediately produced great activity in the suffrage ranks and compelled the opposition to more active measures."[4] For the next twenty-five years, antisuffrage organizations monitored the progress of their opponents, attending suffragists' meetings, subscribing to their journals, and reporting on suffrage association finances and mobilization efforts both at home and abroad. They continued to distance their activity from that of their adversaries by defining remonstrant behaviors in nonpolitical terms, referring to themselves repeatedly as a group of volunteers and amateurs distinct from the "list of salaried workers" found in suffrage organizations and underscoring their own demeanor of "dignified silence" in contrast to the noisy clamor of suffragists.[5]

This opposition tactic had several advantages. By downplaying the extent of their own political activism, antisuffragists hoped to avoid attracting notice to the awkward contradiction they represented—rejecting politics as no place for their sex but nonetheless engaging in that purported disreputable behavior to attain their goal. By placing their own activities above the fray of politics, antisuffragists also hoped to enhance their credibility as nonpartisan, disinterested citizens. They presented a group image consistent with prevailing notions of self-sacrificing womanhood, contrasted with their portrayal of suffragists as self-centered and silly women. One antisuffrage leader explained the gains made by suffrage organizers in rural Massachusetts this way:

> The principal women in a country village are flattered by being made officers and they hold their meetings, sing their suffrage songs, listen to a few burning words, drink the inevitable tea, and go home to hag and tease their men . . .[6]

Antisuffragists presented these divergent female images of the two groups of contestants not only because they genuinely subscribed to these beliefs, but also as a strategy to persuade like-minded women to join the antisuffrage cause. Association efforts to enroll new members acknowledged the reluctance of many women to undertake active work and reassured members that their names would be kept under "lock and key." Antisuffragists professed empathy with the aversion of conservative women to "political strife and to participation in public affairs," but represented women's mobilization against the vote as a pressing duty requiring "some sacrifices" "to aid actively in repelling the danger that threatens."[7]

Despite antisuffragists' attempts to distance themselves from suffragists, the mobilization of both groups derived from the earlier organization of women reformers that converted women's exclusion from electoral politics into a moral virtue. Both sides invoked traditional gender stereotypes, centered on the presumed attributes of the maternal role, to claim that women were particularly well suited to the moral uplift of the citizenry and to slowly carve out a unique female political culture.[8] Following the path of nineteenth-century moral reform groups, remonstrants began recruitment efforts in Massachusetts towns by visiting ministers and requesting meetings with their congregations. At public hearings they excused the poor showing of female protesters by citing maternal demands, reminding legislators repeatedly that "there are hundreds of women—mothers—who have no desire to vote."[9]

The antisuffrage movement evolved very much in step with the emerging female political culture represented by the proliferation of women's clubs. Club networks not only aided recruitment efforts but legitimated political work under the traditional guise of education. The young Massachusetts Association claimed that "our great desire is to promote study of the subject" and promised to give a "candid hearing" to proponents' views. For almost twenty years, the organization declined invitations from suffrage organizations to debate the question, although it frequently furnished materials to opposition debaters who were not its official representatives. One of its first organizational decisions was to create an education committee, which was charged with locating "able and effective speakers" and overseeing the preparation of papers to be read by emissaries. To protect the elite leadership, antisuffrage organizations relied mostly on paid speakers of both sexes to lecture, first at parlor meetings and later in public halls. It was not uncommon for the New York and Massachusetts associations, often acting jointly, to send speakers west to "educate" voters in campaign states. Despite its avowed public education function, in 1898 MAOFESW declared itself not yet ready to sponsor a lecture course in Boston, fearing it would raise controversial "industrial and economic questions in anti-suffrage work."[10]

The specialty of antisuffrage organizations was the production and distribution of literature. Written arguments gave the movement the requisite distance from public activism and reached women separated by domestic seclusion or class position; female authors could directly address the male electorate without violating gender norms. The new education committee devoted its meetings to discussions of pamphlet preparation—choosing topics such as temperance, the home, and the relation of suffrage to industrial life, recruiting authors, and handling delicate negotiations over manuscript revisions in order to insure that the contents of all materials conformed to the organization's image. They monitored the popularity of various titles and directed the updating of leaflets to reflect changed conditions or correct inaccuracies. By the turn of the century, the committee had bound a collection of antisuffrage writings and sent them to state and college libraries throughout the United States as well as to other opposition organizations; they would repeat this practice from time to time, donating antisuffrage periodicals and popular books to library reading rooms. The Massachusetts Association also distributed copies of its annual report and its official journal, the *Remonstrance;* as early as 1901, it reportedly mailed 8,000 pamphlets and over 7,500 copies of the *Remonstrance* to local branch committees, newspapers, and members of the legislature, filling requests from twenty-five states.[11]

Antisuffragists also appreciated early the value of free newspaper publicity. For this task, the Massachusetts Association created a one-person press committee, staffed by a paid organizer whose job was to write personal notes to newspaper editors, usually accompanied by requests for a hearing. Prominent members of the standing committee sometimes contacted directly editors of social acquaintance, and the organization was not above prodding neutral editors off the fence on the suffrage issue by inviting their wives to join that influential committee. They canvassed local newspapers to reserve regular space for antisuffrage news, but usually discarded the idea if acceptance were conditioned upon a similar column for the other side. They subscribed to a clipping service to monitor issue coverage and tried to influence editorial policy through personal notes of gratitude or disapproval. When the *Remonstrance* went quarterly in 1908 and sixty newspaper editorials commented on the change, the leadership congratulated itself for having achieved a new level of public awareness.[12]

In the first stage of organizational development, antisuffrage associations alternated between political boldness and retreat behind gender conventions, attributable in part to constraints on women of their social class. Financial resources enabled them to develop a political movement while maintaining a traditional feminine image for at least a decade into the twentieth century, but not without generating tensions that ultimately forced institutional innovation. After two decades of using hired speakers to represent the organization at legislative hearings, by 1902 the men's committee "unanimously and strongly insisted that an opposition made by women in person at the State House was far more effective than anything that could be said by any paid advocate." The women obliged reluctantly, and after their first outing male advisers objected to speakers' blunt references to the "ignorant vote," which, they opined, risked undermining the support of Irish legislators. The next year, when several branch committee chairwomen were recruited to appear at the hearings, male counselors judged them overly coached and warned against repeated use of "the same phraseology" by different speakers. Although a small cadre of spokeswomen did emerge, antisuffrage representatives at public functions by and large continued to be paid staff, while disapproving male advisers exhorted the women's organizations to show their colors, partly out of the perceived necessity to match "the aggressive methods of the suffragettes."[13]

Leadership wealth supplied the funds necessary to sustain the work of antisuffrage organizations, and even to fund their establishment in other states. It was not unusual for a woman officer to underwrite an office stenographer, speaking tour, or printing and postage to mail literature to a distant state legislature; one MAOFESW president paid an organizer's salary for a year, and another left a bequest that financed a large share of a state referendum campaign. In a financial crisis, they might appeal to male benefactors or simply take pledges from members of the executive committee. But affluence could also handicap their own financial interests; particularly in the early phase, antisuffrage organizations seemed almost revolted by the impropriety of general fund-raising appeals, preferring to follow the model of social and philanthropic organizations and target personal contacts for "sustaining memberships." Increasing demands for literature from active associations in other states finally proved so great that the resulting drain on the treasury spurred the transition to new levels of institutionalization. Following the lead of the New York Association, MAOFESW in 1910 reluctantly developed a schedule of fees for supplying antisuffrage materials. Although the charges were minimal and organizations seemed willing to ignore the policy if antisuffragists in a campaign state could not pay, literature sales were nonetheless a valued source of income; in just one month in 1912, for example, the Massachusetts Association sold twelve thousand pamphlets.[14]

Money also permitted women's antisuffrage associations to indulge their reticence about establishing a higher public profile, a requisite for building a mass organization. Parlor meetings were the norm for most associations even into the new century, and some leaders with palatial residences hosted large luncheon meetings with hundreds of invited guests in attendance. Local committees sent printed invitations to soften the group's political image and present a more genteel, social club appearance. Such tactics may have appealed to reluctant society matrons, but private parlor meetings and personal invitations were additional impediments to the goal of broadening the membership. As the Massachusetts Association grew, residential meetings became logistically impractical, and the organization acceded to the need for greater public visibility in 1907 by renting several rooms in a Boston office building where committee meetings could be held and by using downtown hotels for large gatherings. It took the crisis of a state referendum campaign, though, for more traditional associations such as Maine to approve meetings in public rooms. There were also limits to organizational flexibility. The bylaws of the New Jersey Association explicitly prohibited outdoor meetings, and despite suffrage headway in the state Grange, the Massachusetts leaders in 1904 decided against sending representatives to local fairs because it would place the women workers and the association in an "undignified position." Indicative of their class sentiments regarding conspicuous behavior is the fact that they privately denounced one suffrage fair exhibit for its "lurid pictures and rainbow literature."[15]

During these developmental years, antisuffrage organizations were successful in repelling suffragist demands without deviating too far from conventional gender norms. Not one state passed a suffrage amendment during the first decade of the twentieth century, and only six state antisuffrage organizations existed. Antisuffragists nonetheless felt a sense of unease, in part because proponents showed no signs of surrender; after a defeat in state legislative committees or popular referenda, suffragists would resolutely begin the campaign anew. If anything, the perceived danger increased as a new suffrage organizations proliferated, the activism of female wage earners escalated, and political parties began to endorse women's enfranchisement. Suffrage organizations also began to copy some of the campaign innovations of partisan politics to garner publicity for the cause. In both Massachusetts and New York, suffragists began holding open-air rallies in 1908; the next year, Massachusetts suffragists crisscrossed the state in automobiles, and one female activist even went up in a balloon to advertise the movement.[16]

New York City was the epicenter of much fresh suffrage agitation, and the New York State Association Opposed to Woman Suffrage was the first to express dissatisfaction with the remonstrants' style of activism, perhaps not coincidentally just a few months after Harriot Stanton Blatch began to organize new groups of women for suffrage there early in 1907.[17] The leaders of the New York Association had always been relatively more adventurous than those in other states, as is illustrated by the fact that as early as 1896 one Albany society matron addressed both the Democratic and Republican national conventions and two years later toured the western campaign states as the lone eastern antisuffrage organizer. Complaining that antisuffrage discussion to date had been "on too low and trivial a plane," dissatisfied New York antisuffragists began forming competing organizations, including the League for the Civic Education of Women and the Guidon Study Club.[18] In 1907 New York antis resolved "to take a more open stand as an organization and planned an increase in activity," and incorporated several months later as a step toward institution building. The next year the Albany branch began publishing a quarterly periodical, the *Anti-Suffragist*, and by 1909 New York City leaders broke with convention by engaging proponents in public debates.[19]

Prodded by letters from the New York Association, the Massachusetts leadership concurred that "antisuffrage work is not sufficiently aggressive and enterprising," but its response lacked inspiration; MAOFESW rented office space and voted to publish the *Remonstrance* more frequently and to send two issues per year free to each member. At the instigation of New York, existing state associations discussed plans for a national antisuffrage federation modeled after the General Federation of Women's Clubs, but none seemed willing to devote the time to initiating its formation.[20]

National Coalition and Tactical Innovation

It took defeat to push antisuffrage mobilization to the next stage. Pressure mounted in the spring of 1910 when suffragists presented a petition to the U.S. Congress, signed by over four hundred thousand women, demanding a federal Constitutional amendment. Several months later came the enfranchisement of women in Washington State after a fourteen-year suffrage hiatus nationally, followed the next year by passage of a suffrage referendum in the important state of California.[21] The expanding scope of the suffrage issue pressured opposition organizations toward coalition.

Meeting at the Park Avenue residence of New York Association leader Josephine Jewell Dodge, representatives from five eastern state associations organized the National Association Opposed to Woman Suffrage (NAOWS) in November 1911, just weeks after the California election. The new federation was governed by a board consisting of delegates from each state association, with Mrs. Dodge, nationally known leader of the day nursery movement, as its first president. Such a union, assured the organizers, was a more "efficient" and "modern" method of fighting suffrage, and they promised to avoid interference with the "individual enterprise" of the states. Its first press release announced the slogan of the new organization, "down with the Yellow Peril, Woman's Votes"; the phrase simultaneously threw a barb at recalcitrant California, expressed antiforeign and racist sentiments, and tarred the suffrage movement, whose official color was yellow. Greater numerical strength seemed to embolden antisuffragists to escalate the rhetorical battle, as is illustrated by Mrs. Dodge's initial statement of NAOWS goals invoking themes of disease, war, and patriotism:

> It will follow the yellow flag and endeavor to stamp out the pestilence. Where the contagion is rampant the association will endeavor to check it. Where the malady is only threatened we will inoculate against it.[22]

The national antisuffrage coalition based in New York fostered tactical innovation. Within six months of its founding, NAOWS began publication of a monthly periodical, the *Woman's Protest,* which planned to consolidate all state antisuffrage journals and present a unified front. The *Woman's Protest* published detailed reports of the activities of the various state associations, shared new methods of remonstrance, and, perhaps most important, grounded them in traditional gender norms for easier consumption. The minutes of its monthly board meetings, where state reports were read, political strategies analyzed, and members motivated, were distributed and discussed in state executive committees. Annual NAOWS conventions allowed the development of stronger interpersonal networks among antisuffragists across the country and opportunities for the spread of information.[23]

The national coordination of antisuffrage activities came just in time, as suffragist pressures on state legislatures began to bear fruit and suffragists proceeded to the next step of the amendment process, voter approval. The elections of 1912 saw suffrage referenda on the ballot in six states and defeated in half of them, all important midwestern states. NAOWS played a significant role in turning back suffrage in the 1913 Michigan referendum. Over the next year seven states put woman suffrage on the ballot, but it passed only in the two sparsely-populated western states of Nevada and Montana. The National Association sent literature, organizers, and speakers to the campaign states and often initiated the founding of local antisuffrage societies. The large eastern associations donated staff for speaking tours, and Mrs. Dodge herself visited some of the states. Massachusetts helped by mailing antisuffrage literature to "hundreds of bankers" for the important Ohio referendum, and its branch committees raised money to help defray campaign expenses in several locales.[24]

Above all, the national coalition brought the antisuffrage movement to a new level of political visibility. The storefront windows of its Fifth Avenue publicity room displayed antisuffrage cartoons, posters, and favorable newspaper clippings, while literature and badges were sold inside; within months, NAOWS opened a downtown office on Wall Street targeted at businessmen.[25] With a national spokesperson in Mrs. Dodge, the movement publicly took on the suffrage leadership. After a New York City suffrage parade in 1913, Mrs. Dodge criticized the woman suffrage movement as a socially dangerous "sex disturbance" and censured parade participants for dressing "suggestively"; a month later, NAOWS announced a blacklist of suffrage leader Dr. Anna Howard Shaw for her "wild statements" and "insulting language which no woman should endure." In subsequent press releases, the National Association condemned its suffragist adversaries for "distressing ignorance of political economy," showing "contempt for the very government of the country," and making the "pursuit of vice . . . one of their principal industries." All these statements were duly quoted in the sympathetic *New York Times,* whose editorial policy consistently denounced the fad of "suffragiana." This newspaper also helped legitimize NAOWS by soliciting its reactions to suffrage news; Mrs. Dodge obliged and made headlines by charging suffragists with selfishness, political blackmail, and using the "tactics of a pole-cat."[26] The *Times* granted the movement more free publicity by publishing letters to the editor from prominent antisuffragists who, freed from the constraints of organizational representation, leveled sharply worded allegations against their suffrage foes.[27]

The combination of increased competition, improved antisuffrage networks, and an aggressive national federation spurred state associations to new levels of public activism. These changes came just in time for a severe test: the 1915 referenda drive in four highly populated eastern states with active, but in some cases tradition-bound, antisuffrage associations. NAOWS coordinated the regional campaign in a behind-the-scenes effort to combine resources and identify the most effective opposition techniques. The evolution of the Massachusetts Association during the period is illustrative. In 1912, MAOFESW approved the purchase of ads in three urban newspapers, which progressed over the next three years to streetcar ads, billboards in Harvard Square and Fenway Park, and even a controversial illuminated sign in suburban Brookline's town square. They added pink antisuffrage pencils, buttons, stamps, calendars, matchboxes, and slide shows in moving-picture theaters to counter suffrage films, but prudently drew the line at imprinting sanitary toothpicks with antisuffrage slogans for the 1915 campaign. They established a special committee to develop a plan for uniform window decorations of rented storefronts throughout the state, giving detailed instructions to the branches to garnish them "more attractively" as paeans to feminine domesticity, replete with lattice and roses.[28] They opened an official Boston headquarters and numerous shops throughout the state which, consistent with their maternal image, served tea and sold homemade preserves in addition to antisuffrage literature, of which they distributed over 160 thousand pieces during 1914. The stores also sold pink roses, the new national emblem of the opposition—changed from the red American Beauty after the IWW adopted the red rose—at ten cents apiece.[29]

Advertisements and product merchandising, however creative, did not automatically alter women's behavior, and the transition to an expanded public role was more difficult for Massachusetts antisuffragists. MAOFESW officers in 1913 rejected a plan offered by male advisers to build a mass organization, partly because it required aggressive tactics that the genteel leadership found distasteful. They did concede, with some dissent, to provide photos of the leadership to newspaper reporters in order to generate greater public interest in the movement. The organization also staged publicity tours of the commonwealth and, following the lead of Pennsylvania, held a large regional convention in the western Massachusetts city of Springfield. They finally sent representatives to local fairs beginning in 1913, but retained the ban on outdoor speaking. Fairs became an important element of the 1915 opposition campaign, with one Massachusetts leader reporting triumphantly that a local fair was "a blaze of pink anti-suffrage fans." At fairs they sometimes staffed rest tents for weary mothers and children, at which they distributed literature and collected signatures, cleverly preserving feminine propriety by using "silent speeches" mounted on rollers.[30]

Traditional taboos began to fall in the face of campaign exigencies. Antis reluctantly sent staff to debate suffragists in 1914, because, they explained, it was "the only opportunity to get our side presented" to the local Grange. Their few mass meetings followed a similar policy, although only men spoke outdoors before a largely male audience, and paid chaperones accompanied women speakers. They finally sponsored that Boston lecture course that was deemed so inappropriate two decades earlier. Parade marching was still prohibited, however; in Massachusetts and elsewhere, they protested the "sensationalism" of suffrage parades by countering with a "Rose Day" on the same date in which hired boys sold antisuffrage roses along the parade route, bedecking their constituency in floral protest. Faced with huge campaign expenses, they conceded the need for fund-raising efforts, but usually confined them to their own class. They sponsored theatrical entertainments, "fashion fetes," lawn and bridge parties, and tea dances, which, mindful of modesty, prohibited "all of the new dances." The fund-raising events of the New York Association, ever bolder than its Massachusetts counterpart, included an afternoon children's program and evening "tableaux" in which women performers portrayed famous suffragists with sardonic humor. New York antis showed themselves capable of aggressive political action in the fever of the campaign, such as when two groups of contending Long Island activists engaged in escalating acts of vandalism that made the newspapers.[31]

Antisuffrage participation in electoral politics also evolved over time. From writing and personally interviewing elected officials about proposed suffrage legislation in the nineteenth century, their levels of political engagement escalated during the twentieth. In 1901, Massachusetts antisuffragists worked behind the scenes with the statehouse leadership to compile a list of sympathetic legislators for possible appointment to woman suffrage committees. Almost a decade before the organization of NAOWS, six state antisuffrage associations jointly prepared a mass mailing to eight thousand congressional candidates nationwide, emphasizing the extent of constituents' opposition to woman suffrage. They invited prominent politicians to address their meetings and scrutinized the statements of incumbent presidents for evidence of sympathetic dispositions. When Woodrow Wilson appeared to be leaning toward suffrage in the crucial summer of 1915, they wrote urging him "not to express his views." At national party conventions, they lobbied delegates to block committee hearings on the suffrage issue. As their political experience grew and the battle intensified, antisuffragists became noticeably less deferential toward politicians. When the newly elected New York governor in 1914 revealed himself to be a suffrage supporter, an antisuffrage leader publicly requested that he stand by his party, which had not endorsed woman suffrage; that same year, prosuffrage Boston mayor James Curley refused an invitation to speak at an antisuffrage event, whereupon the Massachusetts Association archly revised its assumption that "he was mayor of all the city."[32]

More explicit political strategies also came to infuse organizational decisions over time, partly in response to increasing suffrage activism. The Massachusetts Association leadership by 1904 had devised a plan to recruit standing committee members so as to cover every legislative district; they then sent letters to legislative candidates asking them to reserve their opinions on suffrage until they had studied the issue carefully, enclosing the standing committee list of influential antisuffragists to guide their deliberations. By 1913, both New York City and Boston remonstrants had made attempts to organize their work by political districts and conducted household canvasses in at least some communities. They ambivalently sought the support of local political bosses, as fearful of revealing the extent of their political activities as of associating with distasteful corrupt politicians.[33]

There were limits to women antisuffragists' participation in politics during this intermediate stage. They could endorse local school board candidates, taking care to stress that such concerns were well within the traditional female domains of children's welfare and education. But as suffragists entered electoral politics and targeted for defeat incumbents with antisuffrage voting records, remonstrants confronted a seemingly irresolvable conundrum. The Massachusetts Association received letters beginning in 1913 from candidates facing suffragist "persecution," requesting official endorsements or even a "monster petition" from the women antis on whose behalf they now risked political extinction. Male advisers pressed the MAOFESW executive committee to act, because the suffragists were backing the Democrats and "now the Republicans want to know what we are going to do for them." The women leaders were unmoved, arguing that is was "impossible for us to go into politics in that way." They agreed to inform their membership of the election contest and to permit local branch committees to take independent action, "if they will." The furthest they would go in the name of the association was to write politicians official letters of appreciation and, if they lost the election, send consoling notes.[34] Antis' perceived constraints on extending political support to their allies in state legislatures help explain how suffrage bills finally began to pass state legislatures and come before the electorate.[35]

Despite a strong antisuffrage campaign effort in 1915, women remonstrants continued to deny vehemently that they were engaged in political work. This was the joint result of strategic decision making and a collective inability to concede that they had drifted from their stated values. In both Massachusetts and Pennsylvania, the state antisuffrage associations granted men political stewardship of the antisuffrage campaign. When the National Association, active for over three years, announced that it would coordinate the four eastern campaigns of 1915, its president expressed publicly "deep regret" that the actions of suffragists made "united work in opposition seem desirable." Along with such allusions to its retiring feminine nature, however, the organization simultaneously drew the first blood of the campaign by linking feminism with socialism, Mormonism, and other "sinister influences." Speaking at its Boston offices shortly before the election, the president of the Massachusetts Association rejected assertions that it was a political headquarters, reiterating old claims of amateur status by contrasting its quiet setting with those of large and well-funded suffrage organizations. The tactic of using professional speakers to protect their ladylike image paid off for antis in the New Jersey campaign, when suffragists begged off debates claiming it unfairly disadvantaged their own volunteers. Even the more progressive New York City antisuffrage wing refused to send women poll watchers on the day of the referendum, calling it unseemly. New York antisuffragists may have led the movement in debating and campaigning outdoors at local fairs, but they were careful not to stray too far from tradition; during the campaign, they spoke of decorating one antisuffrage fair tent like a house—with curtains, window boxes, and even a piano—all under a large sign reading, "Home Rule versus Political Activity."[36]

As these women's organizations waged an increasingly aggressive campaign against suffrage, they paradoxically shielded their actions with tokens of traditionalism. The sacred myth of motherhood incited men's chivalric inclinations and provided a genteel cover for women's political work. Cognizant that its position as an opposition movement had truculent connotations that might undermine its feminine image, NAOWS in 1913 announced a subtitle for the association, "the Conservationists," with a "mission" to preserve the sanctity of the home from the strife that elsewhere plagued modern society. Two years later it adopted the slogan "Representatives of Heaven, Home, and Mother." embracing an epithet leveled by archrival Dr. Anna Howard Shaw. Pressured by the state organizer, MAOFESW changed its name in the midst of the 1915 campaign to the Women's Anti-Suffrage Association of Massachusetts, although the new title never caught on. The divergent labeling tactics of the two sides ironically served the same purpose. Woman suffrage organizations renamed themselves "equal suffrage" societies in order to appear more altruistic and consonant with democratic ideals, and preferred the less politicized term "franchise" in the more conservative southern states. While women proponents felt compelled to downplay gender in order to broaden their appeal, antisuffragists invoked such labels intentionally to garner public sympathy and stake their claim to be serving traditional femininity and, perhaps more expediently, masculinity.[37]

The four decisive victories of 1915 were the high point of the antisuffrage movement. They also altered permanently the political behaviors of its conservative eastern leadership, who would never again retreat to parlor meetings. At the height of the Massachusetts campaign, the state antisuffrage offices distributed over forty thousand pieces of literature a month and organized dozens of speeches. Its executive committee met almost weekly, and one officer alone claimed to have prepared articles for over thirty magazines and newspapers in addition to supplying weekly antisuffrage columns to two local publications.[38] In a turnabout from their previous position, Massachusetts antisuffrage leaders shortly after the 1915 election lamented that their offices were not in a "more conspicuous" place and decided to hang a banner from their windows in order to "attract the notice of the public."[39]

Undermining the euphoria of these victories, however, was the suffrage fight for a federal amendment. Paradoxically, it was the success of the antisuffrage movement in blocking women's enfranchisement on a state-by-state basis that prompted proponents to redirect energies toward a federal amendment. As the site of the contest shifted to Washington, antisuffragists found themselves drawn into the more demanding arena of national politics.

Shifting Fortunes and Organizational Strain

In a burst of confidence immediately following the four victories of 1915, the eastern antisuffrage establishment at first planned to repeal suffrage where the trouble had started, in the key western states of California and Colorado. But the actions of suffragists elsewhere put those plans aside, never to be revisited. Suffrage referenda were scheduled for three states in 1916: Iowa in June, followed by South Dakota and West Virginia in November. NAOWS predicted that the Iowa contest, in particular, would be "bitterly fought," and solicited much-needed funds for campaign literature, advertisements, organizers, and speakers. The Massachusetts Association assembled its most important committees early in the new year and warned its branches of the dangers of complacency. All antisuffragists constitute a "link in the national chain," they counseled, and our "hands cannot be folded," "or else our own work would be wasted." Some branch committees reported "difficulty keeping things together" and grew moribund, but others drew momentum from the recent campaign, sponsoring card parties, dramatic performances ("When Knighthood Was in Flower" was particularly successful), and cookbook sales that by May had raised almost four thousand dollars for the 1916 referenda states. The Massachusetts Association ordered a hundred thousand copies of its campaign book for Iowa, while the Cambridge branch sent its *Anti-Suffrage Notes* to every Harvard graduate in that state, and voters in South Dakota and West Virginia received *The Case against Woman Suffrage.*[40] Their efforts paid off, as suffrage was repelled in all three states, making the scorecard between 1910 and 1916 an impressive nineteen defeats out of twenty-six referenda. Suffragists' adoption of more aggressive campaign tactics proved to be a difficult but useful apprenticeship for "disillusioned" antisuffrage organizers, who found that their paths along the 1916 campaign trail were hardly "strewn with roses."[41]

The experiences of recent campaigns also taught antisuffragists that even nonvoting women now held sufficient stocks of political capital to influence the suffrage stance of male legislators. Although mainstream suffrage organizations publicly disapproved of the Congressional Union's policy of working against Democratic Party candidates across the board, suffragists had shown themselves more willing than the opposition to engage openly in politics, organizing entire states by election district and targeting individual antisuffrage legislators for reelection defeat. Carrie Chapman Catt, head of New York's Woman Suffrage Party, was a major innovator in the transformation of suffrage politics.[42] To counter this suffrage strategy, the antisuffrage movement had to prevent more women from being added to the electorate; this meant mobilizing the full force of its national constituency wherever suffrage threatened. NAOWS coordinated efforts to fight the suffrage advance throughout the United States, including the southern states, where legislatures were giving the question increasing consideration. The association targeted locations needing "special work" and consolidated funds and speakers to aid them. Mrs. Dodge and an expanding staff of women organizers traveled regularly to speak to legislatures considering suffrage bills, while male emissaries of the Men's National Anti-Suffrage Association (but often on the payroll of MAOFESW) supervised distant state referenda campaigns. NAOWS raised money to sustain the work by reminding antisuffragists of their personal stake in the battle—regardless of location, they cautioned, every additional state in the suffrage column moved the United States one step closer to national enfranchisement.[43]

Intensified activity for a federal woman suffrage amendment substantiated the concerns articulated by antisuffragists. Mindful of their new female constituency, representatives from two western suffrage states in 1913 introduced to both houses of Congress simultaneously a formal resolution calling for a Constitutional amendment enfranchising women. Groups of suffragists jumped at the political opportunity; instead of merely collecting petitions, they now delivered them personally in a controversial but widely publicized parade to the U.S. Capitol, in which five thousand women reportedly marched before half a million spectators.[44] Antisuffragists had been writing letters of protest to elected officials for years, but the existence of a national coalition enabled better monitoring of suffrage activities in Washington, and Mrs. Dodge was alarmed by what she observed. She opened an office in the nation's capital, sent state associations copies of the *Congressional Record*, and, just six months after the suffrage march on Congress, delivered "several hundred strong and beautifully gowned" antisuffrage women to lobby the Capitol, descending by the trainload to counter the showy suffrage spectacle.[45]

Congressional hearings were held again in 1914, and suffrage made progress in the U.S. Senate, reaching a floor vote for the first time since 1887 and making newspaper headlines by achieving a bare majority of support, although the result was far from the required two-thirds majority. The House vote the next year was more lopsided against proponents, but despite Mrs. Dodge's wishful prediction that the suffrage "wave of hysteria . . . will be on the wane," quiet canvasses conducted during 1915 showed vote gains for a federal amendment in both houses of Congress and a quickening pace of action on the suffrage question. At the end of 1915, barely a month after the four decisive state referenda defeats, congressional hearings on suffrage were scheduled again, with three separate woman suffrage amendments slated to be introduced into the House of Representatives. Both NAWSA and NAOWS, departing from their New York City base of operations, held meetings in the nation's capital that were timed to coincide with the hearings, and Carrie Chapman Catt regained the NAWSA presidency, a change calculated to revitalize the national movement.[46]

The field of antisuffrage activity was also expanded by the war in Europe. As early as 1914, NAOWS used the European conflict to try to effect a truce with suffragists that amounted to a demobilization of both movements for the war's duration. Although its offer was rejected, the National Association exploited the overture by questioning the patriotism of suffragists and repeatedly blaming them for forcing the antis to carry on an active fight. Vying with NAWSA, which also contributed to the war effort but made women's rights its top priority, Mrs. Dodge announced that she was placing the "entire machinery" of the national and all state associations into the service of the American Red Cross. Antisuffrage organizations took up war relief work, wrapping bandages, making clothes, and raising money for emergency medical services and the support of European orphans. The Massachusetts Association, which had earlier been a strong supporter of U.S. conflicts with Mexico and Spain, and its auxiliary Public Interests League were leaders in the war relief effort, one year raising ten thousand dollars for Polish aid and shipping over one hundred thousand garments to Europe.[47]

Early in 1916 NAOWS went beyond the traditional realm of philanthropy to release a resolution endorsing preparedness, although Mrs. Dodge stopped short of committing association resources to it. Preparing the nation to enter the war seemed to be a political boundary that antisuffrage leaders were hesitant to cross formally, although they did speak at a convention of the conservative National Security League as members of the woman's section of the Movement for National Preparedness, along with representatives of women's patriotic-hereditary societies such as Daughters of the American Revolution and United Daughters of the Confederacy. The NAOWS preparedness resolution, couched in the traditional legitimation that women contribute to military service by teaching their sons respect for authority, was mailed to all state associations along with a letter from Mrs. Dodge encouraging their participation "*as individuals*" in the National Security League. The *Woman's Protest* featured numerous articles praising the work of these groups, and antisuffrage organizations periodically aided soldiers and sailors before the U.S. entered the war.[48]

The NAOWS compilation of expanded activities was expensive to maintain. Headquarters, city storefronts, literature, and preemptive interventions in distant states required paid staff. Support for the war effort, Washington lobbying, and multiple tiers of antisuffrage organizational activity increased the financial demands on activists. As a federation of state associations, the National Association did not have separate membership dues. NAOWS informed the states within a year of its formation that bankruptcy was imminent, and some of the wealthy board members graciously took turns sponsoring the organization for a month at a time. The costly 1915 campaigns, which NAOWS correctly viewed as a watershed event, drained its treasury down to fifteen cents, and after those elections it resolved to secure a more stable financial base.[49]

The only solution was to tithe the state associations. This was usually accomplished by a process of negotiation between the NAOWS leadership and various state executive committees to set a specific dollar amount, which state associations would subsequently pass on to their branch committees as a fund-raising goal; in addition, the national office regularly besieged the states requesting additional money to cover some financial emergency.[50] Increased fiscal demands incited the states to further tactical innovation, chipping away at traditional feminine reserve. To raise money for NAOWS, the Maine Association took a booth at a local Shakespeare revel, while Massachusetts experimented with a traveling food sale from the backs of automobiles and a market day in which remonstrants peddled produce, flowers, baked goods, and antisuffrage postal cards. In conjunction with more conventional personal appeals, their efforts yielded impressive results; during 1916, the Massachusetts Association donated more than six thousand dollars to NAOWS.[51]

Heightened financial demands exacerbated organizational tensions between the national and state associations. Maine antisuffragists were discomforted by NAOWS "offers" to sell them literature and speaker services at steep prices, while they generously shared their own limited resources with the national organization. Another concern was the risk of exhausting the local donor pool. Although the Massachusetts Association instigated the formation of a men's national league and ran it through their male campaign organizer, they nonetheless balked when he detailed plans to fund it through their branch committees. MAOFESW directed periodic "dollar drives" at members, but more commonly left fund-raising to local branch committees, which found it difficult to exhort local constituencies time and again to sacrifice for yet another emergency. The Massachusetts Association at one point in 1916 reported only ten dollars in its own treasury, which it attributed to heavy expenses helping NAOWS. When shortly thereafter the National Association again claimed bankruptcy, the president of MAOFESW reacted with pique, telling her executive committee that the National's debts were a consequence of "its inefficient and loose organization," and advocating changes in "its present lamentable condition." NAOWS reorganized just two months later, creating a tighter management structure and reducing its debt.[52] This action did not completely reassure the Massachusetts organization, which in the fall of 1916 passed resolutions for a new national president and even identified a viable candidate because of "the necessity of having our strongest woman at the head of the National Association." It lobbied within the region but lost when the NAOWS board of directors overwhelmingly supported Mrs. Dodge.[53]

The dissension over the NAOWS presidency revealed another source of strain with the state associations: organizational autonomy. The Massachusetts Association often exhibited proprietorship of the national movement traceable to its heavy share of financial support for NAOWS and its early domination of the antisuffrage cause. Although MAOFESW had interjected itself into the internal politics of other states for at least twenty-five years, it resisted interference in its own affairs. It passed a resolution rejecting NAOWS plans to tour the commonwealth during the 1915 referendum year, assuring the national board that "the campaign in Massachusetts is well organized" and calling outside intervention "unwise," "in view of the strong sentiment in favor of home rule in the state." This did not stop the Massachusetts Association from monitoring and second-guessing the decisions of NAOWS, a situation aggravated by differences in organizational style between the New York and New England antisuffrage contingents. The New York women who dominated NAOWS favored a limited role for men; one of their male staff recalled being instructed to "try to discourage the men from holding meetings and making speeches. They always do us more harm than good." But Massachusetts antisuffragists pressed for greater male participation, instigating the idea of a men's national committee that operated from its own headquarters.[54] Mrs. Dodge also displeased the Massachusetts leadership with her announcement that the agenda of the first NAOWS convention "will NOT be devoted to anti-suffrage propaganda. The speakers are requested to bring out constructive and practical ideals of democracy, citizenship, patriotism, and preparedness, with special regard to the aspirations and achievements of women." Two MAOFESW committees passed resolutions asking Mrs. Dodge to make suffrage opposition the convention's "chief subject" at the 1916 event held in Washington, and her apparent refusal probably fueled efforts for her ouster.[55]

The presidential elections of 1916 were another key event in the political development of the antisuffrage movement, lent added significance by the looming federal amendment. Despite valiant antisuffrage lobbying efforts, both party platforms included woman suffrage, but each stopped short of supporting a federal amendment. The two major parties were possibly influenced by the formation of the National Woman's Party immediately preceding both conventions, an action of the Congressional Union intended to unite women voters from the twelve states with presidential suffrage behind the federal amendment drive. The election season was fraught with irony, as the National Woman's Party voted to oppose Woodrow Wilson's candidacy and in response NAOWS vowed to aid all candidates blacklisted by suffragists, albeit in its typical "quiet way." Mrs. Dodge invited Wilson to speak before NAOWS; he declined, addressing instead a NAWSA convention, which nonetheless voted to maintain political neutrality, citing traditional female nonpartisanship. Both anti and suffrage leaders helped Republican presidential candidate Charles Evans Hughes, who endorsed a federal suffrage amendment. Elizabeth Lowell Putnam, head of the women's auxiliary of the Hughes Alliance, also chaired the Massachusetts Association's education and organization committee, and she offered her resignation rather than embarrass the cause. (It was refused.) Nor was Putnam unique among antisuffragists in proclaiming women's indifference while personally taking advantage of new opportunities to participate in electoral politics. The head of a Massachusetts branch committee reported with consternation that she had inspected the list of women registered to vote on the local school question and found "twenty-five anti-suffrage names."[56]

The escalation of women's political activism during 1916 pressured antisuffrage organizations to consider further innovations in order to stay abreast of the competition. The Ohio Association funded a canvass and issued a press release of its findings that the state's women opposed enfranchisement by a majority of ten to one. During the presidential campaign flurry, the Massachusetts Association voted to appoint a chair for each congressional district, and the Boston committee announced that it was reorganizing by wards. (Neither change was realized.) Branch committees began to conduct evening open-air meetings to accommodate working women. The private records of the Massachusetts Association reveal that such innovations were driven by desperation, the bravado of their public rhetoric notwithstanding. Taking stock early in 1917, MAOFESW headquarters reported difficulties keeping branches in operation, because "active workers feel we have a lost cause," and they could not find a head for the important Boston branch. In addition to these internal troubles, they counted sixteen states where suffrage referenda were in the legislative pipeline, requiring expenditures of time and money. These were the fruits of Mrs. Catt's "Winning Plan," designed to accumulate state victories in preparation for a federal amendment drive. Three states would eventually hold elections on suffrage that fall, including neighboring New York and Maine. By that summer, a number of longtime Massachusetts antisuffrage leaders began to resign their leadership posts, ostensibly discouraged by the relentless toil but possibly also to gain greater latitude in their political activity. Among the first was Elizabeth Lowell Putnam, former Hughes campaign leader.[57]

Antisuffragists' feelings of impending doom were not dispelled by news from Washington reporting progress toward a federal amendment. NAOWS did its best to counter the political momentum behind suffrage, evidenced by one news report that seventy of seventy-three candidates in the recent New York congressional elections were prosuffrage. J. S. Eichelberger, NAOWS publicity representative, prepared literature purporting to demonstrate that women are "more neglectful" voters than men and in any event constitute a "duplicate vote"; he urged its use by the state associations to counteract "the influence of the woman vote" on male legislators, and the *New York Times* obliged with an abridged version of his analysis. NAOWS regularly requested petitions and telegrams for Congress and sent roses and literature to Washington on inauguration day while the Congressional Union demonstrated against President Wilson. When the United States finally entered the war, NAOWS patriotic rhetoric escalated, but its call for a temporary halt to suffrage agitation as a gesture of national loyalty was again rebuffed.[58]

The destabilizing impact of the federal amendment threat was clear by July 1917, when NAOWS moved its headquarters to Washington and replaced its founding president with Alice Hay Wadsworth, head of the local antisuffrage association and wife of the U. S. senator from New York. The *Woman's Protest* instituted a new monthly column, "Washington News and Notes," that monitored congressional action on the suffrage question. Despite a summer of lobbying and the recruitment of Mrs. Robert Lansing, wife of the secretary of state, as NAOWS secretary, the U. S. House in September created a committee on woman suffrage to study the question. Shortly thereafter, pressured by the Massachusetts leadership, NAOWS announced formation of an all-male "advisory council," composed of "distinguished and experienced men," many of them nationally prominent political figures, including a number of U.S. senators.[59]

If antisuffragists found events in Washington dispiriting, the elections of 1917 provided tangible evidence that the tide was turning against them. Convincing referenda defeats in Ohio and Maine were small consolation compared with the passage of suffrage by voters in New York, brain center of the national antisuffrage movement.[60] As political parties scrambled to embrace new women voters, some of whom abandoned their antisuffrage work to enter electoral politics, a stunned NAOWS called an emergency board meeting and created two new committees, one to organize antisuffrage delegations to Congress and another to institute membership dues to fund the national antiratification drive. Further evidence that NAOWS was desperately pulling out all the stops to check a federal amendment was its announcement of a new national platform, in language that signaled a shift to the political right. Alleging that a coalition of suffragists, socialists, and pacifists was behind the recent New York suffrage victory, it called upon Congress to defend the Constitution from this "pro-German-pacifist effort to put through the Susan B. Anthony Amendment." With the United States still at war, these charges were tantamount to labeling suffragists traitors to their country. The Man-Suffrage Association, meanwhile, conceded defeat in New York and reorganized as the American Constitutional League to counter a federal amendment.[61]

Busy with events in Washington and divided over how to react to the New York defeat, NAOWS left the final decision to the state association, which flip-flopped confusedly for the next six months. Its president, Alice Hill Chittenden, at first announced plans to dissolve the organization and establish in its place a nonpartisan, antipacifist women's patriotic league to aid the war effort. A week later, New York antisuffragists recanted these plans, announced Chittenden's retirement from active work (she went to Europe as a Red Cross volunteer), and dedicated themselves to fighting the federal suffrage amendment. They changed tack again in January, reorganizing for a "double campaign" against a federal amendment while also "working to elect a legislature" that would prepare a new state constitutional amendment rescinding woman suffrage in New York. By the spring they had reorganized anew as the Women Voters' Anti-Suffrage Party, headed by Mrs. Charles S. Fairchild, whose husband led the American Constitutional League. The new party ultimately "decided to accept woman suffrage in New York as a fact," after suffragists rattled some sabers of their own and pledged to fight any action to nullify the November referendum results. Antisuffragists vowed to use their new electoral power to combat radicalism in New York State while continuing to oppose woman suffrage elsewhere. In a consummate political paradox, they now proclaimed it woman's moral duty to use her vote to put men in office who would carry out the antisuffrage agenda—that is, men who had not yet lost "all the male instincts of domination and sovereignty." Antisuffragists had come very far from their origins; they now advocated political participation "as a conservative force" to revoke the privilege of voting from their own gender.[62]

The New York victory was a turning point for suffragists as well, as President Wilson in January 1918 publicly backed the Susan B. Anthony Amendment and the House of Representatives passed it with a bare two-thirds majority, despite an impressive assemblage of antisuffrage demonstrators. NAOWS kept the state associations busy with protest petitions and letter-writing campaigns, addressed first to the U. S. House, and later to the Senate. Antisuffrage leaders charged that a "female autocracy has been established in the national capital," based on the empty threat of a "phantom female vote," and called upon the Senate to uphold the country's virility. The national headquarters distributed a list of "doubtful Senators" for special attention, and state associations besieged them with telegrams. They also solicited member donations for a special mailing to "a carefully selected list of men to ask them to help stir up sentiment against the federal amendment." Mrs. Wadsworth and a large delegation of NAOWS women, adorned with pink roses, helped to stall the Senate vote in June, while the Women Voters' Anti-Suffrage Party took out a large ad in the *New York Times* that asked, "Shall this revolutionary change in our form of government be decided by popular vote or dictated by the suffrage lobby?" Antisuffragists beat back suffrage in October by a narrow margin of only two votes, despite President Wilson's Senate address requesting its passage as a war measure, which prompted the Massachusetts Association to send him a resolution protesting his decision to "penalize" patriotic women. The antisuffrage cause was heralded by a group of "heroic Senators" led by Oscar Underwood of Alabama; virtually the only Republicans against the federal amendment were from the northeastern states, stronghold of antisuffragism.[63]

The Senate vote was only a temporary reprieve, and the antis knew it. Underneath their public bluster the die-hard activists, never a large group, were wearying from the long struggle, and organizational cracks were becoming evident. The Massachusetts Association experienced a spate of resignations by longtime officers who said they could not meet the time and travel demands of fighting a federal amendment. The number of women remonstrants who appeared for the Senate vote in October was much reduced from that of the June display. The NAOWS executive committee met more frequently after the House vote, to plan strategy and search quietly for new "chairmen" of major committees. Leadership changes created instability in even the strongest state associations, as both Massachusetts and New York operated with acting presidents during part of the year.[64]

Whatever their reasons for deserting the cause, the peeling away of moderate activists from the antisuffrage movement left behind a more politically extremist group of leaders. This was symbolized by the change in title of the NAOWS periodical the *Woman's Protest,* which in April 1918 merged with *Anti-Suffrage Notes* published by the Cambridge branch of MAOFESW to become the *Woman Patriot,* with a new slogan: "for home and national defense AGAINST woman suffrage, feminism, and socialism." Opposition rhetoric escalated in intensity, with frequent political mudslinging; antisuffrage leaflets mailed to campaign states addressed topics such as "Is Woman's Suffrage Pro-German?" With so many leadership changes, the attachment of state organizations to the National Association also become more tenuous, and tensions arose, especially after Alice Wadsworth threatened to close the Washington office unless the states sent sustaining funds quickly. The Massachusetts organization balked at its already heavy share of financial support and questioned NAOWS political strategies and personnel decisions, pushing for male stewardship of future antisuffrage political campaigns. By the fall of 1918, MAOFESW voted to send no further money until the National Association put its affairs in better order.[65]

The stress of so many setbacks seemed to discourage the troops as well. The Massachusetts Association reported declining literature sales, fewer public meetings, and inactive branch committees. Returning in defeat from a meeting of the National Republican Committee, the MAOFESW delegate lamented, "We do not exist politically," and urged state reorganization, but nothing was done. They planned a mass rally in Boston, but, worried about poor attendance, publicized it as an anti-Bolshevist, antisocialist, *and* antisuffrage meeting, bringing in Senator Wadsworth as a keynote speaker. Massachusetts antis saw suffragists making inroads among immigrant communities and gaining popular approval through well-publicized war work. Competition with suffragists over patriotism spurred them to cross perhaps the last bastion of gender convention—they agreed to participate in parades, although they still refused to march. New York antisuffragists staffed a first aid station along the route of the Preparedness Parade, and in Boston they agreed to ride through the city streets on an antisuffrage float as participants in the Liberty Loan Parade.[66]

There were few traces of optimism in the results of the 1918 elections, where antisuffrage associations waged costly campaigns (NAOWS alone reported expenses of over $30,000 for the year) but in most cases were outspent by a suffrage movement that smelled victory. Of the four states with suffrage referenda, only Louisiana turned back the suffrage threat, while Michigan, Oklahoma, and South Dakota enfranchised women. NAWSA also entered electoral politics by targeting for defeat selected U. S. Senators who had voted against the federal amendment; despite the efforts of MAOFESW, Senators Weeks of Massachusetts and Saulsbury of Delaware were defeated, and others barely survived the suffrage assault. In the coming year, Texas alone had scheduled a suffrage referendum but this was not especially good news, since eight state legislatures had already voted for partial suffrage, bypassing the referenda process and adding to the pressure on political parties. Mrs. Catt's "Winning Plan" would bear more fruit in 1919, when the legislatures of seven states passed presidential suffrage, pressed by a growing army of suffrage picketers. In an ironic twist, antisuffragists tried to counter by forcing state referenda, sometimes through court challenges, which were only partly successful. But the real fight was in the nation's capital, where antisuffragists tried vainly to bolster the recalcitrant Senate, all that stood between them and a federal amendment.[67]

The U. S. Senate voted again in February 1919, and while the amendment just missed the required majority, suffragists picked up the support of another southern Democrat. The news from the other party was little better, as NAOWS reported that the Republican National Committee was planning to organize women even in nonsuffrage states. Antisuffragists tried to derail suffrage momentum through escalating allegations of radicalism, presaging its full-scale red-baiting campaign of the 1920s. NAOWS petitioned the Senate to include woman suffrage organizations in its planned investigation of "Bolshevist, I. W. W., and other radical propaganda," and asked the Massachusetts Association to send state legislatures considering partial suffrage copies of its new pamphlet, *The Suffrage Smoke-Screen,* which linked mainstream suffrage organizations to White House picketers and radical politics. Their attention was almost exclusively focused on the imminent federal amendment, even lobbying to block state legislatures from requiring congressional representatives to vote for it. MAOFESW meeting records reveal extensive amounts of time spent identifying wavering congressmen to be bombarded with telegrams and letters, and appeals for assistance in fighting the Texas referendum underscored the number of representatives that distant state sent to Congress.[68]

In the third stage of the antisuffrage movement, suffrage successes no longer energized the mobilization efforts of reluctant women activists. The long campaign had taken its toll, and the all-out fight of the 1915 campaigns proved an empty victory, spurring suffrage organizations to greater effort instead of capitulation. Antisuffragists were drawn further into public battle in order to keep up with the opposition as suffrage became a truly national issue. Despite their rhetorical bombast, antisuffragists privately struggled to prop up shaky state organizations. An organizer for the Massachusetts Association pleaded with her Vermont colleagues to "hold together" the organization for "the real fight" of the federal ratification campaign, and the NAOWS executive committee voted to send a group of women west to "get in touch" with state associations in anticipation of the next stage. That battle would commence shortly, for in May the U. S. House easily passed the Susan B. Anthony Amendment, followed within a fortnight by the U. S. Senate.[69]

Defeat and Movement Decline

As consideration of woman suffrage reverted back to the states, resistance seemed to disappear. Within the first month, eleven states ratified the Susan B. Anthony Amendment, many of them unanimously. Perhaps most discouraging for antisuffragists was the rapid approval of the amendment in states that had traditionally been bastions of opposition: Wisconsin, Michigan, Ohio, Pennsylvania, New York, and even Massachusetts were among the first states to fall into the suffrage column during June 1919. NAOWS president Alice Hay Wadsworth recommended that antisuffragists bow to the inevitable and abandon all efforts to obstruct ratification. Her comments were tantamount to heresy among antisuffrage true believers and threw the National Association into a crisis. The next month NAOWS moved its headquarters back to New York, appointed a new committee to supervise publication of the *Woman Patriot,* and, citing ill health, replaced Alice Hay Wadsworth with Mary G. Kilbreth, former president of the New York Association.[70]

Hunkering down with the state associations shortly thereafter to devise a strategy to block ratification of the federal amendment, NAOWS publicly professed unconcern if "even a score of legislatures" were to "fall into the suffrage line" and promised an "aggressive fight" to hold the necessary thirteen states. It shared New York headquarters with the Woman Voters' Anti-Suffrage Party, a group that used strong language to make its case. Public statements from both groups accused suffragists of "blackmail and bulldozing," their supporters of "perverting the Constitution," and even charged that political parties "have been prostituted to woman suffrage," a term that had been taboo among genteel remonstrants earlier in the struggle. NAOWS also engaged in its "first definite political war," a public fight with the Republican Party that at first glance appears inexplicable, since both major parties by this time officially supported the Susan B. Anthony Amendment. But the Republicans infuriated antisuffragists by putting a New York suffrage leader in charge of the women's division of its National Committee; moreover, since many anti leaders were prominent eastern women, "wives of men high in the councils of the Republican party," they held some hope of influencing the party by withholding their "work, money and votes."[71]

Behind assertions of national unity, the movement was in collapse. The Massachusetts Association discussed a move to smaller quarters, closed its publicity room, and disbanded the education and organization committee that had been responsible for producing propaganda and recruiting new members almost since its inception. Convinced that Massachusetts was the "firing line" of the national suffrage battle, MAOFESW attempted a petition drive to repeal ratification of the federal amendment. It abandoned the plan after receiving the "most depressing" news that the troops had collected but a fraction of the petition signatures needed; this failure provoked accusations of disloyalty, mass resignations of branch chairwomen, and so many defections from the executive committee that it could not get a quorum for six months. Following the aborted repeal campaign, the Massachusetts officers planned a splashy luncheon meeting at a downtown hotel to raise money for the national antiratification campaign, but attendance was so poor that the event ran a deficit.[72]

For the most part, the strategy to counter the federal ratification drive was piecemeal, devised by individual state associations and their men's league supporters to take advantage of local opportunities but also reflecting the confusion of the national leadership. It included petitions to submit the amendment to public referenda, court challenges to the constitutionality of statutory enactment of both presidential suffrage and the federal amendment, lobbying to preclude governors from calling special legislative sessions to consider ratification, and electoral campaigns to purge state legislatures of advocates of "petticoat government." NAOWS supported all of these efforts, but its most cohesive strategy was to concentrate on "states whose legislatures are considered unfavorable" to suffrage, and that meant going south.[73]

Organized protest in the southern states was late and limited in scale, although the northern antisuffrage establishment began to establish contacts by the turn of the century through the ministry and conservative women's clubs like the United Daughters of the Confederacy. Their reluctance to organize was partly cultural—southern gender norms against political participation were even stronger than in the north—but mostly pragmatic. For a long time, there was little need to protest woman suffrage, given the dearth of suffrage activity in the region. The reorganized NAWSA helped establish suffrage associations in the 1890s, facilitated by a wave of state constitutional conventions called to disfranchise black citizens. Numerous suffragists argued before these conventions that woman suffrage would solve the so-called "Negro problem" by increasing the number of white voters. Those speaking against woman suffrage were almost exclusively male politicians, and women remonstrants were not organized. But the southern states ultimately found other means to ensure white racial dominance, and, except for winning partial suffrage for taxpaying Louisiana women, the movement made little headway. None of the suffrage groups approached statewide organization, and most were defunct before the end of the century.[74]

Suffrage lay dormant in the South until around 1910, when female reformers took up the question again as a means of enacting prohibition and restrictions on child labor. As suffrage revitalization took hold, women opponents in some states mobilized, urged on by their northern sisters. NAOWS and the largest state associations sent money, speakers, and literature, but, cognizant of regional sensitivities, debated about how much to interfere, concurring that, at the very least, men state legislators needed women's "moral backing." Members of the NAOWS federation included Virginia (founded in 1912), Georgia (1914), Texas (1915), and Alabama and Tennessee (1916); not coincidentally, these tended to be the states where suffragists were most active in petitioning legislatures. Although ostensibly state antisuffrage associations, most had less than a thousand members clustered in one or two major cities, and only Virginia built a small network of branch committees that spanned the state.[75]

Southern leaders on both sides of the suffrage question were differentiated less by social background than by political ideology. Typical association officers were active clubwomen from the ruling elite, often related by birth or marriage to powerful politicians, and living embodiments of the southern lady. Suffragists' strategy accommodated local gender norms, complete with promises that voting would not jeopardize genteel womanhood, and the more militant National Woman's Party never caught on in the region. The president of the Equal Suffrage League of Virginia was described as a "piece of Dresden China," and the leaders of the Kentucky suffrage movement were so distinguished that their evening address to a joint session of the state legislature was described as "a brilliant social occasion." The socialite president of the Alabama Equal Suffrage Association pronounced "the leisure class . . . the pillar of the suffrage movement," and even newspapers on record against female enfranchisement gushed that "she presented a splendid picture of a true woman, a noble mother, and a deep thinker."[76]

The woman leaders of the suffrage opposition likewise had impeccable social credentials; they included state officers of patriotic-hereditary societies, wives of prominent local attorneys, businessmen, and state politicians, and daughters of judges and a sitting U. S. senator. They were also accomplished in their own right, such as the Alabama Association officer who was the first woman director of a state department of archives and history. Compared with antis, suffrage activists had stronger alliances with the Woman's Christian Temperance Union and the progressive wing of the Democratic Party; these "silk stocking" reformers certainly demonstrated class and racial prejudices, but antisuffrage leaders, not unlike their northern peers, avoided all challenges to the status quo. As active clubwomen, both sides engaged in preparedness and war relief work; one suffrage group published a wartime cookbook, while antisuffragists took advantage of visits to military bases to distribute literature about their cause.[77]

The southern antisuffrage movement was shaped by class homogeneity that united contestants in a region still stinging from the defeat of the Civil War and the humiliations of Reconstruction. The historical connection between abolition and the suffrage movement exacerbated the tendency toward insularity, and antis aimed most of their hostility at northern suffragists. A revealing exception was an antisuffrage assault on an Alabama activist for criticisms leveled against U. S. Senator Underwood at a Chicago banquet; the suffragist's sin lay not in the substance of her comments, but in their presentation before "enemies and critics of the south." Vitriolic personal attacks on suffragists were commonplace, perhaps also because so much of southern antisuffrage literature was produced by men and was written in the final desperate phase of the effort. Pamphlets and broadsides distributed throughout the southern states suggested sexual liaisons between black abolitionist Frederick Douglass and various suffrage pioneers, lambasted the late Susan B. Anthony for defaming revered war hero Robert E. Lee, and cited the opinion of a "prominent neurologist" that Dr. Anna Howard Shaw had the mental development of an eleven-year-old child. Racial fears were exploited by reprinting photos of white women voters intermingling with blacks at the Chicago polls and quoting a suffragist's address before New York "negro voters" that female enfranchisement was the way to "kill the solid South." These reminders of regional and racial hostility legitimated the entrance of women antisuffragists into politics; newspapers that criticized the public activities of even circumspect southern suffragists lauded the opposition for their "courage and spirit of self sacrifice" as patriotic defenders of southern civilization.[78]

In truth, both sides exploited racist sentiments, but by the second decade of the twentieth century southern suffragists were taking primarily a defensive posture, offering public reassurances that women's enfranchisement was no threat to white supremacy. Antisuffragists, on the other hand, took a more aggressive stance, asserting that "the question of negro women voting is the paramount issue," and that no restrictions—neither literacy tests, property requirements, nor poll taxes—will work "in choking off the colored woman vote." Embedded in racist appeals were those to gender and class interests, as antisuffrage posters presented census data showing the likelihood of black rule over "some very rich and important counties." As suffrage strategy increasingly favored a federal solution, antisuffrage rhetoric escalated and drew attention to "that deadly parallel" between the hated Fifteenth Amendment enfranchising black men and the proposed Anthony Amendment, allegedly devised "for the very purpose of destroying white supremacy in the south."[79]

Historical grievances shaped the structure and strategy of southern antisuffrage organizations, especially during the federal ratification drive. The ostensible issue of women voters was rarely addressed apart from its implications for continued racial dominance. The Alabama Association illustrates how far the movement's focus had shifted away from gender. After congressional passage of the Anthony Amendment, it reorganized as the Woman's Anti-Ratification League, proclaimed a states' rights slogan ("Alabama for Alabamians") and appropriated the official Alabama colors of crimson and white. It began an aggressive membership drive, constituted a men's league of prominent local attorneys with impressive pedigrees, called a few mass meetings where the mostly male speakers threatened retribution of "negro extermination" should suffrage pass, and collected protest petitions for the state legislature. When the Alabama legislature met to consider the federal amendment, the Woman's League refused to testify, submitting instead a genteel "memorial" that was read into the record by a friendly state senator. The testimonial, which claimed to be representing "80 percent of the white women of Alabama," reaffirmed women's patriotic contributions to domestic tranquility and a disciplined citizenry and pleaded for protection from "those who would mongrelize and corrupt Anglo-Saxon civilization." The Alabama legislature rejected the suffrage amendment over the entreaties of fellow Democrat President Wilson.[80]

Energized by this victory, the Alabama Association spearheaded a coalition called the Southern Woman's League for the Rejection of the Susan B. Anthony Amendment. The group encompassed existing NAOWS state associations, although appeals to regional pride did inspire mobilization in previously moribund places like North Carolina. States with the most active antisuffrage organizations—Georgia, Virginia, and Alabama—swapped speakers and contributed propaganda aimed at the particular concerns of southern whites. James Callaway, editor of the Macon (Ga.) *Telegraph,* wrote numerous antisuffrage tracts on the dual themes of states' rights and white supremacy, including one provocatively titled, *Will the States Consent to Blot the Stars from Old Glory, Leaving Only a Meaningless Square of Blue?* Patriotic themes became a key element of the southern campaign against the federal amendment and suggest ties with northern associations; one league notice contained the expert opinion of a Chicago professor that the collapse of male dominance will destroy "American pep" so responsible for the nation's prosperity. Links with NAOWS were never severed, but they were hidden for the sake of expediency. Pamphlets and broadsides from antisuffrage associations outside the region were either stripped of identifying labels or restamped as products of southern organizations. The North Carolina headquarters of the Southern Woman's League bore the same motto as the NAOWS New York headquarters ("Politics Is Bad for Women and Women Are Bad for Politics"), albeit unattributed, and league records reveal frequent consultations with the northern national leadership that were not made public.[81]

The National Association Opposed to Woman Suffrage had a plan for the southern states, which it called "affirmative rejection." Mary Kilbreth's idea was to reverse the ratification process by filing an official rejection of the Susan B. Anthony Amendment with the U. S. secretary of state; to accomplish this, both houses of thirteen state legislatures would have to defeat it. This strategy was actually a bit of rhetorical sleight of hand, since it presented a more difficult goal than merely blocking ratification in the required thirty-six states; its purpose was inspirational and publicity-minded. During 1919, only Alabama qualified as an official rejection state while the border states ratified the amendment quickly: Texas in June, and Missouri and Arkansas in July. In January 1920, Kentucky became the twenty-fourth state to ratify the amendment, followed shortly by Oklahoma and West Virginia (a state whose decision, along with that of Missouri, antisuffragists disputed). After the state legislature of Washington approved the Anthony Amendment in March, only one state was needed to enfranchise U. S. women.[82]

Over the next few months, suffragists pursued a triage plan, targeting only those states with good chances of success. The opposition countered them at every step. NAOWS by this time had overcome its distaste for politics to create Democratic and Republic sections of its organization that lobbied unsuccessfully to keep the federal amendment out of party platforms during the presidential election year. It sent its field secretary to open antisuffrage headquarters where southern legislatures were in session and announced progress toward a planned fifty-thousand-dollar war chest. At its April annual convention, touted as "the greatest meeting in the history of the Association," NAOWS pledged a "new" campaign "to defend the rights of the States and the people against Federalism, feminism and demoralization." The Massachusetts Association distributed thirty thousand pieces of literature in the first year of its federal antiratification drive, which equaled its monthly production at the height of the 1915 state campaign. MAOFESW bolstered northern opposition to special state legislative sessions, subscribed to southern newspapers in order to tailor arguments to local interests, and mailed literature to the legislatures of every state where the amendment was pending, boasting that "Wherever we saw a head we made a point to hit it." The New Jersey Association petitioned southern legislatures to hold firm to their states' rights position, commiserating that "foreigners" were an even more serious problem than "negro voters."[83]

Partly as a result of these efforts, the states available for a suffrage victory grew limited, as the governors of Connecticut and Vermont refused to call special sessions of the legislature and Ohio was tied up in a court challenge. Mississippi rejected the amendment in February, and in June so did Louisiana, thanks to the help of New Orleans suffragist Kate Gordon, who strongly supported states' rights and broke with NAWSA over the Anthony Amendment. Antisuffrage campaigns kept

Delaware and North Carolina from ratifying, and suffragists' attention converged on Tennessee, whose state legislature had recently passed municipal and presidential suffrage and where federal intervention permitted its governor to convene a special legislative session.[84]

Both sides descended on Nashville over the summer to rouse public interest and lobby the legislature, which would not meet until early August. The convergence of antisuffrage organizations was particularly impressive. On the woman's side, it included an illustrious contingent from NAOWS, the Southern Woman's League for the Rejection of the Susan B. Anthony Amendment (with a Tennessee division that claimed to be "several hundred strong"), and southern suffrage turncoats Laura Clay and Kate Gordon. Male opponents included a group of North Carolina legislators who, invigorated by their recent defeat of suffrage, promised to strengthen any "weak knees" among peers in the neighboring state. New York lawyer Everett P. Wheeler organized a Tennessee division of the American Constitutional League under the directorship of a local judge, joined by the Maryland League for State Defense. Opponents of ratification tried to maintain consistency with their states' rights argument by putting local antisuffrage leaders in the visible forefront of the campaign.[85]

The resulting last-ditch battle was aptly dubbed the "War of the Roses" by one suffrage leader. NAOWS president Mary Kilbreth predicted an antisuffrage victory in Tennessee and called the suffrage campaign there a "wild goose chase," while the National Woman's Party retorted that antis were "grasping at straws." Antisuffragists tried a variety of tactics to forestall the inevitable. The *Woman Patriot*, which had heretofore made oblique racist appeals through states' rights, now asserted plainly that the Anthony Amendment means "race peril to the South," as "Negro assertiveness would be doubled." The Southern Woman's League petitioned in vain the national Democratic Party leadership for nonintervention in the Tennessee vote out of respect for "home-loving women of the South, who do not picket, card-index, or blackmail candidates." They mounted a nonpareil propaganda campaign that invoked the standard racial fears, supplemented with pointed appeals to masculine pride and states' rights, producing leaflets that asked, "Can Anybody Terrorize Tennessee Manhood?" and asserting that the amendment could still be defeated if enough "real men" opposed it. Shortly before the vote, the Southern League published a newspaper from women of the eleven southern states pleading for regional loyalty and protection under "the unquestioned chivalry of the South." The NAOWS representative invoked the specter of socialism before a joint legislative hearing, and was the only woman speaker to address a mass meeting organized by the Tennessee Constitutional League. They came close to succeeding, as the Tennessee legislature ratified the amendment by a bare one-vote margin. Antisuffragists refused to quit, trying a number of political and legal interventions to prevent certification, but U.S. Secretary of State Colby proclaimed the Nineteenth Amendment ratified on 26 August 1920.[86]

Antisuffragists reacted to the Tennessee legislature's vote with a mixture of disappointment, denial, and rage. The *Woman Patriot* acknowledged the Tennessee vote with an allegation that suffragists bought legislative votes, and subsequent issues paid more attention to an attempt by the Tennessee House to rescind ratification. The National Association insisted that the Anthony Amendment remained at least three states short of ratification, claiming that the actions of the Tennessee, Missouri, and West Virginia legislatures were unconstitutional. The NAOWS leadership optimistically declared, "our fight has just begun," and reminded antisuffragists of their "duty" to stem this "feminist disease" that turns "both sexes into weak neuters." Privately, however, they were furious over the defeat, and much of their anger was directed toward the Connecticut Republican Party leadership, which abandoned "its manly and patriotic course," called a special legislative session in September, and ratified the amendment; this vote (followed later by that of Vermont) gave suffragists a comfortable margin of victory. Mary Kilbreth told the state associations that they were betrayed by their so-called Connecticut "friends," especially Governor Holcomb and Senator Brandegee, and urged revenge at the ballot box—the only way "to make politicians understand [that] surrender will cost them their offices." Tennessee antisuffragists pursued the same course and took consolation two months later when that governor lost his reelection bid.[87]

With the November presidential elections following so closely behind women's enfranchisement, the antisuffrage rank and file requested guidance on voting. The National Association was curiously silent, although the *Woman Patriot* published the policy of Maryland antisuffragists enjoining its members from working with any women's political organization and from voting for any prosuffrage politicians. As both parties scrambled to embrace the new woman voter, this instruction was impossible to follow in many localities; the best MAOFESW could offer its constituency was a vague resolution about using good judgment. The public seemed to await the new "experiment" with curious anticipation, egged on by national media focused on the historic event of the first presidential election decided by universal suffrage. National magazines speculated on the impact of women voters on democracy, femininity, and the family, and antisuffrage newspapers like the *New York Times* grudgingly accepted the new female electorate but drew a new line in the sand against female office seeking. In perhaps the ultimate irony, the first woman elected to Congress after ratification of the Anthony Amendment was a former vice-president of the Oklahoma Association Opposed to Woman Suffrage.[88]

The antisuffrage movement was in disarray, although the National Association, asserting its continuing relevance, claimed to have seven hundred thousand members in twenty-eight state chapters. Their actual membership figures were much less, judging by organizational collapse in many states following suffrage ratification. A number of prominent antisuffrage leaders abandoned the cause and became active in partisan politics; Alice Hill Chittenden, for example, helped found the Women's National Republican Club and served two terms as its president. The Massachusetts Association discontinued publication of the *Remonstrance,* dismissed some staff, and considered closing the state headquarters. NAOWS president Kilbreth telegrammed, urging them to keep the office open for its "psychological effect," especially given their symbolic value to the movement. The National Association moved its own headquarters back to Washington, ostensibly to be closer to the legal battle, although Kilbreth admitted privately that there was a dispute with the New York landlord over antisuffrage window signs. In the heady postamendment political climate, antisuffragism had become controversial.[89]

Hope for ultimate victory now rested in the courts. While the Anthony Amendment was still before the states, NAOWS publicly warned that it planned to mount a legal challenge. Working behind the scenes with the men's associations, it found a way. In July 1920 the American Constitutional League filed suit in Washington challenging the ratification process as an illegal intrusion on states' rights. Their claim (*Fairchild v. Colby*) was rejected at several levels, and the plaintiffs unsuccessfully petitioned the U.S. Supreme Court to hear the case before the November elections. The Maryland League for State Defense, another men's group composed heavily of lawyers, filed a second legal challenge (*Leser v. Garnett*) after two women registered to vote, in violation of the state's constitution. The National Association proclaimed its faith that the courts would uphold states' rights, and its president touted the legal strategy as a way not just to defeat woman suffrage, but "to kill it beyond power of reviving." "I want a final decision," avowed Kilbreth, and she got it, when the U.S. Supreme Court dismissed both suits and upheld the constitutionality of the Nineteenth Amendment in February 1922.[90]

With the woman suffrage issue settled, NAOWS dissolved quietly. First to leave were southern activists, criticized privately by Kilbreth as "quitters in the Amendment fight—leaving the North to pay all the bills and Maryland and New York to fight the legal battles." The *Woman Patriot* was reduced to a bimonthly publication, and the last national convention, held in September 1921, signaled the future course of the opposition movement. Contending that the vote was but "the first step in the feminist program for a complete social revolution," antisuffrage leaders exhorted conventioneers to continue the fight against the "Feminist-Socialist measures demanded by the Suffrage Lobby." The further turn to the right was evidenced by red-baiting, as Kilbreth alleged a new "deadly parallel" between suffragism and bolshevism. By 1922, Mary Kilbreth described herself as "busy . . . preparing our 'red' charges," and the *Woman Patriot* actively helped discredit the women's movement by linking the League of Women Voters to "international communism," an allegation that helped push the league into a defensive posture of female nonpartisanship. In Boston, the antisuffrage Public Interests League aided this effort by mounting an exhibition of "red propaganda" that included suffrage materials.[91]

The women who remained within the antisuffrage fold in the aftermath of the amendment's passage were die-hard conservatives, both politically and socially. Mary Kilbreth, for example, continued to "object to women in politics—and to myself as much as anyone else." They remained ostensibly nonpartisan, not only because of traditional views about women's roles, but also out of a refusal to associate with former suffragists who dominated partisan organizations and because of their dismissal of mainstream political parties as leftist. They were deeply critical of both conservative Republican administrations of the 1920s; Kilbreth privately derided President Harding as a "weakling" for not standing up to women reformers and snobbishly characterized his successor as "quite uncouth" with a "schoolteacher" wife—not of the "good Coolidge family" that had populated the Boston antisuffrage leadership. In defeat, the movement reverted back to the insularity that characterized its origins. Several wealthy leaders of former state antisuffrage associations reorganized into local Women's Constitutional Leagues to fight socialism and defend the Constitution, by which they meant restricting the power of the federal government. In 1923, a former Massachusetts Association president helped establish a mixed-sex organization called the Sentinels of the Republic; headquartered in the same building as the old MAOFESW, it used the imagery and rhetoric of patriotic-hereditary societies for the goal of "putting strong men into office during the crisis" brought on by an expanded electorate. The Woman Patriot Publishing Company under Kilbreth's leadership helped publicize the mobilization efforts of both conservative groups, but she acknowledged privately that they were severely diminished from their antisuffrage predecessors in both size and resources.[92]

These new patriotic organizations, aided by the voice of the *Woman Patriot*, attacked social welfare policies that former suffragists brought before Congress. These were tarred as radical experiments in socialism and as unconstitutional intrusions upon states' rights. Antisuffragists lobbied throughout the 1920s against mothers' pensions and the establishment of a federal department of education; they accused the National Education Association, allegedly replete with suffragists, of scheming to get political control of the nation's children in order to create a "New World Order." They attacked a child labor bill as an "original socialist draft," and by the end of the decade lobbied to abolish the federal Children's Bureau. They supported immigration and naturalization restrictions and repeal of the federal estate tax, and periodically fulminated on the deleterious effects of the weak-kneed "new man" on national security and foreign policy.[93]

The social welfare issue that became a particular target of fury for these former antisuffragists was the Sheppard-Towner Maternity and Infancy Act, which they charged came "straight from Bolshevist Russia by way of the left-wing radicals of the Republican Party." This law was originally supported by most women's groups, including the General Federation of Women's Clubs; it expanded health services and information to reduce child mortality through grants to the states under the supervision of the Children's Bureau, which was dominated by former suffragists. When Congress passed this premier federal program for social welfare in 1921 over their protests, "women patriots" lobbied among the states against the "Federal Baby Act," and a former president of the Massachusetts Association even filed suit as a federal taxpayer challenging its constitutionality.[94]

These conservative women's organizations were motivated by class interests specific to their gender. The "female dominion in American reform" that advocated the expansion of social welfare programs stood to benefit the most from it and envisioned policy solutions for children's poverty from a vantage point different from that of the conservative women involved in the antisuffrage campaign. The female reformers were college-educated women trained for the most part in the professions of social work and nursing, often with prior experience in settlement work; they were overwhelmingly prosuffrage. While some women leaders of the antisuffrage movement gained national prominence in the development of social services for women and children, they were wealthy volunteers—self-described "amateurs"—not professionals. The expansion of the social welfare state increased employment opportunities for professional women, and its centralized administration undermined the authority and social status of those engaged in traditional private philanthropy. Class differences exacerbated elite women's reactions to these changes; appointed board members who dictated policies carried out by paid staff, they were now being displaced by credentialed daughters of the middle class. From their perspective, the social revolution had occurred, and the servants had taken over the mansion. The resentment of former antisuffrage activists toward this reversal of the social order is revealed in their derisive statements about Sheppard-Towner. They privately denounced social welfare legislation as "women's porkbarrels" and publicly alleged that Sheppard-Towner would benefit not mothers, but "amateurs who will 'investigate' maternity." Coming after decades of proclaiming the advantages of their own amateur status, this particular insult resounds with defensiveness and class antipathy.[95]

In the end, suffragists and antisuffragists both pursued self-interest. Suffragists won the greatest battle, but for a time it appeared that the opposition had won the war. Armed with the resources of privilege, the reduced cadre of right-wing conservative women helped discredit former suffragists and their reform policies. They confronted legislators with the diversity of the female electorate and diminished the perceived political benefits of supporting social welfare legislation. Antisuffragists lost the first round of Sheppard-Towner, but they returned to battle its extension several years later with a coalition of other elite women's patriotic-hereditary societies, including the DAR and the Daughters of 1812. This time they won, and the nation's experiment with social welfare reform ceased until the New Deal legislation of President Franklin D. Roosevelt. It is probably not coincidental that his election coincided with the final issue of the *Woman Patriot*.[96]

Conclusion

The tactical evolution of the antisuffrage movement is striking. From a genteel group meeting in residential parlors for self-study and public education, they increasingly adopted more visible means of promoting the cause. These changes were partly a consequence of pressure from male advisers, competition with suffragists, and demands from political candidates. The establishment of a national coalition in 1911 incited innovation by improving the flow of information and other resources among state antisuffrage associations, but also by multiplying their financial burdens. Suffrage opponents publicly legitimated deviations from traditional gender norms in numerous ways; they blamed suffragists for forcing them into public battle, emphasized distinctions between themselves and their adversaries, or simply denied the obvious political dimensions of their work. Traditional rhetoric extolling motherhood and the sanctity of the home functioned partly to shield the true extent of women's activism from public notice and potential criticism. Women remonstrants commonly appealed to male lawmakers and voters for protection, invoking norms of chivalry that underscored women's dependency and their position as political outsiders.

Both sides adopted a nonpartisan stance, but the suffrage establishment benefited from the existence of a radical flank in the form of the National Woman's Party that absorbed controversy while putting pressure on both parties.[97] There was no parallel organization within the antisuffrage movement; the men's associations, dominated by elite lawyers, largely eschewed electoral politics and sought redress in the courts. Women's antisuffrage organizations repeatedly beseeched politicians for protection, but the policy of nonpartisanship prevented them from bestowing quid pro quo political rewards in the form of candidate endorsements. The perceived political leverage of newly enfranchised women voters prodded many elected officials to endorse suffrage, siphoning off politically moderate antisuffragists for leadership positions in Republican women's associations. The loss of this segment of the antisuffrage movement to party participation illuminates the extent to which the fight against woman suffrage, at least for the privileged leadership, centered less on protecting the home than on preserving group power.

This conclusion is supported by antisuffrage strategies during the declining phase of the movement, when the remaining opposition activists were drawn into political battle. Having lost informal channels of influence stemming from their positions of privilege, antisuffragists had no choice but to compete in the public sphere. They now mounted an overt defense of class interests; the Women Voters' Anti-Suffrage Party focused on fighting radicalism—a code word for antilabor and anti-immigrant sentiments—and so did the official organ of the National Association, renamed the *Woman Patriot*. The home, motherhood, and children's welfare took a backseat to issues of patriotism and socialism; in the southern mobilization against ratification, the defense of southern civilization was paramount. After the passage of the Nineteenth Amendment, their gendered appeals addressed primarily the question of masculinity, excoriating presidents and their policies for being too "soft" on domestic reform or national security. The remaining true believers persisted in the view that women were bad for politics, but this had more to do with differences in political ideology—particularly the successes of female reformers in getting social welfare legislation through Congress—than with the deleterious consequences of enfranchisement for home-loving women and their families. The right-wing associations of the 1920s formed from the ashes of the antisuffrage movement protested their own loss of influence, brought on by the mass empowerment of women as well as the rise of trained female professionals who threatened to displace the society volunteer.

This examination of antisuffrage tactics over time not only challenges the notion of a lockstep reaction by countermovements to the initial movement, but also suggests that the tactical responses of countermovements vary according to the phase in which they occur. For example, suffrage victories when antisuffragists were less mobilized seemed to spur further activation efforts, whereas a referendum defeat coming after a host of significant antisuffrage victories led to organizational conflict and demobilization. The difficulties of holding together suffrage opponents derived not merely from social position or domestic responsibilities, but from the problems confronting all movements of maintaining consensus and dedication over the course of a protracted contest. In this task, the repertoire available to suffragists was less constrained by ideology. Antisuffrage organizations, while more flexible than their rhetoric implied, viewed open political engagement as certain defeat, given their strong moral pronouncements against women's political participation. While we will never know if their assessment was accurate, the exhortation to vote by the Women Voters' Anti-Suffrage Party that began this chapter encapsulates the movement's dilemma as much as its desperation. Antisuffragists' hesitancy to cross that line until so late in the struggle gave suffragists a major tactical advantage and contributed to the successful outcome of women's campaign for political equality.

7

The Politics of Conservative Womanhood

> Feminism is no substitute for traditional marriage. Liberation is no substitute for fidelity. Political Correctness is no substitute for chivalry. Careers are no substitute for children and grandchildren.
>
> —Phyllis Schlafly, 1994

Looking behind the traditional facade of the U. S. antisuffrage movement, this study discovered a more complex reality.[1] Upon closer and more systematic inspection, organized antisuffragists were found to deviate considerably from their traditional self-constructed image as well as from stereotypes promulgated by outsiders. Women antisuffragists were not merely fronts for men, a prevalent myth that has hindered investigation of conservative women's movements more generally. Concerned about possible damage to their positions of public trust and influence, men were even more reluctant to organize permanently and openly against suffrage than were women. Women's associations prodded men into sporadic action for referenda campaigns and sought their assistance for specific purposes, such as fund-raising; behind the scenes, meanwhile, female remonstrants struggled to maintain autonomy in the face of male attempts at control.

Comparisons of men's and women's antisuffrage rhetoric reveal a distinct female point of view on enfranchisement, further challenging the myth of female passivity. While both sexes generally addressed the same topics, men were especially concerned about threats to patriarchal family relations and women objected to the imposition of more work on their already overburdened sex. It may be an overstatement to describe women's antisuffrage arguments as expressing a feminist consciousness, but they often appealed to perceived female concerns.

Men, by contrast, used more threatening and demeaning rhetoric to justify the continued disfranchisement of one sex and preferred to attack suffragists' personalities rather than their politics.

The women who initiated the countermovement against suffrage were not isolated homemakers, but members of an urban upper class who enjoyed easy access to political elites by virtue of kinship and marriage. They served as appointees to numerous state and local boards overseeing the administration of social services and directed private philanthropies endowed by family fortunes. The class position of the antisuffrage leadership constituted a key component of its opposition to women's enfranchisement, but not in the manner described by its rivals. This study argues that female remonstrants had a direct class interest in opposing suffrage rather than one mediated by their husbands' profit motives. The ideology of separate spheres that infused antisuffrage rhetoric enhanced their social influence as cultural arbiters, maintaining the exclusivity of elite social networks while simultaneously promoting new standards of domesticity that enhanced class control. It is probably no accident that many editors of women's magazines and authors of manuals preaching true womanhood to the growing middle classes were avid antisuffragists. Privileged social networks landed antisuffrage leaders influential public positions that only elite volunteers had the resources to fill, although they carefully cloaked their power with the label "amateur" in conformity to contemporary norms for women of their class. Their rhetorical claims that men adequately represented women's interests reflected the experiences of many antisuffrage leaders, who communicated directly with the highest levels of government, assured of prompt and courteous attention.[2]

The organizers of the antisuffrage movement did not reject a political role for all women. From their perspective, the franchise was an inferior form of power to that which they already enjoyed. Along with many men of their class, they distrusted the mass electorate of either sex and feared the imminent loss of their own hegemony. Census counts of foreign-born and black populations incited fears that adding women to the electorate would further diminish the power of their select group. As descendants of early American settlers (and later, Confederate defenders), they saw no distinction between personal and societal interest as they donned patriotic emblems and warned of national calamity from enfranchising women with "handkerchiefs over their heads."[3] Their grievance against suffragists, many of whom were middle class, also embodied a defense of gendered class interests. The antisuffrage establishment was threatened by the educated "new woman" who stood to gain from progressive reforms that would expand the role of government as providers of social services and replace the society volunteer with expert professionals. Following the ratification of the Nineteenth Amendment, the remaining antisuffragists, while also fighting communism, globalism, and immigration, subordinated their professed concern for women, children, and family life to mount an attack on the progressive agenda that sought federal regulation of child labor and education.

Class loyalty shaped more than the ideology of the antisuffrage movement. Organizational development—the founding of branch committees and the recruitment of individual members—was directed principally at affluent women in urban areas. This was partly a deliberate plan to sway public opinion through public endorsements from prominent citizens, but it was also the result of exploiting available interpersonal networks. Class cohesion benefited the antisuffrage movement by enabling the mobilization of women through extended family networks and exclusive social clubs. It may seem puzzling that organizations on both sides of the suffrage issue recruited from women's clubs, but this finding further undermines the claim that antisuffragism was a defense of female seclusion. From a strategic perspective, women's clubs constituted a rare aggregation of affluent women and thus a political opportunity that neither side could ignore. Denied access to full participation in the American republic, women responded by creating a distinct culture and establishing autonomous organizations. They reclaimed the stereotypes used to subordinate them and turned them into rationales for increased participation in social life, demonstrating the dialectical effects of the ideology of separate spheres as both constraint and opportunity.[4] The shared roots of suffragists and remonstrants diverged at some point, however, and antisuffragism found support among women who espoused a more conservative maternalist agenda—those who rejected state regulation of business and its intrusion into social welfare services, explained poverty as a manifestation of weak character, and blamed low female wages on poor performance.

Antisuffragists used the rhetoric of separate spheres to expand beyond the small cadre of elites and solicit support among a broader constituency of women. Their avowed defense of the sanctity of the family and the primacy of motherhood against the divisive effects of modern life took advantage of the gendered class structure that denied most women a living wage. Antisuffrage predictions that woman suffrage would spark male antagonism and ultimately male desertion exploited the anxieties of less privileged women for whom economic independence was an unrealistic goal and at the same time promised respect, security, and comfort for those who submitted to the true womanhood ideal. The sample of antisuffrage recruits examined in chapter 5 contained significant numbers of unmarried women who were typically at the bottom rungs of the middle class. These women were largely native-born and, if employed, worked in shops or offices rather than in factories or professional jobs. These results imply that it was women removed from the harshest conditions of the labor market who were more susceptible to the message of upward mobility contained in antisuffrage endorsements of feminine privilege. Opposition attempts to recruit among immigrant and working-class women never made much headway, and their private records and public rhetoric reveal deep ambivalence about the labor movement. Furthermore, examination of election returns on a sample of state referenda found evidence that male suffrage opposition was more popular among smaller and less privileged communities, although not necessarily immigrant populations. These findings suggest that antisuffragism found support in reactionary and antireform impulses among diverse segments of the population, tapping resentments against middle-class "do-gooders" who avowed that woman suffrage would clean up politics as well as fears that the changes of modern life would disturb the peace of small communities.

This study illustrates and elaborates upon scholarly efforts to reconceptualize gender as not simply a property of individuals, but embedded in institutional structures and in hierarchies of class and ethnicity.[5] Gendered class position suggests motives for female mobilization against the extension of the franchise to others of their gender, the different forms of opposition adopted by men and women remonstrants, and the strategic choices made to influence public opinion and state policy. As others have discovered for different groups of women, the effects of gendered class position are often contradictory. Privilege gained women antisuffragists a receptive hearing in the chambers of statehouses, where male friends and relations prevented many a suffrage petition from going before the voters. Contacts among newspaper publishers, magazine editors, and renowned experts in various fields facilitated access to a broader public. Male emissaries bound by kinship and class interest enabled female opponents of suffrage to maintain an image of self-sacrificing womanhood that obfuscated the true extent of their political activities. Once suffragists began to adopt more overt political tactics, such as targeting antisuffrage legislators for defeat, the constraints of class foretold defeat for the antisuffrage movement. Standard-bearers of a gendered class tradition of true womanhood, they were restricted from openly engaging in electoral politics in support of their allies. They lost control of the suffrage issue when popular referenda in state after state enlarged the terrain for deciding the question, ultimately forcing antisuffragists to adopt more overt political strategies. But it was too late to prevent desertion within the ranks by prominent women seeking power in expanding party structures. A diminished radical group of antisuffragists continued to protest its own political participation into the next decade while using an aggressive arsenal of new political tactics to avenge its defeat.

The mobilization of conservative women against female political equality invites theoretical revisions of countermovements as reactive, static, and single-issue.[6] Antisuffragists coalesced in response to the threat of local suffrage progress, but emergent political opportunities also favored organization, including events far removed from suffragism, such as the development of patriotic-hereditary societies that extended elite women's networks nationwide and provided opportunities to share grievances. Antisuffragists frequently legitimated their cause within the ideology of separate spheres, but its prevalence has been overstated as evidence of countermovements' traditionalism. The antisuffrage rationale encompassed much more than the myth of separate spheres, ruminating on issues of class welfare, national character, and military strength, defending the fairness of the capitalist free market, and proffering an image of the "traditional" woman as political independent rather than submissive homemaker. The ideology of separate spheres also evolved over time in antisuffrage propaganda, and by the new century gender differences were justified almost entirely by science instead of traditional religious orthodoxy.

Antisuffragists' proclaimed defense of homebound women was often at odds with their own political practice, especially in the latter phases of the movement when their activity escalated. Contrary to their image of feminine passivity, antisuffrage organization records present a picture of astute political operatives who knew how to marshal valued resources in service to the cause and alter their conduct to fit different situations and changed political circumstances. Their skilled use of the media was one of their greatest achievements; the antisuffrage movement's near monopoly of endorsements from major journals of the day makes the passage of the Nineteenth Amendment an even more remarkable achievement. And they purposely asserted a new positive image as self-described "conservationists" in order to unhook themselves from the position of caboose following behind the engine of the suffrage movement. Both reactive and proactive strategies characterized the antisuffrage movement, but not every position was strategic; its conservative outlook on gender and class permitted only so much flexibility, and certain boundaries held firm despite their acknowledged harm to the progress of the cause. While their primary goal was to defeat suffrage, they were not a single-issue organization; the political activities of the Woman Patriots during the 1920s remind us that social movements do not end neatly with the loss of their ostensible goal, and that assessments of success or failure require a longer time perspective.

The notion that countermovements monopolize the established myths of society is also belied by the antisuffrage example. Suffragists laid claim to one of the most evocative American ideas—equality—and the antisuffrage movement struggled to defuse its legitimating power. It devised some very creative rebuttals that sometimes granted suffragists credit for their efforts on behalf of women. Antisuffrage counterarguments to the equality rationale very likely pushed the suffrage movement to adjust its own justifications for the vote toward expediency. More generally, the example of antisuffragism suggests that countermovements are not solely reactive movements, but can impel movement innovation.

It is more accurate to describe the relationship between movements and countermovements as interactive, not reactive. A serious problem with the reactive concept is that it narrows the field of vision to the two groups of contestants, whereas both sides actually engaged in a far more complex competition that extended beyond their own boundaries. They sought help from women, male voters and politicians, other organizations, and representatives of influential societal institutions, choosing actions that were sometimes contradictory and often unanticipated in order to gain the upper hand. Antisuffragists' shift to a more public role, for example, not only was a response to suffrage competition, but also met the internal need of raising funds to sustain the national organization. Collectively, these results underscore the complexity of countermovement development and argue for greater scholarly attention to these phenomena. Countermovements are not simply mirror images of the initial proactive movement, but experience phases of mobilization and demobilization that cannot be explained solely as strategic reactions to movement development. This case study of the U. S. antisuffrage movement further demonstrates the responsiveness of movements to countermovement activity. With greater access to channels of elite influence, the antisuffrage movement forced suffragists to respond in ways that scholars now justly criticize. This study does not excuse the documented racism and classism of suffragists, but provides a new angle from which to interpret their actions.

The active opposition of women tied to the elite establishment pushed the public image of the suffrage movement well out of the mainstream, and charges of suffrage radicalism further put them on the defensive, increasing pressures on suffragists to move to the right in order to influence the political process and achieve their goal. Suffrage leaders fought to win the middle ground by presenting a more conservative image that was a strategic response to the countermovement as much as an expression of collective class bias. They offered sporadic reassurances that neither black women in the South nor immigrant women elsewhere would vote in large enough numbers to disturb the hegemony of the dominant group and considered briefly the possibility of educational limitations on women's voting rights to win over anxious voters. NAWSA president Carrie Chapman Catt defended suffrage as a "bourgeois movement with nothing radical about it," and its journal celebrated a referendum victory by thanking the men of Kansas for their "chivalry" toward women, while victorious suffragists burned copies of the popular *Ladies' Home Journal* to protest its antisuffrage endorsement. Expediency rationales based on municipal housekeeping replaced demands for women's natural rights, suffrage posters proclaimed "Votes for Mothers," and the movement succumbed to the cult of domesticity.[7] Although incomplete and often superficial, the ostensible suffrage retrenchment encompassed gender norms, class and racial equity, and political ideology. It suggests the tenuousness of women's gender consciousness and the difficulty of forming cross-class alliances. It is an ironic historical note that attacks by Woman Patriots on the alleged radical alliances of the League of Women Voters impelled the latter group to abandon its goal of creating a female political interest group and adopt a nonpartisan stance consistent with the antisuffragist position. Both goals—the development of a single-sex voting bloc and participation by women from all levels of society—continue to elude the women's movement to the present day.

This study of antisuffragism documents also the utility of broadening the investigation of politics from voting and officeholding, particularly for the study of relatively powerless populations. Women's efforts for and against equal rights unfolded within a common context of exclusion from formal political participation that required a deferential stance toward those with the power to grant their wishes. Segregation and seclusion created a female culture that legitimated its forays into the public sphere by invoking themes of moral superiority, maternal devotion, and public education. Yet differences between suffrage and antisuffrage messages, means, and goals demonstrate the separation between women's culture and women's politics. These results also highlight the need for a more critical examination of the public image of women's political organizations, given the societal context of gender subordination in which they operate.[8] In short, appeals to traditional womanhood are a rational strategic choice where woman's power is both feared and disdained, and should not be taken at face value.

The example of antisuffragism underscores the complexity of political activity during the Progressive Era. The search for order in response to increasing societal diversity provoked some men to call for a restricted electorate and the resurrection of elite hegemony, and their civic reform efforts aimed to strip power from the immigrant voter along with corrupt urban machines. The antisuffrage movement often drew support from this brand of male reformer. The nation also experienced a widespread preoccupation with purity and unity, and sanctified motherhood fulfilled both needs. This female image is a complex component of the dispute over the ballot; from the same source, women with different ideological predispositions spun distinct political mandates for their gender. Prosuffrage reformers expanded the concept of "home" to include anywhere that women were; said one, "Home is the community. The city full of people is the Family. The public school is the real nursery." Antisuffragists rejected this expanded definition of the domestic sphere, in principle if not in practice. The antisuffrage movement generally did not advocate a progressive ideology, even in the broadest sense of the term. In contrast to suffragists, they supported laissez-faire economic policies that upheld the interests of corporate capitalism and typically advocated nonpolitical and individualistic solutions to social problems. While it is fair to judge the elitism of suffragists and other reformers who advocated protective policies that placed "the canons of womanhood at the core of women's political personality" and naive Americanization programs to assimilate the immigrant, their support for social change to benefit less advantaged groups stands in contrast to the opposition's nostalgic embrace of an earlier, simpler, and more homogeneous America.[9]

Contemporary Antifeminism and the Conservative Coalition

As we approach the end of another century, the U. S. political landscape manifests striking parallels to that of the 1890s. Collective anxiety about national identity and economic well-being is reflected in public debate over the merits of cultural diversity, calls for restrictive immigration policies, and publication of "scholarly" discursives on racial inferiority reminiscent of turn-of-the-century interest in eugenics. Controversies over affirmative action and welfare reform that dominate current political discourse evoke nineteenth-century judgments about the importance of virtue, and calls for a severely restricted federal role reiterate the states' rights arguments of an earlier era. Numerous public figures have proposed a reconstituted "Puritan covenant" based on personal character and hierarchical authority as a solution to the complex dilemmas of modern life.[10]

In both historical periods, proposed constitutional amendments to guarantee gender equality were part of a wave of progressive reforms. While antisuffragists battled against an ascendant progressive impulse that culminated in the passage of the Nineteenth Amendment in 1920, the current conservative response represents a backlash against a more recent progressive phase, the civil rights era of the 1960s and early 1970s. Federal laws that mandated governmental intervention to achieve gender and racial equity are now derided as "countercultural" and targeted for eradication. Election results and public opinion polls concur that liberalism is in disrepute, and conservative values increasingly dominate the political agenda, manifested by the visibility and power of a right-wing coalition that helped engineer this ideological transformation. The "culture war" between traditionalists and cosmopolitans parallels the demographic divide revealed in some balloting on suffrage referenda. What is new to the modern era, somewhat paradoxically, is the significant role played by religious institutions in the political mobilization of conservative citizens, as embodied in the frequently used description the New Christian Right.[11]

The organization of antifeminist women constitutes an important albeit less acknowledged component of the New Right coalition, and they share many traits with their antisuffrage predecessors.[12] The two largest women's antifeminist organizations, Eagle Forum and Concerned Women for America (CWA), were both founded to halt ratification of a federal amendment, in this case the proposed Equal Rights Amendment, which passed Congress in 1972 on the heels of other civil rights legislation. As with the earlier antisuffragists, the largest organized protests against the ERA were made by women, and their efforts were more successful than the campaign against the Nineteenth Amendment. A speechwriter for presidential candidate Barry Goldwater in 1964 and more recently national co-chair of Patrick Buchanan's 1996 presidential bid, Phyllis Schlafly established Eagle Forum in 1972, while Beverly LaHaye, long active in her husband's Christian ministry, began CWA in 1979. Both leaders claim that their primary rationale for organizing was to defeat the ERA; Eagle Forum originated STOP-ERA chapters in states considering ratification, and CWA built a national network of anti-ERA prayer chains that sought God's help weekly. After the ratification period for the federal amendment finally lapsed in 1982, both organizations expanded their issue base, but remain vigilant and have helped defeat every proposed state equal rights amendment since.[13]

The rhetorical themes of the contemporary antifeminist movement parallel those of its antisuffrage progenitors, although there is no evidence of any historical connection between the two groups. Both Eagle Forum and CWA present themselves as the true defenders of women's interests, arguing that the feminist agenda "deliberately degrades the homemaker." Schlafly and LaHaye are both relatively privileged and accomplished women in charge of multimillion-dollar budgets who nevertheless denounce careers for other married women, not unlike the disparity found between antisuffragists' rhetoric and conduct. Today's antifeminist organizations likewise ignore women family heads and treat female employment as superfluous and harmful, alleging that women workers usurp the male breadwinner role and threaten family stability. They largely reject the possibility of job discrimination and trace inequities to "the inadequacy of female qualifications." Both uphold the ideology of separate spheres as the "plan of the Divine Architect for the survival of the human race" and the source of women's success and fulfillment. Schlafly has labeled the ERA the "extra responsibilities amendment," a reiteration of the antisuffrage charge that voting constituted an unfair burden on women, and the STOP-ERA acronym reportedly refers to "stop taking our privileges." Both deride feminism as an extremist experiment that threatens the nation's strength with its goal of a "gender-free" society, oppose attempts to "feminize" the military, and apply gender stereotypes to label feminists "bitter" proponents of a "sterile" ideology. Just as antisuffrage women described their suffrage sisters in infantilizing terms, today's antifeminist writings trivialize women's rights activists as "whining" "crybabies."[14]

Antifeminists still attack women's rights activists as selfish and take sharper aim at credentialed professional women, reflecting changes in the opportunity structure. According to Phyllis Schlafly and Beverly LaHaye, feminists are "executive" women in "well-paying jobs," who take employment away from male breadwinners or push a goal of equality that harms women without college degrees. Just as antifeminists argued against federal spending for social programs in the 1920s, today's antifeminists denounce government support for education in the 1990s as a "well-larded pork barrel for the radical feminists to put their people on the public payroll." The gendered class basis of women's opposition to feminism is still apparent, but contemporary rhetoric targets its appeals downward to working-class resentments, charging that policies like Affirmative Action, Comparable Worth, and the Family and Medical Leave Act will advantage "yuppie, two-career couples" at the expense of manual laborers and poor workers. This historical contrast is due partly to differences in leadership between the two movements; no urban aristocracy is in charge of the current wave of antifeminism, and its core activists are a relatively low-status group rather than society women. But as with its earlier manifestation, contemporary antifeminist rhetoric extends a positive ideal to women disadvantaged by the gendered class hierarchy, fashioning a modern image of true womanhood: a virtuous, ladylike "Positive Woman" who has the power to control men without government protection.[15]

New issues have appeared on the feminist agenda since the suffrage campaign: employment equity, reproductive freedom, and gay rights. Antifeminist organizations oppose them all, and a rhetorical connection between the two periods is discernible. The "terrible triplets" of the modern era are not suffragism, socialism, and feminism, but "militant homosexuals," "radical feminists," and "ultraliberals." Homosexual epithets are used to discredit all feminists as lesbians, and a standard anti-ERA argument was that it would legalize homosexual marriages. While gay rights was not a political issue at the turn of the century, ad hominem attacks on suffragists as a "third sex," "freaks," "hybrids," and "Amazons" are replicated in current antifeminist references to "feminoids" and radical lesbians; all these terms question the femininity and hence the legitimacy of feminists as spokespersons for women's interests. The achievement of voting rights and greater public participation by women over time has enlarged the scope of permissible antifeminist discourse, and today's antis abandon ladylike gentility when describing the opposition, routinely denouncing the character, physical appearance, and sexuality of feminists much as men did during the suffrage fight. But if courtesy toward their own gender has diminished over time, so has deference toward men. Harsh words are leveled against men who stray from the conservative course: they are called "hen-pecked," "wimpish politicians" and chided to "stand up and be men."[16]

Besides gender issues, the two waves of antifeminist mobilization share other traits derived from their common roots in political conservatism. In fact, gender issues are a rather low priority in current antifeminist propaganda, judging by the contents of monthly newsletters produced by both CWA and Eagle Forum. The majority of themes in Schlafly's monthly report address prototypical conservative issues, such as a strong defense, low taxes, and the protection of private enterprise, and both groups retain a hard anticommunist stance despite the breakup of the Soviet Union. The names of both Eagle Forum and Concerned Women for America recall the hyperpatriotic title of the earlier Woman Patriots. Tendencies toward ethnocentrism and isolationism, manifested in antisuffragists' anxieties over an incipient "New World Order," reappear verbatim in current antifeminist propaganda; just as the Woman Patriots protested proposals to form a League of Nations, Schlafly and LaHaye oppose United States participation in the United Nations and warn their members that its true mission is to force godless "global values" on American families, dictating "who does the household chores around your home . . . even how a 'family' should be defined."[17]

If international agencies are suspect, antifeminist distrust of the federal government is even stronger; this laissez-faire approach to government's role is very much in line with the U. S. conservative tradition and their antisuffrage forebears, and at variance with expressions of class resentments used to frame gender issues. A common theme is tax relief, and high-income Americans are no longer called spoiled yuppies, but deserving entrepreneurs and lawyers who put in "hard work and long hours" while their employees enjoy leisure. Part of the objection voiced to the Equal Rights Amendment was that it represented a "big grab for vast new federal power," an accusation consistent with states' rights arguments against the Nineteenth Amendment as well as opposition to federal reform legislation during the 1920s. The Woman Patriots' protests against the National Education Association and establishment of a federal Department of Education recur in the rhetoric of both contemporary antifeminist organizations, which demand their abolishment. Education is a major concern of CWA and Eagle Forum; they object especially to "humanist" curricula that teach moral relativism and undermine parental authority through "evil" messages to children "that parents are irrelevant and their savior is the government."[18]

By legitimating an expanded political role for women, the feminist movement has bequeathed a much larger legacy to contemporary political culture: the mobilization of conservative women. I contend that the political activation of antifeminist women is largely responsible but rarely credited for the rise of the New Right in the 1970s. Issues of social conservatism—reproduction, sexuality, pornography, marriage, the family—are the ideological hallmark of the New Right and fit well within the traditional domain of female concerns. Moreover, as Jerome Himmelstein points out, the women's liberation movement of the 1960s and 1970s transformed the personal into the political, generating public controversy that gave conservatives a "cornucopia of social issues" to address in efforts to restore social order and personal discipline. The contemporary antifeminist movement developed in this context, not just to stop the Equal Rights Amendment, but also to create an alternative political agenda for conservative women labeled the "profamily movement." The genius of antifeminist leaders like Phyllis Schlafly lies in their adept use of social issues to educate and mobilize women to work for the more conventional conservative agenda of taxes and defense, often by appealing to female anxieties derived from their disadvantaged position in the gendered class hierarchy.[19] And, just as in the suffrage era, political pundits and scholars alike tend to depoliticize and romanticize their efforts as the actions of a group of homemakers fighting to remain there.

This modern continuation of the antisuffrage movement is a reminder of the ongoing political interaction between both sides of the women's rights movement. Female politics, whether liberal or conservative, are shaped by the contradictions of women's lives embedded in the social context of inequality. This examination of an overlooked group of reactionary women reinforces previous caveats against the conflation of feminism and women's politics.[20] Much work remains to flesh out the dynamics of female activism across the full ideological continuum, especially on the right. Although foes of feminism, the remonstrants have been revealed as political actors of considerable ingenuity and skill. They serve as ironic testimony to feminist assertions of female equality.

Appendices
Notes
Select Bibliography
Index

Appendix 1. Distribution of Major Variables for Massachusetts Towns, 1895 (N = 353)

	Mean	SD	Minimum	Maximum
Referendum results				
Negative vote, total	.60	.11	.26	.97
Men	.65	.09	.33	.89
Women	.04	.13	.00	1.00
Voter turnout				
Men	.44	.11	.14	.73
Women	.04	.06	.00	.91
Demographic variables				
Sex ratio (male/female)	1.01	.13	.53	1.83
Native-born	.99	.11	.49	1.73
Foreign-born	1.14	.49	.40	5.90
Foreign-born voters	.13	.09	.00	.49
Farm population	.21	.16	.00	.69
Youth population	.35	.04	.22	.49
Single adults	.27	.06	.00	.51
Married adults	.60	.07	.08	.76
Ethnic origin (% foreign-born)				
Irish	.30	.16	.00	.79
British	.21	.12	.00	.68
French Canadian	.14	.15	.00	.79
German	.05	.07	.00	.67
Labor force, by gender				
Male participation rate	.64	.05	.37	.85
White-collar	.12	.07	.00	.42
Professional	.02	.01	.00	.08
Manufacturing	.34	.19	.00	.72
Female participation rate	.11	.06	.01	.39
White-collar	.34	.21	.00	1.00
Manufacturing	.53	.25	.00	.94

Appendix 2. County Characteristics for State Referenda Analysis, c. 1910

	West		Kansas		Texas		East	
	Mean	SD	Mean	SD	Mean	SD	Mean	SD
Referenda results								
Negative vote	.43	.08	.47	.07	.50	.15	.56	.11
Voter turnout	.30	.15	.70	.10	.31	.13	.44	.14
Demographic variables								
Male/female ratio	1.43	.23	1.13	.08	1.12	.10	1.04	.07
Urban	.23	.25	.14	.21	.11	.19	.45	.29
Growth	1.19	1.50	.27	.40	8.36	27.72	.33	.50
Foreign-born	.17	.07	.07	.04	.06	.09	.15	.09
Nonwhite	.04	.04	.02	.03	.12	.16	.02	.02
School enrollment	.67	.04	.72	.04	.59	.10	.66	.04
Ethnicity								
German	.14	.05	.22	.08	.18	.14	.15	.09
Irish	.07	.04	.05	.03	.03	.04	.15	.08
Scandinavian	.12	.10	.08	.10	.03	.06	.03	.05
Catholic	.07	.07	.04	.04	.05	.12	.11	.09
N	123		105		235		159	

Notes

Abbreviations

The following abbreviations identify frequently cited archives and publications.

EPW	Everett P. Wheeler Papers, New York Public Library, New York
MAOFESW	Massachusetts Association Opposed to the Further Extension of Suffrage to Women Papers, Massachusetts Historical Society, Boston
EC	Executive Committee meeting
EDC	Education Committee meeting
EOC	Education and Organization Committee meeting
JC	Joint Committee meeting
MAOSW	Maine Association Opposed to Suffrage for Women Papers, Maine Historical Society, Portland
MSA	Man-Suffrage Association Opposed to Political Suffrage for Women Papers, Library of Congress, Washington, D.C.
NCAB	*National Cyclopedia of American Biography*
NYT	*New York Times*
RHJ	Rossiter and Helen Kendrick Johnson Papers, New York Public Library, New York
SWL	Southern Woman's League for the Rejection of the Susan B. Anthony Amendment Papers, Alabama Department of Archives and History, Montgomery, Alabama
WP	*Woman's Protest* (changed its name to *Woman Patriot* in March 1918)

Chapter 1. Introduction: The Paradox of Antifeminism

1. Epigraph, "Women Are Jubilant: Antis Promise Appeal," *NYT,* 19 August 1920, 2.

2. *WP* quoted in "The American Woman Voter Arrives," 10.

3. Catt and Shuler, chap. 10; Yellin; A. Elizabeth Taylor, *Woman Suffrage Movement in Tennessee,* chap. 7.

4. These were Wyoming, Colorado, Utah, and Idaho. Catt and Shuler, 107; Morrison, 54.

5. Quotes in MAOFESW, Annual Report, 30 April 1896; Mrs. Arthur M. Dodge, "Why I Am an Antisuffragist," presidential keynote speech at the Annual Convention of the National Association Opposed to Woman Suffrage, December 1916, box 1, Woman's Suffrage and Women's Rights Collection, Special Collections, Vassar College Libraries. Scholarly interpretations of antisuffragists as cultural traditionalists include Banks, chap. 6; O'Neill, *Everyone Was Brave,* 55–63; Sinclair, 168–71; Chafetz and Dworkin.

6. Hazard, "New York State Association"; "Anti-Suffragists Aroused," *NYT,* 10 December 1911, sec. 3, 16; "Notes on the Year's Work," *WP,* October 1916, 14–15; "Miss Rowe Challenges Suffrage Threat," *WP,* 21 August 1920, 2.

7. Becker; Scharf and Jensen. For a revised view of the so-called doldrums, see Rupp and Taylor.

8. Daniels, xxi.

9. MAOFESW, untitled address, 23 February 1898; Hazard, "New York State Association."

10. On the progressive movement generally, see an overview of the debate by Rodgers. Anthologies of women's actions in the progressive period include Hewitt and Lebsock; DuBois and Ruiz; Frankel and Dye.

11. The conflation of feminism and women's politics is most directly addressed by Cott, "What's in a Name?" The most influential critical analysis of the woman suffrage movement is by the same author. See Cott, *Grounding of Modern Feminism.* Blee; Koonz; Rupp; Klatch.

12. For theoretical treatments of the study of women in public life, see Clemens; Sara M. Evans; Kerber, "Separate Spheres."

13. Recent empirical research finds that women have relatively low levels of solidarity, identification, and grievance on gender issues as compared with race consciousness among blacks, class consciousness among blue-collar workers, and even age solidarity among the elderly. See Kluegel and Smith; Gurin; Gurin and Townsend; Sears and Huddy; Davis and Robinson.

14. The most complete analyses of the failed ERA ratification drive include Mansbridge; Boles, *Politics of the Equal Rights Amendment;* Berry. See also Conover and Gray. The post-ERA activities of antifeminists are examined in Susan E. Marshall, "Who Speaks for American Women."

15. Sapiro, 468. Some major histories of the women's movement that mention antisuffrage, although not necessarily women's organized opposition, include Flexner, chap. 22; Kraditor, chap. 2; O'Neill, *Everyone Was Brave,* 55–63; Cott, *Grounding of Modern Feminism,* 20, 44; Sinclair, 168–73, 201–10, 239–48, 293, 321, 331; Banks, 96, 247; Buechler, 12–14, 20–21, 103, 133, 172–75.

16. Anne Firor Scott, "On Seeing and Not Seeing." A classic sociological statement of feminist epistemology is Dorothy Smith.

17. For example, Cott, *Grounding of Modern Feminism;* DuBois and Ruiz; Frankel and Dye.

18. Of the six volumes documenting the struggle for woman suffrage in the

United States, only the last three volumes address organized antisuffrage activity. See Anthony and Harper, xxix, 16, 168–71, 249, 258, 320, 327, 361, 364, 369, 370, 381, 392, 512, 556, 603, 650, 704, 716, 736–44, 850–61, 888, 895, 971; Harper, 5:xix, 223, 235, 269, 299, 354, 362, 383–92, 436–38, 467–69, 476–79, 536, 583–93, 735–37. Harper, vol. 6, provides state-by-state synopses of the suffrage campaign that are peppered with brief references to antisuffrage activities. See also Catt and Shuler, chap. 10; Blatch and Lutz, 95–97, 140, 227–32, 264; Catt, chap. 6.

19. Anthony and Harper, xxix; Catt and Shuler, 273.

20. Examples of scholarship that have characterized the ideological conflict between feminists and antifeminists in these dichotomous terms are Howard; Susan E. Marshall, "Keep Us on the Pedestal."

21. Anthony and Harper, 361; Harper, 5:299, 392, 471–73, 583, 592, 735–37. See also Blatch and Lutz, 140, 232. For an example of Catt's rejoinders, see "John Hay, Mrs. Catt, and Patriotism," originally published in *Woman Citizen*, 10 November 1917, reprinted in O'Neill, *Woman Movement*, 190–95.

22. Catt and Shuler, 130–59; Snapp. See also Lunardini.

23. Fisher; Firestone; Scott and Scott, 25–27; Wilda M. Smith; Flexner, chap. 22.

24. Kraditor, 12–26; Mayor; Howard; Harrison, chap. 4; Frenier; Susan E. Marshall, "Keep Us on the Pedestal"; idem, "In Defense of Separate Spheres;" Billie Barnes Jensen; Thurner.

25. Cott, *Bonds of Womanhood*, 204; DuBois, *Feminism and Suffrage;* Berg; Epstein; Blair; Melder, *Beginnings of Sisterhood*.

26. Kraditor, chaps. 3, 5. See also O'Neill, *Everyone Was Brave*, 33–44; Richard J. Evans, chap. 4; Banks, chap. 6; Cott, *Grounding of Modern Feminism;* Buechler, chaps. 4, 5; Marlow and Davis, chap. 4; Mink, "Lady and the Tramp."

27. Catt and Shuler, 125; Gertrude Foster Brown, "Decisive Victory Won"; O'Neill, *Everyone Was Brave*, 65–76; Penn, 261–64; Giddings, chap. 7.

28. In fact, in 1917 Carrie Chapman Catt called NAWSA a "bourgeois movement with nothing radical about it," in part to distance NAWSA from the militancy of the National Woman's Party. Quoted in Cott, *Grounding of Modern Feminism*, 60. See also Richard J. Evans, chap. 4; O'Neill, *Everyone Was Brave*, chap. 2.

29. Acker, "Women and Social Stratification"; Hacker.

30. For example, Cott, *Grounding of Modern Feminism;* DuBois and Ruiz; Frankel and Dye; Dye.

31. See Iris Young; Acker, "Women and Stratification"; idem, "Class, Gender, and the Relations of Distribution." Other important early feminist critiques of women's social class placement include West; Comer.

32. For critical reviews of the literature on gender and class, see Acker, "Women and Stratification." For a critique of gender and race conceptualizations, see King.

33. Quote by Acker, "Class, Gender, and the Relations of Distribution," 477; idem, "Gendered Institutions"; Joan Scott; West and Zimmerman; Walby.

34. Milton Gordon; Ransford.

35. Daniels, xxi; Odendahl; Susan A. Ostrander.

36. Sara M. Evans; Baker, *Moral Frameworks of Public Life;* Nancy A. Hewitt; Mary P. Ryan; Anne Firor Scott, *Natural Allies.*

37. Oberschall; Gamson, *Strategy of Social Protest;* McCarthy and Zald, "Resource Mobilization and Social Movements"; Jenkins; McCarthy and Zald, *Trend of Social Movements in America;* Snow, Zurcher, and Ekland-Olson; Cathcart; John Wilson; Turner and Killian, chap. 14.

38. Two noteworthy exceptions to the theoretical neglect of countermovements are Mottl; Lo. Recent research examining the interaction between movement and countermovement include Zald and Useem; Gale.

39. For the national antisuffrage movement, the three historical monographs are Benjamin; Camhi; Jablonsky. There is also a bibliography by Kinnard, and a monograph on British antisuffragism (Harrison, *Separate Spheres*) that is of limited applicability to the United States because woman suffrage there was a parliamentary issue and produced a more centralized antisuffrage effort. Readers are also referred to an unpublished dissertation on the U.S. antisuffrage movement: James J. Kenneally, "The Opposition to Woman Suffrage in Massachusetts, 1868–1920."

40. A partial list of these sources includes MAOFESW; MAOSW; SWL; MSA; RHJ; EPW.

41. The History of Women microfilm collection was especially helpful for collecting the sample, although it was not the only source used. See *History of Women: Guide to the Microfilm Collection.* A useful guide for identifying antisuffrage publications was Kinnard.

42. For identifying women remonstrants, some of the most important sources included John William Leonard, *Woman's Who's Who of America;* Cameron; Edward T. James. Men were researched primarily with *Who's Who in American History,* 21 vols., reprinted as *Who Was Who in America,* 7 vols.; *NCAB;* Johnson and Malone.

Chapter 2. "Women of High Social Standing"

1. Epigraph, speech at 1908 National American Woman Suffrage Association convention, quoted in Harper, 5:223.

2. On suffragist elitism, see Cott, *Grounding of Modern Feminism;* Kraditor, chaps. 6, 7; O'Neill, *Everyone Was Brave,* chap. 2. For examples of research focusing on male antisuffragists, see Flexner; Kraditor; Grimes.

3. See Blair; Clemens; Epstein; Theodora Penny Martin; Melder, "Ladies Bountiful."

4. See Stevenson. For other treatments of the female antisuffrage leadership, see Jablonsky, chap. 4; Camhi, 233–45; Howard; Mambretti; Kenneally,

"Woman Suffrage and the Massachusetts 'Referendum' of 1895"; Susan E. Marshall, "In Defense of Separate Spheres."

5. On countermovements, see Turner and Killian, chap. 16. On social movement networks, see McAdam, McCarthy, and Zald, 707–12; Friedman and McAdam; Clemens, 759–63.

6. See Fisher.

7. Winslow; Burnap; Chapin; Sprague; Sears; Doane, *Sermon Preached at the Commencement of Cottage Hill Seminary;* Todd; Brockett, 93–95, 283; Bushnell, *Women's Suffrage,* 56, 86, 142.

8. Epstein; Lerner; Welter; Easton; Rothman; Smith-Rosenberg.

9. On the canon of domesticity, see Cott, *Bonds of Womanhood,* 66–71. Quotes by Welter, 320, 326.

10. See Woody.

11. Child; Beecher, *Treatise on Domestic Economy;* Sarah Josepha Hale; Bushnell, *Christian Nurture.* See also Sklar, 151–67.

12. "Editors' Table," *Godey's Lady's Book and Magazine,* May 1871, 476.

13. See Sarah Josepha Hale, "Editors' Table," *Godey's Lady's Book and Magazine,* July 1851, 57–58; April 1852, 293; October 1867, 354–55; July 1868, 82–83; October 1869, 359; August 1870, 181; January 1872, 93.

14. Quote from "Editors' Table," *Godey's Lady's Book and Magazine,* May 1871, 476. The claim about the petition's size was made by an antisuffrage activist. See Dahlgren, 3.

15. The petition named Mrs. Senators Corbett (Oregon), Edmunds (Vermont), Scott (Pennsylvania), Sherman (Ohio); Mrs. Jacob D. Cox (former Ohio governor and U.S. secretary of the interior), and Mrs. Rev. Dr. Butler, probably referring to John George Butler. See *Who Was Who in America,* 1:117, 268, 359, 1117.

16. See Sklar; Boydston, Kelley, and Margolis. The 1871 petition in *Godey's* incorrectly listed Catharine Beecher as "Mrs. Beecher." See "Editors' Table," *Godey's Lady's Book and Magazine,* May 1871, 476. Beecher, *Something for Women Better Than the Ballot,* reprinted from advance sheets of *Appleton's Journal,* 4 September 1869, 12; idem, *Woman Suffrage and Woman's Profession;* idem, *Woman's Profession as Mother and Educator.*

17. A biographical sketch of Madeleine Vinton Dahlgren is found in Willard and Livermore, 1:225. On Almira Lincoln Phelps, see Edward T. James, 3:58–60.

18. Phelps, "Woman's Record." See also Phelps, "Woman's Duties and Rights."

19. Flexner, chap. 11.

20. Grimes, chaps. 2, 3.

21. DuBois, *Feminism and Suffrage,* chap. 3; Stanton, Anthony, and Gage, 2:257; Wilda M. Smith. See also *An Appeal against Anarchy of Sex.*

22. DuBois, *Feminism and Suffrage,* chaps. 3, 6; Flexner, 143–53; Morrison, 49–56; Meade.

23. Flexner, 153–54, 168–69.

24. Quote in Phelps, "Woman's Record," 149. For information on Frances Wright, see Flexner, 27–28; Eckhardt.

25. *The True Woman* is described in Kinnard, 181; Moore, 278–306.

26. Stanton, Anthony, and Gage, 1:47; also see Harper, 5:678.

27. For background on the Massachusetts case, see Strom.

28. Mrs. Charles E. Guild, "Address at a Conference of the Executive Committee with Gentlemen, March 30, 1906," MAOFESW; John Lowell; Lord. For a history of Massachusetts remonstrants, see Benjamin, chap. 1; Jablonsky, chap. 1.

29. Clara T. Leonard, *Letter from Mrs. Clara T. Leonard;* Mrs. Charles E. Guild, "Address at a Conference of the Executive Committee with Gentlemen, March 30, 1906," MAOFESW; Parkman, *Some of the Reasons against Woman Suffrage;* J. W. P.; H. M. Goodwin; Mary Abigail Dodge; Frank Foxcroft, *Municipal Suffrage for Women—Why?*

30. MAOFESW, "Report of the Secretary to the Committee of Remonstrants against Woman Suffrage for the Year Ending December 31, 1894."

31. Crocker, *Argument of Hon. George G. Crocker;* idem, *Letter to the Committee;* Tappan.

32. *Remonstrance,* 1890, 1; 1891, 1; Duniway, 117–18.

33. "Recent Defeats of Woman Suffrage" was a feature in each issue of the *Remonstrance* during this period. See also "Suffrage Disappointments in New England" and "A Bad Year for Suffrage," *Remonstrance,* February 1890, 3; "The Defeat in South Dakota," *Remonstrance,* 1891, 4; "Losing Ground," *Remonstrance,* 1893, 2; "Municipal Suffrage Not Constitutional," "The Michigan Decision," *Remonstrance,* 1894, 2. For examples of the failed experiment argument, see "A Fluctuating Factor," *Remonstrance,* February 1890, 4; "Controlled by Emotion," *Remonstrance,* 1893, 2; "Wait for Experiment," *Remonstrance,* 1894, 3. For examples of prominent antisuffragist opinions, see "Goldwin Smith on Suffrage," *Remonstrance,* February 1890, 1–2; "A True and Impartial View," *Remonstrance,* 1892, 4; "Why Indeed?" *Remonstrance,* 1894, 2. For articles purporting to identify weakness among the suffrage opposition, see "Concessions of a Suffragist," *Remonstrance,* 1891, 4; "Have Enough of It," "Not Asked, but Repudiated," *Remonstrance,* 1893, 3, 4.

34. MAOFESW, untitled paper, n.d.; "The Massachusetts 'Referendum,' " *Remonstrance,* 1896, 1; Kenneally, "Woman Suffrage and the Massachusetts 'Referendum.' "

35. MAOFESW, meeting, 1 May 1895; MAOFESW, "Report of the Secretary," 2, 5; Mrs. Charles E. Guild, "Address at a Conference of the Executive Committee with Gentlemen, March 30, 1906," MAOFESW; Hazard, "New York State Association," 84, 85; Benjamin, chap. 2.

36. New York State Association Opposed to the Extension of Suffrage to Women, Brooklyn auxiliary (1902), MAOFESW.

37. Anthony and Harper, 4:995–1004; "Wyoming as an Example," *Remon-*

strance, February 1890, 1; "Woman Suffrage in Wyoming" and "Women Mayors," *Remonstrance,* 1894, 4; "The Four Women Suffrage States," *Anti-Suffragist,* March 1909, 6–7; MAOFESW, Western Report, Summer of 1898, n.d.; Billie Barnes Jensen; Benjamin, chap. 3.

38. Duniway, 117; MAOFESW, Annual Report, January 1900.

39. Corbin, "The Reasons for Remonstrance," *Remonstrance,* 1892, 2.

40. Anthony and Harper, 4:599–601; Mambretti, 168–69.

41. For more on the Woman's Christian Temperance Union and Willard's socialist conversion, see Bordin; Flexner, 182–85; Buhle, chap. 3.

42. Corbin, *Position of Women in the Socialist Utopia;* Illinois Association Opposed to the Extension of Suffrage to Women, *Socialism and Sex.*

43. Wiebe, 51, 91–97; *NCAB,* 1:51–52; Higham, 100–107.

44. *Remonstrance,* 1900, 1.

45. Baltzell, *Philadelphia Gentlemen,* 174; idem, *Puritan Boston,* 40–41, 385–89, 458–69; Jaher, *Urban Establishment,* 20–44, 57–67; idem, "Politics of the Boston Brahmins," 59–78; Higley, 1–30.

46. Baltzell, *Puritan Boston,* 213–35; Jaher, "Politics of the Boston Brahmins," 60; idem, *Urban Establishment,* 50–54, 71–75, 88.

47. The convention among antisuffrage leaders was to refer to themselves publicly by their husbands' full name. I deviate from this practice to provide the reader information about their family backgrounds and to make this history more human. For residential data, I consulted U.S. Department of the Interior, Census Office, *Tenth Census of the United States,* Population Schedules; Baltzell, *Puritan Boston,* 30, 230. For Houghton and Fisk, see Brooks, 100; Mary Caroline Crawford, 1:224–26.

48. The family lineages of antisuffrage women presented in tables 2.1 and 2.2 were collected from the following sources: Baltzell, *Puritan Boston;* Mary Caroline Crawford; Cameron; Edward T. James; *Who Was Who in America; NCAB.*

49. On the Gardner lineage, see Mary Caroline Crawford, 1:83. On the Parkmans, see Van Doren, 796–97. Rev. Lothrop is profiled in *NCAB,* 14:225–26. The Lyman family is mentioned in Curtis, 310. For Elizabeth Sohier, see National Society of the Daughters of the American Revolution, 24:55.

50. For example, the founding committee included two pairs of sisters; in addition to the Lothrop women there were the Winthrop sisters, Susan Swett and Elizabeth Hooker, whose aunt was committee member Adele Thayer Winthrop, third wife of their uncle Robert. Marriage also linked the Crocker women, as Annie Bliss Crocker was the sister-in-law of Sarah Haskell Crocker.

51. Husbands of the Massachusetts antisuffrage leadership were researched through Marquis; Mary Caroline Crawford; Johnson and Malone; *Who Was Who in America; NCAB.*

52. Firey, 106.

53. According to Baltzell, the Eliots, Cabots, and Lowells dominated the stewardship of Harvard University. The brother of one antisuffrage leader, Mrs. William Lowell Putnam, was Abbott Lawrence Lowell, president of Har-

vard from 1909 to 1933, and the husband of another, Judge Francis Cabot Lowell, was a Harvard overseer (1886–95) and fellow (1895–1911). See Baltzell, *Puritan Boston*, 255–60.

54. *Tenth Census of the United States*, Population Schedules.

55. For a profile of Oliver Peabody, see *NCAB*, 26:59. The quote about publisher Henry Houghton is from Green, 28. On the links between Houghton, Crocker, and Thayer, see Johnson and Malone, 2:554–55.

56. Baltzell, *Puritan Boston*, 48, 240; *Proceedings of the Bostonian Society*.

57. For the history of private Boston philanthropy, see Huggins. On Winthrop's civic activities, see Jaher, "Politics of the Boston Brahmins," 65. On Homans, see *Appleton's Cyclopedia of American Biography*, 3:245. On Crocker, see *Who Was Who in America*, 1: 277.

58. Jaher, "Politics of the Boston Brahmins," 66–67; Wiebe, 97–103.

59. On Stone and Peabody, see *NCAB*, 12:350, 24:128. For Smith and Mott, see *NCAB*, 9:171, 2:310.

60. Neither Lucy Stone's husband, Henry Blackwell, nor Seth Wells Cheney, husband of Edna Dow Cheney, was college educated. On Samuel G. Howe, who got his M.D. from Harvard, see *NCAB*, 1:402.

61. O'Neill, *Everyone Was Brave*, 107–10; Anne Firor Scott, *Natural Allies*, 64–65, 75. There were exceptions to this pattern, such as Pauline Agassiz Shaw, the first president of the Boston Equal Suffrage Association for Good Government, daughter of Harvard professor Louis Agassiz, wife of wealthy mine owner Quincy A. Shaw, and sister-in-law of a founding member of the Massachusetts Association. See Strom, 301.

62. DuBois, "Harriot Stanton Blatch," 162–69; Aldrich; Birmingham. Another suffragist of extraordinary wealth was Paulina Wright Davis, wife of a wealthy Rhode Island jewelry manufacturer turned politician, who herself developed a series of anatomy lectures illustrated by the first female models ever brought to the United States. See *NCAB*, 22:327.

63. MAOFESW, untitled address, author unknown, n.d. (c. 1890), 2; "Plan Anti-Suffrage Fight," *NYT*, 8 September 1909, 10. On social life in Newport, see Dwight, 37–69.

64. For a description of upper-class conventions in the latter nineteenth century, see Lash, 37–50; Dwight, 7–70. For a first-person account of upper-class norms among Boston Brahmin women of the period, a valuable resource is the diary of Elizabeth Rogers Mason Cabot, sister-in-law of the first MAOFESW president. See P. A. M. Taylor.

65. Historians have focused their attention on gender norms among the middle classes, and some of the best descriptions of upper-class gender norms remain these American novels: Henry James, *Washington Square* (1881); Edith Wharton, *The House of Mirth* (1905); idem, *The Age of Innocence* (1920).

66. For descriptions of women's space in urban life of the nineteenth century, see Kasson, 128–32; Mary P. Ryan, chap. 2.

67. P. A. M. Taylor, 66–67, 116.

68. Weber, 186–91.

69. Bourdieu; DiMaggio, "Cultural Entrepreneurship in Nineteenth-Century Boston, Part I"; idem, "Cultural Entrepreneurship in Nineteenth-Century Boston, Part II"; Levine.

70. Domhoff, chap. 2.

71. Daniels; Susan A. Ostrander; Odendahl.

72. Trachtenberg, 80.

73. Lears, 31; Wiebe, 69–71.

74. Blodgett, "Yankee Leadership," Kleppner, "From Party to Factions"; Shannon; Jaher, *Urban Establishment*, 88, 96.

75. Henry Adams, 419, quoted in Blodgett, "Yankee Leadership," 101; Wharton, *Age of Innocence*, 124.

76. Lears, 31; Wiebe, 42, 111; Jaher, *Urban Establishment*, 101–9; Aldrich; Birmingham; Porzelt, chap. 1; "Club News and Gossip," *NYT*, 21 August 1891, 14; "Boston's '400' Is '361,' " *NYT*, 18 February 1907, 9.

77. DiMaggio, "Cultural Entrepreneurship in Nineteenth-Century Boston, Parts I and II"; Levine; Harris; Kouwenhoven.

78. Quote by McCarthy, *Noblesse Oblige*, 30. On upper-class marriage rituals, see also Dwight, 7–27; P. A. M. Taylor; Davidoff; Kasson.

79. Quote in Kasson, 60, 185–95; Porzelt, 9.

80. McCarthy, *Noblesse Oblige*, 33; Schlesinger; Rothman; Kasson, 128–32, 165–69; Mary P. Ryan, chap. 2.

81. Ehrenreich and English, 198–203; Kasson, 194–95; P. A. M. Taylor, 262–63; Birmingham, 220–22, 250.

82. For overviews of the club movement, see Blair; Theodora Penny Martin; Anne Firor Scott; *Natural Allies;* Baker, "Domestication of Politics." An excellent primary source on U.S. women's organizations is a special issue of *Chautauquan*, June 1910.

83. Blair, 20–28; Croly, 9, quoted in Clemens, 772–73. See also Theodora Penny Martin, 63.

84. Anne Firor Scott, *Natural Allies*, 114.

85. Blair, 32–56; Anne Firor Scott, *Natural Allies*, 141–58. For a primary source on municipal housekeeping, see Beard.

86. Margaret Gibbons Wilson, 100.

87. Blair, 95–107. See also Linda Gordon; Skocpol; Clemens, 768–70.

88. MAOFESW, EDC, 7 March 1896.

89. See the statement by Georgia state federation president Mrs. G. I. Fitzpatrick, quoted in A. Elizabeth Taylor, "Last Phase of the Woman Suffrage Movement in Georgia." For the Massachusetts Association response, see MAOFESW, EOC, 15 December 1915; MAOFESW, JC, 17 July 1914.

90. Wharton, *House of Mirth*, 455.

91. Wells, "Women in Organizations"; McCarthy, *Lady Bountiful Revisited;* idem, *Noblesse Oblige*, chaps. 1–2; Melder, "Ladies Bountiful"; Mary P. Ryan; Odendahl; Daniels; Susan A. Ostrander.

92. Wells, "Boston Club Woman," 371.

93. *Mayflower Club*, 1–2; *Boston Transcript*, quoted in *Mayflower Club*, 15–16.

94. This is a primary thesis of Elizabeth Wilson, *The Sphinx in the City.*

95. *Mayflower Club*, 33.

96. Aldrich, 42–50; Rotundo, 201–2.

97. The six women were Mrs. Roger Wolcott, wife of the future Massachusetts governor, Mrs. Henry Whitman, Beacon Hill artist and wife of a wealthy wool merchant, Mrs. John Lowell, wife of the judge and antisuffrage activist; the three antisuffrage leaders were Mrs. Homans, Mrs. Peabody, and Mrs. Shaw. U.S. Department of the Interior, Census Office, *Tenth Census of the United States*, Population Schedules. See also *Mayflower Club*, 1.

98. Mrs. Charles E. Guild, "Address at a Conference of the Executive Committee with Gentlemen, March 30, 1906," MAOFESW.

99. Julia Coolidge, Cora Shaw, and Elizabeth Sohier were vice-presidents, Sarah Crocker was a member of the board of government, and Annie Crocker was listed as a charter member of the club. See *Mayflower Club*.

100. Ibid., 3. Quote by Wells, "Women in Organizations."

101. Mary Caroline Crawford, 1:146, 182–87; *NCAB*, 21:320; P. A. M. Taylor, 34.

102. Whitney obituary from *NYT*, 26 January 1923, 17. See also Blodgett, *Gentle Reformers*, 122–24.

103. Description of Mrs. Oliver W. Peabody in *Mayflower Club*, 45. Obituary of Mrs. J. Elliot Cabot from *Remonstrance*, 1902, 1.

104. *Mayflower Club*, 46; "The March Town Meetings," *Woman's Journal*, 11 March 1882, 73; Homans's obituary is in *Remonstrance*, October 1914, 7. Kate Gannett Wells, who served on the Boston antisuffrage committee during the 1880s, was one of the first woman members of the Boston School Committee, a leader in the Woman's Education Association of Boston, and a three-term appointee to the Massachusetts State Board of Education, as well as a well-known author. See Edward T. James, 3: 563–65.

105. For more on the backgrounds of the U.S. suffrage leadership, see Kraditor, 265–82; O'Neill, *Everyone Was Brave*, chap. 4. On comparisons between pro- and antisuffrage leaders, see Stevenson, 90; Jablonsky, 52–57.

106. Agnes Irwin, a descendant of Benjamin Franklin, remained until her death in 1914 the only MAOFESW officer listed by occupational title, although she retired and moved to Philadelphia in 1909. Irwin never attended executive committee sessions, although she once addressed an annual meeting. MAOFESW records indicate that, as early as 1901, Miss Irwin had given permission for the organization to use her name for the antisuffrage cause. Anna L. Dawes was a long-distance officer who corresponded frequently with the MAOFESW leadership from her home in western Massachusetts until her 1919 resignation. She was also director of the Massachusetts Prison Association. See *Who Was Who in America*. 1:304, 620; Edward T. James, 2:253–55; MAOFESW,

EC, 11 January 1901; "Annual Meeting of the Association," *Remonstrance,* June 1907, 1–3.

107. John William Leonard, *Woman's Who's Who,* 666; Cameron, 1:86–87; Michel and Rosen.

108. John William Leonard, *Woman's Who's Who,* 406; obituary in *Remonstrance,* July 1915, 3.

109. She was a Dover, Massachusetts, clubwoman named Caroline Miller (Mrs. Augustin Hamilton) Parker, who served as the chairman of the county committee, charged with organizing the Massachusetts hinterland. John William Leonard, *Woman's Who's Who,* 620. For a study of suffrage and antisuffrage support based on Leonard's document, albeit with a small sample size of questionable reliability in the case of antisuffragist women, see Campbell, 133–42.

110. Kenneally, *Women and American Trade Unions,* 129–34. Quote from Dye, 10; see also chap. 6. On Elizabeth Lowell Putnam, see Michel and Rosen, 368–72.

111. Quotes in MAOFESW, Annual Report, January 1900; MAOFESW, EC, 9 January 1903, 11 December 1903, 14 October 1910, 21 January 1910. On the formation of antisuffrage organizations, see Jablonsky, chap. 2.

112. MAOFESW, EC, 12 April 1901. Mrs. Ely's leadership of the Rhode Island antisuffrage movement ended in 1909, when she was divorced from her husband. See *NCAB,* 37:387–88.

113. Mrs. Pruyn's daughter was Mrs. William Gorham Rice. Bishop Doane's daughter was Mrs. James Terry Gardiner. See Doane, *Sermon Preached at the Commencement of Cottage Hill Seminary.* Mrs. Barclay Hazard was with the New York Association, and Mrs. Roland G. Hazard was associated with the Rhode Island Association. Mrs. William Gammell and Mrs. Robert I. Gammell (the former Eliza A. Hoppin) were members of the Rhode Island standing committee, as was Mrs. Frederick C. Hoppin. At the same time, Miss Louise C. Hoppin served as vice-president. *Remonstrance,* April 1911, 1.

114. These were executive committee member Mrs. Arthur Biddle (the former Julia Biddle, who married her cousin) and recording secretary Mrs. Charles Bingham Penrose (the former Katharine Drexel, whose husband was also a Biddle descendant). *NCAB,* 20:459–60, 30:396–97.

115. For Bertha Koenig Achelis, see *NCAB,* 22:322; on Lilian B. Kiliani, see Hazard, "New York State Association," 84–89; John William Leonard, *Woman's Who's Who,* 455. The biographies of some of the eastern leaders are sketched in Camhi, 235–45.

116. On the New York leadership, see *NCAB,* 28:181; *Who Was Who in America,* 1: 3, 1096. The Oregon Association president, Mrs. R. W. (Alice Dunbar Heustis) Wilbur, was a Bostonian by birth, and Caroline Fairfield Corbin was born in Connecticut. See *NCAB,* 42:665; John William Leonard, *Woman's Who's Who,* 205.

117. Davies, 11, 46–47. For illustrative statements by officers of the Sons and

Daughters of the American Revolution and the Society of Colonial Wars, see 48–49, 79, 285, 294.

118. Davies, 57, 70, 77.

119. Quotes from Davies, 215–48, 283, 296. See also Kenneally, *Women and American Trade Unions*, 135.

120. Davies, 354–55.

121. Colonial Dames members in Albany included Eliza Doane (Mrs. James T.) Gardiner, Isabel Whitney (Mrs. William H.) Sage, and Louisa Lane (Mrs. William Bayard) Van Rensselaer. They are briefly profiled in *Social Register, New York, 1910*, 222, 508, 607. An illuminating example is found in the history of the Mayflower Club. Its leadership claimed that the club was named for the spring flower and was bemused when a Kentucky woman wrote asserting her Pilgrim heritage and requesting membership. Yet the club reported losing many members after the founding of the Chilton Club, named for the first woman to leave the Mayflower. *Mayflower Club*, 4, 34.

122. In Minneapolis, Florence Welles (Mrs. E. L.) Carpenter; in Maryland, Mary Buchanan Coale (Mrs. Francis T.) Redwood; in Georgia, Eugenia Blount (Mrs. Walter D.) Lamar; in Virginia, Jane Meade Rutherford. John William Leonard, *Woman's Who's Who*, 162, 676, 709; *Who's Who in the South and Southwest*, 542.

123. DAR members included, in Washington, Eliza Ferry (Mrs. John) Leary, president of the Seattle association, and Martha A. Gallup (Mrs. Chauncey W.) Griggs, president of the Tacoma association; in Oregon, Alice Heustis (Mrs. R. W.) Wilbur; in Montana, Jane Hutchins (Mrs. Clinton H.) Moore; in Wisconsin, Mary Clark (Mrs. Frank W.) Hoyt, president of the Madison committee in 1913, and Miss Mary Louise Atwood, state president in 1914; Illinois antisuffrage association founder Caroline Fairchild Corbin; in Ohio, Mary Jane Whiton (Mrs. Herman Milton) Hubbard; in Iowa, Garaphelia Burnham (Mrs. Joseph H.) Merrill; in Nebraska, Mary E. Bishop (Mrs. Edward Porter) Peck; in Georgia, Miss Caroline Patterson; in Pennsylvania, Debbie Norris Coleman (Mrs. Horace) Brock; in New Jersey, Miss Anna Dayton; in New York, Mrs. Charles S. Fairchild, president in 1918; in Connecticut, Grace Upson Goodrich (Mrs. Daniel A.) Markham; in Vermont, Mary Ellen Jones (Mrs. David Sloan) Conant; in the District of Columbia, Lillian Lash (Mrs. Arthur Wallace) Dunn. The Mayflower Descendant Society member who served as New York State president was Miss Alice Hill Chittenden. See *Directory of the National Society of the Daughters of the American Revolution; Social Register, New York, 1910; NYT*, 3 October 1945, 19.

124. William S. Stryker, a founder of the SAR, was married to the former Helen B. Atterbury, vice-president of the New Jersey antisuffrage association; Daniel Rogers Noyes, married to Minnesota antisuffrage vice-president Helen A. Gilman, was Minnesota's SAR president; John Thompson Spencer, married to Rebecca Blackwell Willing, Pennsylvania antisuffrage association vice-president, served as state governor for the Society of Colonial Wars. *NCAB*, 45:274–75; *Who Was Who in America*, 1: 907; Davies, 52. Catherine S. Davis, vice-

president of the Oregon Association, married Wallace McCamant. *NCAB,* 34:34; *Directory of the National Society of the DAR.*

125. The two attorneys were Edith M. (Mrs. Charles E.) Conant of Wells, Minnesota, and Frances May (Mrs. L. B. Dochterman) of Williston, Minnesota, whose occupation was listed as "abstractor of titles" and "real estate law." For the backgrounds of the career women mentioned, see John William Leonard, *Woman's Who's Who,* 197, 250, 326; Edward T. James, 3:511–12; Harper, 6:44, 139; Yellin, 20. Quote about Mariana Van Rensselaer is from Dwight, 35. Dwight (69) also suggests that such travel accounts were the most socially acceptable form of writing for "ladies" at that time.

126. Harriot Stanton Blatch had a master's degree from Vassar College, and Dr. Anna Howard Shaw earned two doctorates. Kraditor, 265–82.

127. NAOWS president Josephine Marshall Jewell Dodge is described in John William Leonard, *Woman's Who's Who,* 250–51; Michel; Alice Hay Wadsworth is profiled in Cameron, 32.

128. MAOFESW, EC, 14 October 1910; MAOFESW, Annual Meeting, 22 April 1914. In North Dakota, federation and antisuffrage officers included Ida Clarke (Mrs. Newton Clarence) Young and Frances May (Mrs. L. B.) Dochterman; in Wisconsin it was Agnes Haskell (Mrs. George H.) Noyes and Mary Newton (Mrs. Joseph H.) Hobbins. See John William Leonard, *Woman's Who's Who,* 250, 393, 604, 913.

129. The Ohio leader was Susan Platt (Mrs. Herman Milton) Hubbard, as described in John William Leonard, *Woman's Who's Who,* 411. The quote about the Maryland Association president, Mary Sloan Frick (Mrs. Robert) Garrett, is from *NCAB,* 18:4–5.

130. "Distinguished Women Build Magnificent Clubhouse," *NYT,* 17 February 1907, sec. 3, 3; "Women's New Club, The Colony, Opened," *NYT,* 12 March 1907, 9; "Says Suffragettes Lean to Socialism," *NYT,* 1 April 1908, 7; "Antis Denounce the 'Noisy Minority,' " *NYT,* 26 February 1913, 10.

131. In addition to the list of Bostonian ministers' daughters that counted Mrs. Homans, Mrs. Peabody, Miss Parkman, and Kate Gannett Wells, those with fathers in the ministry included Grace Duffield Goodwin (N.Y. and Washington, D.C.), Jeannette L. Gilder (N.Y.), Eliza Doane Gardiner (N.Y.), and Caroline Bushnell Hazard (R.I.). Daughters of military officers included Winifred Brent Lyster (Mich.), Helena de Kay Gilder (N.Y.), and Bertha Lane Scott (N.Y.). Alabama leader Nina (Mrs. James S.) Pinckard was the daughter of a prominent judge. *NCAB,* 1:312–13, 8:441, 16:308, 23:190–91, 30:151, 43:332–33; John William Leonard, *Woman's Who's Who,* 333, 723.

132. Alice Gilman (Mrs. Everett P. Wheeler, N.Y.), daughter of university president Daniel Coit Gilman; Sarah Cooper (Mrs. Abram S. Hewitt, N.Y.); Kathryn Riis (Mrs. Oscar Owre, Minn.). *NCAB,* 12:53, 39:622; *Social Register, New York, 1910,* 273.

133. Marshall Jewell, the father of Mrs. Josephine Jewell Dodge, was a Connecticut governor (1869–79, 1871–73) who endorsed improvements in female

education and advocated legislation granting women rights to property. The president of the Washington State Association, Eliza Ferry (Mrs. John) Leary, was the daughter of the first governor of Washington State, Elisha Peyre Ferry. The fathers of both Agnes Irwin and Harriet Pruyn (Mrs. William Gorham) Rice served in the U.S. Congress (from Pennsylvania and New York, respectively), while U.S. Senator Henry Laurens Dawes was the father of Massachusetts antisuffrage leader Anna Dawes. Cabinet members included John W. Foster, secretary of state under Harrison, father of Mrs. Robert Lansing, president of the Maryland Association and later secretary of NAOWS. Sobel and Raimo, 1:180, 4:1675; Edward T. James, 1:492–93, 2:253–54; *NCAB*, 25:277–78; *Who Was Who in America*, 1:304; John William Leonard, *Who's Who in America; WP*, September 1917, 3; Cameron, 1: 32.

134. The Alabama daughter of John Bankhead was Mrs. Thomas M. Owen, and Mrs. Augustus Peabody (Constance) Gardner was the daughter of Henry Cabot Lodge. See *Who Was Who in America*, 1:439; Allen.

135. Illustrating the prevalence of colonial ancestry, the husband of Alabama Association president Mrs. James S. Pinckard was descended from early Virginia settlers, and the family of Texan James B. Wells, husband of the state association founder, were New England Puritans. The Rhode Island president was Mrs. William Ely, the Delaware president was Mrs. Henry B. Thompson, and the Pennsylvania president was Mrs. Horace Brock. The Nebraska and Maine presidents were Mrs. Edward Porter Peck and Mrs. Sidney Warren Thaxter. The Minnesota and Oregon vice-presidents were Mrs. Alfred Pillsbury and Mrs. Chauncey Wright Griggs, respectively. The Michigan president was married to Dr. Henry G. Lyster. Some of the Yale professor husbands of Connecticut officers included William Beebe (math), A.S. Cook (English), Henry Wolcott Farnam (economics), J. Mason Hoppin (art history), and E. W. Hopkins (philology). *NCAB*, 3:294–95, 27:73, 30:151, 37:387–88; *Who Was Who in America*, 1:77, 253, 385, 438, 439, 586, 587, 951, 974; Marquis; Webb, 2:877–78; Hoffecker, 158.

136. The president of the Maine Association was Mrs. John F. A. Merrill, whose husband was a U.S. attorney; the Minnesota president was Mrs. J. B. Gilfillan; the Oregon president was Mrs. R. W. Wilbur; her Tennessee counterpart was Mrs. John J. Vertrees. The Wisconsin leader was Mrs. Charles E. Estabrook. James B. Wells, Jr., of Brownsville, Texas, was a leader in the state Democratic Party. States whose top leadership were married to railroad executives included Maine, Maryland, Minnesota, New York, North Dakota, Pennsylvania, Washington, and Wisconsin. Those with financier husbands included another Pennsylvania president who was married to a member of the prominent Cassatt family, and Rhode Island Association president Mrs. Robert Ives Gammell. *Who Was Who in America*, 1:957; *NCAB*, 5:552, 16:308, 17:20–21, 18:4–5, 21:390, 25:277–78, 42:665; *NYT*, 3 January 1944, 22; *NYT*, 7 April 1911, 13; A. Elizabeth Taylor, "Short History of the Woman Suffrage Movement in Tennessee"; McBride, 239.

137. The president of the Nevada Association was Mrs. Jewett Adams, whose husband was governor of the state from 1882 to 1886. The wives of former governors were listed as officers of antisuffrage associations in the following states: Iowa (Mrs. Frank D. Jackson), Illinois (Mrs. Richard Oglesby), Maine (Mrs. John F. Hill), and Massachusetts (Mrs. Eben S. Draper). The widows were both vice-presidents of the New Jersey Association: Mrs. Thomas J. Preston, Jr. (the former Mrs. Grover Cleveland), and Mrs. Garrett A. Hobart, whose husband was a vice-president in the McKinley administration. Many other officers were married to state legislators. Constance Lodge Gardner is profiled in John William Leonard, *Woman's Who's Who,* 315.

138. Daniels; Odendahl.

139. Mrs. J. P. Morgan quoted in "Mrs. J. P. Morgan Protests," *NYT,* 23 December 1911, 1. Mrs. Guild recalled that Anna L. Dawes "did not approve of active work in Pittsfield," Massachusetts, and that Mrs. Corbin of the Illinois Association "was not a believer in the association of women" for antisuffrage activism. Mrs. Charles Eliot Guild, "The Early Days of the Remonstrants against Woman Suffrage: A Memory Sketch by Their First Secretary," September 1916, MAOFESW.

140. "Anti's Denounce the 'Noisy Minority,' " *NYT,* 26 February 1913, 10; MAOFESW, EC, 28 February 1902, 27 March 1902.

141. MAOFESW, "To Be Used at Meetings," speech text, n.d.; MAOFESW, EC, 22 February 1901.

142. Quotes from "Red Rose as Anti's Badge," *NYT,* 5 May 1914, 13; Mrs. Charles Eliot Guild, "Address to Legislative Hearings," 2 February 1905, MAOFESW.

143. MAOFESW, EC, 17 December 1901, 11 November 1910; J. S. Eichelberger to E. P. Wheeler, box 8, EPW.

144. Quotes from MAOFESW, untitled paper, n.d.; MAOFESW, EC, 9 December 1910; "The Taste of Woman Suffrage," *Anti-Suffragist,* January 1912, 1. The deliberate strategy to gain credit for the cause by cataloguing the civic contributions of antisuffrage leaders is illustrated in the preface to the compendium, ed. and introd. Ernest Bernbaum, *Anti-Suffrage Essays by Massachusetts Women.*

145. These included Jeannette L. Gilder, Helena deKay Gilder, and Louise Caldwell Jones. Jones, "Some Impediments to Woman Suffrage"; MAOFESW, EC, 25 September 1908.

146. These two ostensibly nonpolitical societies were not totally independent; Louise Caldwell Jones of the Civic Education League served as Guidon vice-president. "The Guidon," *Anti-Suffragist,* December 1908, 6–7; "New Anti-Suffrage Organizations," *Remonstrance,* June 1908, 4.

147. MAOFESW, EC, 3 April 1914, 8 May 1914, 11 September 1914, 23 October 1914; MAOFESW, EOC, 25 October 1916.

148. Baker, "Domestication of Politics," 625.

149. The self-interest of female reformers is a primary thesis of Muncy.

Chapter 3. Gentleman Suffrage

1. Epigraph, Nebraska Men's Association Opposed to Woman Suffrage, *Manifesto,* 6 July 1914, in Harper, 6:873–75.

2. Among scholarly treatments of antisuffrage, see Flexner, chap. 22; Grimes, chap. 4; Kraditor, 14–42. One scholar who dismisses the suffrage claims of an association between women antis and liquor interests is O'Neill, *Everyone Was Brave,* 55–63. Suffrage accounts include Catt and Shuler, chap. 10; Anthony and Harper, 4:888; Harper, 6:513. A suffrage report on the Montana campaign claimed that a NAOWS organizer met privately with an organ of the liquor industry. See Harper, 6:365. For contemporary analyses, see Stewart; Youmans. See also *Brewing and Liquor Interests.*

3. McDonagh and Price; Thomas G. Ryan; Mahoney; Kenneally, "Woman Suffrage and the Massachusetts 'Referendum,' " 622.

4. George Glover Crocker served as a member of the Massachusetts House of Representatives from 1873 to 1875, as a member of the State Senate from 1880 to 1884, and as president of the Senate from 1883 to 1884. See *Who Was Who in America,* 1: 277. Quotes by MAOFESW, untitled paper, n.d.; Mrs. Charles E. Guild, "Address at a Conference of the Executive Committee with Gentlemen, March 30, 1906," MAOFESW.

5. Quote in MAOFESW, untitled address, author unknown, n.d. (c. 1890), 3. See also Crocker, *Argument of Hon. George G. Crocker;* idem, *Letter to the Committee;* John Lowell. Thornton K. Lothrop read a paper on 29 January 1884 by Clara T. Leonard, *Letter from Mrs. Clara T. Leonard.* For biographical sketches of Lowell and Lothrop, see *NCAB,* 11:550, 14:225–26. For a collection of addresses before state legislative hearings on woman suffrage in 1886, see Frothingham et al. Sprague was president of the State Senate during 1890–91. For biographical information on Dana, Ropes, Herford, and Sprague, see *NCAB,* 11:404, 14:195, 24:178–79, 27:34.

6. Quote in MAOFESW, untitled address, author unknown, n.d. (c. 1890), 4. See Lord.

7. Quotes in MAOFESW, untitled address, author unknown, n.d. (c. 1890), 3.

8. Sohier was state legislator from 1888 to 1891; Eben Draper served as governor from 1909 to 1911. For biographical information on Draper and Sohier, see Marquis; on Burnett and Wheelright, see *Who Was Who in America,* 1:169, 1329–30; on Warren, see Garraty, suppl. 5:730–31.

9. Lowell served as state legislator from 1895 to 1898, and he was appointed to the judiciary in 1898. His life is summarized in *NCAB,* 21:320–21; Mrs. Charles E. Guild, "Address at a Conference of the Executive Committee with Gentlemen, March 30, 1906," MAOFESW. Charles Saunders served in the state legislature from 1898 to 1901. The quote is in Marquis.

10. Judge John Lowell served as director of the Harvard Alumni Association and treasurer of the Harvard Loan Fund. See *NCAB,* 11:550. Some exceptions

to the Harvard educational pattern were Eben Draper and William Sohier, both of whom graduated from the Massachusetts Institute of Technology, although Sohier earned a law degree from Harvard. See Marquis. For a biographical sketch of Brandeis, see *NCAB,* 36:1–5.

11. Story, 89–120, 149–59.

12. Before it changed ownership and moved to New York in 1878, *North American Review* was edited by Harvard professors, including Brahmins James Russell Lowell (1863–72), Charles Eliot Norton (1863–68), and Henry Adams (1870–76). Henry Cabot Lodge served as assistant editor under Adams (1873–76). Mott, 4:229–61. The *Atlantic Monthly,* described as standing "more distinctly for culture than any other American magazine" in the 1890s, was published by Houghton and then Houghton Mifflin Company, owned by the husband and father of remonstrance leaders, until 1908. Mott, 2:493–515; quote from 4:44.

13. Quote by Choate's longtime headmaster Seymour St. John from Aldrich, 83; Story, 110–120, 163–66.

14. A sampling of their better-known titles includes Francis C. Lowell's biography *Joan of Arc* (1896), John C. Ropes's *The Campaign of Waterloo* (1892) and *Story of the Civil War,* 2 vols. (1894–99), and J. T. Wheelright's *Rollo's Journey to Cambridge* (1880) and *A Bad Penny* (1895).

15. For example, see Dana, "Substitutes for the Caucus," 491–501; idem, "American View of the Irish Question"; Francis C. Lowell, "Legislative Shortcomings"; idem, "American Boss." The newspaper president (*Boston Journal,* 1895–1900) was William D. Sohier. See *NCAB,* 29:118. The *Boston Journal* published from 1833 to 1917, when it merged with the *Boston Herald* (see Gregory).

16. DiMaggio, "Cultural Entrepreneurship in Nineteenth-Century Boston, Part I and II." For a different view of elite motivations, see Harris.

17. Richard H. Dana served as president of the New England Conservatory of Music from 1891 to 1898, raising large sums of money for the institution. He also organized the fund-raising for construction of Harvard's Emerson Hall. The military historian was John Codman Ropes, who reportedly amassed the largest private library of military archives in the United States. *NCAB,* 11:404, 24:178; Huggins.

18. Wheelright was chairman of the Board of Gas and Electric Light Commissioners (1896–1900), and Sohier headed the Massachusetts Highway Commission (1911–19). Saunders served on the elections board between 1901 and 1905, and Warren chaired the state's Civil Service Commission between 1905 and 1911. On Saunders' prohibitionism, see Jablonsky, 75. Quote is by Parkman, "Failure of Universal Suffrage." On changing Boston politics of the period, see Kleppner, "From Party to Factions"; Shannon; Burns; Charles H. Trout. As Boston mayor during the 1915 woman suffrage referendum, Curley endorsed woman suffrage. "Bay State Likely to Beat Suffrage," *NYT,* 29 October 1915, 5. On Warren, see Garraty, suppl. 5:730–31.

19. On Eben Draper, see Sobel and Raimo, 2: 722–23. Quote by Parkman,

"Failure of Universal Suffrage," 18. For a discussion of the upper-class view of the importance of breeding, see Aldrich, 92. On the elite reform movement in Boston, see Burns.

20. The other league founders were Prescott Farnsworth Hall and Robert DeCourcy Ward, whose name appeared on Massachusetts antisuffrage literature into the twentieth century. The literacy restriction finally passed Congress in 1917. On the Immigration Restriction League and the Harvard quota system, see Barbara Miller Solomon, 100–24, 204–5; Pavalko.

21. Pavalko, 63–64; Charles R. Saunders to MAOFESW EC, 30 October 1895, MAOFESW.

22. Quoted in "Extraordinary Protest against Woman-Suffrage." See also Massachusetts Man Suffrage Association, *Privileges of Women in Massachusetts.*

23. "Extraordinary Protest against Woman-Suffrage."

24. MAOFESW, EC, 15 April 1910.

25. Francis M. Scott, *Address of Francis M. Scott.* He also contributed an essay to the New York Association entitled *Woman and the Law.* Scott was New York State supreme court justice between 1898 and 1918. For a brief biographical sketch, see *Who Was Who in America,* 1:1094. The women's report to the state constitutional convention is found in Mrs. Francis M. Scott et al.

26. *NCAB,* 26:1–5. Root, *Address Delivered by the Hon. Elihu Root;* quote in Leopold, 20. The Union League is described in Fairfield, 106–38.

27. Quotes by Root, "Address as President." *Century Association Year-Book 1969,* 46–7.

28. Wheeler chaired the New York State Civil Service Reform Association from 1880 to 1899, and his tenure as chair of the New York City Civil Service Commission spanned the years 1884–89, 1894–96. See *NCAB,* 12:53; Everett P. Wheeler, *Sixty Years of American Life,* 359. Other antisuffragist leaders on the executive committee of the Citizen's Union were Charles S. Fairchild, Richard Watson Gilder, and Abram S. Hewitt. "Everett P. Wheeler an Anti," *NYT,* 2 May 1913, 2; Harper, 5:680.

29. Munroe Smith, *Questionnaire to Professors in Universities and Colleges.*

30. Other corporate attorneys on the executive committee of Man-Suffrage included John R. Dos Passos and George W. Seligman. Their lives are profiled in *NCAB,* 2:406, 11:100–101, 14:411–12, 14:503, 15:277–78, 15:306, 22:322, 25:273–74, 30:264, 39:484–85, F: 442, G:322; *Who Was Who in America,* 1:328.

31. Babbott and Wheeler served on the New York City Board of Education, Fairchild was president of the New York Reform Club, and Satterlee presided over the Grant Monument Association. Achelis was president of the German (later Lenox Hill) Hospital, Babbot was director of the Brooklyn Library and president of the Brooklyn Free Kindergarten Society, Fairchild was president of the State Charity Aid Association, Prentice was vice-president of the New York Society for the Relief of Ruptured and Crippled, Satterlee was a trustee of Columbia University, Stetson was a trustee of Williams College, Seligman was a member of the executive committee of the National Urban League, and

Wheeler was one of the founders of the East Side settlement house and the Bar Association. Fritz Achelis also donated a valuable collection of Rembrandt and Dürer etchings to Yale University.

32. Harper, 6:308, 873–75; Fox.

33. The president of the New Jersey league was Col. William Libbey, a Princeton geology professor; other executive officers included former Princeton chancellor William J. Magie and his son, Princeton physics professor William F. Magie. On the New Jersey antis, see *NCAB*, 10:401–2, 12:425, 18:95–96. Frank Jackson was Iowa governor from 1894 to 1896; Clyde Herring was Iowa governor from 1933 to 1937, and U.S. senator from 1937 to 1943. The real estate tycoon was Richard R. Rollins, banker and railroad president was Harry H. Polk, and the oil company lawyer, who was also a bank director, was Nathan E. Coffin. On the Iowa mobilization, see "Iowa Association of Men Opposed to Woman Suffrage," *Republican*, 9 March 1916, box 7, Anna and William Lawther Collection, Iowa State Historical Society, Iowa City; *NCAB*, 11:434, 23:165, 34:125–26, 39:336–37.

34. See Camhi, chap. 5; Jablonsky, chap. 5.

35. Charles R. Saunders, *Taxpaying Suffrage*. The MAOFESW collection documents regular correspondence between Charles Saunders and the MAOFESW leadership, primarily reporting on antisuffrage victories in the state legislature and confirming strategy.

36. Mrs. Cabot was related by marriage to Senator Lodge, and it was she who initiated the correspondence. MAOFESW, EC, 26 January 1900. On Lodge and Wadsworth's political activism against suffrage, see Catt and Shuler, 252–59.

37. See also O'Neill, *Everyone Was Brave*, 55–63; Jablonsky, 70–75; Benjamin, 176–90.

38. Quote in MAOFESW, untitled address, author unknown, n.d. (c. 1890), 4.

39. See Marquis. The Good Government Association is detailed in Burns.

40. MAOFESW, EC, 12 October 1900, 24 May 1901, 27 September 1901, 13 June 1902, 13 January 1905.

41. MAOFESW, EC, 26 January 1906, 23 February 1906, 9 March 1906.

42. Quote by Mrs. Charles E. Guild, "Address at a Conference of the Executive Committee with Gentlemen, March 30, 1906," MAOFESW. The request came from Judge Francis C. Lowell. See MAOFESW, EC, 25 May 1906.

43. MAOFESW, EC, 14 June 1907, 27 September 1907, 10 January 1908, 19 February 1909, 15 January 1909.

44. One fund-raising letter, dated 15 November 1906, was signed by gentlemen's committee members George G. Crocker, Laurence Minot, and Charles Warren, and requested that all monies be sent to Mrs. Codman, MAOFESW treasurer. MAOFESW, EC, 12 October 1906, 13 March 1908, 21 May 1909, 4 June 1909, 29 October 1909, 3 November 1909, 4 February 1910.

45. Mrs. Guild to the EC, 20 February 1910, MAOFESW; MAOSW, Annual Report, December 1915.

46. Quote in "Red Rose as Antis' Badge," *NYT,* 5 May 1914, 13. For elite studies, see Hunter; Mills.

47. Acker, "Class, Gender, and the Relations of Distribution"; idem, "Gendered Institutions"; Joan Scott; West and Zimmerman.

48. MAOFESW, EC, 27 October 1911, 29 December 1911, 23 February 1912. Quote in Mrs. Guild to the EC, 20 February 1910, MAOFESW.

49. On the formation of the men's association, see "A Welcome Ally," *Remonstrance,* July 1912, 4. For a biographical sketch of William T. Sedgwick, see *NCAB,* 13:290–91. The Lowell Institute, founded by the great-uncle of Judge Lowell, sponsored scholarly lectures for the Boston elite and established the careers of many Brahmin academics. See Story, 14–17.

50. MAOFESW, JC, 24 October 1913; MAOFESW, EC, 8 May 1914, 17 July 1914. Mr. Prendergast is sketched in Marquis. On financial hegemony, see Story, 11, 16.

51. MAOFESW, EC, 13 September 1912, 27 September 1912, 11 October 1912, 10 January 1913, 10 October 1913.

52. "A Welcome Ally," *Remonstrance,* July 1912, 4. At their annual meeting in April 1913, MAOFESW reported a treasury balance of $44, and by September of that year projected a $600 deficit. In the fall of 1914 and 1915 this deficit-spending pattern was repeated, largely because of high staff expenses. MAOFESW, Annual Report, 23 April 1913; MAOFESW, EC, 26 September 1913, 25 September 1914, 17 September 1915.

53. MAOFESW, EC, 12 December 1913, 3 April 1914, 17 April 1914; MAOFESW, JC, 17 July 1914, 21 August 1914.

54. "Time to Show One's Colors," *Remonstrance,* July 1914, 1; MAOFESW, EC, 24 October 1913, 1 May 1914, 8 May 1914, 15 May 1914, 12 March 1915, 14 May 1915, 28 May 1915, 9 July 1915, 24 September 1915; MAOFESW, EOC, 7 April 1915, 20 October 1915; MAOFESW, JC, 17 July 1914, 21 August 1914.

55. MAOFESW, EC, 9 October 1914, 30 October 1914, 26 February 1915.

56. Quote in MAOFESW, EOC, 25 October 1916. Both Jacobus and Thompson graduated from Princeton in 1877. *NCAB,* 26:47, 27:419. For more about Mary Wilson Thompson, see Higgins; Hoffecker, 149, 158–60; "The National Convention," *Remonstrance,* January 1917, 6–7.

57. Among the names listed were U.S. Secretary of State Robert Lansing; West Virginia governor A. D. Fleming; former Ohio governor J. B. Foraker; railroad president Edmund Pennington; Judge N. C. Young of Fargo, North Dakota; Minneapolis manufacturer Alfred Pillsbury; and John G. Adams, vice-chairman of the Republican National Committee. "Tells of Organization Opposed to Suffrage," *Indiana News,* 16 February 1917, box 7, Lawther Collection, Iowa State Historical Society, Iowa City; "Suffragists Seek Funds," *NYT,* 18 September 1917, 8; MAOFESW, EOC, 7 February 1917; "The National Convention," *Remonstrance,* January 1917, 6–7.

58. MAOFESW, EC, 14 January 1916, 7 February 1917, 28 July 1917; MAOFESW, EOC, 7 February 1917, 4 April 1917, 2 May 1917, 2 April 1919; MAOSW, executive committee, 7 March 1917.

59. "Anti-Suffrage Meetings," *NYT,* 23 September 1913, 7; "Everett P. Wheeler an Anti," *NYT,* 2 May 1913, 2.

60. "Antis at Capitol Oppose Suffrage," *NYT,* 5 December 1913, 3. For the full text, see Everett P. Wheeler, *Brief before the Committee on Rules.*

61. Everett P. Wheeler, *Case against Woman Suffrage.* Man-Suffrage Association printed at least twenty-one essays between 1914 and 1916; see MSA.

62. "Anti-Suffrage Apology," *NYT,* 25 October 1915, 7; "An Apology Shouldn't Be Grudging," editorial, *NYT,* 26 October 1915, 10. This was not the end of the incident, as the editorial engendered a flurry of letters whose authors included antisuffragists Mrs. William Forse Scott and Everett P. Wheeler. See *NYT,* 27 October 1915, 10. For document in question, see MSA.

63. "Suffragists Fear Jersey Vote," *NYT,* 16 October 1915, 7; "Union League Votes 'No,' " *NYT,* 10 April 1914, 1. Examples of Wheeler's letters include those to the editor of the *NYT,* 7 January 1915, 25 February 1915, 23 August 1920; *New York Tribune,* 3 May 1915; and the *New York Sun,* 7 January 1915, box 1, EPW.

64. "Anti-Suffragists Spend $31,159.27," *NYT,* 21 November 1915, 16; "Spent $7,790 to Defeat Suffrage," *NYT,* 27 November 1915, 16; Benjamin, 235, 244.

65. Franklin Carter, Jr., for Man-Suffrage Special Committee, 7 January 1916; J. S. Eichelberger to Everett P. Wheeler, n.d.; Everett P. Wheeler to Alice Hill Chittenden, 16 June 1917; Everett P. Wheeler for Man-Suffrage Association, n.d., box 8, EPW; "E. P. Prentice Heads Men 'Antis,' " *NYT,* 5 March 1916, sec. 1, 4; "Anti-Suffrage Men Unite," *NYT,* 28 September 1917, 4.

66. Everett P. Wheeler for Man-Suffrage Association, 1 December 1917, box 8, EPW.

67. Everett P. Wheeler for American Constitutional League, 14 December 1917, box 8, EPW.

68. "Antis Start Fight to Lose the Vote," *NYT,* 29 January 1918, 7.

69. The most complete study of this organization is Edwards, 5–13, 35–57, 97, 114–15. Choate was one of Root's first idols, whom he eulogized in Root, "Joseph H. Choate." The Iowa officer was Harry H. Polk. See *NCAB,* 39:336. The Iowa state chairman was former senator Lafayette Young. For analysis of the imperialist proclivities of prominent male antisuffrage leaders, see Benjamin, chap. 4.

70. Quotes in Edwards, 37–57, 104–5. See also Root, "Letter to the President of the National Security League," and "Speech before the National Security League."

71. Catt and Shuler, chaps. 24, 29; "Opens Court Fight against Suffrage," *NYT,* 8 July 1920, 17; "To Fight Suffrage on Tennessee Vote," *NYT,* 6 September 1920, 7; Everett P. Wheeler, "Suffrage Amendment," *NYT,* 21 July 1920, 12.

72. At the last annual meeting of the women's national antisuffrage associa-

tion (NAOWS) in 1920, the men who led the legal battle against the federal amendment were reportedly thanked for "working for us without pay." MAOFESW, EC, 6 May 1920; Mary Kilbreth to Mrs. Frank Foxcroft, 3 October 1920, MAOFESW. "Woman's Suffrage Amendment Valid," *NYT,* 28 February 1922, 9; "Anti-Suffragists Lose," *NYT,* 5 October 1920, 10; "Testing Validity of Suffrage Law," *NYT,* 24 January 1922, 14.

73. MAOFESW, *Opinions of Eminent Persons against Woman Suffrage.*

74. Vertrees; see also A. Elizabeth Taylor, "Short History of the Woman Suffrage Movement in Tennessee."

75. Parkman, *Some of the Reasons against Woman Suffrage: Printed at the Request of an Association of Women,* from Parkman, "Woman Question." The article was answered by suffragists Howe, Stone, Stanton, Higgins, and Phillips, "The Other Side of the Woman Question," but Parkman got the last word. See Parkman, "Woman Question Again"; "For the Sake of Womanhood," *Remonstrance,* 1893, 4.

76. Francis Parkman was the author of many books, including the critically acclaimed *The Oregon Trail: Sketches of Prairie and Rocky Mountain Life,* based on his youthful travels, and *Montcalm and Wolfe* (1884). He was president of the Massachusetts Horticultural Society and developed a lily that was named for him. *NCAB,* 1:431–32. Quotes from Parkman, "Woman Question," 316.

77. Mrs. Charles E. Guild, "The Early Days of the Remonstrants against Woman Suffrage: A Memory Sketch by Their First Secretary," September 1916, MAOFESW. MAOFESW, EC, 27 September 1901; MAOFESW, EOC, 2 February 1910.

78. These included Dr. C. H. Parkhurst, whose column in the *Ladies' Home Journal* regularly articulated antisuffrage views; Edward Bok, publisher of the *Ladies' Home Journal;* reformer Jacob Riis; and Sen. Henry Cabot Lodge. All four men refused. Rev. Lyman Abbott, publisher of the *Outlook,* promised to write an article for MAOFESW on "What Women Can Do for Politics without the Ballot," but there is no evidence that the article was completed. MAOFESW, EDC, 12 December 1896, 30 January 1897, 24 November 1899; MAOFESW, EOC, 8 October 1909; MAOFESW, EC, 18 June 1909, 6 August 1915.

79. For example, the education and organization committee reported a telegram from the Los Angeles association requesting "immediate shipment" of fifteen hundred pamphlets in November 1910, and in four months in 1912 they reported 138 requests for literature from twenty-five states. MAOFESW, EOC, 3 November 1910; MAOFESW, Room Report, 27 December 1912.

80. On clerical support for the anti position, see "Extraordinary Protest against Woman-Suffrage"; MAOFESW, JC, 22 May 1912; "Clash on Suffrage at Rabbi's Council," *NYT,* 24 April 1917, 11; Frothingham, "Real Case of the 'Remonstrants.' " See also idem, "Women versus Women"; Frothingham et al. O. B. Frothingham was also related by marriage to the Committee of Remonstrants; his niece Ann married Mrs. Guild's son, Charles Eliot Guild II. A biographical sketch of Frothingham is in *Who Was Who in America,* 1:193.

81. Doane, "Why Women Do Not Want the Ballot"; idem, "Some Later Aspects of Woman Suffrage." Bishop Doane's life is chronicled in *NCAB*, 4:489. Buckley, "Wrongs and Perils of Woman Suffrage"; idem, *Wrong and Peril;* idem, "Moral Objections to Woman Suffrage," 177–79. A biographical sketch of Buckley is found in *NCAB*, 12:191–92.

82. Henry A. Stimson, "Is Woman's Suffrage an Enlightened and Justifiable Policy," reprinted by the Brooklyn Auxiliary of New York State Association Opposed to Woman Suffrage, 1910. Henry A. Stimson's life is described in *NCAB*, 13:531–32.

83. See John Tracy Ellis. Gibbons, "Relative Condition of Woman under Pagan and Christian Civilization"; idem, "Pure Womanhood"; idem, "Restless Woman."

84. John Tracy Ellis, 2:539–43; MAOSW monthly meeting, 1 March 1915; MAOFESW, EC, 6 August 1915, 15 June 1917; "Priest Attacks Equal Suffrage," *Dubuque Times*, 1 May 1916, box 7, Lawther Collection, Iowa State Historical Society, Iowa City; "Gibbons Condemns Votes for Women," *NYT*, 28 June 1915, 9. James Nugent was the party leader. He was one of the alleged "wet" interests targeted by suffragists as evidence of corruption within the antisuffrage movement. See Catt and Shuler, 258–59.

85. "Root and Gibbons Oppose Suffrage," *NYT*, 8 December 1916, 7; *Eminent Catholic Prelates Oppose Woman Suffrage*. A publication for the 1917 New York referendum used quotes from Protestant, Roman Catholic, and Jewish leaders. *Appeal to the Electors of the State of New York;* Nebraska Men's Association Opposed to Woman Suffrage, *Nebraska Clergymen Condemn Suffrage*. A copy of Cardinal Gibbons' message to the "antis" read at the NAOWS convention is found in box 1, Woman's Suffrage and Women's Rights Collection, Special Collections, Vassar College Libraries.

86. "Suffrage Plea to Gibbons," *NYT*, 14 February 1917, 7; "Gibbons Hears Suffragist," *NYT*, 15 February 1917, 20; "Suffrage Interests Cardinal Gibbons," *NYT*, 16 February 1917, 6.

87. Ira V. Brown, 99–112, 161–77; Wiebe, 234, 274. Abbott quote in Edwards, 11.

88. Ira V. Brown, 3–9, 18, 73. Jacob Abbott also wrote children's stories, including the popular Rollo series that emphasized the importance of fathers for the proper socialization of sons. Byars, 61.

89. The Abbott quotation is from an editorial, "Do Women Wish to Vote?" The number of antisuffrage articles by Lyman Abbott is too great to be listed here, but the titles listed in the bibliography are indicative of his output.

90. Lyman Abbott, "Why Women Do Not Wish the Suffrage"; idem, *Home Builder*. The Massachusetts Association originally requested an article on "What Women Can Do for Politics without the Ballot," but Everett P. Wheeler eventually published a similar piece, entitled "What Women Have Done without the Ballot," which is found in MSA. See also MAOFESW, EDC, 12 December 1896. Lyman Abbott, "Anti-Suffrage Movement"; idem, "Woman's Protest against Woman Suffrage."

91. Rev. Parkhurst is profiled in *NCAB*, 4:402–3. See also Abbott's editorial in *Outlook*, 17 November 1894, 788. For examples of Parkhurst's antisuffrage writings for women's magazines, see the bibliography.

92. The *Ladies' Home Journal* is profiled in Wood, 105–17. For a biographical sketch of Edward W. Bok, see *NCAB*, 23:41–42. On women's mass-market publishing more generally, see Waller-Zuckerman.

93. Wood, 109–15. Although a Dutch immigrant, Bok married the only child of his publisher, Cyrus Curtis, and became a generous benefactor of cultural and educational institutions, including Harvard. Fittingly, his grandson Derek Bok became president of Harvard in the 1960s. Baltzell, *Puritan Boston*, 289.

94. For examples of Bok's editorials, see the bibliography.

95. Examples of Bok's work on these themes are listed in the bibliography.

96. Cleveland, "Woman's Mission and Woman's Clubs"; idem, "Would Woman Suffrage Be Unwise?"; Roosevelt, "American Woman as a Mother."

97. John, 1–6, 198–228; Everett P. Wheeler, *Sixty Years of American Life*, 360; Edwards, 9.

98. John, 2–3, 76–83, 90–93, 146–48, 221.

99. Ibid., 20, 121, 153, 218. "Women"; Shinn; Frances M. Abbott.

100. [Richard Watson Gilder], "Moral Power of Women"; idem, "Woman Suffrage"; idem, "New Woman-Suffrage Movement"; John, 219; Hoar; Buckley, "Wrongs and Perils of Woman Suffrage," 613–23.

101. For example, Bok, *Real Opponents;* Schurz, "Woman Suffrage," reprinted by MAOFESW; Bissell, "Woman Suffrage in Colorado"; Seawell, "Ladies' Battle"; Deland; Clara T. Leonard, "What Women Can Do Best."

102. Jones, "Some Impediments to Woman Suffrage"; Mrs. William Forse Scott; Wood, 111.

103. Mrs. Charles E. Guild, "Address at a Conference of the Executive Committee with Gentlemen, March 30, 1906," MAOFESW. Frank Foxcroft was also a department editor at the *Youth's Companion*, editor of (Littell's) *Living Age*, and state civil service commissioner. See Marquis. MAOFESW pamphlets with his authorship included *Objections to License Suffrage from a No-License Point of View. Address before the Massachusetts Legislative Committee* (1898), *The Check to Woman Suffrage in the United States*, which originally appeared in 1904 in a London periodical (*Nineteenth Century*), and *Municipal Suffrage for Women: Why?*

104. English professor Barrett Wendell assisted MAOFESW in placing articles in *Atlantic Monthly*, the organ of Boston's literary establishment. *NCAB*, 6:428, 9:207–8; Bernbaum; MAOFESW, EC, 27 May 1910, 25 April 1913, 12 December 1913, 23 October 1914; MAOFESW, Annual Meeting, 23 April 1913.

105. Mrs. Charles E. Guild, "Address at a Conference of the Executive Committee with Gentlemen, March 30, 1906," MAOFESW; John, 18.

106. Cope, who died in 1897, was cited in 1895 campaign materials distributed by MAOFESW. See Cope, *Relation of the Sexes to Government;* idem, "Relation of the Sexes to Government." For a biographical profile of E. D. Cope, see

NCAB, 7:474. For a summary of neo-Lamarckianism, see Russett, 55, 68, 158–59, 200–201.

107. Barbara Miller Solomon, 90, 130; Brooks, 421.

108. Solomon, 65; Chase, 8, 111–14, 517.

109. Chase, 105.

110. Barbara Miller Solomon, 64–65; Spencer, "Psychology of the Sexes"; Goldwin Smith, "Is Universal Suffrage a Failure?"; idem, "Female Suffrage."

111. "Professor Goldwin Smith on Suffrage," *Remonstrance,* February 1890, 1–2; "Proof Is Wanted," *Remonstrance,* 1894, 2; "Herbert Spencer's Changed His Views," *Remonstrance,* 1892, 3; Münsterberg, "American Woman"; idem, "Is Co-Education Wise for Girls?" See also *NCAB,* 13:85–86; MAOFESW, EC, 28 June 1901, 20 March 1914.

112. Chase, 12–15, 138–44; *NCAB,* 25:274.

113. Lutz, 1–37; Rotundo, 85–93; Dwight; Mitchell.

114. William T. Sedgwick, 7–8; Mrs. Charles E. Guild, "Address at a Conference of the Executive Committee with Gentlemen, March 30, 1906," MAOFESW; idem, "The Early Days of the Remonstrants against Woman Suffrage: A Memory Sketch by Their First Secretary," September 1916, MAOFESW; Mrs. Mary K. Sedgwick.

115. *Pamphlets Printed and Distributed by the Women's Anti-Suffrage Association; Why Women Do Not Want the Ballot;* Oregon State Association Opposed to the Extension of Suffrage to Women; *Opinions of Eminent Persons; Views on Woman Suffrage;* Illinois Association Opposed to the Extension of Suffrage to Women, *Where Woman's Work Is Most Needed;* Mrs. Annie Riley Hale; *Appeal to the Electors of the State of New York.*

116. Mrs. Guild to the executive committee, 20 February 1910, MAOFESW; MAOFESW, EC, 25 April 1902, 8 April 1910, 2 December 1910, 12 March 1915; MAOFESW, Organizer's Report, 12 January 1919; "Some of the Women Who Oppose," *Remonstrance,* October 1915, 5; "Miss Gilder Helps Campaign of Antis," *NYT,* 24 August 1915, 11.

117. This pessimistic view of the future among Boston Brahmins at the turn of the century was described in Brooks, 418–41.

118. Lears, xiii. See also Wiebe; Trachtenberg; Hofstadter, *Age of Reform.*

119. Quote from Root, "Address as President." Male clubs during the period are discussed also in Aldrich, 49–53; Rotundo, 201–2.

120. See Huggins. Quote in Brooks, 437.

121. See Tomsich.

Chapter 4. A Menace to Civilization

1. Epigraph, Mrs. Arthur M. Dodge, "Why I Am an Antisuffragist," 1916, box 1, Woman's Suffrage and Women's Rights Collection, Special Collections, Vassar College Libraries.

2. For example, see Flexner, chap. 22; Kraditor, chap. 2; Howard; Susan E. Marshall, "In Defense of Separate Spheres"; Billie Barnes Jensen; Frenier; Mayor.

3. Billie Barnes Jensen, 44; Howard, 467. See also Chafe, *American Woman,* 231–32; O'Neill, *Everyone Was Brave,* 63; Mayor.

4. Studies that suggest a prioritization of antisuffrage arguments according to frequency include Frenier; Thurner. Susan E. Marshall, "In Defense of Separate Spheres," subjects antisuffrage rhetoric to systematic content analysis, but her data are limited to the official NAOWS journal, the *Woman's Protest,* published between 1912 and 1918.

5. As Stevenson notes, Flexner and Sinclair focused on male antisuffragists and Kraditor combined men's and women's arguments "without appreciating the distinctiveness of women's thought." This was also true of the analyses of Frenier and Mayor. Those who focused exclusively on women include Howard, Marshall, and Thurner. Stevenson, 80; Susan E. Marshall, "In Defense of Separate Spheres."

6. Cathcart; Gregg; John Wilson.

7. For example, see Albrecht; Griswold.

8. Snow, Rochford, Worden, Benford; Ferree and Miller; Gamson, "Political Discourse and Collective Action"; Zald and Useem; Gale.

9. Many of the earlier articles and organizational documents were accessed through the *History of Women* microfilm collection.

10. There was money to be made in antisuffragism. Macmillan offered MAOFESW special rates for large orders of *The Book of Women's Power,* prefaced by Ida Tarbell. MAOFESW, EC, 29 December 1911. For the life of Ida Tarbell, see Brady; Camhi, 145–78.

11. Where the publication date was unknown, in most cases Kinnard's estimates were used to categorize the time period of each writing. See Kinnard.

12. Because the analysis relies on relative frequencies, these distributions have been taken into account when analyzing trends in antisuffrage rhetoric.

13. Lipset and Raab; Mottl; Turner and Killian, 318–19.

14. For a comparison of the mobilization dilemmas of the antisuffrage and anti-ERA movements, see Susan E. Marshall, "Ladies against Women."

15. Kraditor, chap. 3. For an overview of the Seneca Falls convention and the ideology of the Declaration of Sentiments, see DuBois, *Feminism and Suffrage,* chap. 1; Flexner, 71–77; Griffith, 51–57.

16. *New York State Association Opposed,* reprinted from *Outlook,* 31 March 1894, 7 April 1894, 14 April 1894; Mrs. Francis M. Scott et al.; Seawell, *Ladies' Battle,* 11.

17. NAOWS, *Some Facts about California's Experiment with Woman Suffrage;* Eliza A. White, 262; Lily Rice Foxcroft, *Why Are Women Opposing.*

18. Massachusetts Man Suffrage Association, *Why Should Suffrage Be Imposed on Women;* Brock.

19. Grace Duffield Goodwin, 18; Jones, "Some Facts about Suffrage," 498; Clara T. Leonard, *Letter from Mrs. Clara T. Leonard.*

20. See MacIntire.

21. Letter from Richard H. Dana, in Frothingham et al.; Henry A. Stimson, *Is Woman's Suffrage an Enlightened and Justifiable Policy.*

22. Bushnell, *Women's Suffrage;* Abram Stevens Hewitt; Lord; Mrs. Arthur M. Dodge, *Case against Votes.*

23. For an example of an early expediency counterargument by antisuffragists, see Bushnell, *Women's Suffrage,* 44. For some early examples of the use of the term expediency in antisuffrage arguments, see Root, *Address Delivered by the Hon. Elihu Root;* Frothingham et al. Adeline Knapp suggested that the term originated with former U.S. Supreme Court Chief Justice Marshall, whom she allegedly quotes. Knapp, *Do Working Women Need the Ballot?*

24. Kraditor, 43–54.

25. Root, *Address Delivered by the Hon. Elihu Root;* Frothingham et al.

26. Both *History of Woman Suffrage* and *Woman's Journal* reported on and rebutted the opposition while simultaneously dismissing them as irrelevant to the suffrage campaign. As early as the 1880s, suffragist D. P. Livermore wrote a book with a decided defensive tone, rebutting objections to female enfranchisement and devoting a chapter to antisuffrage arguments. Livermore, *Woman Suffrage Defended by Irrefutable Arguments.*

27. Mrs. Arthur M. Dodge, "Woman Suffrage Opposed"; Caswell; Helen Kendrick Johnson, *Woman and the Republic,* 60–66; Brock, 4; Sams, 284; Lyman Abbott, "Why the Vote Would Be Injurious"; Terry, 48; Dicey.

28. Brockett; Bushnell, *Women's Suffrage,* 35–37; Tarbell, 212–13; Lyman Abbott, "Women's Rights"; Terry, 10; William Parker, 16; Mrs. Arthur M. Dodge, "Woman Suffrage Opposed," 101; Owen, 38–40; Brock, 5.

29. Bissell, *Talk to Every Woman;* Jones, "Position of the Anti-Suffragists"; Pennsylvania Association Opposed to Woman Suffrage, *A Talk on the Tax-Paying Woman;* Terry, 46.

30. Kraditor, 52–74.

31. Lyman Abbott, "Why the Vote Would Be Injurious," 22; Sams, 305–6; Hubbard, 253; Grace Duffield Goodwin, 75–76; Van Rensselaer, 11.

32. Knapp, 3–4; Eliza A. White, 194; Helen Kendrick Johnson, *Woman and the Republic,* 182–86, 238; Van Rensselaer, 15; Bissell, *Talk to Every Woman,* 18–19; William Parker, 57–60; Corbin, *Women's Rights in America.*

33. See Zald and Useem.

34. Grace Duffield Goodwin, 31–32, 67–68; Edward Sandford Martin, 19; Bronson; *Woman Suffrage and the Liquor Question;* Foley; Robert S. Taylor; Terry, 52; Robinson; MAOFESW, *Mothering the Community.*

35. Carver, 2; Owen, 7; Grace Duffield Goodwin, 17–18; Hubbard, 144; Chittenden, *Inexpediency of Granting the Suffrage,* 10–11.

36. Illinois Association Opposed to the Extension of Suffrage to Women, *To the Voters of the Middle West,* 6; [Corbin], *Home versus Woman Suffrage,* 7; Helen

Kendrick Johnson, *Woman and the Republic,* 100; idem, *Woman's Progress,* 2; Edward Sandford Martin, 13–15; *Protest against Woman Suffrage in Alabama.*

37. Corbin, *Position of Women;* idem, *Home versus Woman Suffrage,* 7; Seawell, *Ladies' Battle,* 14, 73–74; William Parker, 30, 114; NAOWS, *The Red behind the Yellow.*

38. Mrs. Clarence Hale, 3.

39. Hubbard; Corbin, *Position of Women,* 12; Illinois Association Opposed to the Extension of Suffrage to Women, *To the Voters of the Middle West,* 3; Dahlgren, 13; Helen Kendrick Johnson, *Woman's Progress,* 3; Bushnell, *Women's Suffrage,* 152; William Parker, 43, 62–68; Dodge, *Case against Votes,* 5; Buckley, *Wrong and Peril,* 110; Owen, 230, 255; Edward Sandford Martin, 116–21.

40. Bok, *Real Opponents,* 9; Bissell, *Talk to Every Woman,* 21; Bushnell, *Women's Suffrage,* 89; Pyle, *Christian Civilization in the Balance.*

41. Terry, 54; Tarbell, 218; Buckley, *Wrong and Peril,* 118–19; Nebraska Association Opposed to Woman Suffrage; Lily Rice Foxcroft, *Why Are Women Opposing,* 7–8; Helen Kendrick Johnson, *Woman and the Republic,* 211. Antisuffragists' antipathy to Charlotte Perkins Gilman was partly a response to Gilman's own assaults on the movement. In her major work, *Women and Economics,* published in 1898, Gilman referred to the newly organized women's antisuffrage associations as the "crowning imbecility of history." Quoted in Conn, 168.

42. George, 27; Bissell, *Talk to Every Woman,* 22; Brock, 6; Tarbell, chap. 2.

43. Lord, 3; Helen Kendrick Johnson, *Woman and the Republic,* 282–83; Sams, 162–63; Straube, 30; Owen, 126; Helen Kendrick Johnson, *Woman's Progress,* 4.

44. Straube, 40; Simkins; Helen Kendrick Johnson, *Woman and the Republic,* 50; Birdsall; Mary Dean Adams, 3; Saunders, 2; MAOFESW, *Address to the Judiciary Committees,* 4.

45. Oregon State Association Opposed to the Extension of Suffrage to Women, 11–12; Robinson; Pyle, *Should Women Vote;* Bok, *Real Opponents,* 1–12; "Famed Biologist's Warning," 59–62; Bock; Seawell, *Ladies' Battle,* 9, 34; Hubbard, 273–74; Terry, 55.

46. Cudell; Van Rensselaer, 15; *Appeal against Anarchy of Sex;* Parkhurst, *Woman;* Sams, 280; Hubbard, 214; anonymous address, Boonville, Missouri, n.d. (c. 1885), folder 1, Suffrage Papers, Joint Collection, University of Missouri Western Historical Manuscript Collection and Columbia and State Historical Society of Missouri Manuscripts, Columbia.

47. Hazard, *How Women Can Best Serve the State,* 8; Buckley, *Wrong and Peril,* 104; Mrs. Augustin H. Parker, 81; Corbin, *Woman's Rights in America.*

48. Corbin, *Woman Movement in America;* idem, *Anti-Suffrage Movement;* Dos Passos, 3; Frothingham, "Real Case of the 'Remonstrants' "; Van Rensselaer, 5; Buckley, *Wrong and Peril,* 57–60.

49. Mrs. Lyman Abbott, 6; *Why Women Do Not Want to Vote,* 3; Crannell, *Address of Mrs. W. Winslow Crannell,* 1; Bissell, *Talk to Every Woman,* 12; Corbin, *Woman's Rights in America;* Chittenden, *Inexpediency of Granting the Suffrage,* 3.

50. Lyman, 120; Scott and Adams, 3; Van Rensselaer, 5; Bissell, *Talk to Every*

Woman, 3–4, 12, 23; Mrs. Lyman Abbott, 5–6; Mrs. Arthur M. Dodge, "Why I Am an Antisuffragist," box 1, Woman's Suffrage and Women's Rights Collection, Special Collections, Vassar College Libraries.

51. For an overview of the political opportunity framework for analyzing social movements, see Gamson and Meyer. For a summary of the political climate during World War I, see Painter, chap. 11; Wiebe, chap. 11. For a description of the links between socialism, suffragism, and war opposition, see Buenker, "Politics of Mutual Frustration;" Buhle, chap. 6; O'Neill, *Everyone Was Brave,* chap. 6; Allen F. Davis, chap. 11.

52. Turner and Killian, 319.

53. Ibid, 318.

54. Baker, *Moral Frameworks of Public Life,* 24–29, 41; Kann, 202–7; Pugh, 102–4; Rotundo, 271–74; Hofstadter, *Anti-Intellectualism in American Life,* 179–91; Trachtenberg, 163–65.

55. Illinois Association Opposed to the Extension of Suffrage to Women, *Protest against the Granting of Municipal Suffrage,* 10; Baker, "Domestication of Politics"; Kann, 227; Hofstadter, *Anti-Intellectualism in American Life,* 186–89; Douglas.

56. William Parker, 17; Frothingham, "Real Case of the 'Remonstrants' "; Frothingham et al., 10; Lyman Abbott, "Why Women Do Not Wish the Suffrage"; Parkhurst, "Inadvisability of Woman Suffrage"; Kate McBeth, untitled antisuffrage address, n.d., Kate McBeth Collection, Joint Collection, University of Missouri Western Historical Manuscript Collection and Columbia and State Historical Society of Missouri Manuscripts, Columbia; Massie, 87; Brock, 7.

57. Crocker, *Letter to the Committee,* 6; Women Remonstrants of the State of Illinois, 3; Parkman, *Some of the Reasons against Woman Suffrage: Printed,* 16; Parkhurst, *Woman,* 10; William Parker, 17; Bock, 10; *New York State Association Opposed,* 5.

58. Helen Kendrick Johnson, *Woman's Progress,* 4; Wilbur, 7; Scott and Adams, 3; Pyle, *Should Women Vote,* 10; Bissell, *Talk to Women,* 3; Parkhurst, *Woman,* 4; idem, *"Inadvisability of Woman Suffrage,"* 36.

59. Henry A. Stimson, *Is Woman's Suffrage An Enlightened,* 4; Mrs. Arthur M. Dodge, "Woman Suffrage Opposed," 99; William Parker, 25; Brock, 6; Owen, 265.

60. MacIntire, 6.

61. Kann, 88, 137–41; Coontz, 62; Nebraska Men's Association Opposed to Woman Suffrage, *Nebraska Clergymen Condemn Suffrage,* 11. See also Everett P. Wheeler, *Right and Wrong of Woman Suffrage,* 11; Sams, 92–93; William Parker, 36; Owen, 150.

62. Illinois Association Opposed to the Extension of Suffrage to Women, *Why the Home Makers Do Not Want to Vote,* 4; Clement, 30; Seawell, *Ladies' Battle,* 107–8; Jones, "Some Impediments to Woman Suffrage"; NAOWS, *Some Facts about California's Experiment;* Helen Kendrick Johnson, *Woman and the Republic,* 312–16; Sams, 97; Buckley, *Wrong and Peril,* 106.

63. Eliza A. White, 30–31; Lily Rice Foxcroft, "Suffrage a Step Toward Feminism," 152; Illinois Association Opposed to the Extension of Suffrage to Women, *One Woman's Experience of Emancipation,* 4–5; Corbin, *Home versus Woman Suffrage,* 10.

64. Guild, *Municipal Suffrage for Women,* 2; Bissell, *Talk to Women,* 5; Caswell; Oregon State Association Opposed to the Extension of Suffrage to Women, 10; Terry, 52–53; Straube, 19; William Parker, 123; Simkins, 326–27.

65. Grace Duffield Goodwin, 103–4; Van Rensselaer, 10; Brock, 8; Bissell, *Talk to Every Woman,* 21.

66. Pyle, *Christian Civilization in the Balance,* 2; Frothingham et al., 12, 28; Doane, *Extracts from Addresses of the Rt. Rev. William Croswell Doane,* 4; Nott, 3–4; Terry, 5–6; *Appeal against Anarchy of Sex,* 21; Hubbard, 196; Lyman Abbott, *Why Women Do Not Wish the Suffrage,* 3; Cuyler, 4; Bushnell, *Women's Suffrage,* 136; Buckley, *Wrong and Peril,* 103; Nebraska Men's Association Opposed to Woman Suffrage, *Nebraska Clergymen Condemn Suffrage,* 4.

67. Grace Duffield Goodwin, 100; Women Remonstrants of the State of Illinois, 4; Chittenden, *Inexpediency of Granting the Suffrage,* 8; Helen Kendrick Johnson, *Woman and the Republic,* 284; Henry A. Stimson, *Is Woman's Suffrage an Enlightened,* 8; Parkhurst, *Woman,* 9; Sanford, 2.

68. Grace Duffield Goodwin, 92; Mrs. Lyman Abbott, 4; Dahlgren, 9–21; Bock, 10; Beecher, *Woman Suffrage and Woman's Profession,* 195; Kate McBeth, untitled antisuffrage address, n.d., Kate McBeth Collection, Joint Collection University of Missouri Western Historical Manuscript Collection and Columbia and State Historical Society of Missouri Manuscripts, Columbia.

69. Hubbard, 273–74; Straube, 69; Parkman, *Some of the Reasons against Woman Suffrage: Printed,* 13; Vertrees, 10; Nebraska Men's Association Opposed to Woman Suffrage, *Manifesto,* 6–8; Everett P. Wheeler, *Address of Everett P. Wheeler,* 6; idem, "Federal Woman Suffrage Amendment."

70. Melvin, 42; Owen, 136; Hubbard, 208; Bok, *Real Opponents,* 5.

71. Vertrees, 8; Massachusetts Man Suffrage Association, *Why Should Suffrage Be Imposed;* Frothingham et al., 22; Van Rensselaer, 12; Crocker, *Letter to the Committee,* 5; Jeannette Leonard Gilder, 1.

72. Russett, 40–41, 55, 81–92, 189; Darwin; Cope, *Origin of the Fittest.*

73. Russett, 33–39, chap. 6; Owen, 136; Havelock Ellis, *Studies in the Psychology of Sex;* idem, *Man and Woman.* For more on Havelock Ellis, see Rowbotham and Weeks.

74. Spencer, "Psychology of the Sexes," 31–36; idem, *Principles of Sociology;* Lutz; Grace Duffield Goodwin, 92; Vertrees, 8; Oregon State Association Opposed to the Extension of Suffrage to Women, 12. On Herbert Spencer, see Peel. For further discussion of the U.S. eugenics movement, see Chase, chap. 6.

75. Women Remonstrants of the State of Illinois, 4; MacIntire, 6; Brock, 4; *Letter to the Honorable Henry W. Blair;* Bissell, *Talk to Women,* 2; Lyman, 121; Mrs. Lyman Abbott, 5–6.

76. Tappan, 1; Edward Marshall, 3; Illinois Association Opposed to the Extension of Suffrage to Women, *Protest against the Granting of Municipal Suffrage*, 16; Gulick; Lyman Abbott, *Why Women Do Not Wish the Suffrage;* Terry, 14, 24; Root, *Address Delivered by the Hon. Elihu Root*, 3; Mrs. Arthur M. Dodge, *Case against Votes*, 5; Illinois Association Opposed to the Extension of Suffrage to Women, *To the Voters of the Middle West*, 3; Dos Passos, 6; Russett, 195; "To Raise New Race Is Woman's Problem," *NYT*, 19 March 1911, 12.

77. Mrs. Francis M. Scott, *Extension of the Suffrage to Women;* Straube, 20, 34; Tarbell, 77, 216; Mrs. Horace A. Davis; Beecher, *Woman Suffrage and Woman's Profession;* Helen Kendrick Johnson, *Woman and the Republic*, 318; Mrs. Lyman Abbott, 4.

78. For examples of support for the principle of equal pay for equal work, see Dahlgren; Helen Kendrick Johnson, *Woman and the Republic*, 190; Beecher, *Woman Suffrage and Woman's Profession*, 38. The person who advocated paying women workers more than men was Eliza A. White, 225–26. For an example of the denunciation of equal pay as a "suffragist cry," see Bissell, *Talk to Every Woman*, 9; Seawell, *Ladies' Battle*, 79. Male opposition to women professionals is illustrated by Brockett, 151–67, 195–96; Bushnell, *Women's Suffrage*, 19–27.

79. Seawell, *Ladies' Battle*, 79–80; Mrs. Henry Preston White; MacIntire, 5–6; Henry A. Stimson, *Is Woman's Suffrage Enlightened*, 6; Wilbur, 4; Illinois Association Opposed to the Extension of Suffrage to Women, *Protest Against the Granting of Municipal Suffrage*, 14; Grace Duffield Goodwin, 52–55; Chittenden, "Counter Influence to Woman Suffrage"; Wadlin; Bissell, *Help or a Hindrance*, 4.

80. Brockett, 236; Helen Kendrick Johnson, *Woman and the Republic*, 189–90; Bissell, *Help or a Hindrance*, 7; idem, *Talk to Every Woman*, 7; MacIntire, 6; Mrs. Henry Preston White, "Ballot and the Woman in Industry," 32–33; Grace Duffield Goodwin, 53–58.

81. Bissell, *Help or a Hindrance*, 5; idem, *Talk to Every Women*, 5; Mary Dean Adams, 5; Henry Billings Brown, 4; Birdsall, 1; Brockett, 141–44, 348; Beecher, *Woman Suffrage and Woman's Profession*, 51.

82. Massie, 85–86; Van Rensselaer, 15; NAOWS, *Truth about Wage-Earning Women;* Jones, "Position of the Anti-Suffragists," 18; Bock, 7.

83. Mrs. Henry Preston White, 33; Owen; Ten Eyck, 8; Bissell, *Help or a Hindrance*, 3; Grace Duffield Goodwin, 39; Mary Dean Adams, 6.

84. Seawell, *Ladies' Battle*, 47; Sams, 273–74; Jones, "Some Facts about Suffrage," 504; Lyman Abbott, "Women's Rights," 787; Bissell, *Help or a Hindrance*, 5; Terry, 51; Melvin, 40; Sanford, 3.

85. Baker, "Domestication of Politics." See also Lebsock, "Women and American Politics"; Clemens; Blair.

86. Coontz; Goffman; Wolf.

87. Mink, "Lady and the Tramp"; Kann, 17, 82.

88. Helen Kendrick Johnson, *Woman and the Republic*, 325–26; Kerber, *Women of the Republic;* Norton; Kann, 15–31, 252; Ashcraft.

89. Kann, 262; Edward Sandford Martin, 13–15.

90. Bissell, *Talk to Every Woman,* 4–7; Grace Duffield Goodwin, 135–36; Clara T. Leonard, *Letter from Mrs. Clara T. Leonard,* 4; Corbin, *Anti-Suffrage Movement,* 2; Caswell, 2; Hazard, *How Women Can Best Serve,* 2, 7–8; Illinois Association Opposed to the Extension of Suffrage to Women, *Why the Home Makers Do Not Want to Vote,* 1; Everett P. Wheeler, *What Women Have Done without the Ballot.*

91. Hubbard, 238; Meyer, *Woman's Assumption of Sex Superiority,* 5; Frothingham et al., 28; Sanford, 2; Buckley, *Wrong and Peril,* 99; Robinson; Lily Rice Foxcroft, *Why Are Women Opposing,* 3; George, 26–27; Massachusetts Man Suffrage Association, *Privileges of Women in Massachusetts;* Scott et al., 5; MAOFESW, *Address to the Judiciary Committees,* 5–8.

92. Dicey, 75; Jones "Some Facts about Suffrage," 495; Lyman Abbott, *Why Women Do Not Wish the Suffrage,* 4; Henry L. Stimson, *Suffrage Not a Natural Right,* 1–2; Mrs. Arthur M. Dodge, "Woman Suffrage Opposed," 99; Bernbaum, x; NAOWS, *Some Facts about California's Experiment,* 5; Hartwell.

93. Robinson, 10–12; Lily Rice Foxcroft, *Why Are Women Opposing,* 4–6; Bushnell, *Women's Suffrage,* 131; Henry A. Stimson, *Is Woman's Suffrage Enlightened,* 10; *Appeal against Anarchy of Sex,* 10–11; Mrs. Arthur M. Dodge, *Case against Votes,* 7; Frothingham, "Real Case of the 'Remonstrants,' " 178; Buckley, "Wrongs and Perils of Woman Suffrage"; Seawell, *Ladies' Battle;* Crannell, *Wyoming;* MAOFESW, *Woman Suffrage in Practice;* Cuyler, 2.

94. Quotation from Mrs. H. P. White in "Anti-Suffrage Meeting," n.p., n.d., box 7, William and Anna Lawther Collection, Iowa State Historical Society, Iowa City; *Appeal against Anarchy of Sex,* 12; Frothingham et al., 14; Illinois Association Opposed to the Extension of Suffrage to Women, *To the Voters of the Middle West,* 10; NAOWS, *Some Facts about California's Experiment;* MacIntire.

95. Schurz, *Woman Suffrage,* 2.

96. Grace Duffield Goodwin, 45–47; Scott and Adams, 5–7; "Antisuffragists in a National Union," *NYT,* 29 November 1911, 6; Seawell, *Ladies' Battle,* 18; Sams, 305; Tucker, 95; *Protest against Woman Suffrage in Alabama.*

97. Bissell, *Talk to Every Woman,* 11–12.

98. Helen Kendrick Johnson, *Woman and the Republic,* 134; Buckley, *Wrong and Peril,* 96; William Parker, 38; Frothingham et al., 12; Putnam; Bushnell, *Women's Suffrage,* 176; Tarbell, 198; Matthew Hale.

99. Bok, *Real Opponents,* 8; Bock, 3–4; *Appeal against Anarchy of Sex,* 12; Brock, 3; Rossiter Johnson, 8; Crocker, *Letter to the Committee,* 7.

100. Kann, 271; Bloch.

101. Seawell, *Ladies' Battle,* 27–29; Crannell, *Address of Mrs. W. Winslow Crannell,* 3; Massie, 87; Rossiter Johnson, 4; Jamison; Buckley, *Wrong and Peril,* 94; Munroe Smith, "Consent of the Governed"; Conaway; Carver, 16.

102. Terry, 63; Straube, 102; Owen, 33; circular from the Men's Patriotic Association, Pittsburgh, 31 December 1919, described in "Books and Things"; "Turns against Suffrage," *NYT,* 9 July 1920, 3; Tappan, 1; Lily Rice Foxcroft, *Why Are Women Opposing,* 10; George; Lord; Pennsylvania Association Opposed to Woman Suffrage, *Defeats and Failures of Woman Suffrage; Appeal against Anarchy of Sex,* 20.

103. For some examples of this literature, see A. Elizabeth Taylor, "Short History of the Woman Suffrage Movement in Tennessee"; idem, *Woman Suffrage Movement in Tennessee,* 110–14. The Georgia Association also produced some materials that explicitly addressed white supremacy, such as *The Vulnerability of the White Primary,* by its vice-president, Mrs. Walter D. Lamar; see A. Elizabeth Taylor, "Last Phase of the Woman Suffrage Movement in Georgia."

104. Bissell, *Talk to Every Woman,* 3; idem, *Talk to Women,* 2, 7; Illinois Association Opposed to the Extension of Suffrage to Women, *To the Voters of the Middle West,* 10; Beecher, *Woman Suffrage and Woman's Profession,* 12; Brockett, 298; Grace Duffield Goodwin, 38–47; Bock, 9; Elihu Root, speech before the NAOWS national convention, Washington, D.C., December 7–8, 1916, read by Alice Hill Chittenden, as reported by Maine delegate Annie Frances Harrod Boyd, in box 1, Woman's Suffrage and Women's Rights Collection, Special Collections, Vassar College Libraries. Everett P. Wheeler, *Home Rule,* 5; Mrs. Lyman Abbott, 2; *Protest against Woman's Suffrage in Alabama;* Tucker.

105. Everett P. Wheeler, "Federal Woman Suffrage Amendment"; idem, *Home Rule;* Seawell, "Two Suffrage Mistakes"; Pennsylvania Association Opposed to Woman Suffrage, *Talk on the Tax-Paying Woman;* Jones, "Some Facts about Suffrage," 501; Terry, 21.

106. Brock, 3, 8; Hubbard; Helen Kendrick Johnson, *Woman and the Republic;* Crannell, *Address of Mrs. W. Winslow Crannell,* 4; Sams, 309.

107. On the incorporation of labor into the U.S. party system, see Mink, *Old Labor and New Immigrants.* The function of the republican mother for taming male passions is elaborated by Kann; Kerber, *Women of the Republic;* Norton; Bloch; Coontz.

108. Mink, "Lady and the Tramp," 96; Rotundo, 254.

109. See Hartmann.

110. Scholars who have addressed these themes in the suffrage movement include DuBois, *Feminism and Suffrage;* Cott, *Grounding of Modern Feminism;* O'Neill, *Everyone Was Brave;* Grimes; Buechler.

111. Mrs. Arthur M. Dodge, "Why I Am an Antisuffragist," box 1, Woman's Suffrage and Women's Rights Collection, Special Collections, Vassar College Libraries.

112. See Zald and Useem.

113. Baker found a similar style among rural New York State female petitioners of nineteenth-century officeholders and also interprets it as acknowledgment of their position of political weakness as nonvoters. See Baker, *Moral Frameworks of Public Life,* 86–87.

Chapter 5. Mobilizing a Majority

1. Epigraph, "Votes for Men," broadside, n.d. (est. 1915), box 1, Woman's Suffrage and Women's Rights Collection, Special Collections, Vassar College Libraries.

2. On the rise of partisan politics, see Chambers and Burnham; Kleppner, *Who Voted,* chap. 2. For specific reference to women and partisan politics, see Baker, *Moral Frameworks of Public Life,* chap. 2; Mary P. Ryan.

3. Berg; Bordin; Cott, *Bonds of Womanhood;* DuBois, *Feminism and Suffrage;* Epstein; Melder, *Beginnings of Sisterhood.*

4. Buechler; Gould, *Progressive Era;* Richard Jensen; Lemons, chap. 1; Sochen.

5. For example, see Goldberg; Graham; Schaffer, "New York City Woman Suffrage Party"; idem, "Montana Woman Suffrage Campaign"; Snapp.

6. Grimes; Hofstadter, *Age of Reform.* See also Gusfield; Wiebe.

7. Anthony and Harper, 4:493–94, 896; Schaffer, "Montana Woman Suffrage Campaign," 14.

8. Baker, *Moral Frameworks of Public Life;* Berman; Buenker, "Urban Political Machine and Woman Suffrage"; McDonagh and Price; Mahoney; Thomas G. Ryan.

9. Buechler; Buenker, "Politics of Mutual Frustration"; Cott, *Grounding of Modern Feminism;* DuBois, "Harriot Stanton Blatch"; Dye; Schaffer, "Problem of Consciousness in the Woman Suffrage Movement"; Tax. One source of information on women's sentiments is Richard Jensen, although the women included in his survey are all civic leaders.

10. See Merk.

11. Benjamin, 3–4; Jablonsky, 6–8; "Editorial Notes," *Woman's Journal,* 25 May 1895, 161; "The Sham Referendum," *Woman's Journal,* 9 November 1895, 355–56.

12. "Not the Same Thing," *Remonstrance,* 1894, 1; Mrs. Charles E. Guild, "Address at a Conference of the Executive Committee with Gentlemen, March 30, 1906," MAOFESW; MAOFESW, untitled paper, n.d.

13. Kenneally, "Woman Suffrage and the Massachusetts 'Referendum.' " Concerning the clergy's position on woman suffrage, Kenneally notes that the Episcopal bishop of Massachusetts, William Lawrence, was included on a Man Suffrage Association mailing listing prominent male antisuffragists, and that Rev. Thomas Scully, leader of the Catholic temperance movement, was the first and for a long time the only Catholic priest on record for woman suffrage.

14. Kenneally, "Woman Suffrage and The Massachusetts 'Referendum' "; "The Sham Referendum," *Woman's Journal,* 9 November 1895, 355–56.

15. Referendum election results were collected from "The Sham Referendum," *Women's Journal,* 9 November 1895, 355–56. Data on 353 Massachusetts municipalities come from *Census of the Commonwealth of Massachusetts—1895.*

16. The number of eligible male voters for each town was counted in the *Census of the Commonwealth,* 1 (1896): 239–66. Women, however, were counted as having "no political condition" in the 1895 state census. To estimate the female turnout rates, this analysis used the percentage of the female native-born population (aged twenty and older) who voted. This narrower base of eligible voters was used because a poll tax was imposed on

propertyless women as an eligibility requirement for casting ballots on school suffrage. See Merk.

17. These conclusions are based on multiple regression models. Assessments of the relative strength of association among variables utilize standardized regression coefficients (signified as Beta values on the tables).

18. In table 5.1, the number of cases for women is reduced because no women voted on the Wellman bill in forty-five towns. They are included in table 5.2 and assigned a value of zero.

19. Sex ratios are calculated for both the total and foreign-born population (which varied more widely), with the total number of men in the numerator and the total number of women in the denominator. The foreign-born vote is calculated by the percentage of male eligible voters who are naturalized citizens. Population size for each town is logged to normalize the distribution. Rural residence is measured by the percentage engaged in agriculture among the male labor force (the 1895 state census recorded only twelve women engaged in agriculture). Appendix 1 summarizes the descriptive statistics for the variables included in the analysis.

20. The analysis includes the four most populous ethnic categories among the Massachusetts foreign-born population in 1895: Ireland (33.8% of foreign-born in the state; Great Britain (England, Scotland, Wales, English Canada, and other British possessions, 21.5%); French Canada (14.3%); Germany (4.1%). All ethnicity indicators are calculated as the percentage of the foreign-born population in each town. The choice of foreign-born population instead of total population as the denominator for the ethnicity variables had two advantages. First, it eliminated the problem of multicollinearity with the percentage of foreign-born voters in each town. These four ethnicity indicators were weakly and negatively intercorrelated (zero-order correlations ranged from −.02 to −.26), suggesting segregated patterns of immigrant settlement. Second, it increased the variance of ethnicity measures. For example, the highest share of any town's population that were Irish was 21 percent, while the greatest percentage of Irish among a town's foreign-born population was 79 percent.

21. The Boston-based *Woman's Journal,* quoting from the Boston *Herald,* opined that half of the majority against the referendum was "rolled up in our city." They also published a "roll of honor" of forty-six Massachusetts towns, most of them in the "country districts," that voted a majority for woman suffrage. See *Woman's Journal,* 9 November 1895, 356, and 16 November 1895, 361.

22. Labor force participation rates were estimated by adding the number of residents of each sex who were employed in ten classified occupations and dividing by the population of each sex aged 15–59. The ten occupations are government, professional, personal service, trade, transportation, agriculture, fisheries, manufactures, mining, and laborers. Scholars were not included because the numbers were high and suggested these were not all paid workers. Domestic service was deleted as an occupational category because the 1895 census included unpaid homemakers in this category. A breakdown of this

category into housewives, private domestic servants, and boarding and lodging services was given for the state as a whole and indicated that 91.7 percent of the women in this category were housewives. Only 392 men were listed in this occupational category. Hence, the labor force participation rates of women probably underestimate their actual level of economic activity. *Census of the Commonwealth*, 7 (1900). The average estimated labor force participation rate in Massachusetts towns was 11 percent for women and 64 percent for men. See appendix 1.

23. Men's and women's white-collar employment was estimated by a composite measure of professional and trade occupations as a percentage of workers in each sex. In the 1895 Massachusetts census, the trade category included bankers, accountants, brokers, dealers, and merchants. Blue-collar employment was measured for women workers only, owing to the high correlation between men's and women's participation in manufacturing (r = .76) in towns of the commonwealth.

24. In 1895, women's employment rates in Massachusetts were inversely related (r = −.25) to female professional employment. In other words, the relative share of women's higher-status employment was greater in towns where fewer women were employed, probably because manufacturing and domestic service were the two most common sources of female wage earning.

25. Low voter turnout among women might also reflect female apathy, identified privately by both sides as the greatest challenge to their mobilization efforts. Mrs. Charles E. Guild, "Address at a Conference of the Executive Committee with Gentlemen, March 30, 1906," MAOFESW; Schaffer, "Problem of Consciousness in the Woman Suffrage Movement."

26. Sex ratios are broken down into native-born and foreign-born categories, and two indicators assess the impact of family status on voter turnout: the percentage of the population under twenty years of age (youth population), which generally indicates higher child-rearing demands on adult women, and the percentage of the married adult population. The percentage of men in elite occupations is specified further as professional employment. The numerator for men's professional employment is professional occupations only, whereas the women's white-collar measurement includes both professional and trade occupations in the numerator.

27. This is shown by the larger proportion of variance explained for each sex, connoted by the Adjusted R-square on each table.

28. See Burris; Huber, Rexroat, and Spitze.

29. See Goertzel; Wirls; Conover; Mueller.

30. Kenneally, "Woman Suffrage and the Massachusetts 'Referendum' "; idem, "Catholicism and Woman Suffrage in Massachusetts."

31. These reportedly included Lyman Abbott, Edward Bok, Grover Cleveland, and Theodore Roosevelt. See Kenneally, "Woman Suffrage and the Massachusetts 'Referendum,' " 632.

32. See Beeton.

33. The thirteen defeated state referenda between 1910 and 1914 are Louisiana (limited suffrage, defeated 1912), Michigan (1912, 1913), Missouri, Nebraska, North Dakota (1914), Ohio (1912, 1914), Oklahoma (1910), Oregon (1910), South Dakota (1910, 1914), Wisconsin (1912). For more on the western suffrage victories, see Benjamin, chap. 3.

34. Studies that failed to find a strong rural-urban split on woman suffrage referenda include Baker, *Moral Frameworks of Public Life;* Mahoney; Thomas G. Ryan; Schaffer, "Problem of Consciousness in the Woman Suffrage Movement."

35. Thomas G. Ryan; Mahoney; Berman.

36. See McDonagh and Price.

37. The Kansas referendum of 1867 was important in the history of the woman suffrage movement because the campaign split the suffrage movement over the question of black male suffrage, which was also on the ballot. See DuBois, *Feminism and Suffrage,* chap. 3.

38. Although it was rare, the legislatures of several other southern states did pass suffrage bills mandating an election on the woman suffrage question: Oklahoma (1910), Louisiana (1912), and West Virginia (1916). All referenda failed, although Oklahoma subsequently added a woman suffrage amendment to the state constitution in 1918.

39. On California's suffrage history, see Englander, 73–76; Schaffer, "Problem of Consciousness in the Woman Suffrage Movement," 481–84. On Oregon, see Duniway; Anthony and Harper, 4:895, 971; Benjamin, chap. 5; *Woman's Journal,* 26 November 1910, 216; MAOFESW, EC, 9 February 1906, 2 December 1910, 24 February 1911.

40. Goldberg; Wilda M. Smith.

41. Camhi, 197; A. Elizabeth Taylor, "Woman Suffrage Movement in Texas."

42. Benjamin, chap. 13; Camhi, 122; Jablonsky, 17–27; MAOFESW, Account of Work, Room 615, September 1915, November 1915; NAOWS, board of directors meeting, 2 September 1915, MAOSW.

43. NAOWS, board of directors meeting, 2 September 1915, MAOSW; "Suffrage Recruits Gained on Bowery," *NYT,* 2 May 1915, sec. 7, 11.

44. Woman suffrage referenda results are tabulated from the following sources: "The Washington Vote," *Woman's Journal,* 10 December 1910, 229; "Suffragists Win by a Narrow Margin," *San Francisco Examiner,* 13 October 1911, 1; "Oregon's Vote by Counties," *Woman's Journal,* 4 January 1913, 7; "Total Kansas Vote Arrives," *Woman's Journal,* 4 January 1913, 3; MAOFESW, *Special Report on the 1915 Massachusetts Referendum,* n.d.; "Vote by Counties," *NYT,* 5 November 1915, 6; "Suffrage Vote in Detail," *NYT,* 25 December 1915, 5; "Jersey Reports Final Returns," *Woman's Journal,* 6 November 1915, 352; Baker, *Moral Frameworks of Public Life,* 179–82; A. Elizabeth Taylor, *Citizens at Last,* 189–92. Incomplete election results for some states necessitated deleting the following counties from the analysis: Alpine, Modoc, and Siskiyou (California); Clearfield, Indiana, Sullivan, Tioga (Pennsylvania); Cochran, Crane, Glasscock, Hockley,

Loving, Moore, Stonewall, Upton (Texas). The final county totals for the western sample are California (54); Oregon (33); Washington (36). For the eastern sample, the county totals are Massachusetts (14); New Jersey (21); New York (61); Pennsylvania (63). County-level information is collected from U.S. Department of the Interior, Census Office, *Thirteenth Census of the United States,* vol. 1, *General Report and Analysis,* and vols. II and III, *Reports by States.*

45. Sex ratios, as before, represent the number of males relative to females, with the highest values indicating a relative surplus of males. We measure urbanization by the 1910 census definition, expressed as the percentage of county residents in places with 2,000 or more population. Population growth between 1890 and 1910 is expressed as a percentage in positive (for growth) or negative (for population loss) values. Counties not established in 1890 were deleted from the analysis. This resulted in exclusion of the following counties: Benton and Grant (Washington); Hood River (Oregon); Imperial (California); Reagan, Terrell (Texas). Race and ethnicity are indicated by the percent nonwhite and the percent foreign-born in each county, and school enrollment refers to the percent aged 6–20 attending school.

46. Kleppner, *Who Voted,* 58–68; Kousser, 29–57.

47. Country of origin includes first- and second-generation immigrants of each county. This is measured by the percentage of each nationality among county residents who are foreign-born or the offspring of immigrant parents, an indicator that more broadly captures ethnic influences within the new-stock community. In the interests of parsimony, only those countries of origin that achieved statistical significance in the models for at least one region are presented here. Religious estimates were calculated as the percentage Roman Catholic of the total population in each county in 1890. Catholicism is commonly associated with certain immigrant populations at the time and with traditional views toward women. U.S. Department of the Interior, Census Office *Eleventh Census of the United States,* vol. 3, *Report on Statistics of Churches in the United States,* table 2.

48. Voter turnout is measured as the percentage of voting-age men in each county who cast ballots on state suffrage referenda. Number of voting-age males by county in 1910 is found in U.S. Department of the Interior, Census Office, *Thirteenth Census of the United States,* 1: 231–46.

49. For example, voters in Washington State approved female enfranchisement by the widest margin (64 percent) and with the lowest voter turnout (20 percent) in the sample; Oregon, with the highest average voter turnout (50 percent), also had the largest share of counties rejecting the amendment (about one-third) in the western sample.

50. Duniway, 243; Englander, 76; Schaffer, "Problem of Consciousness in the Woman Suffrage Movement," 490.

51. Moreover, antisuffragists in the eastern states were more successful at getting out the opposition vote; Pennsylvania, the state with the lowest turnout (32 percent), also had the closest election returns, with 54 percent voting down the referendum.

52. Letter from Mrs. Charles Eliot Guild, in MAOFESW, EC, 24 January 1913; MAOFESW, EOC, 21 July 1915; MAOFESW, EC, 9 July 1915; "Bay State Likely to Beat Suffrage," *NYT*, 29 October 1915, 5; "Suffrage Recruits Gained on Bowery," *NYT*, 2 May 1915, sec. 7, 11; NAOWS, board of directors meeting, 2 September 1915, 30 September 1915, MAOSW.

53. Bordin, 118–22, 134–35, 151–57; Catt and Shuler, chap. 10; Duniway, 99–101, 179, 224–32; Englander, 73–79; Schaffer, "Problem of Consciousness in the Woman Suffrage Movement."

54. Flexner, 296–98; Camhi, chap. 5; Jablonsky, 72–75; Grace Wilbur Trout; Youmans; McBride, 239–40; Caruso, 210–11; Wilda M. Smith, 87–89; Mahoney, 154–58; Ohio Association Opposed to Woman's Suffrage, memorandum, n.d. (est. 1914), Harriet Taylor Upton Papers, Western Reserve Historical Society, Cleveland, Ohio.

55. Berman; McDonagh and Price; Caruso.

56. Gilman M. Ostrander, 117; Englander, 141.

57. Gould, *Progressives and Prohibitionists*, 254–59; Marburger, 4; McKay, 85. The defeat of woman suffrage in Ohio in 1917 was also explained by the presence of a prohibition amendment on the same ballot. See "Charles McLean Returns from East," *Dubuque Telegraph-Herald*, 12 November 1917, box 7, Lawther Collection, Iowa State Historical Society, Iowa City.

58. The tally on the Texas prohibition referendum is taken from "Vote on Constitutional Amendments by Counties," *Dallas Morning News*, 1 June 1919, 3. Because of incomplete returns, twenty counties were eliminated from the analysis.

59. McDonagh and Price; McKay, 82–86.

60. On the Congressional Union's partisan strategy, see Cott, *Grounding of Modern Feminism*, chap. 2; Snapp. For party endorsement histories, see Beeton, 113; Buenker, "Politics of Mutual Frustration," 119; Buhle, chap. 3; Flexner, 262.

61. Berman; Flexner, 261; Gould, *Progressives and Prohibitionists*, 234–48; Gilman M. Ostrander, 116; Grace Wilbur Trout.

62. State legislatures that implemented presidential suffrage include Michigan, North Dakota, Nebraska, Rhode Island (1917); Indiana, Maine, Missouri, Iowa, Minnesota (1919). See National American Woman Suffrage Association, appendix 4.

63. Beeton, 108–13, 139–43; Boles, "Systemic Factors Underlying Legislative Responses"; Goldberg.

64. Buenker, "Politics of Mutual Frustration," 119–21.

65. These are the gubernatorial election of 1914 and the vote for state attorney general in 1917. Source for the county-level political variables is Baker, *Moral Frameworks of Public Life*, 179–82. The third parties included are the Prohibition, Progressive, Socialist, and Industrial Labor parties for 1914, and the Socialist and Prohibition parties for 1917. Ethnicity was not significant and is not included in either equation.

66. In addition, the antisuffrage vote of rural counties in 1915 rewarded the

New York Association's arduous summer work at county fairs and the Chautauqua Circuit. NAOWS, board of directors meeting, 2 September 1915, 30 September 1915, MAOSW.

67. "Bay State Likely to Beat Suffrage," *NYT,* 29 October 1915, 5.

68. See Buenker, "Urban Political Machine and Woman Suffrage," 268; idem, "Politics of Mutual Frustration"; DuBois, "Harriot Stanton Blatch"; Schaffer, "New York City Woman Suffrage Party."

69. MAOFESW, EC, 22 March 1901, 24 May 1901, 27 December 1901.

70. MAOFESW, EC, 28 June 1901, 25 October 1901, 27 December 1901, 10 January 1902, 27 March 1902, 24 May 1907.

71. MAOFESW, EDC, 7 March 1906; MAOFESW, EC, 12 February 1904.

72. Standing committee membership lists are from MAOFESW, untitled brochures, 1905, 1910, 1915.

73. The regional breakdowns were calculated by county, as follows: the western region included Berkshire, Franklin, Hampden, and Hampshire Counties; the central region constituted Worcester County; the eastern region included all towns in Middlesex, Essex, Norfolk, and Plymouth Counties that were not previously listed in Boston or in greater Boston, as well as the southeastern Massachusetts counties of Barnstable and Dukes.

74. MAOFESW, Annual Report, 30 April 1896.

75. MAOFESW, untitled pamphlet, n.d. (est. 1897).

76. MAOFESW, EOC, 10 March 1910; MAOFESW, Special Report, 23 May 1910; MAOFESW, EC, 13 March 1914; MAOSW, executive committee meeting, 1 August 1916, 27 March 1917; MAOSW, business meeting, 4 April 1917.

77. The information on number and location of branch committees was taken from MAOFESW, EDC, 7 March 1906; *Remonstrance,* January 1915, 6.

78. MAOFESW, EOC, 17 May 1909.

79. The dependent variable is an ordinal scale varying from 0 to 3; towns scored 1 had a branch committee in place by 1915, those coded 2 were organized as early as 1906, and the highest score was reserved for the few towns with multiple branch committees as of 1915. For the towns included in the analysis represented in table 5.7, the frequency distribution of the dependent variable, branch committee organization, is as follows: no organization by 1915 (code 0): 73.7%; organization in 1915 (code 1), 17%; organization in 1906 (code 2), 7.6%; multiple organization in one town (code 3), 1.7%. The town characteristics are derived from *Census of the Commonwealth of Massachusetts*. The sociodemographic variables and 1895 referendum results have been previously described in the discussion of tables 5.1 and 5.2. The one exception is the percentage of female workers in professional occupations, which is measured as described for men; see note 26 in this chapter.

80. MAOFESW, EC, 10 May 1901, 11 April 1902, 25 April 1902, 23 May 1902.

81. MAOFESW, EC, 11 April 1913; MAOFESW, EDC, 7 March 1906; MAOFESW, EOC, 1 February 1915; MAOFESW, JC, 5 January 1916; Alice N. George to branch committees, 11 December 1903, MAOFESW.

82. MAOFESW, EC, 17 December 1909, 24 March 1911, 25 April 1913; MAOFESW, JC, 20 November 1906, 22 March 1909.

83. Owing to missing election returns, sixty-four towns are eliminated from this analysis. The data source for the 1915 election is MAOFESW, Special Report, 2 November 1915.

84. MAOFESW, Annual Report, 30 April 1896, 26 April 1917; MAOFESW, untitled pamphlet, January 1902; MAOFESW, EDC, 7 March 1906; MAOFESW, Account of Work, Room 615, November 1915; *Remonstrance,* January 1915, 6.

85. MAOFESW, EDC, 7 March 1896; MAOFESW, EOC, 22 November 1909, 11 May 1911; MAOFESW, EC, 2 February 1904, 27 May 1904, 26 May 1905, 16 January 1914, 5 February 1915; MAOFESW, Organizer's Report, 23 February 1919.

86. Annie Nathan Meyer tried to market her book *The Dominant Sex* through the Massachusetts Association, which declined. See MAOFESW, EC, 12 May 1911. For a sketch of her life, see John William Leonard, *Woman's Who's Who,* 559. A sampling of her views is found in Meyer, *Woman's Work in America.* For more on the role of women's colleges in maintaining the ideology of domesticity, see Wein.

87. MAOFESW, EDC, 12 December 1896, 30 January 1897, 2 April 1897, 3 February 1898; MAOFESW, EC, 9 May 1913.

88. MAOFESW, EOC, 21 December 1909, 21 May 1913, 20 May 1914, 13 December 1916, 18 July 1917; MAOFESW, EC, 31 May 1912, 20 February 1914, 15 May 1914; "Anti-Suffrage Campaign On," *NYT,* 9 September 1909, 7.

89. One such pamphlet was Frances J. Dyer's "The Ballot for Wage-Earning Women." Miss Dyer was also a MAOFESW speaker. See MAOFESW, EDC, 11 January 1896, 2 April 1897; MAOFESW, EOC, 21 January 1914; MAOFESW, EC, 27 March 1902, 24 January 1908, 14 February 1908, 10 February 1911, 27 November 1914. As for gaining entrée to employee meetings, the daughter of the president of Plymouth Cordage Company invited the Massachusetts Association to speak to the workers. See MAOFESW, Special Report, 9 November 1910.

90. MAOFESW, EC, 16 April 1909, 31 October 1913; MAOFESW, EOC, 6 December 1911, 15 March 1916.

91. MAOFESW, EC, 14 March 1913, 27 March 1914, 10 March 1916, 17 May 1918; MAOFESW, EDC, 30 November 1897; MAOFESW, EOC, 30 November 1909, 20 March 1912, 6 November 1912, 19 March 1913, 3 June 1914, 3 March 1915.

92. The quote is from Mrs. William Lowell Putnam. See MAOFESW, Annual Meeting, 23 April 1913.

93. MAOFESW, EC, 11 June 1904; MAOFESW, JC, 5 January 1916; MAOSW, Annual Meeting, 3 May 1915.

94. The comment about colleges is attributed to Mrs. John Balch, former MAOFESW president (1915) and later delegate to NAOWS. It is found in NAOWS, Delegate's Report, 7 December 1916, MAOSW. See also MAOSW, Annual Report, 1 December 1915; MAOFESW, EC, 27 October 1905; MAOFESW,

EOC, 19 March 1913, 7 March 1917; MAOFESW, Special Report, 9 November 1910; MAOFESW, Organizer's Report, 10 August 1918, 2 February 1919.

95. MAOSW, Monthly Meeting, 6 April 1914; MAOSW, Executive Committee meeting, 22 April 1914; MAOSW, Annual Report, 15 December 1915; MAOFESW, Organizer's Report, 1 September 1915.

96. The taxpayer, Mrs. John Fremont (Laura Colman Liggett) Hill, president of the Augusta branch, was the daughter of the U.S. secretary of agriculture under Grover Cleveland, and her husband was a two-time governor of Maine. After his death in 1912, records uncovered in his estate papers became the focus of an antitrust scandal involving his steamship and railroad investments. Mrs. Hill moved to Boston in 1916, whereupon she was invited to join the MAOFESW executive committee. Mrs. John F. A. Merrill, MAOSW president between 1916 and 1917, was the wife of the U.S. district attorney for Maine and former state senator. Mrs. Clarence (Margaret Rollins) Hale, chair of the committee on literature, printing, and legislature, was married to a federal judge from a distinguished New England family. See *NYT,* 17 March 1912, 15; 10 October 1914, 12; 16 October 1914, 12; 23 March 1915, 5; 19 October 1915, 6; 10 April 1934, 23; 3 January 1944, 22; "Bingham Leads in Maine," *NYT,* 3 September 1925, 2; MAOFESW, EC, 8 June 1916.

97. MAOSW, Monthly Meeting, 7 December 1914; MAOSW, Organizer's Report, n.d. (est. April 1917); MAOFESW, EOC, 18 July 1917.

98. The undated MAOSW organizers' report, which was in the form of a handwritten "book," with members listed by town, was compiled for the 1917 referendum. The collection also includes several organization registration cards dated as late as August 1917 which have been added to the book totals. The total number of signatures collected for Maine was 3,546, of which 56 percent (1,987) had Portland addresses.

99. Boston was the nation's fifth largest city in 1910, with 74 percent of its population of foreign birth or foreign parentage. U.S. Department of the Interior, Census Office, *Thirteenth Census of the United States,* Abstract of the Census with Supplement for Maine, table V; *Thirteenth Census of the United States,* 4: tables III and IV.

100. The registration cards for Portland contained more complete address listings, making identification possible by matching addresses to census population schedules. To draw the sample, we first selected every third listing from the association's Portland membership roster, and the address of each selected case was researched on a city map to locate its census enumeration district; 566 members were matched with an enumeration district by this method. The next stage examined the population schedules by enumeration district to collect individual and household information for each case, yielding a final sample of 252 members. This number represents 13 percent of the listed MAOSW members in the city. Snahel Patel and Kyong Murchison assisted in the data collection. U.S. Department of the Interior, Census Office, *Thirteenth Census of the United States,* Population Schedules, National Archives Microfilm Publication #T624.

101. Part of the problem with sample attrition was the fact that the membership lists ranged from 1913 to 1917, and changes of residence made matching difficult using the decennial manuscript census. Checking attrition rates between stages 1 and 2 indicates that the loss of data was slightly lower in the wealthier neighborhoods. Hence, the sample probably underenumerates more mobile members, such as boarding house residents, and for that reason is likely to be skewed in favor of more affluent and older members.

102. MAOSW, untitled organizer's report, undated (est. April 1917).

103. As the sample sizes shown on the bottom of table 5.8 indicate, these two categories constitute 82 percent of the sample. The two groups not examined in detail are widowed women ($N = 29$) and all men ($N = 13$). Marital status was not identified for two cases. Because of small sample sizes, results for these two subsamples are omitted, although they are counted in the sample statistics presented in the first panel of table 5.8.

104. In 1910, 13 percent of employed males in Portland were in professional and managerial jobs. U.S. Department of the Interior, Census Office, *Thirteenth Census of the United States,* 4: table III.

105. Because of the time interval between census enumeration and membership, it is possible that a small percentage of nonemployed women might have been employed by the time of their MAOSW membership. This is probably not a large number of single women, however, since many were middle-aged even in 1910.

106. Jablonsky, 75.

Chapter 6. From Parlors to Parades

1. Epigraph, statement by Mrs. Charles S. Fairchild, in "New York Suffrage Accepted by Antis," *NYT,* 9 May 1918, 13.

2. "Anti-Suffragists Aroused," *NYT,* 10 December 1911, sec. 3, 16.

3. MAOFESW, untitled address, anon., n.d. (c. 1890).

4. Mrs. Charles E. Guild, "Address at a Conference of the Executive Committee with Gentlemen, March 30, 1906," MAOFESW; Hazard, "New York State Association," 85.

5. Hazard, "New York State Association"; "Anti-Suffragists Aroused," *NYT,* 10 December 1911, sec. 3, 16; MAOFESW, Western Report for the Summer of 1898; MAOFESW, EC, 22 November 1901, 2 February 1902, 11 December 1903, 11 June 1904, 3 November 1909.

6. MAOFESW, untitled address, n.d. (c. 1890).

7. MAOFESW, EC, 1 November 1909; MAOFESW, untitled pamphlet, n.d. (c. 1897); MAOSW, executive committee meeting, 27 March 1917; "Time to Show One's Colors," *Remonstrance,* July 1914, 1.

8. See Skocpol; Koven and Michel.

9. MAOFESW, EC, 28 June 1901, 29 April 1910; MAOFESW, EOC, 20 March 1912.

10. MAOFESW, Annual Report, 30 April 1896; MAOFESW, EC, 12 October 1900, 10 May 1901, 25 March 1904, 13 January 1905, 10 November 1911, 8 December 1911; MAOFESW, EDC, 11 January 1896, 9 November 1898, 15 December 1898; MAOFESW, EOC, 4 October 1911.

11. MAOFESW, EDC, 7 March 1896, 7 January 1898, 9 November 1898, 15 December 1898, 8 December 1899, 22 January 1904; MAOFESW, EOC, 2 February 1910, 4 October 1911, 6 March 1912; MAOFESW, EC, 12 April 1901, 27 September 1901, 7 January 1904.

12. The press committee was staffed by Mrs. A. J. George, who was also a paid antisuffrage organizer, speaker, and writer. See George memo, n.d. (est. 1903), and Charles R. Saunders to Mrs. Charles Eliot Guild, 1 March 1906, MAOFESW; MAOFESW, EDC, 3 February 1898, 1 March 1898; MAOFESW, EOC, 5 October 1910, 6 March 1912; MAOFESW, EC, 10 May 1901, 28 February 1902, 25 April 1902, 27 April 1906, 14 February 1908, 12 May 1911.

13. MAOFESW, untitled address, n.d. (c. 1890); MAOFESW, EC, 8 February 1901, 27 December 1901, 10 January 1902, 13 March 1903, 22 January 1904, 29 January 1909.

14. Mrs. Charles E. Guild, "Address at a Conference of the Executive Committee with Gentlemen, March 30, 1906," MAOFESW; MAOFESW, EC, 11 January 1901, 26 April 1901, 14 March 1902, 19 June 1908, 19 March 1909, 27 January 1911, 26 April 1912, 8 November 1912, 8 May 1914, 23 October 1914, 3 December 1915; MAOFESW, EOC, 3 November 1910.

15. MAOFESW, Boston committee meeting, 17 January 1901, 12 March 1902; MAOFESW, EC, 2 May 1902, 23 September 1904, 14 October 1904, 24 October 1907, 14 October 1910; MAOSW, executive committee meeting, 12 December 1916; "Suffrage Campaign Is Carried to Polls," *NYT,* 19 October 1915, 1.

16. As of April 1910, state antisuffrage associations existed in Massachusetts, New York, Illinois, Iowa, Oregon, and Pennsylvania. There were also committees in Rhode Island and Washington. See *Remonstrance,* April 1910, 1. McGerr; Buenker, "Politics of Mutual Frustration"; Buhle.

17. DuBois, "Harriot Stanton Blatch"; Schaffer, "New York City Woman Suffrage Party."

18. Jones, "Some Impediments to Woman Suffrage;" "Guidon," *Anti-Suffragist,* December 1908, 6–7; MAOFESW, EC, 27 March 1908, 25 September 1908, 4 December 1908. The Albany activist was Mrs. W. Winslow Crannell, and the western campaign states in 1898 were South Dakota and Washington. See Benjamin, 20–33, 87–88.

19. The early debater was Mrs. William Forse Scott; one of the woman suffragists she would subsequently debate was Mrs. Thomas Hepburn, president of the Connecticut Woman Suffrage Association and mother of actor Katharine Hepburn. See "Suffragettes Meet the Antis in Debate," *NYT,* 24 April 1909, 3; "Anti-Suffrage Campaign On," *NYT,* 9 September 1909, 7; "Charges Suffrage Increases Divorce," *NYT,* 6 January 1915, 15; Jablonsky, 23.

20. MAOFESW, EC, 12 April 1907, 11 October 1907, 19 June 1908, 20 Novem-

ber 1908, 3 December 1909, 4 February 1910. The five state associations were New York, Massachusetts, Pennsylvania, Illinois, Iowa, and Oregon. There were also two committees, in Maine and Rhode Island.

21. The suffrage petition for a federal amendment is described in Flexner, 249; MAOFESW, EC, 15 April 1910. California was important because it had a relatively large population among the western states, at twice the electoral college vote of Washington State. Antis were also more organized there, and actively lobbied the legislature against suffrage. See Harper, 6:27–58.

22. The five states represented were New York, Massachusetts, Maryland, Rhode Island, and Pennsylvania. Letters of approval were sent by the Illinois, Oregon, and Northern and Southern California Associations. The statement by Mrs. Dodge is from "Anti-Suffragists in a National Union," *NYT,* 29 November 1911, 6. See also MAOFESW, EC, 13 October 1911, 24 November 1911. For more on NAOWS, see Benjamin, chap. 6; Jablonsky, chap. 6.

23. MAOFESW, EC, 8 December 1911, 26 April 1912, 31 May 1912, 25 April 1913, 10 March 1916; NAOWS, board of directors meeting, 2 September 1915, MAOSW.

24. In the 1912 elections, state suffrage was passed in Arizona, Kansas, and Oregon, and defeated in Michigan, Ohio, and Wisconsin. In 1913, Michigan again placed woman suffrage on the ballot, and it was defeated. In addition to Nevada and Montana voting for suffrage in 1914, the following states defeated it: Missouri, Ohio, Nebraska, North Dakota, and South Dakota. During this period, the Illinois legislature (1913) also granted presidential suffrage to women without a referendum. Harper, 6:10–15, 200–201, 307–8, 365–66, 375–82, 397, 506–13, 543–47, 591, 703–5; Caruso; Fox; Schaffer, "Montana Woman Suffrage Campaign"; Mary Semple Scott; Grace Wilbur Trout; Youmans; MAOFESW, EC, 28 June 1912, 13 September 1912, 6 December 1912, 28 March 1913, 24 October 1913, 9 October 1914, 13 November 1914; MAOFESW, JC, 17 July 1914, 21 August 1914; "Predicts Anti Victory," *NYT,* 14 September 1914, 8.

25. "An Anti-Suffrage Annex," *NYT,* 5 April 1913, 17; "Antis Move Downtown," *NYT,* 25 May 1913, sec. 2, 8; MAOFESW, EC, 23 May 1913.

26. "Antis Condemn Paraders," *NYT,* 6 May 1913, 10; "Says Suffrage Idea Is Only Sex Fad," *NYT,* 12 May 1913, 2; Edward Marshall, "Our Suffrage Movement Is Flirtation on a Big Scale," *NYT,* 25 May 1913, sec. 5, 2; "Antis Boycott Anna Shaw," *NYT,* 16 June 1913, 3; "Antis Explain Attitude," *NYT,* 4 August 1913, 2; "Fear Pankhurst Visit," *NYT,* 8 September 1913, 3; "Blame Suffragists for Vice Publicity," *NYT,* 22 September 1913, 9; "Raise 'Free Love' Cry," *NYT,* 25 May 1914, 11; "Antis Answer Suffragists," *NYT,* 1 June 1914, 10; "Calls Suffragists Selfish," *NYT,* 10 August 1914, 6; "Attacks Belmont Meeting," *NYT,* 24 August 1914, 8; "Antis Assail Blacklist," *NYT,* 31 August 1914, 6; "Calls Dr. Shaw Untruthful," *NYT,* 9 September 1915, 12; "Suffragiana," *NYT,* 29 September 1915, 2; "Mrs. Dodge Charges Poison-Pen Plot," *NYT,* 30 October 1916, 9; "Antis Again Attack Suffrage Leaders," *NYT,* 21 October 1917, sec. 1, 3.

27. Examples of antisuffrage letters to the editor of the *NYT* include E. P.

Wheeler, "Dyspeptic Suffragists," 28 December 1913, 14; idem, "Suffragists' Unfitness," 26 September 1914, 10; idem, "Russian Women and Suffrage," 10 August 1917, 8; Alice N. George, "Anti-Suffrage Speaker Misquoted," 17 January 1914, 8; Helen K. Johnson, ""The Suffrage Menace," 23 May 1915, sec. 7, 1; Alice Hill Chittenden, "The Fat Suffrage Purse," 27 June 1916, 10.

28. MAOFESW, EC, 14 February 1913, 28 March 1913, 11 April 1913, 27 November 1914, 5 March 1915, 16 April 1915, 23 July 1915, 3 September 1915, 24 September 1915; MAOFESW, EOC, 3 January 1912, 16 April 1913, 7 May 1913, 1 October 1913, 21 April 1915, 19 May 1915, 4 August 1915, 18 August 1915; MAOFESW, JC, 17 July 1914.

29. MAOFESW, EC, 28 February 1913, 11 April 1913, 20 February 1914, 3 April 1914, 9 April 1914, 8 May 1914, 12 March 1915, 24 September 1915; MAOFESW, EOC, 17 March 1915; "Red Rose as Anti's Badge," *NYT,* 5 May 1914, 13; "Anti-Suffrage Rose Named 'Mrs. Dodge,' " *NYT,* 6 April 1915, 4.

30. MAOFESW, JC, 18 July 1913; MAOFESW, EC, 25 September 1914; NAOWS, board of directors meeting, 2 September 1915, MAOSW; "Progress of the Campaign," *WP,* September 1915, 12–13; "Intensive Work in Campaign States," *WP,* October 1915, 13–14; "Antis State Convention," *NYT,* 1 May 1914, 5; "Anti-Suffragists Rally," *NYT,* 10 June 1915, 11.

31. MAOFESW, EC, 13 February 1914, 3 April 1914, 27 November 1914, 11 December 1914, 26 March 1915, 8 October 1915; MAOFESW, EOC, 17 December 1913, 1 April 1914, 6 January 1915, 19 May 1915, 21 July 1915, 3 November 1915; "Anti-Suffrage Rose Named 'Mrs. Dodge,' " *NYT,* 6 April 1915, 4; "Tear Down Suffrage Sign," *NYT,* 24 September 1915, 11.

32. MAOFESW, EDC, 4 November 1905; MAOFESW, EOC, 9 April 1909; MAOFESW, EC, 27 December 1901, 28 February 1902, 11 November 1904, 15 May 1908, 30 September 1910; 11 October 1912; 28 March 1913; 30 October 1914, 23 July 1915; "Taft to Speak for Antis," *NYT,* 15 February 1914, 11; "Antis Address Wilson," *NYT,* 29 June 1914, 9; "Whitman Favors Woman Suffrage," *NYT,* 9 December 1914, 1.

33. MAOFESW, JC, 15 August 1913; MAOFESW, EDC, 28 September 1904; MAOFESW, EOC, 7 May 1913; MAOFESW, EC, 9 December 1910, 27 September 1912, 9 October 1914; NAOWS, board of directors meeting, 2 September 1915, MAOSW; "Anti-Suffrage Meetings," *NYT,* 23 September 1913, 7.

34. MAOFESW, EC, 9 December 1910, 27 June 1913, 10 October 1913, 24 October 1913, 14 November 1913, 24 April 1914, 9 October 1914, 30 October 1914.

35. This was certainly the case in Massachusetts, where many antisuffrage state legislators were defeated in the 1912 elections, and those remaining feared being labeled obstructionists by suffragists. In strategy sessions with the men's committee, the MAOFESW leadership recognized the inevitability of the bill's passage. They agreed that it should not go through unopposed, so they proposed an amendment to open the referendum to both sexes, hoping to garner the "stay-at-home women vote." Their amendment was defeated, but

not without putting on record that antisuffragists alone were willing to let women voters settle the question. MAOFESW, EC, 26 December 1913, 16 January 1914, 27 February 1914.

36. "Big Suffrage Fight Promised by Antis," *NYT,* 24 March 1915, 11; "Bay State Likely to Beat Suffrage," *NYT,* 29 October 1915, 5; NAOWS, board of directors meeting, 2 September 1915, 30 September 1915, MAOSW.

37. MAOFESW, JC, 18 July 1913; MAOFESW, EC, 16 April 1915, 31 December 1915; MAOFESW, Annual Meeting, 27 April 1916; "The Antis Become 'Conservationists,' " *NYT,* 11 August 1913, 2; "Suffrage Recruits Gained on Bowery," *NYT,* 2 May 1915, sec. 7, 11; Englander, 73; Schaffer, "Problem of Consciousness in the Women Suffrage Movement"; A. Elizabeth Taylor, "The Woman Suffrage Movement in Florida."

38. MAOFESW, EC, 20 August 1915; MAOFESW, Room Report, 30 September 1915.

39. MAOFESW, EOC, 2 February 1916; MAOFESW, EC, 25 August 1916.

40. MAOFESW, JC, 5 January 1916; MAOFESW, EC, 11 February 1916, 25 February 1916, 24 March 1916; MAOFESW, EOC, 17 November 1915, 16 February 1916, 15 March 1916, 7 April 1916, 18 April 1916, 17 May 1916, 25 October 1916; MAOFESW, Room Report, 31 August 1916.

41. Catt, chap. 4; "Iowa Rejects Suffrage," *NYT,* 7 June 1916, 7; "Iowa Suffragists Admit Defeat," *NYT,* 8 June 1916, 5; "South Dakota," *NYT,* 8 November 1916, 2; "West Virginia," *NYT,* 8 November 1916, 3; "The Iowa Victory," *WP,* June 1916, 3; "Suffrage Routed in Two More States," *WP,* November 1916, 3; NAOWS Delegate's Report, 7 December 1916, MAOSW.

42. Flexner, 251–54, 265–70; McGerr, 871–78; Schaffer, "New York City Woman Suffrage Party"; Snapp; "To Defeat All Antis," *NYT,* 23 October 1913, 7; "Women Blacklist Foes in Congress," *NYT,* 30 August 1914, sec. 2, 13; "Women War on Democrats," *NYT,* 21 September 1914, 6.

43. Allen; Graham; A. Elizabeth Taylor, "Woman Suffrage Movement in Texas"; idem, "Woman Suffrage Movement in Florida"; idem, "Revival and Development of the Woman Suffrage Movement in Georgia" idem, "Last Phase of the Woman Suffrage Movement in Georgia"; idem, "Woman Suffrage Movement in North Carolina: Part I"; idem, "South Carolina and the Enfranchisement of Women"; Thomas, 152–73; "Anti-Suffrage Men Unite," *NYT,* 28 September 1917, 4; MAOFESW, EC, 28 July 1916; NAOWS, board of directors meeting, 2 September 1915, 30 September 1915, MAOSW.

44. "Suffrage Invasion Is On in Earnest," *NYT,* 2 March 1913, sec. 2, 15; "5,000 Women March, Beset by Crowds," *NYT,* 4 March 1913, 5; "Impressive March of Suffrage 531," *NYT,* 8 April 1913, 7; "Suffrage Autos Off," *NYT,* 22 July 1913, 3; "To Defeat All Antis," *NYT,* 23 October 1913, 7.

45. Flexner, 272–75; MAOFESW, EC, 18 March 1910, 21 April 1913; "Suffrage Rivals Meet," *NYT,* 21 February 1913, 8; "Suffrage Invasion Is On in Earnest," *NYT,* 2 March 1913, sec. 2, 15; "Suffragists Gain Allies," *NYT,* 13 April 1913, sec. 3, 3; "Senate Hearing from Foes of Suffrage," *NYT,* 20 April 1913, sec.

2, 5; "Bay State Antis Storm Washington," *NYT,* 3 December 1913, 10; "Antis at Capitol Oppose Suffrage," *NYT,* 5 December 1913, 3; "Final Appeals to Congress," *NYT,* 6 December 1913, 10.

46. MAOFESW, EC, 13 March 1914; "Suffrage Loses in Senate Vote," *NYT,* 20 March 1914, 1; "Suffrage Gains in House," *NYT,* 17 September 1915, 7; "Suffragists Renew Siege of President," *NYT,* 7 December 1915, 13; "J. W. Foster Argues against Suffrage," *NYT,* 14 December 1915, 5.

47. Flexner, 272–75; MAOFESW, EC, 20 February 1914, 18 December 1914; MAOFESW, EOC, 16 December 1914; MAOFESW, JC, 5 January 1916; NAOWS, Delegate's Report, 7 December 1916, MAOSW; "New Jersey Antis Volunteer," *NYT,* 30 April 1914, 4; "Antis and the Red Cross," *NYT,* 4 September 1914, 6. Massachusetts Association records indicate total donations of over $2,600 to the Massachusetts Volunteer Aid Association, chaired by its ally, future governor Eben S. Draper, "to assist the civil and military authorities of the Commonwealth in furnishing supplies and relief to the men of the army and navy during the war with Spain." MAOFESW, memorandum, 10 October 1898.

48. MAOFESW, EC, 23 June 1916; MAOFESW, EOC, 5 July 1916; MAOSW, monthly meeting, 7 March 1916; Josephine Dodge to Mrs. Sidney W. Thaxter, 1 February 1916, MAOSW; "Antis for Preparedness," *NYT,* 29 January 1916, 10; Mrs. Lindon Bates, "Woman's Duty to Preparedness," *WP,* February 1916, 5–6; Agnes Repplier, "Women and Preparedness," *WP,* March 1916, 8–9.

49. MAOFESW, EC, 29 December 1911, 11 October 1912, 11 December 1914, 29 October 1915.

50. MAOFESW, EC, 26 December 1913, 30 October 1914, 19 November 1915, 14 April 1916, 12 May 1916, 8 June 1916; MAOFESW, EOC, 17 November 1915, 19 January 1916, 4 December 1918; MAOSW, executive committee meeting, 1 August 1916; NAOWS Delegate's Report, 7 December 1916, MAOSW; NAOWS finance committee to Mrs. Sidney W. Thaxter, 24 November 1915, MAOSW.

51. MAOFESW, EC, 12 May 1916, 8 June 1916, 28 July 1916; MAOFESW, EOC, 18 April 1916, 25 October 1916; MAOSW, executive committee meeting, 27 October 1916; NAOWS Delegate's Report, 7 December 1916, MAOSW.

52. MAOFESW, EOC, 15 December 1915, 4 October 1916, 7 February 1917, 4 September 1918, 6 November 1918, 4 December 1918; MAOFESW, EC, 12 May 1916, 28 July 1916; MAOSW, executive committee meeting, 1 August 1916, 4 October 1916, 28 March 1917, 11 April 1917.

53. MAOFESW, EC, 27 October 1916, 24 November 1916; MAOFESW, EOC, 8 November 1916.

54. J. S. Eichelberger to Everett P. Wheeler, n.d., box 8, EPW; MAOFESW, EC, 31 December 1915, 14 January 1916; MAOFESW, EOC, 25 October 1916; NAOWS Delegate's Report, 7 December 1916, MAOSW; "The National Convention," *Remonstrance,* January 1917, 6–7.

55. MAOFESW, EC, 30 April 1915, 13 October 1916; MAOFESW, EOC, 25 October 1916; Mrs. Arthur M. Dodge to Miss Alice Wood, 7 October 1916,

MAOSW; "Antis' to Invade Capital," *NYT,* 20 November 1916, 4; "Anti-Suffragists Move," *NYT,* 3 December 1916, 12; "Voting Delegates," *WP,* December 1916, 13. As it turned out, speakers at the first NAOWS convention, like Elihu Root, did interject some antisuffrage messages, although the speakers also included Mabel Boardman of the American Red Cross and an officer of the National Security League. Texts of several convention speeches are found in *WP,* December 1916. See also "Root and Gibbons Oppose Suffrage," *NYT,* 8 December 1916, 7.

56. Flexner, 276–78; Catt and Shuler, chap. 17; "Republicans Modify Plank on Suffrage," *NYT,* 9 June 1916, 3; "Convention Ends; Platform Voted Raps Hyphenism," *NYT,* 17 June 1916, 1; "Hughes Suits Antis and Suffragists," *NYT,* 7 July 1916, 6; "Full Text of Mr. Hughes's Speech of Acceptance," *NYT,* 1 August 1916, 6; "Antis Will Help Wilson," *NYT,* 11 August 1916, 3; "Suffragists Vote to Oppose Wilson," *NYT,* 12 August 1916, 3; "Suffragists Keep Neutral in Politics," *NYT,* 7 September 1916, 9; "Wilson Pledges His Aid to Women in Fight for Vote," *NYT,* 9 September 1916, 1; "Thanks Antis for Support," *NYT,* 18 November 1918, 7. MAOFESW, EC, 13 October 1916; MAOFESW, EOC, 25 October 1916; NAOWS, Delegate's Report, 7 December 1916, MAOSW.

57. MAOFESW, EC, 25 August 1916, 3 August 1917; MAOFESW, EOC, 7 June 1916, 8 November 1916, 3 January 1917, 7 February 1917; Park; "Ohio Women against Suffrage," *NYT,* 11 December 1916, 6.

58. J. S. Eichelberger to Mrs. John F. A. Merrill, 23 January 1917, MAOSW; J. S. Eichelberger, "Analysis of Woman Vote in 1916 Upsets Theories," *NYT Magazine,* 21 January 1917, 8; "Suffragists Take a Poll," *NYT,* 7 October 1916, 9; "Anti-Suffragists Heard," *NYT,* 3 May 1917, 15; "Antis Denounce Militant Pickets," *NYT,* 24 July 1917, 10; Henry A. WiseWood, "Government a Man's Job," *WP,* May 1917, 3; Mrs. Margaret C. Robinson, "Suffrage in Relation to Patriotic Service," *WP,* May 1917, 10–11; Rabbi Joseph Silverman, "The Patriotism America Needs," *WP,* June 1917, 3; Mrs. A. J. George, "Anti-Suffragism and the War," *WP,* September 1917, 6–7; "Foes of America," *WP,* September 1917, 15–17. On the antisuffrage campaign in Congress, see Benjamin, chap. 11.

59. MAOFESW, EC, 23 February 1917; "New Head for the 'Antis,' " *NYT,* 1 July 1917, sec. 1, 5; "Mrs. Lansing Joins Antis," *NYT,* 23 September 1917, sec. 1, 19; "House Moves for Woman Suffrage," *NYT,* 25 September 1917, 11; "Antis Again Attack Suffrage Leaders," *NYT,* 21 October 1917, sec. 1, 3; "Wartime Gains of the Suffragists," *Survey,* 28 April 1917, 97; "Our New Headquarters in Washington," *WP,* July/August 1917, 3; Mrs. George F. Richards, "Washington News and Notes," ibid., 6; "Our New Secretary, Mrs. Lansing," *WP,* September 1917, 3; "The Advisory Council," *Remonstrance,* October 1917, 3.

60. "Maine Rejects Suffrage 2 to 1," *NYT,* 11 September 1917, 1; "Lays Maine Defeat to 'Picketing,' " *NYT,* 16 September 1917, 6; "Ohio May Go Wet," *NYT,* 7 November 1917, 1; "Suffrage Fight Won in Cities," *NYT,* 8 November 1917, 1; "Ohio Wets Leading on Face of Returns," *NYT,* 9 November 1917, 9; "Suffrage Won by 102,344," *NYT,* 1 January 1918, 12; "Women Capture the Empire State,"

Current Opinion, December 1917, 363–64; J. B. Murdock, "Woman Suffrage: A Protest," letter to the editor, *Outlook,* 21 November 1917, 457–58; "Suffragists Take New York State," *Literary Digest,* 17 November 1917, 14–15; "The Maine Victory," *WP,* September 1917, 3; "The Third Anti-Suffrage Victory in Ohio," *WP,* November 1917, 3.

61. MAOFESW, EC, 26 November 1917, 28 December 1917; Gertrude Foster Brown, "Decisive Victory Won"; Catt and Shuler, chap. 19; "Declares Pacifists Helped Women to Win," *NYT,* 8 November 1917, 3; "Many State Jobs Go to Women," *NYT,* 15 November 1917, 1; "Suffrage Victory Laid to Germans," *NYT,* 19 November 1917, 11; "Suffragists Deny Pro-German Help," *NYT,* 20 November 1917, 13; "Women Condemn Suffrage Pacifism," *NYT,* 23 November 1917, 5; "No Peace Prospect in Suffrage Victory," *NYT,* 24 November 1917, 13; "Suffrage Opponents Divide on Policy," *NYT,* 11 December 1917, 15; "Antis to Fight On," *NYT,* 12 December 1917, 10; Rheta Childe Dorr, "The Democracy in Russia Which Suffragists Laud," *WP,* October 1917, 6; "German Kaiser's Alleged Cousin Led Prussian and Woman Suffrage Campaign among New York Germans," *WP,* 3 August 1918, 1–2; "Alice Chittenden of Red Cross Dead," *NYT,* 31 October 1945, 19.

62. "New Suffrage Drive Planned by Women," *NYT,* 7 November 1917, 3; "Antis Will Open Fight on Pacifism," *NYT,* 16 November 1917, 6; "Antis Report Rush to Join New League," *NYT,* 17 November 1917, 4; "Antis Now to Fight National Suffrage," *NYT,* 28 November 1917, 13; "Antis Not to Fight Women's Vote Here," *NYT,* 3 December 1917, 13; "Anti Sees Danger in Woman Autocracy," *NYT,* 12 January 1918, 12; "Women Plan Ballot Fight," *NYT,* 23 January 1918, 5; "Antis Start Fight to Lose the Vote," *NYT,* 29 January 1918, 7; "Antis Renew War on Suffragists," *NYT,* 24 March 1918, sec. 1, 9; "Repeal of Suffrage Sought by Women," *NYT,* 3 April 1918, 11; "New York Suffrage Accepted by Antis," *NYT,* 9 May 1918, 13; MAOFESW, EC, 11 January 1918, 8 February 1918; MAOFESW, Annual Meeting, 24 April 1918.

63. Flexner, 307–8; Scott and Scott, 161–63; MAOFESW, EC, 28 December 1917, 25 January 1918, 8 February 1918, 28 June 1918, 20 September 1918; MAOFESW, EOC, 2 January 1918, 5 June 1918, 2 October 1918, 4 December 1918; MAOFESW, Room Report, 31 January 1918; "House Test Shows Suffrage Gains," *NYT,* 8 January 1918, 13; "Suffrage Measure Reported to House," *NYT,* 9 January 1918, 12; "Wilson Backs Amendment on Woman Suffrage," *NYT,* 10 January 1918, 1; "Anti Sees Danger in Woman Autocracy," *NYT,* 12 January 1918, 12; "How Suffrage Vote Was Distributed," *NYT,* 13 January 1918, 18; "Suffrage Drive Begun in Senate," *NYT,* 14 March 1918, 1; "Antis Stave Off Suffrage Vote," *NYT,* 28 June 1918, 6; "Suffrage Vote to Wait," *NYT,* 29 June 1918, 5; "Antis Send Protest to the President," *NYT,* 12 August 1918, 8; "Suffrage Beaten by the Senate," *NYT,* 2 October 1918, 1; "Statistics of the Year in the World's Activities," *NYT,* 2 January 1919, 11; "Women Voters' Anti-Suffrage Party Appeals to the President against Intolerable Distraction during War," *WP,* 17 August 1918, 1–2. The Women Voters' Anti-Suffrage Party advertisement,

headed "Suffrage Federal Amendment: The People vs. The Lobby," was published in the *NYT*, 25 September 1918, 8.

64. MAOFESW, EC, 30 November 1917, 14 December 1917, 8 February 1918, 8 March 1918, 5 April 1918, 18 April 1918, 23 August 1918; MAOFESW, EOC, 1 May 1918.

65. Jablonsky, 97; MAOFESW, EC, 21 February 1918, 4 October 1918, 18 October 1918, 15 November 1918, 6 December 1918; MAOFESW, EOC, 10 July 1918; "The Woman Patriot," *Remonstrance*, July 1918, 3.

66. MAOFESW, EC, 8 February 1918, 21 February 1918, 22 March 1918, 14 March 1919, 28 March 1919, 23 April 1919; MAOFESW, EOC, 5 June 1918, 10 July 1918, 6 November 1918, 8 January 1919; MAOFESW, Room Report, 31 March 1918, 30 September 1918, 30 November 1915; "Anti-Suffrage—For Patriotism and Preparedness," *WP*, June 1916, 5–6; "A Great Mass Meeting in Boston," *Remonstrance*, July 1919, 2.

67. MAOFESW, EC, 3 January 1919, 17 January 1919; MAOFESW, EOC, 4 December 1918; "Women Oppose Baird," *NYT*, 31 October 1918, 6; "Woman's Party in Fight," *NYT*, 4 November 1918, 10; "Baird Wins in New York," *NYT*, 6 November 1918, 4; "Louisiana Defeats Suffrage Amendment," *NYT*, 6 November 1918, 4; "Women Apparently Win Vote in Michigan," *NYT*, 7 November 1918, 15; "Suffrage Wins in South Dakota," *NYT*, 7 November 1918, 15; "Badly Beaten in Oklahoma," *NYT*, 7 November 1918, 15; "Thanks Antis for Support," *NYT*, 18 November 1918, 7; Flexner, 310–11; Harper, 6:307–8, 528–29; Scott and Scott, 166–68. The states where antisuffragists challenged legislative enactment of partial suffrage include Illinois, Ohio, Nebraska, and Indiana. They were most successful in Ohio, where they forced a referendum in 1917, which was defeated. See Gertrude Foster Brown, "Opposition Breaks"; Catt and Shuler, chap. 14; Harper, 6:375–82; "Nebraska Suffrage Law in Effect," *NYT*, 26 January 1919, 18; "Ohio Suffrage Bill Signed by Governor," *NYT*, 22 February 1917, 8.

68. MAOFESW, EC, 3 January 1919, 17 January 1919, 14 February 1919, 28 February 1919, 28 March 1919, 23 April 1919, 23 May 1919; MAOFESW, EOC, 5 February 1919, 2 April 1919; "Plan Blow at Suffragists," *NYT*, 8 February 1919, 3; "Senate Again Beats Suffrage," *NYT*, 11 February 1919, 1; "Women Voters' Anti-Suffrage Party Asks Will Hays If Republicans Have Been 'Roped, Thrown, and Tied' by Suffrage," *WP*, 18 January 1919, 1–2; "Bolsheviki Meetings Arranged by Suffragists Arouse Senate to Investigate Radical Propaganda," *WP*, 8 February 1919, 1–2.

69. MAOFESW, EC, 28 March 1919; MAOFESW, Organizer's Report, 23 February 1919; "Suffrage Wins Easily in House; Vote 304 to 89," *NYT*, 22 May 1919, 1; "Suffrage Wins in Senate; Now Goes to States," *NYT*, 5 June 1919, 1.

70. MAOFESW, EC, 3 July 1919; "Suffragists Turn to Legislature," *NYT*, 6 June 1919, 15; "Antis Assail Suffrage Vote," *NYT*, 17 June 1919, 9; Mary G. Kilbreth, "Mrs. Wadsworth Still an Anti-Suffragist," letter to the editor, *NYT*, 22 September 1919, 10; "Miss Mary Kilbreth, Opposed Suffrage," *NYT*, 28 June 1957, 23.

71. "Fight on Suffrage Goes On," *NYT,* 3 July 1919, 16; "Women Lay Plans for Ballot Fight," *NYT,* 12 September 1919, 12; "Antis to Continue Fight on Suffrage," *NYT,* 18 September 1919, 8; "Protests against Miss Hay," *NYT,* 26 November 1919, 3; "Asks Hays to Oust Miss Mary G. Hay," *NYT,* 21 December 1919, sec. 2, 1; "Anti-Suffragists Again Fight Hays," *NYT,* 8 February 1920, sec. 2, 1; Mary G. Kilbreth, "The Suffrage Issue," letter to the editor, *NYT,* 16 February 1920, 10; "Anti-Suffragists Seeks Hays's Scalp," *New York World,* 2 February 1920, box 1, Woman's Suffrage and Women's Rights Collection, Special Collections, Vassar College Libraries.

72. MAOFESW president Frothingham was blunt before the executive committee on the failure of the repeal petition drive, stating that "one man who had promised 2000 [signatures] sent in 138." MAOFESW, EC, 3 July 1919, 14 July 1919, 25 July 1919, 8 August 1919, 5 September 1919, 3 October 1919, 31 October 1919; MAOFESW, EOC, 8 January 1919, 7 May 1919, 31 July 1919; Mrs. Charles F. Strong, "Suffrage in New England," letter to the editor, *NYT,* 24 September 1919, 16; Lily R. Foxcroft, memorandum, 15 October 1923, MAOFESW.

73. MAOFESW, EC, 26 April 1920; "Antis Want Vote on Suffrage Law," *NYT,* 14 July 1919, 6; "Women Lay Plans for Ballot Fight," *NYT,* 12 September 1919, 12; "Obstructing Federal Suffrage," *NYT,* 12 October 1919, sec. 3, 3; "Ohio Suffragists Lose," *NYT,* 12 November 1919, 6; "Asks Hays to Oust Miss Mary G. Hay," *NYT,* 21 December 1919, sec. 2, 1; "Will Test Suffrage," *NYT,* 15 February 1920, 8; "Two Anti-Suffrage Suits," *NYT,* 17 February 1920, 17; "Suffrage Struggle Likely in Delaware," *NYT,* 12 March 1920, 18; "Suffrage Ratified by Washington, the 35th State," *NYT,* 23 March 1920, 1; "Connecticut Republicans," *NYT,* 26 March 1920, 12; "Antis Will Renew Fight," *NYT,* 2 May 1920, sec. 7, 2; "For Suffrage Amendment," *NYT,* 4 June 1920, 2; Alabama Division of SWL, meeting, 16 March 1920, SWL.

74. MAOFESW, EC, 24 May 1901, 9 May 1902, 24 April 1903, 27 January 1905, 7 December 1906, 13 December 1907. On the culture of southern womanhood, see Anne Firor Scott, *Southern Lady from Pedestal to Politics.* Ironically, the idea of using the argument that woman suffrage would preserve white racial dominance seems to have been first proposed by former abolitionist Henry Blackwell, who wrote southern legislatures in 1867, detailing the numerical advantage of white over black women in the region. For accounts of the suffrage movement in the southern United States, see Marjorie Spruill Wheeler; Fuller; A. Elizabeth Taylor, *Woman Suffrage Movement in Tennessee;* Thomas; Lebsock, "Woman Suffrage and White Supremacy"; Graham; Kenneth R. Johnson. For an analysis of racism in the national woman suffrage movement, see Andolsen; Giddings, chaps. 7–9; Terborg-Penn.

75. NAOWS, Delegate's Report, 30 September 1915, 7 December 1916, MAOSW; MAOFESW, EC, 22 March 1912, 12 December 1913, 25 February 1916; MAOFESW, EOC, 5 July 1916; MAOFESW, Room Report, 28 February 1918, 31 May 1918; "Important Work by State Associations," *WP,* June 1915, 20–21; "A Successful Year's Work against Suffrage," *WP,* January 1916, 15–18; "The Prog-

ress of the Campaign," *WP,* February 1916, 16–17; "The State Campaigns," *WP,* March 1916, 16–17; "States' Evidence against Woman Suffrage," *WP,* April 1916, 11–13; Graham, 233–36; Lebsock, "Woman Suffrage and White Supremacy," 69–70; A. Elizabeth Taylor, "Short History of the Woman Suffrage Movement in Tennessee"; idem, "Woman Suffrage Movement in Texas," 7–8; Thomas, 195; Marjorie Spruill Wheeler, 312–402.

76. Quoted in Marjorie Spruill Wheeler, 103, 141; Thomas, 164; Graham, 229. The social backgrounds and strategies of southern suffrage leaders are described in Marjorie Spruill Wheeler, 89–148, 178–81; Thomas, 138–40, 160–64, 182–85; Graham, 229–30.

77. Information on antisuffrage leaders is found in *NCAB,* 30: 151; *Who's Who in the South and Southwest,* 542; A. Elizabeth Taylor, "Last Phase of the Woman Suffrage Movement in Georgia," 16–17; idem, "Short History of the Woman Suffrage Movement in Tennessee," 206–7; Allen, 94–96; "Three Montgomery Women Win Honors," n.d., unattributed newspaper clipping, Woman's Anti-Ratification League of Alabama Scrapbook, Alabama Department of Archives and History, Montgomery. On war work, see "Anti-Suffrage Aid to Preparedness," *WP,* July 1916, 13–14; "Notes from the States," *WP,* July/August 1917, 11–14; Marjorie Spruill Wheeler, 178; Thomas, 182–87.

78. One of the most prominent male antisuffragists in Alabama was Selma attorney Martin L. Calhoun, grandnephew of John C. Calhoun. Others were Montgomery attorney and future U.S. senator J. Lister Hill, former Alabama court of appeals judge John R. Tyson, Montgomery judge E. Perry Thomas, and former Andalusia solicitor H. L. Brassell. See Thomas, 195–98. Broadsides, "Dr. Anna Howard Shaw and Frederick Douglass"; "How many of these will your county and state produce under federal suffrage?"; "Shall History Repeat Itself?"; J. B. Evans, "Some Facts about Suffrage Leaders"; James Callaway, "Character of Robert E. Lee Defamed"; "Mrs. Gould Speaks to Negro Voters," Swann-Cavett Family Papers, Mitchell Memorial Library, Mississippi State University. Information concerning reactions to the Alabama suffragists' comments in Chicago is from "Alabama Suffragette Angers Tennesseans," n.d., "Southern Women's League Resents Mrs. Jacob's Act," n.d., unattributed newspaper clippings, Woman's Anti-Ratification League of Alabama Scrapbook, Alabama Department of Archives and History, Montgomery. See also, "Important Work by State Associations," *WP,* June 1915, 20–21; James Callaway, "The Preservation of Southern Civilization," *WP,* November 1917, 6.

79. For an overview of southern suffragists' racial strategies, see Marjorie Spruill Wheeler, 235–92; Whites; Lebsock, "Woman Suffrage and White Supremacy." Quotes are from "Notes from the States," *WP,* November 1917, 15; "That Deadly Parallel," Swann-Cavett Family Papers, Mitchell Memorial Library, Mississippi State University; "Legislators Urged to Defeat Susan B. Anthony Amendment," 25 June 1919, unattributed newspaper clipping, Woman's Anti-Ratification League of Alabama Scrapbook, Alabama Department of Archives and History, Montgomery. See also "The State Campaigns," *WP,* March 1916, 16.

80. Assorted newspaper clippings, Woman's Anti-Ratification League of Alabama Scrapbook, Alabama Department of Archives and History, Montgomery; Woman's Anti-Ratification League of Alabama meeting, July 1919, SWL; "Alabama Senate Rejects Suffrage," *NYT,* 18 July 1919, 3; "Two States Reject Suffrage," *NYT,* 4 September 1919, 16; Thomas, 200–202.

81. Evidence for North Carolina's mobilization under the Southern League is found in the Romulus P. Nunn Papers, North Carolina Division of Archives and History, Raleigh. See letter in this collection from Mary Hilliard Hinton to Romulus P. Nunn, 12 July 1920. Also, A. Elizabeth Taylor, "Woman Suffrage Movement in North Carolina, Part II." The NAOWS motto is quoted in "Antis to Continue Fight," *NYT,* 18 September 1919, 8. For a broad sampling of southern antisuffrage materials, including many by James Callaway, see Swann-Cavett Family Papers, Mitchell Memorial Library, Mississippi State University. The *Woman Patriot* dedicated a memorial number on the occasion of his death; see *WP,* 26 June 1920. An example from the Swann-Cavett collection of an anonymous pamphlet that was actually contributed by the Pennsylvania Association Opposed to Woman Suffrage is *A Talk on the Tax-Paying Woman.* See also *A Protest against Woman's Suffrage in Alabama, by Alabama Democrats on Behalf and in Defense of the Large Unorganized Majority of the Women of Alabama,* n.d.; assorted newspaper clippings, Woman's Anti-Ratification League of Alabama Scrapbook, Alabama Department of Archives and History, Montgomery. Marjorie Spruill Wheeler, 59–60; SWL and Alabama Division of SWL, joint meeting, 20 February 1920, 2 March 1920, SWL; Alabama Division of SWL, meeting, 16 March 1920, 20 April 1920, SWL; "America When Feminized," undated postcard, SWL; Woman's Anti-Ratification League of Alabama, financial records, June to November 1919, Woman's Anti-Ratification League of Alabama Scrapbook. MAOFESW, Room Report, 31 July 1919. Alabama antisuffrage leaders also wrote letters to northern newspapers; see N. V. Baker, "Anti-Suffrage," *NYT,* 6 August 1920, 8.

82. In 1919, Georgia's legislature also defeated the amendment, but slight differences in wording between its two houses invalidated the vote. One house of the Virginia legislature rejected the Anthony Amendment in September, but the other never voted. See "Two States Reject Suffrage," *NYT,* 4 September 1919, 16; "Asks Hays to Oust Miss Mary G. Hay," *NYT,* 21 December 1919, sec. 2, 1; "Three More States Sure for Suffrage," *NYT,* 22 February 1920, sec. 2, 1; "Suffrage Ratified by Washington, the 35th State," *NYT,* 23 March 1920, 1; "Not Obstruction, but Rejection the Anti-Suffrage Aim," *Remonstrance,* January 1920, 4; A. Elizabeth Taylor, "Woman Suffrage Movement in Arkansas"; idem, "Woman Suffrage Movement in Texas"; Mary Semple Scott.

83. MAOFESW, EC, 9 April 1920; MAOFESW, Office Report, 1 May 1920; "The Anti-Ratification Luncheon," *Remonstrance,* January 1920, 2; "A New Anti-Suffrage Campaign," *Remonstrance,* July 1920, 5; "Asks Suffrage Rejection," *NYT,* 24 July 1920, 12; "Anti-Suffragists Also Rap Harding," *NYT,* 16 July 1920, 1.

84. Flexner, 317–24; "Three More States Sure for Suffrage," *NYT,* 22 February 1920, sec. 2, 1; "Ohio Court Backs Referendum on Suffrage and Prohibition," *NYT,* 20 June 1919, 17; "Ohio Suffragists Lose," *NYT,* 12 November 1919, 16; "Mississippi Senate Rejects Suffrage," *NYT,* 19 February 1920, 15; "Antis Will Renew Fight," *NYT,* 2 May 1920, sec. 7, 2; "For Suffrage Amendment," *NYT,* 4 June 1920, 2; "Defeat for Suffrage," *NYT,* 9 June 1920, 3; A. Elizabeth Taylor, *Woman Suffrage Movement in Tennessee,* 101; idem, "Woman Suffrage Movement in Florida"; Marjorie Spruill Wheeler, 312–77; Kenneth R. Johnson. For a review of legislative defeats in the southern states, see Catt and Shuler, chap. 31.

85. The Tennessee ratification campaign is described in A. Elizabeth Taylor, *Woman Suffrage Movement in Tennessee,* 110–25; Marjorie Spruill Wheeler, 61–64; "Antis and Drys to Join," *NYT,* 29 June 1920, 2; "Turns against Suffrage," *NYT,* 9 July 1920, 3; "Send Anti-Suffrage Envoy," *NYT,* 16 August 1920, 11; "An Insult to Tennesseeans," *WP,* 3 July 1920, 4; "Anti-Suffragists Expect Victory in Tennessee," *WP,* 31 July 1921, 1. For the perspective of the winning side, see Peek; Harper, 6:621; Catt and Shuler, 456–61. Southern suffragist opposition to the federal amendment is addressed also in Fuller, 148–61; Kenneth R. Johnson.

86. Catt and Shuler, 441; "Antis and Drys to Join," *NYT,* 29 June 1920, 2; "Opens Court Fight against Suffrage," *NYT,* 8 July 1920, 17; "Southern Antis Ask Hearing from Cox," *NYT,* 29 July 1920, 3; "Suffragists Aim to End Injunction," *NYT,* 23 August 1920, 11; "Court Refuses to Delay Suffrage," *NYT,* 26 August 1920, 1; "Cox Finds Cheer in Roosevelt Tone," *NYT,* 10 August 1920, 3; "Force Bills and Race Prejudice," *WP,* 10 July 1920, 4; "Ratification Wins by Narrow Margin in Tennessee," *WP,* 21 August 1920, 1; A. Elizabeth Taylor, *Woman Suffrage Movement in Tennessee,* 111–24.

87. "Women are Jubilant: Antis Promise Appeal," *NYT,* 19 August 1920, 2; Everett P. Wheeler, "Holcomb Asked to Be Firm," letter to the editor, *NYT,* 31 August 1920, 5; idem, "Suffrage Ratification," letter to the editor, *NYT,* 20 September 1920, 14; "Tennessee Record Sent," *NYT,* 4 September 1920, 4; "To Fight Suffrage on Tennessee Vote," *NYT,* 6 September 1920, 7; "Moves to Dismiss 'Anti's' Appeal," *NYT,* 22 September 1920, 1; "Our Fight Has Just Begun," *WP,* 21 August 1920, 4; "Tennessee House Reconsiders and Rejects Suffrage," *WP,* 4 September 1920, 1–2; "The Amendment Situation," *WP,* 4 September 1920, 7; "Tennessee Antis Wage Campaign against Roberts," *WP,* 16 October 1920, 1–2; "Election Returns Prove Strength of Anti-Suffragists," *WP,* 6 November 1920, 1. Mary G. Kilbreth to Lily Rice Foxcroft, 3 October 1920, MAOFESW.

88. MAOFESW, EC, 15 October 1920; "Maryland Antis to Support Real Men," *WP,* 16 October 1920, 3; "Election Returns Prove Strength of Anti-Suffragists," *WP,* 6 November 1920, 1; Rose Young; "To Educate Our Rulers," editorial, *NYT,* 16 August 1920, 10; "Picturesque Canvass for Tomorrow's Vote in Maine," *NYT,* 12 September 1920, sec. 7, 1; "Republicans Sweep Maine by 65,000 with Women Casting a Heavy Vote," *NYT,* 14 September 1920, 1; "American Woman Voter Arrives"; Dawson.

89. MAOFESW, EC, 9 April 1920, 3 September 1920, 3 October 1920, 15 October 1920; Mary G. Kilbreth to MAOFESW, telegram, n.d., MAOFESW; Mary G. Kilbreth to Lily Rice Foxcroft, 3 October 1920, MAOFESW; "Miss Rowe Challenges Suffrage Threat," *WP,* 21 August 1920, 2; "National Association Moves to Washington," *WP,* 9 October 1920, 2; Mary G. Kilbreth to Rossiter Johnson, 19 October 1920, box 4, RHJ; "Alice Chittenden of Red Cross Dead," *NYT,* 31 October 1945, 19.

90. "Asks Hays to Oust Miss Mary G. Hay," *NYT,* 21 December 1919, sec. 2, 1; "Two Anti-Suffrage Suits," *NYT,* 17 February 1920, 17; "Antis Will Renew Fight," *NYT,* 2 May 1920, sec. 7, 2; "Open Court Fight against Suffrage," *NYT,* 8 July 1920, 17; "Suffragists Aim to End Injunction," *NYT,* 23 August 1920, 11; "Court Refuses to Delay Suffrage," *NYT,* 26 August 1920, 1; "Suffrage Tangles Don't Worry Colby," *NYT,* 2 September 1920, 15; "Antis Lose Quick Appeal," *NYT,* 4 September 1920, 4; "To Fight Suffrage on Tennessee Vote," *NYT,* 6 September 1920, 7; "Moves to Dismiss 'Anti's' Appeal," *NYT,* 22 September 1920, 1; "Anti-Suffragists Lose," *NYT,* 5 October 1920, 10; "Supreme Court Denies Anti-Suffrage Motion," *NYT,* 19 October 1920, 4; "Try to Stop Women's Vote," *NYT,* 31 October 1920, sec. 2, 6; "Test Suffrage Amendment," *NYT,* 15 December 1920, 14; "Replies to Suffrage Suit," *NYT,* 21 January 1922, 12; "Testing Validity of Suffrage Law," *NYT,* 24 January 1922, 14; "End Suffrage Argument," *NYT,* 25 January 1922, 7; "Woman's Suffrage Amendment Valid," *NYT,* 28 February 1922, 9; "Faith in the Supreme Court," *WP,* 16 October 1920, 4; "Maryland League for State Defense Starts Great Suit," *WP,* 6 November 1920, 2; "The Maryland Case against the Anthony Amendment," *WP,* 27 November 1920, 1–2; "A Review of the Court Decision," *WP,* 5 February 1921, 5; "Maryland Suffrage Decision," *WP,* 1 July 1921, 7–8; J. S. Eichelberger to Mary G. Kilbreth, 6 April 1920, box 8, EPW; Mary G. Kilbreth to Rossiter Johnson, 19 October 1920, box 4, RHJ; Rossiter Johnson to Mary G. Kilbreth, 23 November 1920, box 4, RHJ.

91. "The Need of Further Organization," *WP,* 23 October 1920, 4; "The Deadly Parallel of Suffragism and Bolshevism," *WP,* 27 November 1920, 1–2; "National Anti-Suffrage Meeting," *WP,* 1 October 1921, 2; "The Woman's Party and Communism," *WP,* 1/15 October 1922, 12–13; Donald Alexander, "How Reds Are Organizing Women," *WP,* 1 February 1923, 1; "Organizing Women for Class and Sex War," *WP,* 15 April 1923, 2–7; "Exhibition of Red Propaganda," *WP,* 1 February 1924, 7; "Miss Kilbreth Denounces as Bolshevists Women Urging Congress to Reduce the Army," *NYT,* 25 April 1922, 21; Mary G. Kilbreth to Rossiter Johnson, 29 March 1921, 29 March 1922, box 4, RHJ. On the League of Women Voters during this period, see Cott, *Grounding of Modern Feminism,* chap. 3.

92. Mary G. Kilbreth to Rossiter Johnson, 3 April 1922, 11 June 1922, Labor Day 1922, 8 June 1923, 3 August 1923, box 4, RHJ; "News from the Women's Constitutional Leagues," *WP,* 15 November 1921, 5; "Sentinels of the Republic," *WP,* 1/15 September 1922, 2; "Sentinels of the Republic Announce Organization Plans," *WP,* 1 July 1923, 1. When Mary Kilbreth died, her obituary noted

that she actively opposed the entry of various aliens into the United States, including Albert Einstein. "Miss Mary Kilbreth, Opposed Suffrage," *NYT,* 28 June 1957, 23.

93. "To Make Motherhood a Governmental Institution," *WP,* 16 October 1920, 6; "The Political Plot to Nationalize the Schools," *WP,* 11 December 1920, 1–2; "The New Man—And National Defense," *WP,* 25 December 1920, 7; "Radical Congressional Program in Next Session," *WP,* 1 December 1923, 1; "Farm Organizations Oppose Federal Control of Children," *WP,* 1 March 1924, 1–2; "Child Labor Amendment Means Federal Control of Schools," *WP,* 15 March 1924, 1–2; "Petition against Child Labor Amendment," *WP,* 15 May 1924, 1–5; "Communists Prematurely Unmask 'Child' Labor Amendment," *WP,* 1 November 1924, 1–2; "The Children's Bureau's 'Expanding Program' Self-Revealed," *WP,* 1 April 1927, 49–56; "N.E.A. Bloc Dictatorship, Not Federal Control, Aim of Education Bill," *WP,* 15 June 1928, 89–96; Mary G. Kilbreth and Mrs. Randolph Frothingham, "Why Present Federal Estate Tax Should Be Repealed," *WP,* 1 April 1928, 49–56; "United States of America v. Rosika Schwimmer," *WP,* 1 October 1928, 89–149; "Statement against the Griffin Bill," *WP,* 1 July 1930, 65–104; "Emasculating Our Foreign Policy," *WP,* April 1931, 1–12; "American Allegiance without Alien Reservations Again Upheld," *WP,* June 1931, 1–11.

94. For more about the Sheppard-Towner Act, see Lemons, chap. 6; Muncy, 93–140; Skocpol, chap. 9; "To Ask Jury Duty on Behalf of Women," *NYT,* 23 January 1921, sec. 2, 1; "Motherhood Deaths Grow," *NYT* 29 January 1921, 7; "Assail Maternity Bill," *NYT,* 6 May 1921, 17; "Saving Young Mothers," *NYT,* 8 May 1921, sec. 7, 3; "Women Oppose Maternity Bill," *NYT,* 2 June 1921, 32; Margaret D. Fayerweather, "The 'Welfare Bills,' " letter to the editor, *NYT,* 4 June 1921, 14; "Federal Midwifery," *NYT,* 24 January 1922, 14; Mary G. Kilbreth, "Investigating Motherhood—As a Political Business," *WP,* 8 January 1921, 5–6; "Bolshevist 'Welfare' Program Vigorously Opposed," *WP,* 15 May 1921, 1–2; "President Receives Anti-Suffrage Delegation," *WP,* 1 June 1921, 1–2; "Roll of Honor," *WP,* 1 December 1921, 8; "Three States Refuse to Submit to Federal Baby Act," *WP,* 15 March 1922, 1–2; "Organizing Revolution through Women and Children," *WP,* 1/15 September 1922, 3; "Supreme Court Declines to Pass on Maternity Act," *WP,* 1 June 1923, 1–3.

95. See Muncy. For two examples of antisuffrage leaders who were also nationally known philanthropists in women and children's welfare, see Michel; Michel and Rosen. The antisuffrage quotes about Sheppard-Towner are from Mary G. Kilbreth to Rossiter Johnson, 18 May 1921, box 4, RHJ; Mary G. Kilbreth, "Investigating Motherhood—As a Political Business," *WP,* 8 January 1921, 5–6.

96. On the defeat of the extension of the Sheppard-Towner Act, see Muncy, 124–50; Skocpol, 513–20; "A Petition to the United States Senate—Part I," *WP,* 5 May 1926, 73–80.

97. The influence of radical factions within social movements on public support for moderate groups is documented by Haines.

Chapter 7. The Politics of Conservative Womanhood

1. Epigraph, "The Feminists Have a Terrible Identity Crisis," *Phyllis Schlafly Report,* December 1994, 1.

2. This was the experience of Elizabeth Sohier, whom the Massachusetts governor appointed to the state's library committee after receiving her note suggesting its formation. See *Mayflower Club,* 46.

3. Quote in MAOFESW, Hearing Report, 2 February 1905.

4. For a review of this argument, see Kerber, "Separate Spheres."

5. Acker, "Gendered Institutions"; idem, "Class, Gender, and Relations of Distribution"; Joan Scott; West and Zimmerman.

6. For important theoretical treatments of countermovements, see Turner and Killian, 317–19; Mottl; Lo; Zald and Useem.

7. Catt quote in Cott, *Grounding of Modern Feminism,* 60; "Chivalry Shown by Kansas Men," *Woman's Journal,* 5 November 1912, 353; "Bok's Journal Feeds Bonfire," *Woman's Journal,* 7 December 1912, 385; O'Neill, *Everyone Was Brave,* 32–38.

8. On conservative maternalism, see Michel; Michel and Rosen. On the distinction between women's culture and politics, see DuBois, "Politics and Culture in Women's History." An interesting recent discussion of the impact of this reformist orientation on women's political power more generally is Chafe, "Women's History and Political History."

9. Quotes from Baker, "Domestication of Politics," 632; Mink, "Lady and the Tramp," 101. See also Wiebe.

10. For expressions of this conservative worldview, see Brimelow; Herrnstein and Murray; Bennett. Two recent journalistic treatments that make the connection between contemporary nativist anxieties and an earlier period are Mead; Lind. Analysis of the new Puritan covenant is from Hatheway.

11. On the rise of the New Right, see Alan Crawford; Liebman and Wuthnow; Wilcox; Himmelstein; Tom W. Smith.

12. For exceptions to this overall pattern, see Conover and Gray; Klatch; Susan E. Marshall, "Keep Us on the Pedestal"; idem, "Who Speaks for American Women"; idem, "Confrontation and Co-optation in Antifeminist Organizations"; idem, "Marilyn vs. Hillary."

13. For the background of Phyllis Schlafly, see Felsenthal; on Beverly LaHaye, see Paige.

14. Quotes from Schlafly, *Power of the Positive Woman,* 11, 86, 104, 131; Martha Solomon, 49; Beverly LaHaye to CWA membership, August 1995; "The Feminization of the U.S. Military," *Phyllis Schlafly Report,* September 1989; "Insights into Feminist Ideology," *Phyllis Schlafly Report,* December 1989, 1; "Time to Tell the Feminists Bye-Bye," *Phyllis Schlafly Report,* December 1990, 1–2; "Feminist Goals vs. Fairness and Truth," *Phyllis Schlafly Report,* April 1992, 2–3; "Feminists Try to Stamp Out the Radical Truth," *Phyllis Schlafly Report,* July 1995, 1; "The Feminists Have a Terrible Identity Crisis," *Phyllis Schlafly Report,* December 1994, 1.

15. Quotes in Beverly LaHaye to CWA membership, August 1995; *Congressional Digest*, 67 (November 1988), 275; "Comparable Worth: Unfair to Men and Women," *Humanist*, May–June 1986, 12; "Parental Leave—A Windfall for Yuppies," *Phyllis Schlafly Report*, November 1986; "Feminist Falsehoods, Follies, and Funding," *Phyllis Schlafly Report*, July 1991; "The Feminists Have a Terrible Identity Crisis," *Phyllis Schlafly Report*, December 1994, 4. See also Schlafly, *Power of the Positive Woman*, 66–71. On the social backgrounds of antifeminist women activists, see Arrington and Kyle; Mueller and Dimieri; Tedin, Brady, Buxton, Gorman, and Thompson.

16. Quotes in Beverly LaHaye to CWA membership, January 1993; Schlafly, *Power of the Positive Woman*, 34, 166; "The Feminization of the U.S. Military," *Phyllis Schlafly Report*, September 1989, 4; "Sending Mothers to the Gulf War!" *Phyllis Schlafly Report*, March 1991, 1; "Feminism Falls on Its Face," *Phyllis Schlafly Report*, November 1991; "Feminist Falsehoods, Follies, and Funding," *Phyllis Schlafly Report*, July 1991, 3; "Feminist Goals vs. Fairness and Truth," *Phyllis Schlafly Report*, April 1992, 2–3; "Feminists Try to Stamp Out the Radical Truth," *Phyllis Schlafly Report*, July 1995, 1.

17. The content analysis of CWA and Eagle Forum publications is reported in Susan E. Marshall, "Marilyn vs. Hillary." Quote is from Marian Wallace, "United Nations Re-Designing Women," *Family Voice*, July 1995, 4. See also "The United Nations—An Enemy in Our Midst," *Phyllis Schlafly Report*, November 1995; "Reaganism vs. the New World Order," *Phyllis Schlafly Report*, January 1992; "The New World Order Wants Your Children," *Phyllis Schlafly Report*, March 1993.

18. Quotes are from Schlafly, *Power of the Positive Woman*, 35; "Are All Our Children at Risk?" *Phyllis Schlafly Report*, October 1995, 4; "Taxes and Tactics of the Class War," *Phyllis Schlafly Report*, April 1993, 1. See also "NEA Disrespect for Home and Parents," *Phyllis Schlafly Report*, August 1991; "Let's Abolish the Department of Education," *Phyllis Schlafly Report*, September 1995; "The NEA Steps Up Its Anti-Parent Policies," *Phyllis Schlafly Report*, September 1993; Rosaline Bush, "Making the Grade," *Family Voice*, September 1995, 4.

19. Himmelstein, 89, 99–106.

20. See Cott, "What's In a Name."

Select Bibliography

Abbott, Frances M. "College Women and Matrimony, Again." *Century,* March 1896, 796–97.

Abbott Lyman. "Answer to the Arguments in Support of Woman Suffrage." *Annals of the American Academy of Political Science* 35 (May 1910): S28–S32.

Abbott, Lyman. "An Anti-Suffrage Movement." *Outlook,* 28 April 1894, 738–39.

Abbott, Lyman. "The Assault on Womanhood." *Outlook,* 3 April 1909, 784–88.

Abbott, Lyman. "Don't Ask Her." *Outlook,* 10 May 1913, 54–55.

Abbott, Lyman. "Do Women Wish to Vote?" *Outlook,* 19 February 1910, 375–77.

Abbott, Lyman. "Has Woman Renounced Her Job?" *Outlook,* 11 February 1920, 233.

Abbott, Lyman. *The Home Builder.* New York: Houghton Mifflin, 1908.

Abbott, Lyman. "The Right of Suffrage." *Outlook,* 27 July 1901, 711–12.

Abbott, Lyman. "The Right of the Silent Woman." *Outlook,* 18 May 1912, 105–6.

Abbott, Lyman. "Why the Vote Would Be Injurious to Women." *Ladies' Home Journal,* February 1910, 21–22.

Abbott, Lyman. *Why Women Do Not Wish the Suffrage.* Boston: MAOFESW, 1904.

Abbott, Lyman. "Why Women Do Not Wish the Suffrage." *Atlantic Monthly,* September 1903, 289–96.

Abbott, Lyman. "A Woman's Protest against Woman Suffrage." *Outlook,* 28 April 1894, 760.

Abbott, Lyman. "Woman's Suffrage in Oregon." *Outlook,* 27 June 1908, 402.

Abbott, Lyman. "Woman Suffrage in New Hampshire." *Outlook,* 21 February 1903, 418.

Abbott, Lyman. "Women's Rights." *Outlook,* 10 February 1912, 302–4.

Abbott, Mrs. Lyman. *Mrs. Lyman Abbott on Woman Suffrage: Address Before the Anti-Woman Suffrage Society of Albany, New York.* Albany, N.Y., n.d.

Acker, Joan. "Class, Gender, and the Relations of Distribution." *Signs* 13 (Spring 1988): 473–97.

Acker, Joan. "Gendered Institutions: From Sex Roles to Gendered Institutions." *Contemporary Sociology* 21 (September 1992): 565–69.

Acker, Joan. "Women and Social Stratification: A Case of Intellectual Sexism." *American Journal of Sociology* 78 (January 1973): 936–45.

Acker, Joan. "Women and Stratification: A Review of Recent Literature." *Contemporary Sociology* 9 (January 1980): 25–39.

Adams, Henry. *The Education of Henry Adams.* 1918; reprint ed., New York: Modern Library, 1931.

Adams, Mary Dean. *Wages and the Ballot.* New York: New York State Association Opposed to Woman Suffrage, 1909.

Albrecht, Milton C. "The Relationship of Literature and Society." *American Journal of Sociology* 59 (March 1954): 425–36.

Aldrich, Nelson W., Jr. *Old Money: The Mythology of America's Upper Class.* New York: Alfred A. Knopf, 1988.

Allen, Lee N. "The Woman Suffrage Movement in Alabama, 1910–1920." *Alabama Review* 11 (April 1958): 83–99.

"The American Woman Voter Arrives." *Literary Digest*, 28 August 1920, 9–11.

Andolsen, Barbara Hilkert. *"Daughters of Jefferson, Daughters of Bootblacks": Racism and American Feminism.* Macon, Ga.: Mercer University Press, 1986.

Anthony, Susan B., and Ida Husted Harper, eds. *The History of Woman Suffrage,* vol. 4. Rochester, N.Y.: Susan B. Anthony, 1902.

An Appeal against Anarchy of Sex to the Constitutional Convention and the People of the State of New York, by a Member of the Press. New York: J. A. Gray & Green, 1867.

An Appeal to the Electors of the State of New York to Vote against Woman Suffrage on 6 November 1917. New York: n.p., 1917.

Appleton's Cyclopedia of American Biography. 7 vols. New York: D. Appleton, 1888.

Arrington, Theodore S., and Patricia A. Kyle. "Equal Rights Amendment Activists in North Carolina." *Signs* 3 (Spring 1978): 666–80.

Ashcraft, Richard. *Revolutionary Politics and Locke's Two Treatises of Government.* Princeton, N.J.: Princeton University Press, 1986.

Baker, Paula. "The Domestication of Politics: Women and American Political Society, 1780–1920." *American Historical Review* 89 (June 1984): 620–47.

Baker, Paula. *The Moral Frameworks of Public Life: Gender, Politics, and the State in Rural New York, 1870–1930.* New York: Oxford University Press, 1991.

Baltzell, E. Digby. *Philadelphia Gentlemen: The Making of a National Upper Class.* Glencoe, Ill.: Free Press, 1958.

Baltzell, E. Digby. *Puritan Boston and Quaker Philadelphia.* New York: Free Press, 1979.

Banks, Olive. *Faces of Feminism: A Study of Feminism as a Social Movement.* Oxford, England: Martin Robertson, 1981.

Beard, Mary Ritter. *Woman's Work in Municipalities.* New York: D. Appleton, 1915.

Becker, Susan D. *The Origins of the Equal Rights Amendment: American Feminism between the Wars.* Westport, Conn.: Greenwood Press, 1981.

Beecher, Catharine E. *Something for Women Better Than the Ballot.* New York: D. Appleton, 1869.

Beecher, Catharine E. *A Treatise on Domestic Economy for the Use of Young Ladies at Home and at School*. Boston: T. H. Webb, 1843.

Beecher, Catharine E. *Woman's Profession as Mother and Educator with Views in Opposition to Woman Suffrage*. Philadelphia: George Maclean, 1872.

Beecher, Catharine E. *Woman Suffrage and Woman's Profession*. Hartford, Conn.: Brown & Gross, 1871.

Beeton, Beverly. *Women Vote in the West: The Woman Suffrage Movement, 1869–1896*. New York: Garland, 1986.

Benjamin, Anne M. *A History of the Anti-Suffrage Movement in the United States from 1895 to 1920*. Lewiston, N.Y.: Edwin Mellen Press, 1991.

Bennett, William J., ed. *The Book of Virtues: A Treasury of Great Moral Stories*. New York: Simon and Schuster, 1993.

Berg, Barbara. *The Remembered Gate: Origins of American Feminism*. New York: Oxford University Press, 1978.

Berman, David R. "Male Support for Woman Suffrage: An Analysis of Voting Patterns in the Mountain West." *Social Science History* 11 (Fall 1987): 281–94.

Bernbaum, Ernest. "Introduction." In *Anti-Suffrage Essays by Massachusetts Women*, ed. Bernbaum. Boston: Forum Publications, 1916. ix–xvii.

Berry, Mary Frances. *Why ERA Failed: Politics, Women's Rights, and the Amending Process of the Constitution*. Bloomington: Indiana University Press, 1986.

Birdsall, Mrs. William W. *Woman Suffrage and the Working Woman*. N.p., n.d.

Birmingham, Stephen. *America's Secret Aristocracy*. Boston: Little, Brown, 1987.

Bissell, Emily P. [Priscilla Leonard]. *A Help or a Hindrance*. New York: New York State Association Opposed to Woman Suffrage, n.d.

Bissell, Emily P. *A Talk to Every Woman*. Richmond: Virginia Association Opposed to Woman's Suffrage, n.d.

Bissell, Emily. *A Talk to Women on the Suffrage Question*. New York: New York State Association Opposed to Woman Suffrage, 1909.

Bissell, Emily P. [Priscilla Leonard]. "Woman Suffrage in Colorado." *Outlook*, 20 March 1897, 789–92.

Blair, Karen J. *The Clubwoman as Feminist: True Womanhood Redefined, 1868–1914*. New York: Holmes and Meier, 1980.

Blatch, Harriet Stanton, and Alma Lutz. *Challenging Years: The Memoirs of Harriet Stanton Blatch*. New York: G. P. Putnam's Sons, 1940.

Blee, Kathleen M. *Women of the Klan: Racism and Gender in the 1920s*. Berkeley: University of California Press, 1991.

Bloch, Ruth H. "The Gendered Meanings of Virtue in Revolutionary America." *Signs* 13 (Autumn 1987): 37–58.

Blodgett, Geoffrey. *The Gentle Reformers: Massachusetts Democrats in the Cleveland Era*. Cambridge: Harvard University Press, 1966.

Blodgett, Geoffrey. "Yankee Leadership in a Divided City: Boston, 1860–1910." In *Boston, 1700–1980: The Evolution of Urban Politics*, ed. Ronald P. Formisano and Constance K. Burns. Westport, Conn.: Greenwood Press, 1984. 87–110.

Bock, Annie. *Woman Suffrage: Address to the Committee on Woman Suffrage*. United States Senate, 63d Congress, Document no. 160. Washington, D.C.: U.S. Government Printing Office, 1913.

Bok, Edward W. "Are Girls Overdoing Athletics?" *Ladies' Home Journal*, May 1906, 16.

Bok, Edward W. "Behold, the Emancipated Woman!" *Ladies' Home Journal*, April 1906, 20.

Bok, Edward W. "The College and the Stove." *Ladies' Home Journal*, April 1903, 16.

Bok, Edward W. "Death's New Clutch on Woman." *Ladies' Home Journal*, October 1907, 8.

Bok, Edward W. "The Job That Was Too Big." *Ladies' Home Journal*, July 1912, 3.

Bok, Edward W. "My Quarrel with Women's Clubs." *Ladies' Home Journal*, January 1910, 5–6.

Bok, Edward W. "One Reason for the Saloon." *Ladies' Home Journal*, October 1913, 6.

Bok, Edward W. *Real Opponents to the Suffrage Movement Are the Women Themselves Whose Peculiar Field of Work Lies Outside of Politics*. New York: New York State Association Opposed to Woman Suffrage, 1909.

Bok, Edward W. "The Signal Failure of Woman Suffrage." *Ladies' Home Journal*, June 1912, 6.

Bok, Edward W. "When Work Fits Woman." *Ladies' Home Journal*, February 1896, 14.

Bok, Edward W. "Woman or Mother? Woman's Real Progress." *Ladies' Home Journal*, October 1909, 6.

Bok, Edward W. "The Woman Who Really Holds a Man." *Ladies' Home Journal*, March 1913, 6.

Boles, Janet K. *The Politics of the Equal Rights Amendment: Conflict and the Decision Process*. New York: Longman, 1979.

Boles, Janet K. "Systemic Factors Underlying Legislative Responses to Woman Suffrage and the Equal Rights Amendment." *Women and Politics* 2 (Spring/Summer 1982): 5–22.

"Books and Things." *New Republic*, 11 February 1920, 319.

Bordin, Ruth. *Woman and Temperance: The Quest for Power and Liberty, 1873–1900*. Philadelphia: Temple University Press, 1981.

Bourdieu, Pierre. *Reproduction in Education, Society, Culture*. Beverly Hills, Calif.: Sage, 1977.

Boydston, Jeanne, Mary Kelley and Anne Margolis. *The Limits of Sisterhood: The Beecher Sisters on Women's Rights and Woman's Sphere*. Chapel Hill: University of North Carolina Press, 1988.

Brady, Kathleen. *Ida Tarbell: Portrait of a Muckraker.* New York: Seaview/Putnam, 1984.

Brewing and Liquor Interests, and German and Bolshevik Propaganda. Report and Hearings of the Subcommittee on the Judiciary, United States Senate, 65th Congress, 1st Session, vol. 1, 1918.

Brimelow, Peter. *Alien Nation: Common Sense about America's Immigration Disaster.* New York: Random House, 1995.

Brock, Mrs. Horace. *Must All Women Bear the Burden of the Ballot to Give Some Women Political Prominence?* Philadelphia: Pennsylvania Association Opposed to Woman Suffrage, n.d.

Brockett, Linus Pierpont. *Woman: Her Rights, Wrongs, Privileges, and Responsibilities.* 1869; reprint ed. Plainview, N.Y.: Books for Libraries Press, 1976.

Bronson, Minnie. *Woman Suffrage and Child Labor Legislation.* New York: NAOWS, 1914.

Brooks, Van Wyck. *New England: Indian Summer.* 1940; reprint ed., New York: E. P. Dutton, 1965.

Brown, Gertrude Foster. "A Decisive Victory Won." In *Victory: How Women Won It,* ed. NAWSA. New York: H. W. Wilson, 1940. 107–20.

Brown, Gertrude Foster. "The Opposition Breaks." In *Victory: How Women Won It,* ed. NAWSA. New York: H. W. Wilson, 1940. 83–94.

Brown, Henry Billings. *Woman Suffrage. A Paper Read by Ex-Justice Brown before the Ladies' Congressional Club of Washington, D.C., April 1910.* Boston: MAOFESW, 1910.

Brown, Ira V. *Lyman Abbott: Christian Evolutionist.* Cambridge: Harvard University Press, 1953.

Buckley, James M. "Moral Objections to Woman Suffrage." *Current Literature,* February 1910, 177–79.

Buckley, James M. *The Wrong and Peril of Woman Suffrage.* New York: Fleming H. Revell, 1909.

Buckley, James M. "The Wrongs and Perils of Woman Suffrage, with Postscript." *Century,* August 1894, 613–23, 625–26.

Buechler, Steven M. *The Transformation of the Woman Suffrage Movement: The Case of Illinois, 1850–1920.* New Brunswick, N.J.: Rutgers University Press, 1986.

Buenker, John D. "The Politics of Mutual Frustration: Socialists and Suffragists in New York and Wisconsin." In *Flawed Liberation: Socialism and Feminism,* ed. Sally M. Miller. Westport, Conn.: Greenwood Press, 1981. 113–44.

Buenker, John D. "The Urban Political Machine and Woman Suffrage: A Study in Political Adaptability." *Historian* 33 (February 1971): 264–79.

Buhle, Mari Jo. *Women and American Socialism, 1870–1920.* Urbana: University of Illinois Press, 1981.

Burnap, George Washington. *Lectures on the Sphere and Duties of Woman and Other Subjects.* Baltimore: J. Murphy, 1841.

Burns, Constance K. "The Irony of Progressive Reform: Boston, 1898–1910." In *Boston, 1700–1980: The Evolution of Urban Politics,* ed. Ronald P. Formisano and Constance K. Burns. Westport, Conn.: Greenwood Press, 1984. 133–64.

Burris, Val. "Who Opposed the ERA? An Analysis of the Social Bases of Antifeminism." *Social Science Quarterly* 64 (June 1983):305–17.

Bushnell, Horace. *Christian Nurture.* 1860; reprint ed., New York: Scribner, Armstrong, 1876.

Bushnell, Horace. *Women's Suffrage: The Reform against Nature.* New York: Charles Scribner, 1869.

Byars, Ronald Preston. *The Making of the Self-Made Man: The Development of Masculine Roles and Images in Ante-Bellum America.* Ann Arbor, Mich.: University Microfilm International, 1979.

Cameron, Mabel Ward. *Biographical Cyclopedia of American Women.* 2 vols. New York: Halvord, 1924.

Camhi, Jane Jerome. *Women against Women: American Anti-Suffragism, 1880–1920.* Brooklyn, N.Y.: Carlson, 1994.

Campbell, Barbara Kuhn. *The "Liberated" Woman of 1914: Prominent Women in the Progressive Era.* Ann Arbor, Mich.: UMI Research Press, 1979.

Caruso, Virginia Ann Paganelli. *A History of Woman Suffrage in Michigan.* Ann Arbor, Mich.: University Microfilms International, 1986.

Carver, Thomas Nixon. *Women Suffrage from a Neutral Point of View. Address Delivered at the Annual Meeting of the Cambridge Branch of the Women's Anti-Suffrage Association of Massachusetts, May 13, 1918.* Boston: A. T. Bliss, 1918.

Caswell, Mrs. George A. *Address in Opposition to Woman Suffrage.* Boston: MAOFESW, 1913.

Cathcart, Robert S. "New Approaches to the Study of Social Movements: Defining Movements Rhetorically." *Western Speech* 36 (Spring 1972): 82–88.

Catt, Carrie Chapman. *Woman Suffrage by Federal Constitutional Amendment.* New York: National Woman Suffrage Publishing Company, 1917.

Catt, Carrie Chapman, and Nettie Rogers Shuler. *Woman Suffrage and Politics: The Inner Story of the Suffrage Movement.* 1923; reprint ed., Seattle: University of Washington Press, 1970.

Census of the Commonwealth of Massachusetts—1895. 7 vols. Prepared by Horace G. Wadlin. Boston: Wright and Potter Printing Co., 1896–1900.

The Century Association Year-Book 1969. New York: Century Association, 1969.

Chafe, William H. *The American Woman: Her Changing Social, Economic, and Political Roles, 1920–1970.* New York: Oxford University Press, 1972.

Chafe, William H. "Women's History and Political History: Some Thoughts on Progressivism and the New Deal." In *Visible Women: New Essays on American Activism,* ed. Nancy A. Hewitt and Suzanne Lebsock. Urbana: University of Illinois Press, 1993. 101–18.

Chafetz, Janet Saltzman, and Anthony Gary Dworkin. "In the Face of Threat: Organized Antifeminism in Comparative Perspective." *Gender and Society* 1 (March 1987): 33–60.

Chambers, William Nisbet, and Walter Dean Burnham, eds. *The American Party Systems: Stages of Political Development.* New York: Oxford University Press, 1967.

Chapin, Edwin Hubbell. *Duties of Young Women.* Boston: G. W. Briggs, 1848.

Chase, Allan. *The Legacy of Malthus: The Social Costs of the New Scientific Racism.* Urbana: University of Illinois Press, 1980.

Child, Lydia Maria. *The American Frugal Housewife.* Boston: Charter, Hendee, 1832.

Chittenden, Alice Hill. "The Counter Influence to Woman Suffrage." *Independent,* 29 July 1909, 246–49.

Chittenden, Alice Hill. *The Inexpediency of Granting the Suffrage to American Women: Address at the Tenth Biennial of the General Federation of Women's Clubs, Cincinnati, May 14, 1910.* New York: New York State Association Opposed to Woman Suffrage, 1910.

Clemens, Elisabeth S. "Organizational Repertoires and Institutional Change: Women's Groups and the Transformation of U.S. Politics, 1890–1920." *American Journal of Sociology* 98 (January 1993): 755–98.

Clement, Cora. *A Woman's Reasons Why Women Should Not Vote.* Boston: J. E. Farwell, 1868.

Cleveland, Grover. "Woman's Mission and Woman's Clubs." *Ladies' Home Journal,* May 1905, 3–4.

Cleveland, Grover. "Would Woman Suffrage Be Unwise?" *Ladies' Home Journal,* October 1905, 7–8.

Comer, Lee. "Women and Class: The Question of Women and Class." *Women's Studies International Quarterly* 1 (1978): 165–73.

Conaway, Waitman Harrison. *The Subjugation of Man through Woman Suffrage.* N.p., 1919.

Conn, Peter. *The Divided Mind: Ideology and Imagination in America, 1898–1917.* Cambridge: Oxford University Press, 1983.

Conover, Pamela Johnston. "Feminists and the Gender Gap." *Journal of Politics* 50 (November 1988): 985–1010.

Conover, Pamela Johnston, and Virginia Gray. *Feminism and the New Right: Conflict over the American Family.* New York: Praeger, 1983.

Coontz, Stephanie. *The Social Origins of Private Life: A History of American Families, 1600–1900.* London: Verso, 1988.

Cope, Edward D. *The Origin of the Fittest.* 1887; reprint ed., New York: Arno Press, 1974.

Cope, Edward D. *The Relation of the Sexes to Government.* New York: DeVinne Press, 1888.

Cope, Edward D. "The Relation of the Sexes to Government." *Popular Science Monthly,* October 1888, 721–30.

Corbin, Caroline Elizabeth. *The Anti-Suffrage Movement.* Chicago: Illinois Association Opposed to the Extension of Suffrage to Women, 1908.

[Corbin, Caroline Elizabeth.] *The Home versus Woman Suffrage.* Boston, 1896.

Corbin, Caroline Elizabeth. *The Position of Women in the Socialistic Utopia.* Chicago, 1901.

Corbin, Caroline Elizabeth. *The Woman Movement in America.* Chicago: Illinois Association Opposed to the Extension of Suffrage to Women, 1900.

Corbin, Caroline Elizabeth. *Woman's Rights in America, A Retrospect of Sixty Years, 1848–1908*. Chicago: Illinois Association Opposed to Woman Suffrage, 1909.

Cott, Nancy F. *The Bonds of Womanhood: "Woman's Sphere" in New England, 1780–1835*. New Haven: Yale University Press, 1977.

Cott, Nancy F. *The Grounding of Modern Feminism*. New Haven: Yale University Press, 1987.

Cott, Nancy F. "What's in a Name? The Limits of 'Social Feminism'; or, Expanding the Vocabulary of Women's History." *Journal of American History* 76 (December 1989): 809–29.

Crannell, Elizabeth Keller. *Address of Mrs. W. Winslow Crannell, Chairman of the Executive Committee of the Third Judicial District of the State of New York, Before the Committee on Resolutions of the Republican National Convention at St. Louis, 16 June 1896*. Albany, N.Y.: Anti-Suffrage Association of the Third Judicial District of the State of New York, 1896.

Crannell, Elizabeth Keller. *Wyoming*. Albany, N.Y.: Albany Anti-Suffrage Association, 1895.

Crawford, Alan. *Thunder on the Right: The "New Right" and the Politics of Resentment*. New York: Pantheon, 1980.

Crawford, Mary Caroline. *Famous Families of Massachusetts*. 2 vols. Boston: Little, Brown, 1930.

Crocker, George G. *Argument of Hon. George G. Crocker, at the Hearing before the Committee on Woman Suffrage*. N.p., 1884.

Crocker, George G. *Letter to the Committee on Woman Suffrage from George G. Crocker*. Boston: Rand Avery, 1887.

Croly, Mrs. J. C. *The History of the Women's Club Movement in America*. New York: Henry G. Allen, 1898.

Cudell, F. E. *A House of Ladies for Ohio*. Cleveland, 1912.

Curtis, John Gould. *History of the Town of Brookline*. Boston: Houghton Mifflin, 1933.

Cuyler, Theodore L. *Shall Women Be Burdened with the Ballot?* New York: Brooklyn Auxiliary of the New York State Association Opposed to the Extension of Suffrage to Women, n.d.

Dahlgren, Madeleine Vinton. *Thoughts on Female Suffrage and in Vindication of Woman's True Rights*. Washington, D.C.: Blanchard, Mohun, 1869.

Dana, R. H. "American View of the Irish Question." *Forum*, August 1892, 709–17.

Dana, R. H. "Substitutes for the Caucus." *Forum*, December 1886, 491–501.

Daniels, Arlene Kaplan. *Invisible Careers: Women Civic Leaders from the Volunteer World*. Chicago: University of Chicago Press, 1988.

Darwin, Charles. *The Descent of Man, and Selection in Relation to Sex*. 2d ed. New York: P. F. Collier and Son, 1900.

Davidoff, Leonore. *The Best Circles: Society Etiquette and the Season*. London: Croom Helm, 1973.

Davies, Wallace Evan. *Patriotism on Parade: The Story of Veterans' and Hereditary*

Organizations in America, 1783–1900. Cambridge: Harvard University Press, 1955.

Davis, Allen F. *Spearheads for Reform: The Social Settlements and the Progressive Movement,* 1890–1914. New York: Oxford University Press, 1967.

Davis, Mrs. Horace A. "The True Function of the Normal Woman." In *Anti-Suffrage Essays by Massachusetts Women,* ed. Ernest Bernbaum. Boston: Forum Publications, 1916. 123–27.

Davis, Nancy J., and Robert V. Robinson. "Men's and Women's Consciousness of Gender Inequality: Austria, West Germany, Great Britain, and the United States." *American Sociological Review* 56 (February 1991): 72–84.

Dawson, J. W. "Woman Suffrage." *Catholic World,* November 1920, 145–56.

Deland, Margaret. "The New Woman Who Would Do Things." *Ladies' Home Journal,* September 1907, 17.

Dicey, A. V. "Woman Suffrage." *Living Age,* 10 April 1909, 67–84.

DiMaggio, Paul. "Cultural Entrepreneurship in Nineteenth-Century Boston, Part I: The Creation of an Organizational Base for High Culture in America." *Media, Culture, and Society* 4 (January 1982): 33–50.

DiMaggio, Paul. "Cultural Entrepreneurship in Nineteenth-Century Boston, Part II: The Classification and Framing of American Art." *Media, Culture, and Society* 4 (October 1982): 303–22.

Directory of the National Society of the Daughters of the American Revolution. Washington, D.C.: Memorial Continental Hall, 1911.

Doane, William Croswell. *Extracts from Addresses of the Rt. Rev. William Croswell Doane, D.D., Bishop of Albany, to the Classes Graduated from St. Agnes' School, Albany, June 6th, 1894, and June 6th, 1895.* Albany, N.Y.: Albany Anti-Suffrage Association, 1895.

Doane, William Croswell. *A Sermon Preached at the Commencement of Cottage Hill Seminary for Ladies, Poughkeepsie, New York, 19 June 1867.* Poughkeepsie, N.Y.: Telegraph Steam Presses, 1867.

Doane, William Croswell. "Some Later Aspects of Woman Suffrage." *North American Review,* November 1896, 537–48.

Doane, William Croswell. "Why Women Do Not Want the Ballot." *North American Review,* September 1895, 257–67.

Dodge, Mary Abigail [Gail Hamilton]. *Letter from Gail Hamilton.* N.P., 1886.

Dodge, Mrs. Arthur M. *The Case against Votes for Women.* New York: New York State Association Opposed to Woman Suffrage, 1915.

Dodge, Mrs. Arthur M. "Woman Suffrage Opposed to Woman's Rights." *Annals of the American Academy of Political and Social Science* 56 (November 1914): 99–104.

Domhoff, G. William. *The Higher Circles: The Governing Class in America.* New York: Random House, 1970.

Dos Passos, John R. *Equality of Suffrage Means the Debasement Not Only of Women but of Men.* New York: NAOWS, n.d.

Douglas, Ann. *The Feminization of American Culture.* New York: Knopf, 1977.

DuBois, Ellen Carol. *Feminism and Suffrage: The Emergence of an Independent Women's Movement in America, 1848–1869.* Ithaca, N.Y.: Cornell University Press, 1978.

DuBois, Ellen Carol. "Harriot Stanton Blatch and the Transformation of Class Relations among Women Suffragists." In *Gender, Class, Race, and Reform in the Progressive Era,* ed. Noralee Frankel and Nancy S. Dye. Lexington: University Press of Kentucky, 1991. 162–79.

DuBois, Ellen Carol. "Politics and Culture in Women's History: A Symposium." *Feminist Studies* 6 (Spring 1980): 28–36.

DuBois, Ellen Carol, and Vicki L. Ruiz, eds. *Unequal Sisters: A Multicultural Reader in U.S. Women's History.* New York: Routledge, 1990.

Duniway, Abigail Scott. *Path Breaking: An Autobiographical History of the Equal Suffrage Movement in Pacific Coast States.* 1914; reprint ed., New York: Source Book Press, 1970.

Dwight, Eleanor. *Edith Wharton: An Extraordinary Life.* New York: Harry N. Abrams, 1994.

Dye, Nancy Schrom. *As Equals and As Sisters: Feminism, the Labor Movement, and the Women's Trade Union League of New York.* Columbia: University of Missouri Press, 1980.

Easton, Barbara. "Industrialization and Femininity: A Case Study of Nineteenth-Century New England." *Social Problems* 23 (April 1976): 389–401.

Eckhardt, Celia Morris. *Fanny Wright: Rebel in America.* Cambridge: Harvard University Press, 1984.

Edwards, John Carver. *Patriots in Pinstripe: Men of the National Security League.* Washington, D.C.: University Press of America, 1982.

Ehrenreich, Barbara, and Deidre English, *For Her Own Good: 150 Years of the Experts' Advice to Women.* Garden City, N.Y.: Doubleday, 1978.

Ellis, Havelock. *Man and Woman: A Study of Human Secondary Sexual Characteristics.* London: Walter Scott, 1894.

Ellis, Havelock. *Studies in the Psychology of Sex.* 4 vols. New York: Random House, 1936.

Ellis, John Tracy. *The Life of James Cardinal Gibbons, Archbishop of Baltimore, 1834–1921.* 2 vols. Milwaukee, Wis.: Bruce Publishing Company, 1952.

Eminent Catholic Prelates Oppose Woman Suffrage. Boston: Massachusetts Anti-Suffrage Committee, 1915.

Englander, Susan. *Class Conflict and Coalition in the California Woman Suffrage Movement, 1907–1912: The San Francisco Wage Earners' Suffrage League.* Lewiston, N.Y.: Edwin Mellon Press, 1992.

Epstein, Barbara Leslie. *The Politics of Domesticity: Women, Evangelism, and Temperance in Nineteenth Century America.* Middletown, Conn.: Wesleyan University Press, 1981.

Evans, Richard J. *The Feminists: Women's Emancipation Movements in Europe, America, and Australasia, 1840–1920.* New York: Barnes & Noble, 1977.

Evans, Sara M. "Women's History and Political Theory: Toward a Feminist

Approach to Public Life." In *Visible Women: New Essays on American Activism*, ed. Nancy A. Hewitt and Suzanne Lebsock. Urbana: University of Illinois Press, 1993. 119–39.

"Extraordinary Protest against Woman-Suffrage." *Literary Digest*, 26 October 1895, 5.

Fairfield, Francis Gerry. *The Clubs of New York*. 1873; reprint ed., New York: Arno Press, 1975.

"A Famed Biologist's Warning of the Peril in Votes for Women." *Current Literature*, July 1912, 59–62.

Felsenthal, Carol. *The Sweetheart of the Silent Majority*. Garden City, N.Y.: Doubleday, 1981.

Ferree, Myra Marx, and Frederick D. Miller. "Mobilization and Meaning: Toward an Integration of Social Psychological and Resource Perspectives on Social Movements." *Sociological Inquiry* 55 (Winter 1985): 39–61.

Firestone, Shulamith. "The Women's Rights Movement in the United States: A New View." In *Voices from Women's Liberation*, ed. Leslie B. Tanner. New York: Signet, 1970. 433–43.

Firey, Walter. *Land Use in Central Boston*. 1947; reprint ed., New York: Greenwood Press, 1968.

Fisher, Marguerite J. "Mid-Nineteenth-Century Attitudes against Woman Suffrage." *Social Studies* 44 (May 1953): 184–87.

Flexner, Eleanor. *Century of Struggle: The Woman's Rights Movement in the United States*. 1959; reprint ed., Cambridge: Harvard University Press, 1975.

Foley, Monica. "How Massachusetts Fosters Public Welfare." In *Anti-Suffrage Essays by Massachusetts Women*, ed. Ernest Bernbaum. Boston: Forum Publications, 1916. 53–61.

Fox, Karolena M. "History of the Equal Suffrage Movement in Michigan." *Michigan History Magazine*, January 1918, 90–109.

Foxcroft, Frank. *The Check to Woman Suffrage in the United States*. Boston: MAOFESW, n.d.

Foxcroft, Frank. *Municipal Suffrage for Women—Why?* Boston: MAOFESW, n.d.

Foxcroft, Frank. *Objections to License Suffrage from a No-License Point of View. Address before the Massachusetts Legislative Committee*. Boston: MAOFESW, 1898.

Foxcroft, Lily Rice. "Suffrage a Step toward Feminism." In *Anti-Suffrage Essays by Massachusetts Women*, ed. Ernest Bernbaum. Boston: Forum Publications, 1916. 141–52.

Foxcroft, Lily Rice. *Why Are Women Opposing Woman Suffrage?* Boston: Women's Anti-Suffrage Association of Massachusetts, 1917.

Frankel, Noralee, and Nancy S. Dye, eds. *Gender, Class, Race, and Reform in the Progressive Era*. Lexington: University Press of Kentucky, 1991.

Frenier, Mariam Darce. "American Anti-Feminist Women: Comparing the Rhetoric of Opponents of the Equal Rights Amendment with That of Opponents of Women's Suffrage." *Women's Studies International Forum* 7 (1984): 455–65.

Friedman, Debra, and Doug McAdam. "Collective Identity and Activism: Networks, Choices, and the Life of a Social Movement." In *Frontiers in Social Movement Theory,* ed. Aldon D. Morris and Carol McClurg Mueller. New Haven: Yale University Press, 1992. 156–73.

Frothingham, O. B. "The Real Case of the 'Remonstrants' against Woman Suffrage." *Arena,* July 1890, 175–81.

Frothingham, O. B. "Women versus Women." *Nation,* 3 October 1867, 276–77.

Frothingham, O. B., et al. *Woman Suffrage, Unnatural and Inexpedient.* Boston, 1894.

Fuller, Paul E. *Laura Clay and the Woman's Rights Movement.* Lexington: University Press of Kentucky, 1975.

Gale, Richard P. "Social Movements and the State: The Environmental Movement, Countermovement, and Governmental Agencies." *Sociological Perspectives* 29 (April 1986): 202–40.

Gamson, William A. "Political Discourse and Collective Action." In *International Social Movement Research,* ed. Bert Klandermans, Hanspeter Kriesi, and Sidney Tarrow. Greenwich, Conn.: JAI Press, 1988. 219–44.

Gamson, William A. *The Strategy of Social Protest.* Homewood, Ill.: Dorsey, 1975.

Gamson, William A., and David S. Meyer. "Framing Political Opportunity." In *Comparative Perspectives on Social Movements: Political Opportunities, Mobilizing Structures, and Cultural Framings,* ed. Doug McAdam, John D. McCarthy, and Mayer N. Zald. New York: Cambridge University Press, 1996. 275–90.

Garraty, John A., ed. *Dictionary of American Biography.* New York: Charles Scribner's Sons, 1977.

George, Mrs. A. J. "Suffrage Fallacies." In *Anti-Suffrage Essays by Massachusetts Women,* ed. Ernest Bernbaum. Boston: Forum Publications, 1916. 24–30.

Gibbons, James Cardinal. "Pure Womanhood." *Cosmopolitan,* September 1905, 559–61.

Gibbons, James Cardinal. "Relative Condition of Woman under Pagan and Christian Civilization." *American Catholic Quarterly,* October 1886, 651–65.

Gibbons, James Cardinal. "The Restless Woman." *Ladies' Home Journal,* January 1902, 6.

Giddings, Paula. *When and Where I Enter: The Impact of Black Women on Race and Sex in America.* New York: William Morrow, 1984.

Gilder, Jeannette Leonard. *Why I Am Opposed to Woman's Suffrage.* Boston: MAOFESW, 1894.

Gilder, Richard Watson. "The Moral Power of Women: Editorial." *Scribner's Monthly,* June 1874, 238–39.

Gilder, Richard Watson. "The New Woman-Suffrage Movement: Editorial." *Century,* July 1894, 469–70.

Gilder, Richard Watson. "Woman Suffrage: Editorial." *Scribner's Monthly,* March 1875, 628–29.

Goertzel, Ted George. "The Gender Gap: Sex, Family Income, and Political

Opinions in the Early 1980s." *Journal of Political and Military Sociology* 11 (Fall 1983): 209–22.

Goffman, Erving. *Interaction Ritual: Essays on Face-to-Face Behavior.* Garden City, N.Y.: Doubleday, 1967.

Goldberg, Michael L. "Non-Partisan and All-Partisan: Rethinking Woman Suffrage and Party Politics in Gilded Age Kansas." *Western Historical Quarterly* 25 (Spring 1994): 21–44.

Goodwin, Grace Duffield. *Anti-Suffrage: Ten Good Reasons.* New York: Duffield, 1912.

Goodwin, H. M. "Women's Suffrage." *New Englander,* 4 March 1884, 193–212.

Gordon, Linda, ed. *Women, the State, and Welfare.* Madison: University of Wisconsin Press, 1990.

Gordon, Milton. *Assimilation in American Life: The Role of Race, Religion, and National Origins.* New York: Oxford University Press, 1964.

Gould, Lewis L. *Progressives and Prohibitionists: Texas Democrats in the Wilson Era.* Austin: University of Texas Press, 1973.

Gould, Lewis L., ed. *The Progressive Era.* Syracuse, N.Y.: Syracuse University Press, 1974.

Graham, Sara Hunter. "Woman Suffrage in Virginia: The Equal Suffrage League and Pressure Group Politics, 1909–1920." *Virginia Magazine of History and Biography* 101 (April 1993): 227–50.

Green, Martin. *The Mount Vernon Street Warrens: A Boston Story, 1860–1910.* New York: Scribner's, 1989.

Gregg, Richard B. "The Ego-Function of the Rhetoric of Protest." *Philosophy and Rhetoric* 4 (Spring 1971): 71–91.

Gregory, Winifred, ed. *American Newspapers, 1821–1936.* New York: H. W. Wilson, 1937.

Griffith, Elisabeth. *In Her Own Right: The Life of Elizabeth Cady Stanton.* New York: Oxford University Press, 1984.

Grimes, Alan P. *The Puritan Ethic and Woman Suffrage.* New York: Oxford University Press, 1967.

Griswold, Wendy. "American Character and the American Novel: An Expansion of Reflection Theory in the Sociology of Literature." *American Journal of Sociology* 86 (January 1981): 740–65.

Guild, Mrs. Charles E. *Municipal Suffrage for Women. An Address before the Massachusetts Legislative Committee on Election Laws, January 27, 1904, by Mrs. Charles E. Guild, President of the Massachusetts Association Opposed to the Further Extension of Suffrage to Women.* Boston, 1904.

Gulick, Mrs. Charles Burton. "The Imperative Demand upon Women in the Home." In *Anti-Suffrage Essays by Massachusetts Women,* ed. Ernest Bernbaum. Boston: Forum Publications, 1916. 128–34.

Gurin, Patricia. "Women's Gender Consciousness." *Public Opinion Quarterly* 49 (Summer 1985): 143–63.

Gurin, Patricia, and Aloen Townsend. "Properties of Gender Identity and

Their Implications for Gender Consciousness." *British Journal of Social Psychology* 25 (June 1986): 139–48.

Gusfield, Joseph R. *Symbolic Crusade: Status Politics and the American Temperance Movement.* Urbana: University of Illinois Press, 1963.

Hacker, Helen Meyer. "Women as a Minority Group." *Social Forces* 30 (October 1951): 60–69.

Haines, Herbert H. "Black Radicalization and the Funding of Civil Rights: 1957–1970." *Social Problems* 32 (October 1984): 31–43.

Hale, Matthew. *Why Women Should Not Vote.* Albany: Anti-Woman Suffrage Association of Albany, n.d.

Hale, Mrs. Annie Riley. *Woman Suffrage: An Article on the Biological and Social Aspects of the Woman Question.* Washington, D.C.: U.S. Government Printing Office, 1917.

Hale, Mrs. Clarence. *Against Woman Suffrage, An Argument by Mrs. Clarence Hale of Maine.* Maine Association Opposed to Suffrage for Women, n.d.

Hale, Sarah Josepha, ed. *Keeping House and House Keeping: A Story of Domestic Life.* New York: Harper and Bros., 1845.

Harper, Ida Husted, ed. *The History of Woman Suffrage.* Vols. 5 and 6. New York: National American Woman Suffrage Association, 1922.

Harris, Neil. "The Gilded Age Revisited: Boston and the Museum Movement." *American Quarterly* 14 (Winter 1962): 545–66.

Harrison, Brian. *Separate Spheres: The Opposition to Woman's Suffrage in Britain.* New York: Holmes and Meier, 1978.

Hartmann, Edward George. *The Movement to Americanize the Immigrant.* 1948; reprint ed., New York: AMS Press, 1967.

Hartwell, Edward M. *Small Interest Taken by Women. Reprinted from Boston Sunday Globe, January 19, 1913.* Boston: MAOFESW, 1913.

Hatheway, Jay. "The Puritan Covenant II: Anti-Modernism and the 'Contract with America.' " *Humanist,* July–August 1995, 24–33.

Hazard, Mrs. Barclay. *How Women Can Best Serve the State: An Address before the State Federation of Women's Clubs, Troy, New York, 30 October 1907.* New York: New York State Association Opposed to Woman Suffrage, 1907.

Hazard, Mrs. Barclay. "New York State Association Opposed to Woman Suffrage." *Chautauquan,* June 1910, 84–89.

Herrnstein, Richard J., and Charles Murray. *The Bell Curve: Intelligence and Class Structure in American Life.* New York: Free Press, 1994.

Hewitt, Abram Stevens. *Statement in Regard to the Suffrage.* New York: New York State Association Opposed to Woman Suffrage, 1894.

Hewitt, Nancy A. *Women's Activism and Social Change: Rochester, New York, 1822–1872.* Ithaca, N.Y.: Cornell University Press, 1984.

Hewitt, Nancy A., and Suzanne Lebsock, eds. *Visible Women: New Essays on American Activism.* Urbana: University of Illinois Press, 1993.

Higgins, Anthony, ed. "Mary Wilson Thompson Memoir, Part 4." *Delaware History* 18 (Fall-Winter 1979): 238–66.

Higham, John. *Strangers in the Land: Patterns of American Nativism, 1860–1925.* New Brunswick, N.J.: Rutgers University Press, 1955.

Higley, Stephen Richard. *Privilege, Power, and Place: The Geography of the American Upper Class.* London: Rowman and Littlefield, 1995.

Himmelstein, Jerome L. *To the Right: The Transformation of American Conservatism.* Berkeley: University of California Press, 1990.

History of Women: Guide to the Microfilm Collection. Woodbridge, Conn.: Research Publications, 1983.

Hoar, George F. "The Right and Expediency of Woman Suffrage." *Century,* August 1894, 605–13.

Hoffecker, Carol E. "Delaware's Woman Suffrage Campaign." *Delaware History* 20 (Spring–Summer 1983): 149–67.

Hofstadter, Richard. *The Age of Reform: From Bryan to F.D.R.* New York: Vintage, 1955.

Hofstadter, Richard. *Anti-Intellectualism in American Life.* New York: Vintage, 1963.

Howard, Jean. "Our Own Worst Enemies: Women Opposed to Woman Suffrage." *Journal of Sociology and Social Welfare* 9 (September 1982): 463–74.

Howe, Julia Ward, Lucy Stone, Elizabeth Cady Stanton, Thomas Wentworth Higgins, and Wendell Phillips. "The Other Side of the Woman Question." *North American Review,* November 1879, 413–46.

Hubbard, B. V. *Socialism, Feminism, and Suffragism: The Terrible Triplets, Connected by the Same Umbilical Cord, and Fed from the Same Nursing Bottle.* Chicago: American Publishing, 1915.

Huber, Joan, Cynthia Rexroat, and Glenna Spitze. "A Crucible of Opinion on Women's Status: ERA in Illinois." *Social Forces* 57 (December 1978): 549–65.

Huggins, Nathan Irvin. *Protestants against Poverty: Boston's Charities, 1870–1900.* Westport, Conn.: Greenwood, 1971.

Hunter, Floyd. *Community Power Structure.* Chapel Hill: University of North Carolina Press, 1953.

Illinois Association Opposed to the Extension of Suffrage to Women. *One Woman's Experience of Emancipation.* Chicago: Illinois Association Opposed to the Extension of Suffrage to Women, 1912.

Illinois Association Opposed to the Extension of Suffrage to Women. *A Protest against the Granting of Municipal Suffrage to Women in the City of Chicago, Addressed to the Honorable the Committee on Municipal Elections of the Charter Convention.* Chicago: Illinois Association Opposed to the Extension of Suffrage to Women, 1906.

Illinois Association Opposed to the Extension of Suffrage to Women. *Socialism and Sex.* Chicago: Illinois Association Opposed to the Extension of Suffrage to Women, 1910.

Illinois Association Opposed to the Extension of Suffrage to Women. *To the Voters of the Middle West.* Chicago: Illinois Association Opposed to the Extension of Suffrage to Women, 1909.

Illinois Association Opposed to the Extension of Suffrage to Women. *Where Woman's Work Is Most Needed.* Chicago: Illinois Association Opposed to the Extension of Woman Suffrage to Women, 1912.

Illinois Association Opposed to the Extension of Suffrage to Women. *Why the Home Makers Do Not Want to Vote.* Chicago: Illinois Association Opposed to the Extension of Suffrage to Women, 1909.

Jablonsky, Thomas J. *The Home, Heaven, and Mother Party: Female Antisuffragists in the United States, 1868–1920.* Brooklyn, N.Y.: Carlson, 1994.

Jaher, Frederic Cople. "The Politics of the Boston Brahmins: 1800–1860." In *Boston, 1700–1980: The Evolution of Urban Politics,* ed. Ronald P. Formisano and Constance K. Burns. Westport, Conn.: Greenwood Press, 1984.

Jaher, Frederic Cople. *The Urban Establishment: Upper Strata in Boston, New York, Charleston, Chicago, and Los Angeles.* Urbana: University of Illinois Press, 1982.

James, Edward T., ed. *Notable American Women, 1607–1950: A Biographical Dictionary.* 3 vols. Cambridge, Mass.: Belknap Press, 1971.

James, Henry. *Washington Square.* New York: Harper and Brothers, 1881.

Jamison, Heloise. *The Wrong of Suffrage.* N.p., 1894.

Jenkins, J. Craig. "Resource Mobilization Theory and the Study of Social Movements." In *Annual Review of Sociology.* Vol. 9. Ed. Ralph H. Turner and James F. Short. Palo Alto, Calif.: Annual Reviews, 1983. 527–53.

Jensen, Billie Barnes. " 'In the Weird and Wooly West': Anti-Suffrage Women, Gender Issues, and Woman Suffrage in the West." *Journal of the West* 32 (July 1993): 41–51.

Jensen, Richard. "Family, Career, and Reform: Women Leaders in the Progressive Era." In *The American Family in Social-Historical Perspective,* ed. Michael Gordon. 2d ed. New York: St. Martin's, 1978. 267–80.

John, Arthur. *The Best Years of the Century: Richard Watson Gilder, Scribner's Monthly, and the Century Magazine, 1870–1909.* Urbana: University of Illinois Press, 1981.

Johnson, Allen, and Dumas Malone, eds. *Dictionary of American Biography.* 11 vols. New York: Charles Scribner's Sons, 1929–64.

Johnson, Helen Kendrick. *Woman and the Republic: A Survey of the Woman-Suffrage Movement in the United States and a Discussion of the Claims and Arguments of Its Foremost Advocates.* New York: D. Appleton, 1897.

Johnson, Helen Kendrick. *Woman's Progress versus Woman Suffrage.* New York: New York State Association Opposed to Woman Suffrage, 1899.

Johnson, Kenneth R. "Kate Gordon and the Woman Suffrage Movement in the South." *Journal of Southern History* 38 (August 1972): 365–92.

Johnson, Rossiter. *The Blank-Cartridge Ballot.* New York: New York State Association Opposed to Woman Suffrage, 1894.

Jones, Mrs. Gilbert E. "The Position of the Anti-Suffragists." *Annals of the American Academy of Political and Social Science* 35 (May 1910): S16–S22.

Jones, Mrs. Gilbert E. "Some Facts about Suffrage and Anti-Suffrage." *Forum,* May 1910, 495–504.

Jones, Mrs. Gilbert E. "Some Impediments to Woman Suffrage." *North American Review,* August 1909, 158–69.

J.W.P. *A Remonstrant View of Woman Suffrage.* Cambridge, Mass.: J. Wilson, 1884.

Kann, Mark E. *On the Man Question: Gender and Civic Virtue in America.* Philadelphia: Temple University Press, 1991.

Kasson, John F. *Rudeness and Civility: Manners in Nineteenth-Century Urban America.* New York: Hill and Wang, 1990.

Kenneally, James J. "Catholicism and Woman Suffrage in Massachusetts." *Catholic Historical Review* 53 (April 1967): 43–57.

Kenneally, James J. "The Opposition to Woman Suffrage in Massachusetts, 1868–1920." Ph.D. diss., Boston College, 1963.

Kenneally, James J. "Woman Suffrage and the Massachusetts 'Referendum' of 1895." *Historian* 30 (August 1968): 617–33.

Kenneally, James J. *Women and American Trade Unions.* Montreal: Eden Press Women's Publications, 1981.

Kerber, Linda K. "Separate Spheres, Female Worlds, Woman's Place: The Rhetoric of Women's History." *Journal of American History* 75 (June 1988): 9–39.

Kerber, Linda K. *Women of the Republic: Intellect and Ideology in Revolutionary America.* New York: W. W. Norton, 1980.

King, Deborah K. "Multiple Jeopardy, Multiple Consciousness: The Context of a Black Feminist Ideology." *Signs* 14 (Autumn 1988): 42–72.

Kinnard, Cynthia D. *Antifeminism in American Thought: An Annotated Bibliography.* Boston: G. K. Hall, 1986.

Klatch, Rebecca E. *Women of the New Right.* Philadelphia: Temple University Press, 1987.

Kleppner, Paul. "From Party to Factions: The Dissolution of Boston's Majority Party, 1876–1908." In *Boston, 1700–1980: The Evolution of Urban Politics,* ed. Ronald P. Formisano and Constance K. Burns. Westport, Conn.: Greenwood Press, 1984. 11–64.

Kleppner, Paul. *Who Voted? The Dynamics of Electoral Turnout, 1870–1980.* New York: Praeger, 1982.

Kluegel, James R., and Eliot R. Smith. *Beliefs about Inequality: Americans' Views of What Is and What Ought to Be.* New York: Aldine, 1986.

Knapp, Adeline. *Do Working Women Need the Ballot? An Address to the Senate and Assembly Judiciary Committees of the New York Legislature, February 19, 1908.* New York: New York State Association Opposed to Woman Suffrage, 1908.

Koonz, Claudia. *Mothers in the Fatherland: Women, the Family, and Nazi Politics.* New York: St. Martin's Press, 1987.

Kousser, J. Morgan. *The Shaping of Southern Politics: Suffrage Restriction and the*

Establishment of the One-Party South, 1880–1910. New Haven: Yale University Press, 1974.

Kouwenhoven, John A. *Made in America: The Arts in Modern Civilization*. Garden City, N.Y.: Doubleday, 1948.

Koven, Seth, and Sonya Michel, eds. *Mothers of a New World: Maternalist Politics and the Origins of Welfare States*. New York: Routledge, 1993.

Kraditor, Aileen S. *The Ideas of the Woman Suffrage Movement, 1890–1930*. 1965; reprint ed., New York: W. W. Norton, 1981.

Lash, Joseph P. *Love, Eleanor: Eleanor Roosevelt and Her Friends*. Garden City, N.Y.: Doubleday, 1982.

Lears, T. J. Jackson. *No Place of Grace: Antimodernism and the Transformation of American Culture, 1880–1920*. New York: Pantheon, 1981.

Lebsock, Suzanne. "Woman Suffrage and White Supremacy: A Virginia Case Study." In *Visible Women: New Essays on American Activism*, ed. Nancy A. Hewitt and Suzanne Lebsock. Urbana: University of Illinois Press, 1993. 62–100.

Lebsock, Suzanne. "Women and American Politics, 1880–1920." In *Women, Politics, and Change*, ed. Louise A. Tilly and Patricia Gurin. New York: Russell Sage Foundation, 1990. 35–62.

Lemons, J. Stanley. *The Woman Citizen: Social Feminism in the 1920s*. Urbana: University of Illinois Press, 1973.

Leonard, Clara T. *Letter from Mrs. Clara T. Leonard, in Opposition to Woman Suffrage*. 1884; reprint ed., Boston: MAOFESW, n.d.

Leonard, Clara T. "What Women Can Do Best." *Century*, January 1895, 475–76.

Leonard, John William, ed. *Who's Who in America, 1899–1900*. Chicago: A. N. Marquis, 1899.

Leonard, John William, ed. *Woman's Who's Who of America. A Biographical Dictionary of Contemporary Women of the United States and Canada, 1914–1915*. New York: American Commonwealth, 1914.

Leopold, Richard W. *Elihu Root and the Conservative Tradition*. Boston: Little, Brown, 1954.

Lerner, Gerda. "The Lady and the Mill Girl: Changes in the Status of Women in the Age of Jackson, 1800–1840." In *A Heritage of Her Own: Toward a New Social History of American Women*, ed. Nancy F. Cott and Elizabeth H. Pleck. New York: Simon and Schuster, 1979. 182–96.

Letter to the Honorable Henry W. Blair, U.S. Senator from New Hampshire. Albany, N.Y.: Anti-Suffrage Association, n.d.

Levine, Lawrence, W. *Highbrow/Lowbrow: The Emergence of Cultural Hierarchy in America*. Cambridge: Harvard University Press, 1988.

Liebman, Robert C., and Robert Wuthnow, eds. *New Christian Right: Mobilization and Legitimation*. New York: Aldine, 1983.

Lind, Michael. "American by Invitation." *New Yorker*, 24 April 1995, 107–10.

Lipset, Seymour Martin, and E. Raab. *The Politics of Unreason: Right-Wing Ex-*

tremism in America, 1790–1970. 2d ed. Chicago: University of Chicago Press, 1978.

Livermore, D. P. *Woman Suffrage Defended by Irrefutable Arguments.* Boston: Lee and Shepard, 1885.

Lo, Clarence Y. H. "Countermovements and Conservative Movements in the Contemporary United States." In *Annual Review of Sociology,* vol. 8, ed. Ralph H. Turner and James F. Short. Palo Alto, Calif.: Annual Reviews, 1982. 107–34.

Lord, Arthur. *Argument of Arthur Lord before the Legislative Committee on Woman Suffrage, 1890, in Behalf of the Remonstrants against Municipal Suffrage for Women.* Boston: G. H. Ellis, 1890.

Lowell, Francis C. "The American Boss." *Atlantic Monthly,* September 1900, 289–99.

Lowell, Francis C. "Legislative Shortcomings." *Atlantic Monthly,* March 1897, 466–77.

Lowell, John. *Address of Hon. John Lowell, Delivered before the Committee on Woman Suffrage, in Boston, March 9, 1885.* The Remonstrants, n.d.

Lunardini, Christine A. *From Equal Suffrage to Equal Rights: Alice Paul and the National Woman's Party, 1912–1928.* New York: New York University Press, 1986.

Lutz, Tom. *American Nervousness, 1903: An Anecdotal History.* Ithaca, N.Y.: Cornell University Press, 1991.

Lyman, Mrs. Herbert. "The Anti-Suffrage Ideal." In *Anti-Suffrage Essays by Massachusetts Women,* ed. Ernest Bernbaum. Boston: Forum Publications, 1916. 118–22.

MacIntire, Mary A. J. *Of No Benefit to Woman. She Is Far Greater Power without Suffrage.* Boston: n.p., 1895.

Mahoney, Joseph F. "Woman Suffrage and the Urban Masses." *New Jersey History* 87 (Autumn 1969): 151–72.

Mambretti, Catherine Cole. "The Battle against the Ballot: Illinois Women Antisuffragists." *Chicago History* 9 (Fall 1980): 168–77.

Mansbridge, Jane J. *Why We Lost the ERA.* Chicago: University of Chicago Press, 1986.

MAOFESW. *Address to the Judiciary Committees of the Senate and Assembly of the State of New York, February 22, 1899, presented by the Association Opposed to the Extension of Suffrage to Women.* Boston: MAOFESW, 1899.

MAOFESW. *Mothering the Community.* Boston: MAOFESW, n.d.

MAOFESW. *Opinions of Eminent Persons against Woman Suffrage.* Boston: MAOFESW, 1909.

MAOFESW. *Woman Suffrage in Practice. A Criticism of "What Have Women Done with the Vote?" by George Creel in the Century Magazine for March, 1914.* Boston: MAOFESW, 1914.

Marburger, Harold J. *Texas Elections, 1918–1954.* Austin: Texas State Library, 1956.

Marlow, H. Carleton, and Harrison M. Davis. *The American Search for Woman.* Santa Barbara, Calif.: Clio, 1976.

Marquis, Albert Nelson, ed. *Who's Who in New England.* 1st ed. Chicago: A. N. Marquis, 1909.

Marshall, Edward. *A Woman Tells Why Woman Suffrage Would Be Bad.* New York: New York State Association Opposed to Woman Suffrage, n.d.

Marshall, Susan E. "Confrontation and Co-optation in Antifeminist Organizations." In *Feminist Organizations,* ed. Myra Marx Ferree and Patricia Yancey Martin. Philadelphia: Temple University Press, 1995. 323–35.

Marshall, Susan E. "In Defense of Separate Spheres: Class and Status Politics in the Antisuffrage Movement." *Social Forces* 65 (December 1986): 327–51.

Marshall, Susan E. "Keep Us on the Pedestal: Women against Feminism in Twentieth-Century America." In *Women: A Feminist Perspective,* ed. Jo Freeman. 5th ed. Mountain View, Calif.: Mayfield, 1994. 547–60.

Marshall, Susan E. "Ladies against Women: Mobilization Dilemmas of Antifeminist Women." *Social Problems* 32 (April 1985): 348–62.

Marshall, Susan E. "Marilyn vs. Hillary: Women's Issues and New Right Politics in the 1992 Campaign." *Women and Politics* 16 (Spring 1996): 55–75.

Marshall, Susan E. "Who Speaks for American Women? The Future of Antifeminism." *Annals of the American Academy of Political and Social Science* 515 (May 1991): 50–62.

Martin, Edward Sandford. *The Unrest of Women.* New York: Appleton, 1913.

Martin, Theodora Penny. *The Sound of Our Own Voices: Women's Study Clubs, 1860–1910.* Boston: Beacon Press, 1987.

Massachusetts Man Suffrage Association. *Privileges of Women in Massachusetts.* Boston: Massachusetts Man Suffrage Association, n.d.

Massachusetts Man Suffrage Association. *Why Should Suffrage Be Imposed on Women?* Boston: Massachusetts Man Suffrage Association, n.d.

Massie, Edith M. "A Woman's Plea against Woman Suffrage." *Living Age,* 11 April 1908, 84–88.

The Mayflower Club, 1893–1931. Cambridge, Mass.: Riverside Press, 1933.

Mayor, Mara. "Fears and Fantasies of the Anti-Suffragists." *Connecticut Review* 7 (April 1974): 64–74.

McAdam, Doug, John D. McCarthy, and Meyer N. Zald. "Social Movements." In *Handbook of Sociology,* ed. Neil J. Smelser. Beverly Hills, Calif.: Sage, 1988. 695–737.

McBride, Genevieve G. *On Wisconsin Women: Working for Their Rights from Settlement to Suffrage.* Madison: University of Wisconsin Press, 1993.

McCarthy, John D., and Mayer N. Zald. "Resource Mobilization and Social Movements: A Partial Theory." *American Journal of Sociology* 82 (May 1977): 1212–41.

McCarthy, John D., and Mayer N. Zald. *The Trend of Social Movements in America: Professionalization and Resource Mobilization.* Morristown, N.J.: General Learning Press, 1973.

McCarthy, Kathleen D. *Noblesse Oblige: Charity and Cultural Philanthropy in Chicago, 1849–1929*. Chicago: University of Chicago Press, 1982.

McCarthy, Kathleen D., ed. *Lady Bountiful Revisited: Women, Philanthropy, and Power.* New Brunswick, N.J.: Rutgers University Press, 1990.

McDonagh, Eileen L., and H. Douglas Price. "Woman Suffrage in the Progressive Era: Patterns of Opposition and Support in Referenda Voting, 1910–1918." *American Political Science Review* 79 (June 1985): 415–35.

McGerr, Michael. "Political Style and Women's Power, 1830–1930." *Journal of American History* 77 (December 1990): 864–85.

McKay, Seth Shepard. *Texas Politics, 1906–1944, with Special Reference to the German Counties.* Lubbock: Texas Tech Press, 1952.

Mead, Walter Russell. "Forward to the Past." *New York Times Magazine,* 4 June 1995, 48.

Meade, Marion. *Free Woman: The Life and Times of Victoria Woodhull.* New York: Knopf, 1976.

Melder, Keith E. *Beginnings of Sisterhood: The American Woman's Rights Movement, 1800–1850.* New York: Schocken, 1977.

Melder, Keith E. "Ladies Bountiful: Organized Benevolence in Early Nineteenth-Century America." *New York History* 48 (July 1967): 231–54.

Melvin, Edith. "A Business Woman's View of Suffrage." In *Anti-Suffrage Essays by Massachusetts Women,* ed. Ernest Bernbaum. Boston: Forum Publications, 1916. 38–42.

Merk, Lois. "Boston's Historic Public School Crisis." *New England Quarterly* 31 (March 1958): 172–99.

Meyer, Annie Nathan. *Woman's Assumption of Sex Superiority.* N.p.: North American Review Publishing, 1904.

Meyer, Annie Nathan, ed. *Woman's Work in America.* New York: Henry Holt, 1891.

Michel, Sonya. "The Limits of Maternalism: Policies toward American Wage-Earning Mothers during the Progressive Era." In *Mothers of a New World: Maternalist Politics and the Origins of Welfare States,* ed. Seth Koven and Sonya Michel. New York: Routledge, 1993. 277–320.

Michel, Sonya, and Robyn Rosen, "The Paradox of Maternalism: Elizabeth Lowell Putnam and the American Welfare State." *Gender and History* 4 (Autumn 1992): 364–86.

Mills, C. Wright. *The Power Elite.* New York: Oxford University Press, 1956.

Mink, Gwendolyn. "The Lady and the Tramp: Gender, Race, and the Origins of the Welfare State." In *Women, the State, and Welfare,* ed. Linda Gordon. Madison: University of Wisconsin Press, 1990. 92–122.

Mink, Gwendolyn. *Old Labor and New Immigrants in American Political Development: Union, Party, and State, 1875–1920.* Ithaca, N.Y.: Cornell University Press, 1986.

Mitchell, S. Weir, "When the College Is Hurtful to a Girl." *Ladies' Home Journal,* June 1900, 14.

Moore, Frank. *Women of the War; Their Heroism and Self-Sacrifice.* Hartford, Conn.: S.S. Scranton, 1866.

Morrison, Mary Foulke. "That Word Male." In *Victory: How Women Won It*, ed. NAWSA. New York: H. W. Wilson, 1940. 49–56.

Mott, Frank Luther. *A History of American Magazines.* 5 vols. Cambridge: Harvard University Press, 1938.

Mottl, Tahi L. "The Analysis of Countermovements." *Social Problems* 27 (June 1980): 620–35.

Mueller, Carol, ed. *The Politics of the Gender Gap: The Social Construction of Political Influence.* Newbury Park, Calif.: Sage, 1988.

Mueller, Carol, and Thomas Dimieri. "The Structure of Belief Systems among Contending ERA Activists." *Social Forces* 60 (March 1982): 657–75.

Muncy, Robyn. *Creating a Female Dominion in American Reform, 1890–1935.* New York: Oxford University Press, 1991.

Münsterberg, Hugo. "The American Woman." *International Monthly*, May-June 1901, 607–33.

Münsterberg, Hugo. "Is Co-Education Wise for Girls?" *Ladies' Home Journal*, 15 May 1911, 16, 32.

Murdock, J. B. "Woman Suffrage: A Protest." *Outlook*, 21 November 1917, 457–58.

NAOWS. *The Red behind the Yellow: Socialism in the Wake of Suffrage.* New York: NAOWS, n.d.

NAOWS. *Some Facts about California's Experiment with Woman Suffrage.* New York: NAOWS, n.d.

NAOWS. *The Truth about Wage-Earning Women.* New York: NAOWS, n.d.

National American Woman Suffrage Association (NAWSA), ed. *Victory: How Women Won It.* New York: H. W. Wilson, 1940.

National Cyclopedia of American Biography. 63 vols. New York: James T. White, 1898–1984.

National Society of the Daughters of the American Revolution. *Lineage Book.* Washington, D.C., 1898.

Nebraska Association Opposed to Woman Suffrage. *Woman Suffrage and the Feminist Movement.* Omaha: Nebraska Association Opposed to Woman Suffrage, 1913.

Nebraska Men's Association Opposed to Woman Suffrage. *Manifesto.* Omaha: Nebraska Men's Association Opposed to Woman Suffrage, 1914.

Nebraska Men's Association Opposed to Woman Suffrage. *Nebraska Clergymen Condemn Suffrage.* Omaha: Nebraska Men's Association Opposed to Woman Suffrage, 1914.

New York State Association Opposed to Woman Suffrage. Brooklyn, N.Y.: Brooklyn Auxiliary of the New York State Association Opposed to the Extension of Suffrage to Women, 1894.

Norton, Mary Beth. *Liberty's Daughters: The Revolutionary Experience of American Women, 1750–1800.* Boston: Little, Brown, 1980.

Nott, Charles C. *The New Woman and the Late President of Williams. Letter to the Editor of the Religious Herald.* N.p., 1895.

Oberschall, Anthony. *Social Conflict and Social Movements.* Englewood Cliffs, N.J.: Prentice-Hall, 1973.

Odendahl, Teresa. *Charity Begins at Home: Generosity and Self-Interest among the Philanthropic Elite.* New York: Basic, 1990.

O'Neill, William L. *Everyone Was Brave: The Rise and Fall of Feminism in America.* Chicago: Quadrangle, 1969.

O'Neill, William L. *The Woman Movement: Feminism in the United States and England.* New York: Barnes & Noble, 1969.

Opinions of Eminent Persons; Views on Woman Suffrage. Albany, N.Y.: Anti-Suffrage Association, n.d.

Oregon State Association Opposed to the Extension of Suffrage to Women. *An Appeal to Voters and Arguments against Equal Suffrage Constitutional Amendment.* Portland: Oregon State Association Opposed to the Extension of Suffrage to Women, n.d.

Ostrander, Gilman M. *The Prohibition Movement in California, 1848–1933.* Berkeley: University of California Press, 1957.

Ostrander, Susan A. *Women of the Upper Class.* Philadelphia: Temple University Press, 1984.

Owen, Harold. *Woman Adrift: A Statement of the Case against Suffragism.* New York: E. P. Dutton, 1912.

Paige, Connie. "The Amazing Rise of Beverly LaHaye." *Ms.*, February 1987, 24–28.

Painter, Nell Irvin. *Standing at Armageddon: The United States, 1877–1919.* New York: W. W. Norton, 1987.

Pamphlets Printed and Distributed by the Women's Anti-Suffrage Association of the Third Judicial District of the State of New York. 1905; reprint ed., Littleton, Colo.: Fred D. Rothman, 1990.

Park, Maud Wood. "The Winning Plan." In *Victory: How Women Won It,* ed. NAWSA. New York: H. W. Wilson, 1940. 123–39.

Parker, Mrs. Augustin H. "Are Suffragists Sincere Reformers?" In *Anti-Suffrage Essays by Massachusetts Women,* ed. Ernest Bernbaum. Boston: Forum Publications, 1916. 81–84.

Parker, William. *The Fundamental Error of Woman Suffrage.* New York: Fleming H. Revell, 1915.

Parkhurst, Charles H. "Andromaniacs." *Ladies' Home Journal,* February 1895, 15.

Parkhurst, Charles H. "College Training for Women." *Ladies' Home Journal,* May 1895, 15.

Parkhurst, Charles H. "The Inadvisability of Woman Suffrage." *Annals of the American Academy of Political and Social Science* 35 (May 1910): S36–S37.

Parkhurst, Charles H. "The True Mission of Woman." *Ladies' Home Journal,* April 1895, 15.

Parkhurst, Charles H. *Woman: An Address Delivered in Mendelssohn Hall, December 17, 1909.* New York: Irving Press, n.d.

Parkhurst, Charles H. "Women without the Ballot." *Ladies' Home Journal,* June 1895, 15.

Parkman, Francis. "The Failure of Universal Suffrage." *North American Review,* July–August 1878, 1–20.

Parkman, Francis. *Some of the Reasons against Woman Suffrage.* Boston: Massachusetts Man Suffrage Association, n.d.

Parkman, Francis. *Some of the Reasons against Woman Suffrage: Printed at the Request of an Association of Women.* Boston: MAOFESW, n.d.

Parkman, Francis. "The Woman Question." *North American Review,* October 1879, 303–21.

Parkman, Francis. "The Woman Question Again." *North American Review,* January 1880, 16–30.

Pavalko, Ronald M. "Racism and the New Immigration: A Reinterpretation of the Assimilation of White Ethnics in American Society." *Sociology and Social Research* 65 (October 1980): 56–77.

Peek, Mary Gray. "The Secretary Has Signed the Proclamation." In *Victory: How Women Won It,* ed. NAWSA. New York: H. W. Wilson, 1940. 143–54.

Peel, J. D. Y. *Herbert Spencer: The Evolution of a Sociologist.* New York: Basic Books, 1971.

Pennsylvania Association Opposed to Woman Suffrage. *Defeats and Failures of Woman Suffrage.* Pennsylvania Association Opposed to Woman Suffrage, n.d.

Pennsylvania Association Opposed to Woman Suffrage. *A Talk on the Tax-Paying Woman, by the Antis.* Pennsylvania Association Opposed to Woman Suffrage, n.d.

Phelps, Almira Lincoln. "Woman's Duties and Rights." *National Quarterly Review* 29 (June 1875): 29–54.

Phelps, Almira Lincoln. "Woman's Record." *Godey's Lady's Book and Magazine,* August 1871, 149.

Porzelt, Paul. *The Metropolitan Club of New York.* New York: Rizzoli, 1982.

Proceedings of the Bostonian Society at Annual Meeting, January 10, 1899. Boston: Old State House, 1899.

A Protest against Woman Suffrage in Alabama, by Alabama Democrats on Behalf and in Defense of the Large Unorganized Majority of the Women of Alabama. N.p., n.d.

Pugh, David G. *Sons of Liberty: The Masculine Mind in Nineteenth-Century America.* Westport, Conn.: Greenwood Press, 1984.

Putnam, Mrs. William Lowell. "Suffrage and the Sex Problem." In *Anti-Suffrage Essays by Massachusetts Women,* ed. Ernest Bernbaum. Boston: Forum Publications, 1916. 135–40.

Pyle, Joseph Gilpin. *Christian Civilization in the Balance.* Pennsylvania Association Opposed to Woman's Suffrage, n.d.

Pyle, Joseph Gilpin. *Should Women Vote? Remarks Made at a Meeting of the Informal Club, St. Paul, 28 March 1913.* N.p., 1913.

Ransford, H. Edward. *Race and Class in American Society: Black, Chicano, Anglo.* Cambridge, Mass.: Schenkman, 1977.

Robinson, Margaret C. *Woman Suffrage a Menace to Social Reform.* Boston: Women's Anti-Suffrage Association of Massachusetts, n.d.

Rodgers, Daniel T. "In Search of Progressivism." *Reviews in American History* 10 (December 1982): 113–32.

Roosevelt, Theodore. "The American Woman as a Mother." *Ladies' Home Journal,* July 1905, 3–4.

Root, Elihu. "Address as President on the Seventy-Fifth Anniversary of the Century Association." In *Men and Policies: Addresses by Elihu Root,* ed. Robert Bacon and James Brown Scott. 1925; reprint ed., Freeport, N.Y.: Books for Libraries Press, 1968. 99–104.

Root, Elihu. *Address Delivered by the Hon. Elihu Root, before the New York State Constitutional Convention on August 15, 1894.* New York: New York State Association Opposed to Woman Suffrage, 1894.

Root, Elihu. "Joseph H. Choate." In *Men and Policies: Addresses by Elihu Root,* ed. Robert Bacon and James Brown Scott. 1925; reprint ed., Freeport, N.Y.: Books for Libraries Press, 1968. 17–48.

Root, Elihu. "Letter to the President of the National Security League, February 16, 1918." In *Men and Policies: Addresses by Elihu Root,* ed. Robert Bacon and James Brown Scott. 1925; reprint ed., Freeport, N.Y.: Books for Libraries Press, 1968. 169–72.

Root, Elihu. "Speech before the National Security League in Philadelphia, April 24, 1918." In *Men and Policies: Addresses by Elihu Root,* ed. Robert Bacon and James Brown Scott. 1925; reprint ed., Freeport, N.Y.: Books for Libraries Press, 1968. 178–89.

Rothman, Sheila M. *Woman's Proper Place.* New York: Basic Books, 1978.

Rotundo, E. Anthony. *American Manhood: Transformations in Masculinity from the Revolution to the Modern Era.* New York: Basic Books, 1993.

Rowbotham, Sheila, and Jeffrey Weeks. *Socialism and the New Life: The Personal and Sexual Politics of Edward Carpenter and Havelock Ellis.* London: Pluto Press, 1977.

Rupp, Leila J. *Mobilizing Women for War: German and American Propaganda, 1939–1945.* Princeton: Princeton University Press, 1978.

Rupp, Leila J., and Verta Taylor. *Survival in the Doldrums: The American Women's Rights Movement, 1945 to the 1960s.* New York: Oxford University Press, 1987.

Russett, Cynthia Eagle. *Sexual Science: The Victorian Construction of Womanhood.* Cambridge: Harvard University Press, 1989.

Ryan, Mary P. *Women in Public: Between Banners and Ballots, 1825–1880.* Baltimore: Johns Hopkins University Press, 1990.

Ryan. Thomas G. "Male Opponents and Supporters of Woman Suffrage: Iowa in 1916." *Annals of Iowa* 45 (Winter 1981): 537–50.

Sams, Conway Whittle. *Shall Women Vote? A Book for Men*. New York: Neale Publishing, 1913.

Sanford, John B. *Extracts from a Speech against Woman Suffrage in the California State Senate*. N.p., n.d.

Sapiro, Virginia. *Women in American Society: An Introduction to Women's Studies*. 3d ed. Mountain View, Calif.: Mayfield, 1994.

Saunders, Charles R. *Taxpaying Suffrage*. Boston: MAOFESW, 1903.

Schaffer, Ronald. "The Montana Woman Suffrage Campaign, 1911–14." *Pacific Northwest Quarterly* 55 (January 1964): 9–15.

Schaffer, Ronald. "The New York City Woman Suffrage Party, 1909–1919." *New York History* 43 (July 1962): 269–87.

Schaffer, Ronald. "The Problem of Consciousness in the Woman Suffrage Movement: A California Perspective." *Pacific Historical Review* 45 (November 1976): 469–93.

Scharf, Lois, and Joan Jensen, eds. *Decades of Discontent: The Women's Movement, 1920–1940*. Westport, Conn.: Greenwood Press, 1983.

Schlafly, Phyllis. "Comparable Worth: Unfair to Men and Women." *Humanist*, May–June 1986, 12–13, 30.

Schlafly, Phyllis. *The Power of the Positive Woman*. New Rochelle, N.Y.: Arlington House, 1977.

Schlafly, Phyllis. "Should the Congress Adopt the Proposed 'Act for Better Child Care Services of 1988?' " *Congressional Digest*, November 1988, 271–74.

Schlesinger, Arthur M. *Learning How to Behave: A Historical Study of American Etiquette Books*. New York: Macmillan, 1946.

Schurz, Carl. "Woman Suffrage." *Harper's Weekly*, 16 June 1894, 554.

Schurz, Carl. *Woman Suffrage*. Boston: Massachusetts Association Opposed to the Extension of Woman Suffrage, 1894.

Scott, Anne Firor. *Natural Allies: Women's Associations in American History*. Urbana: University of Illinois Press, 1991.

Scott, Anne Firor. "On Seeing and Not Seeing: A Case of Historical Invisibility." *Journal of American History* 71 (June 1984): 7–21.

Scott, Anne Firor. *The Southern Lady from Pedestal to Politics, 1830–1930*. Chicago: University of Chicago Press, 1970.

Scott, Anne Firor, and Andrew M. Scott. *One Half the People: The Fight for Woman Suffrage*. Philadelphia: Lippincott, 1975.

Scott, Francis M. *Address of Francis M. Scott to Committee on Suffrage, New York Constitutional Convention, 14 June 1894*. N.p., 1894.

Scott, Francis M. *Woman and the Law*. New York: New York State Association Opposed to Woman Suffrage, 1895.

Scott, Joan. "Gender: A Useful Category of Historical Analysis." *American Historical Review* 91 (December 1986): 1053–75.

Scott, Mary Semple, ed. "History of Woman Suffrage in Missouri." *Missouri Historical Review* 14 (April–July 1920): 281–384.

Scott, Mrs. Francis M. *Extension of the Suffrage to Women. Address Delivered before the Judiciary Committee of the New York Senate, April 10, 1895, by Mrs. Francis M. Scott.* N.p., n.d.

Scott, Mrs. Francis M., et al. *To the Constitutional Convention.* New York: n.p., 1894.

Scott, Mrs. William Forse. "Woman's Relation to Government." *North American Review,* April 1910, 549–58.

Scott, Mrs. William Forse, and Miss Mary Dean Adams. *In Opposition to Woman Suffrage: Two Papers Read at Albany, 24 February 1909, before the Joint Senate and Assembly Judiciary Committee.* New York: New York State Association Opposed to Woman Suffrage, 1909.

Sears, Barnas. "Characteristics, Duties, and Culture of Woman." *Bibliotheca Sacra,* July 1853, 433–47.

Sears, David O., and Leonie Huddy. "On the Origins of Political Disunity among Women." In *Women, Politics, and Change,* ed. Louise A. Tilly and Patricia Gurin. New York: Russell Sage, 1990. 249–77.

Seawell, Molly. "The Ladies' Battle." *Atlantic Monthly,* September 1910, 289–303.

Seawell, Molly. *The Ladies' Battle.* New York: Macmillan, 1911.

Seawell, Molly. "Two Suffrage Mistakes." *North American Review,* March 1914, 366–82.

Sedgwick, Mrs. Mary K. "Some Scientific Aspects of the Woman Suffrage Question." *Gunton's Magazine,* April 1901, 333–44.

Sedgwick, William T. *Feminist Revolutionary Principle Biologically Unsound.* 1914; reprint ed., New York: Man-Suffrage Association, n.d.

Shannon, William V. "Boston's Irish Mayors: An Ethnic Perspective." In *Boston, 1700–1980: The Evolution of Urban Politics,* ed. Ronald P. Formisano and Constance K. Burns. Westport, Conn.: Greenwood Press, 1984. 199–214.

Shinn, Millicent Washburn. "The Marriage Rate of College Women." *Century,* October 1895, 946–48.

Simkins, M. W. "Suffrage and Anti-Suffrage: A Woman Worker's Appeal." *Living Age,* 6 February 1909, 323–29.

Sinclair, Andrew A. *The Better Half: The Emancipation of American Women.* New York: Harper and Row, 1965.

Sklar, Kathryn Kish. *Catharine Beecher: A Study in American Domesticity.* New York: W. W. Norton, 1976.

Skocpol, Theda. *Protecting Soldiers and Mothers: The Political Origins of Social Policy in the United States.* Cambridge: Belknap Press of Harvard University Press, 1992.

Smith, Dorothy. "A Sociology for Women." In *The Prism of Sex: Essays in the Sociology of Knowledge,* ed. Julia A. Sherman and Evelyn Tarton Beck. Madison: University of Wisconsin Press, 1979. 135–87.

Smith, Goldwin. "Female Suffrage." *Popular Science Monthly,* August 1874, 427–43.

Smith, Goldwin. "Is Universal Suffrage a Failure?" *Atlantic Monthly,* January 1879, 71–83.

Smith, Munroe. "Consent of the Governed." *Proceedings of the Academy of Political Science* 5 (October 1914): 82–88.

Smith, Munroe. *Questionnaire to Professors in Universities and Colleges*. New York: Man-Suffrage Association, n.d.

Smith, Tom W. "Liberal and Conservative Trends in the United States since World War II." *Public Opinion Quarterly* 54 (Winter 1990): 479–507.

Smith, Wilda M. "A Half Century of Struggle: Gaining Woman Suffrage in Kansas." *Kansas History* 4 (Summer 1981): 74–95.

Smith-Rosenberg, Carroll. *Disorderly Conduct: Visions of Gender in Victorian America*. New York: Knopf, 1985.

Snapp, Meredith A. "Defeat the Democrats: The Congressional Union for Woman Suffrage in Arizona, 1914 and 1916." *Journal of the West* 14 (October 1975): 131–39.

Snow, David A., E. Burke Rochford, Jr., Steven K. Worden, Robert D. Benford. "Frame Alignment Processes, Micromobilization, and Movement Participation." *American Sociological Review* 51 (August 1986): 464–81.

Snow, David A., Louis A. Zurcher, and Sheldon Ekland-Olson. "Social Networks and Social Movements: A Microstructural Approach to Differential Recruitment." *American Sociological Review* 45 (October 1980): 787–801.

Sobel, Robert, and John Raimo, eds. *Biographical Dictionary of the Governors of the United States, 1789–1978*. 4 vols. Westport, Conn.: Meckler Books, 1978.

Sochen, June, ed. *The New Feminism in Twentieth-Century America*. Lexington, Mass.: D. C. Heath, 1971.

Social Register, New York, 1910. New York: Social Register Association, 1909.

Solomon, Barbara Miller. *Ancestors and Immigrants: A Changing New England Tradition*. Cambridge: Harvard University Press, 1956.

Solomon, Martha. "The Rhetoric of Stop ERA: Fatalistic Reaffirmation." *Southern Speech Communication Journal* 44 (Fall 1978): 42–59.

Spencer, Herbert. *Principles of Sociology*. New York: D. Appleton, 1888.

Spencer, Herbert. "Psychology of the Sexes." *Popular Science Monthly*, November 1873, 30–38.

Sprague, William B. *The Excellent Woman As Described in the Book of Proverbs*. Boston: Gould & Lincoln, 1851.

Stanton, Elizabeth Cady, Susan B. Anthony, and Matilda Joslyn Gage, eds. *History of Woman Suffrage*. Vols. 1 and 2. New York: Fowler and Wells, 1881, 1882.

Stevenson, Louise L. "Women Anti-Suffragists in the 1915 Massachusetts Campaign." *New England Quarterly* 52 (March 1979): 80–93.

Stewart, Ella S. "Woman Suffrage and the Liquor Traffic." *Annals of the American Academy of Political Science* 56 (November 1914): 134–52.

Stimson, Henry A. "Is Woman's Suffrage an Enlightened and Justifiable Policy for the State?" *Bibliotheca Sacra*, April 1910, 335–46.

Stimson, Henry A. *Is Woman's Suffrage an Enlightened and Justifiable Policy for the*

State? Brooklyn, N.Y.: Brooklyn Auxiliary, New York State Association Opposed to Woman Suffrage, 1910.

Stimson, Henry L. *Suffrage Not a Natural Right. A Letter from Henry Lewis Stimson, Formerly Secretary of War, May 24, 1915, to Alice Hill Chittenden.* New York: New York Association Opposed to Woman Suffrage, 1915.

Story, Ronald. *The Forging of an Aristocracy: Harvard and the Boston Upper Class, 1800–1870.* Middletown, Conn.: Wesleyan University Press, 1980.

Straube, Melvin M. *A Scientific Demonstration of the Dangers of Woman Suffrage.* Huntsville, Mo.: Times Publishing, 1921.

Strom, Sharon Hartman. "Leadership and Tactics in the American Woman Suffrage Movement: A New Perspective from Massachusetts." *Journal of American History* 62 (September 1975): 296–315.

"Suffragists Take New York State." *Literary Digest,* 17 November 1917, 14–15.

Tappan, William H. *Minority Report of the Committee on Woman Suffrage in Opposition to the Bill Reported to the Massachusetts Legislature of 1885.* N.p., 1885.

Tarbell, Ida M. *The Business of Being a Woman.* New York: Macmillan, 1912.

Tax, Meredith. *The Rising of the Women: Feminist Solidarity and Class Conflict, 1880–1917.* New York: Monthly Review Press, 1980.

Taylor, A. Elizabeth. *Citizens at Last: The Woman Suffrage Movement in Texas.* Austin, Texas: Ellen C. Temple, 1987.

Taylor, A. Elizabeth. "The Last Phase of the Woman Suffrage Movement in Georgia." *Georgia Historical Quarterly* 43 (March 1959): 11–28.

Taylor, A. Elizabeth. "Revival and Development of the Woman Suffrage Movement in Georgia." *Georgia Historical Quarterly* 42 (December 1958): 339–54.

Taylor, A. Elizabeth. "A Short History of the Woman Suffrage Movement in Tennessee." *Tennessee Historical Quarterly* 2 (September 1943): 195–215.

Taylor, A. Elizabeth. "South Carolina and the Enfranchisement of Women: The Early Years." *South Carolina Historical Magazine* 77 (April 1976): 115–26.

Taylor, A. Elizabeth. "The Woman Suffrage Movement in Arkansas." *Arkansas Historical Quarterly* 15 (Spring 1956): 17–52.

Taylor, A. Elizabeth. "The Woman Suffrage Movement in Florida." *Florida Historical Quarterly* 36 (July 1957): 42–60.

Taylor, A. Elizabeth. "The Woman Suffrage Movement in North Carolina, Part I." *North Carolina Historical Review* 38 (January 1961): 45–62.

Taylor, A. Elizabeth. "The Woman Suffrage Movement in North Carolina, Part II." *North Carolina Historical Review* 38 (April 1961): 173–89.

Taylor, A. Elizabeth. *The Woman Suffrage Movement in Tennessee.* New York: Bookman Associates, 1957.

Taylor, A. Elizabeth. "The Woman Suffrage Movement in Texas." *Journal of Southern History* 17 (May 1951): 194–215.

Taylor, P. A. M., ed. *More Than Common Powers of Perception: The Diary of Elizabeth Rogers Mason Cabot.* Boston: Beacon Press, 1991.

Taylor, Robert S. *Woman Suffrage: An Argument against It.* N.p., n.d.

Tedin, Kent L., David W. Brady, Mary E. Buxton, Barbara M. Gorman, and Judy

L. Thompson. "Social Background and Political Differences between Pro- and Anti-ERA Activists." *American Politics Quarterly* 5 (July 1977): 395–407.

Ten Eyck, John C. *Suffrage and Government.* New York: Guidon Club Opposed to Woman Suffrage, 1914.

Terborg-Penn, Rosalyn. "Discontented Black Feminists: Prelude and Postscript to the Passage of the Nineteenth Amendment." In *Decades of Discontent: The Women's Movement, 1920–1940,* ed. Lois Scharf and Joan M. Jensen. Westport, Conn.: Greenwood Press, 1983. 261–78.

Terry, Edmund R. *Votes for Women, Why?* New York: Hamilton Press, 1917.

Thomas, Mary Martha. *The New Woman in Alabama: Social Reforms and Suffrage, 1890–1920.* Tuscaloosa: University of Alabama Press, 1992.

Thurner, Manuela. " 'Better Citizens without the Ballot': American Antisuffrage Women and Their Rationale during the Progressive Era." *Journal of Women's History* 5 (Spring 1993): 33–60.

Todd, John. *Woman's Rights.* Boston: Lee & Shepard, 1867.

Tomsich, John. *A Genteel Endeavor: American Culture and Politics in the Gilded Age.* Stanford, Calif.: Stanford University Press, 1971.

Trachtenberg, Alan. *The Incorporation of America: Culture and Society in the Gilded Age.* New York: Hill and Wang, 1982.

Trout, Charles H. "Curley of Boston: The Search for Irish Legitimacy." In *Boston, 1700–1890: The Evolution of Urban Politics,* ed. Ronald P. Formisano and Constance K. Burns. Westport, Conn.: Greenwood Press, 1984. 165–95.

Trout, Grace Wilbur. "Side Lights on Illinois Suffrage History." *Journal of the Illinois State Historical Society* 13 (April 1920): 145–79.

Tucker, Henry St. George. *Woman's Suffrage by Constitutional Amendment.* New Haven: Yale University Press, 1916.

Turner, Ralph H., and Lewis M. Killian. *Collective Behavior.* 3d ed. Englewood Cliffs, N.J.: Prentice-Hall, 1987.

U.S. Department of the Interior, Census Office. *Report on Statistics of Churches in the United States at the Eleventh Census, 1890.* Washington, D.C.: U.S. Government Printing Office, 1894.

U.S. Department of the Interior, Census Office. *Tenth Census of the United States, Population Schedules.* Washington, D.C.: National Archives Microfilm Publications, n.d.

U.S. Department of the Interior, Census Office. *Eleventh Census of the United States.* Washington, D.C.: U.S. Government Printing Office, 1892.

U.S. Department of the Interior, Census Office. *Thirteenth Census of the United States.* Washington, D.C.: U.S. Government Printing Office, 1913.

U.S. Department of the Interior, Census Office. *Thirteenth Census of the United States, Abstract of the Census with Supplement for Maine.* Washington, D.C.: U.S. Government Printing Office, 1912.

Van Doren, Charles, ed. *Webster's American Biographies.* Springfield, Mass.: G. and C. Merriam, 1974.

Van Rensselaer, Mrs. Schuyler. *Should We Ask for the Suffrage?* New York: J. J. O'Brien and Son, 1894.

Vertrees, John J. *An Address to the Men of Tennessee on Female Suffrage.* Nashville: n.p., 1916.

Views on Woman Suffrage. Albany: Anti-Suffrage Association, n.d.

Wadlin, Horace G. *Extract from an Address Delivered in 1903 before the Massachusetts Federation of Women's Clubs.* Boston: MAOFESW, 1903.

Walby, Sylvia. "Gender, Class, and Stratification: Towards a New Approach." In *Gender and Stratification,* ed. Rosemary Crompton and Michael Mann. Cambridge, England: Polity, 1986. 23–39.

Waller-Zuckerman, Mary Ellen. " 'Old Homes, in a City of Perpetual Change': Women's Magazines, 1890–1916." *Business History Review* 63 (Winter 1989): 715–56.

"Wartime Gains of the Suffragists." *Survey,* 28 April 1917, 97.

Webb, Walter Prescott, ed. *The Handbook of Texas.* 2 vols. Austin: Texas State Historical Association, 1952.

Weber, Max. *From Max Weber: Essays in Sociology.* Ed. and trans. H. H. Gerth and C. Wright Mills. New York: Oxford University Press, 1975.

Wein, Roberta. "Women's Colleges and Domesticity, 1875–1918." *History of Education Quarterly* 14 (Spring 1974): 31–47.

Wells, Kate Gannett. "The Boston Club Woman." *Arena,* August 1892, 369–71.

Wells, Kate Gannett. "Women in Organizations." *Atlantic Monthly,* September 1880, 360–67.

Welter, Barbara. "The Cult of True Womanhood, 1820–1860." In *The American Family in Social-Historical Perspective,* ed. Michael Gordon. 2d ed. New York: St. Martin's, 1978. 313–33.

West, Candace, and Don H. Zimmerman. "Doing Gender." *Gender and Society* 1 (June 1987): 125–51.

West, Jackie. "Women, Sex, and Class." In *Feminism and Materialism: Women and Modes of Production,* ed. Annette Kuhn and Ann Marie Wolpe. London: Routledge and Kegan Paul, 1978. 220–53.

Wharton, Edith. *The Age of Innocence.* New York: Grosset & Dunlap, 1920.

Wharton, Edith. *The House of Mirth.* New York: Charles Scribner's Sons, 1905.

Wheeler, Everett P. *Address of Everett P. Wheeler, Public Meeting, Berkeley Lyceum, March 6th, 1913, For the Preservation of the Home.* New York: New York State Association Opposed to Woman Suffrage, 1913.

Wheeler, Everett P. *Brief before the Committee on Rules, House of Representatives, December, 1913.* New York: Man-Suffrage Association, 1914.

Wheeler, Everett P. *The Case against Woman Suffrage: A Manual for Speakers, Debaters, Writers, Lecturers, and Anyone Who Wants the Facts and Figures.* New York: Man-Suffrage Association, 1915.

Wheeler, Everett P. "The Federal Woman Suffrage Amendment." *Arbitrator,* December 1918, 6–10.

Wheeler, Everett P. *Home Rule: Brief of Everett P. Wheeler on Argument before Judi-*

ciary Committee, House of Representatives, March 1914, against Proposition for Constitutional Amendment Compelling the States to Adopt Woman Suffrage. New York: Man Suffrage Association, 1914.

Wheeler, Everett P. *The Right and Wrong of Woman Suffrage: Address by E. P. Wheeler, Delivered under the Auspices of the New York State Association Opposed to Woman Suffrage at a Meeting of Men and Women at the Residence of Mr. Justice Bischoff on the Evening of February 17, 1912.* New York: New York State Association Opposed to Woman Suffrage, 1912.

Wheeler, Everett P. *Sixty Years of American Life. Taylor to Roosevelt, 1850 to 1910.* New York: E. P. Dutton, 1917.

Wheeler, Everett P. *What Women Have Done without the Ballot.* New York: Man Suffrage Association, n.d.

Wheeler, Marjorie Spruill. *New Women of the New South: The Leaders of the Woman Suffrage Movement in the Southern States.* Ann Arbor, Mich.: University Microfilms International, 1990.

White, Eliza A. ["Alex"]. *As It Should Be.* Philadelphia: J. B. Lippincott, 1874.

White, Mrs. Henry Preston. "The Ballot and the Woman in Industry." In *Anti-Suffrage Essays by Massachusetts Women,* ed. Ernest Bernbaum. Boston: Forum Publications, 1916. 31–37.

Whites, LeeAnn. "Rebecca Latimer Felson and the Problem of 'Protection' in the New South." In *Visible Women: New Essays on American Activism,* ed. Nancy A. Hewitt and Suzanne Lebsock. Urbana: University of Illinois Press, 1993. 41–61.

Who's Who in the South and Southwest. Chicago: A. N. Marquis, 1950.

Who Was Who in America. 7 vols. Chicago: A. N. Marquis, 1966–81.

Why Women Do Not Want the Ballot. 2 vols. New York: J. J. O'Brien and Son, n.d.

Why Women Do Not Want to Vote: Talk to Legislators by a Tax-Paying Woman Not New and Not Strenuous. Albany, N.Y.: Anti-Suffrage Association of the Third Judicial District, 1905.

Wiebe, Robert H. *The Search for Order, 1877–1920.* New York: Hill and Wang, 1967.

Wilbur, Alice Heustis. *Woman Suffrage Not Wanted in Oregon. Outline of a Talk Given by Mrs. R. W. Wilbur at a Parlor Meeting of the Oregon State Association Opposed to the Extension of the Suffrage of Women, on March 10th, 1900.* Portland, Ore.: Press of the Irwin-Hudson Co., n.d.

Wilcox, Clyde. *God's Warriors: The Christian Right in Twentieth-Century America.* Baltimore: Johns Hopkins University Press, 1992.

Willard, Frances E., and Mary A. Livermore, eds. *American Women.* 2 vols. 1897; reprint ed., Detroit: Gale Research, 1973.

Wilson, Elizabeth. *The Sphinx in the City: Urban Life, the Control of Disorder, and Women.* London: Virago Press, 1991.

Wilson, John. *Introduction to Social Movements.* New York: Basic Books, 1973.

Wilson, Margaret Gibbons. *The American Woman in Transition: The Urban Influence, 1870–1920.* Westport, Conn.: Greenwood Press, 1979.

Winslow, Hubbard. *Woman As She Should Be.* Boston: T. H. Carter, 1838.

Wirls, Daniel. "Reinterpreting the Gender Gap." *Public Opinion Quarterly* 50 (Fall 1986): 316–30.

Wolf, Charlotte. "Social Class, Status, and Prestige." In *Social Control for the 1980s: A Handbook for Order in a Democratic Society,* ed. Joseph S. Roucek. Westport, Conn.: Greenwood Press, 1978. 135–46.

"A Woman's Protest against Woman Suffrage." *Outlook,* 28 April 1894, 760.

Woman Suffrage and the Liquor Question. Facts Show That Women's Votes Have Not Aided Prohibition. New York: Women's Anti-Suffrage Association, 1915.

"Women." *Century,* February 1891, 631–2.

"Women Capture the Empire State." *Current Opinion,* December 1917, 363–64.

Women Remonstrants of the State of Illinois. *To the Honorable the Senate and the House of Representatives of the State of Illinois, Greeting.* Chicago: n.p., 1891.

Wood, James Playsted. *Magazines in the United States.* 2d ed. New York: Ronald Press, 1956.

Woody, Thomas. *A History of Women's Education in the United States.* 2 vols. New York: Octagon Books, 1966.

Yellin, Carol Lynn. "Countdown in Tennessee, 1920." *American Heritage,* December 1978, 12–23, 26–35.

Youmans, Theodora W. "How Wisconsin Won the Ballot." *Wisconsin Magazine of History* 5 (1921–22): 3–32.

Young, Iris. "Beyond the Unhappy Marriage: A Critique of the Dual Systems Theory." In *Women and Revolution: The Unhappy Marriage of Marxism and Feminism,* ed. Lydia Sargent. Boston: South End Press, 1981. 43–69.

Young, Rose. "The End of a Great Adventure." *Ladies' Home Journal,* February 1920, 37, 60.

Zald, Meyer N., and Bert Useem. "Movement and Countermovement Interaction: Mobilization, Tactics, and State Involvement." In *Social Movements in an Organizational Society,* ed. Meyer N. Zald and John D. McCarthy. New Brunswick, N.J.: Transaction Books, 1987. 247–72.

Index

AVON FREE PUBLIC LIBRARY
3 2529 06722 4063